SOLARO

STUDY GUIDE

MW01614404

hematics 9 Academic
ciples of Mathematics (MPM1D)

SOLARO Study Guide is designed to help students achieve success in school. The content in each study guide is 100% curriculum aligned and serves as an excellent source of material for review and practice. To create this book, teachers, curriculum specialists, and assessment experts have worked closely to develop the instructional pieces that explain each of the key concepts for the course. The practice questions and sample tests have detailed solutions that show problem-solving methods, highlight concepts that are likely to be tested, and point out potential sources of errors. ***SOLARO Study Guide*** is a complete guide to be used by students throughout the school year for reviewing and understanding course content, and to prepare for assessments.

Copyright © 2013 Castle Rock Research Corporation

All rights reserved. No part of this book covered by the copyright hereon may be reproduced or used in any form or by any means graphic, electronic, or mechanical, including photocopying, recording, taping, or information storage and retrieval systems without the express permission of the publisher.

Rao,Gautam,1961 –
SOLARO STUDY GUIDE – Mathematics 9 Academic
Principles of Mathematics

1. Mathematics – Juvenile Literature. I. Title

Castle Rock Research Corporation
2410 Manulife Place
10180 – 101 Street
Edmonton, AB T5J 3S4

1 2 3 PP 15 14 13

Redeeming Your Free 14-Day Trial

Congratulations on your purchase of a SOLARO Study Guide!

As a thank you from us, we are pleased to offer our book customers a free 14-day trial of SOLARO.com, our online study tool for math, science, and English language arts for 3rd to 12th grades.

Please visit
www.solaro.com/trial2013
to redeem your
free trial now!

Publisher
Gautam Rao

Contributors
Alan Jones
Betty Morris
Ruth Rancier

CASTLE ROCK
RESEARCH CORP

Dedicated to the memory of Dr. V. S. Rao

Not for Reproduction

SOLARO STUDY GUIDE

Each ***SOLARO STUDY GUIDE*** consists of the following sections:

Key Tips for Being Successful at School gives examples of study and review strategies. It includes information about learning styles, study schedules, and note taking for test preparation.

Class Focus includes a unit on each area of the curriculum. Units are divided into sections, each focusing on one of the specific expectations, or main ideas, that students must learn about in that unit. Examples, definitions, and visuals help to explain each main idea. Practice questions on the main ideas are also included. At the end of each unit is a test on the important ideas covered. The practice questions and unit tests help students identify areas they know and those they need to study more. They can also be used as preparation for tests and quizzes. Most questions are of average difficulty, though some are easy and some are hard—the harder questions are called *Challenger Questions*. Each unit is prefaced by a ***Table of Correlations***, which correlates questions in the unit (and in the practice tests at the end of the book) to the specific curriculum expectations. Answers and solutions are found at the end of each unit.

Key Strategies for Success on Tests helps students get ready for tests. It shows students different types of questions they might see, word clues to look for when reading them, and hints for answering them.

Practice Tests includes one to three tests based on the entire course. They are very similar to the format and level of difficulty that students may encounter on final tests. In some regions, these tests may be reprinted versions of official tests, or reflect the same difficulty levels and formats as official versions. This gives students the chance to practice using real-world examples. Answers and complete solutions are provided at the end of the section.

For the complete curriculum document (including specific expectations along with examples and sample problems), visit http://www.edu.gov.on.ca/eng/curriculum/

SOLARO STUDY GUIDE *Study Guides* are available for many courses. Check www.castlerockresearch.com for a complete listing of books available for your area.

For information about any of our resources or services, please call Castle Rock Research at 1.800.840.6224 or visit our website at http://www.castlerockresearch.com.

At Castle Rock Research, we strive to produce an error-free resource. If you should find an error, please contact us so that future editions can be corrected.

CONTENTS

Key Tips for being Successful at School

Copyright Protected

KEY TIPS FOR BEING SUCCESSFUL AT SCHOOL

KEY FACTORS CONTRIBUTING TO SCHOOL SUCCESS

In addition to learning the content of your courses, there are some other things that you can do to help you do your best at school. You can try some of the following strategies:

- **Keep a positive attitude:** Always reflect on what you can already do and what you already know.
- **Be prepared to learn:** Have the necessary pencils, pens, notebooks, and other required materials for participating in class ready.
- **Complete all of your assignments:** Do your best to finish all of your assignments. Even if you know the material well, practice will reinforce your knowledge. If an assignment or question is difficult for you, work through it as far as you can so that your teacher can see exactly where you are having difficulty.
- **Set small goals for yourself when you are learning new material:** For example, when learning the parts of speech, do not try to learn everything in one night. Work on only one part or section each study session. When you have memorized one particular part of speech and understand it, move on to another one. Continue this process until you have memorized and learned all the parts of speech.
- **Review your classroom work regularly at home:** Review to make sure you understand the material you learned in class.

- **Ask your teacher for help:** Your teacher will help you if you do not understand something or if you are having a difficult time completing your assignments.
- **Get plenty of rest and exercise:** Concentrating in class is hard work. It is important to be well-rested and have time to relax and socialize with your friends. This helps you keep a positive attitude about your schoolwork.
- **Eat healthy meals:** A balanced diet keeps you healthy and gives you the energy you need for studying at school and at home.

Not for Reproduction

How to Find Your Learning Style

Every student learns differently. The manner in which you learn best is called your learning style. By knowing your learning style, you can increase your success at school. Most students use a combination of learning styles. Do you know what type of learner you are? Read the following descriptions. Which of these common learning styles do you use most often?

- **Linguistic Learner:** You may learn best by saying, hearing, and seeing words. You are probably really good at memorizing things such as dates, places, names, and facts. You may need to write down the steps in a process, a formula, or the actions that lead up to a significant event, and then say them out loud.
- **Spatial Learner:** You may learn best by looking at and working with pictures. You are probably really good at puzzles, imagining things, and reading maps and charts. You may need to use strategies like mind mapping and webbing to organize your information and study notes.
- **Kinesthetic Learner:** You may learn best by touching, moving, and figuring things out using manipulatives. You are probably really good at physical activities and learning through movement. You may need to draw your finger over a diagram to remember it, tap out the steps needed to solve a problem, or feel yourself writing or typing a formula.

Copyright Protected

SCHEDULING STUDY TIME

You should review your class notes regularly to ensure that you have a clear understanding of all the new material you learned. Reviewing your lessons on a regular basis helps you to learn and remember ideas and concepts. It also reduces the quantity of material that you need to study prior to a test. Establishing a study schedule will help you to make the best use of your time.

Regardless of the type of study schedule you use, you may want to consider the following suggestions to maximize your study time and effort:

- Organize your work so that you begin with the most challenging material first.
- Divide the subject's content into small, manageable chunks.
- Alternate regularly between your different subjects and types of study activities in order to maintain your interest and motivation.
- Make a daily list with headings like "Must Do," "Should Do," and "Could Do."
- Begin each study session by quickly reviewing what you studied the day before.
- Maintain your usual routine of eating, sleeping, and exercising to help you concentrate better for extended periods of time.

Not for Reproduction

Creating Study Notes

Mind-Mapping or Webbing

Use the key words, ideas, or concepts from your reading or class notes to create a mind map or web (a diagram or visual representation of the given information). A mind map or web is sometimes referred to as a knowledge map. Use the following steps to create a mind map or web:

1. Write the key word, concept, theory, or formula in the centre of your page.
2. Write down related facts, ideas, events, and information, and link them to the central concept with lines.
3. Use coloured markers, underlining, or symbols to emphasize things such as relationships, timelines, and important information.

The following examples of a Frayer Model illustrate how this technique can be used to study vocabulary.

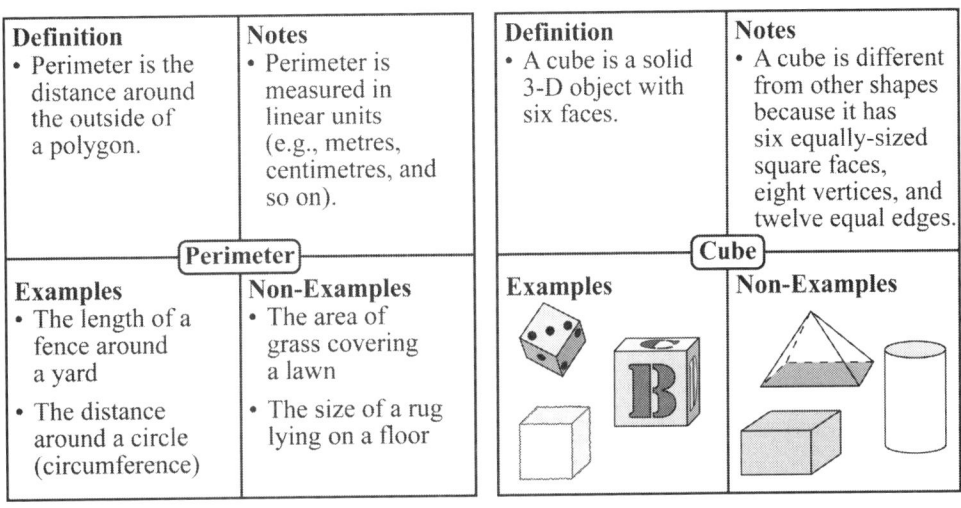

Perimeter

Definition	**Notes**
• Perimeter is the distance around the outside of a polygon.	• Perimeter is measured in linear units (e.g., metres, centimetres, and so on).
Examples	**Non-Examples**
• The length of a fence around a yard • The distance around a circle (circumference)	• The area of grass covering a lawn • The size of a rug lying on a floor

Cube

Definition	**Notes**
• A cube is a solid 3-D object with six faces.	• A cube is different from other shapes because it has six equally-sized square faces, eight vertices, and twelve equal edges.
Examples	**Non-Examples**
	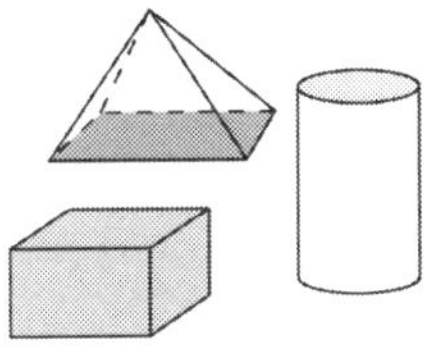

Copyright Protected

Index Cards

To use index cards while studying, follow these steps:

1. Write a key word or question on one side of an index card.
2. On the reverse side, write the definition of the word, answer to the question, or any other important information that you want to remember.

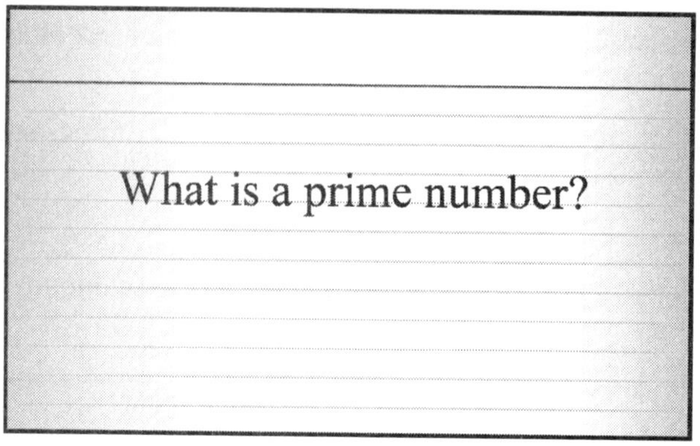

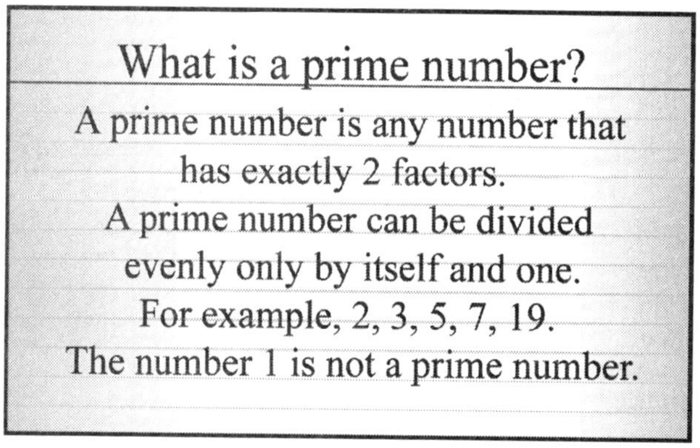

Symbols and Sticky Notes—Identifying Important Information

Use symbols to mark your class notes. The following are some examples:

- An exclamation mark (!) might be used to point out something that must be learned well because it is a very important idea.
- A question mark (?) may highlight something you are not certain about
- A diamond (◊) or asterisk (*) could highlight interesting information that you want to remember.

Sticky notes are useful in the following situations:

- Use sticky notes when you are not allowed to put marks in books.
- Use sticky notes to mark a page in a book that contains an important diagram, formula, explanation, or other information.
- Use sticky notes to mark important facts in research books.

Not for Reproduction

MEMORIZATION TECHNIQUES

- **Association** relates new learning to something you already know. For example, to remember the spelling difference between dessert and desert, recall that the word *sand* has only one *s*. So, because there is sand in a desert, the word *desert* has only one *s*.
- **Mnemonic** devices are sentences that you create to remember a list or group of items. For example, the first letter of each word in the phrase "Every Good Boy Deserves Fudge" helps you to remember the names of the lines on the treble-clef staff (E, G, B, D, and F) in music.

- **Acronyms** are words that are formed from the first letters or parts of the words in a group. For example, RADAR is actually an acronym for Radio Detecting and Ranging, and MASH is an acronym for Mobile Army Surgical Hospital. HOMES helps you to remember the names of the five Great Lakes (Huron, Ontario, Michigan, Erie, and Superior).
- **Visualizing** requires you to use your mind's eye to "see" a chart, list, map, diagram, or sentence as it is in your textbook or notes, on the chalkboard or computer screen, or in a display.
- **Initialisms** are abbreviations that are formed from the first letters or parts of the words in a group. Unlike acronyms, an initialism cannot be pronounced as a word itself. For example, GCF is an initialism for **G**reatest **C**ommon **F**actor.

KEY STRATEGIES FOR REVIEWING

Reviewing textbook material, class notes, and handouts should be an ongoing activity. Spending time reviewing becomes more critical when you are preparing for a test. You may find some of the following review strategies useful when studying during your scheduled study time:

- Before reading a selection, preview it by noting the headings, charts, graphs, and chapter questions.
- Before reviewing a unit, note the headings, charts, graphs, and chapter questions.
- Highlight key concepts, vocabulary, definitions, and formulas.
- Skim the paragraph, and note the key words, phrases, and information.
- Carefully read over each step in a procedure.
- Draw a picture or diagram to help make the concept clearer.

Copyright Protected

KEY STRATEGIES FOR SUCCESS: A CHECKLIST

Reviewing is a huge part of doing well at school and preparing for tests. Here is a checklist for you to keep track of how many suggested strategies for success you are using. Read each question, and put a check mark (✓) in the correct column. Look at the questions where you have checked the "No" column. Think about how you might try using some of these strategies to help you do your best at school.

Key Strategies for Success	Yes	No
Do you attend school regularly?		
Do you know your personal learning style—how you learn best?		
Do you spend 15 to 30 minutes a day reviewing your notes?		
Do you study in a quiet place at home?		
Do you clearly mark the most important ideas in your study notes?		
Do you use sticky notes to mark texts and research books?		
Do you practise answering multiple-choice and written-response questions?		
Do you ask your teacher for help when you need it?		
Are you maintaining a healthy diet and sleep routine?		
Are you participating in regular physical activity?		

Number Sense and Algebra

Copyright Protected

NUMBER SENSE AND ALGEBRA

Table of Correlations

Specific Expectation		Practice Questions	Unit Test Questions	Practice Test 1	Practice Test 2
9NAV.01	Operating with Exponents				
9NA1.01	*substitute into and evaluate algebraic expressions involving exponents*	1, 2	1, 2	15	
9NA1.02	*describe the relationship between the algebraic and geometric representations of a single-variable term up to degree three*	3, 4	3, 4, 5		17
9NA1.03	*derive, through the investigation and examination of patterns, the exponent rules for multiplying and dividing monomials, and apply these rules in expressions involving one and two variables with positive exponents*	5, 6	6		18
9NA1.04	*extend the multiplication rule to derive and understand the power of a power rule, and apply it to simplify expressions involving one and two variables with positive exponents*	7, 8, 9a, 9b	7, 8	16	
9NAV.02	Manipulating Expressions and Solving Equations				
9NA2.01	*simplify numerical expressions involving integers and rational numbers, with and without the use of technology*	10	9		
9NA2.02	*solve problems requiring the manipulation of expressions arising from applications of percent, ratio, rate, and proportion*	11, 12	10a, 10b, 11, 12, 13	17	19, 20
9NA2.03	*relate their understanding of inverse operations to squaring and taking the square root, and apply inverse operations to simplify expressions and solve equations*	13, 14	14, 15		21
9NA2.04	*add and subtract polynomials with up to two variables, using a variety of tools*	15	16		
9NA2.05	*multiply a polynomial by a monomial involving the same variable, using a variety of tools*	16	17		
9NA2.06	*expand and simplify polynomial expressions involving one variable using a variety of tools*	17, 18	18, 19, 20	18, 19a, 19b	
9NA2.07	*solve first-degree equations, including equations with fractional coefficients, using a variety of tools and strategies*	19, 20	21		
9NA2.08	*rearrange formulas involving variables in the first degree, with and without substitution*	21, 22	22		
9NA2.09	*solve problems that can be modelled with first-degree equations, and compare algebraic methods to other solution methods*	23, 24, 25a, 25b	23, 24, 25	20	22

Not for Reproduction

9NA1.01 substitute into and evaluate algebraic expressions involving exponents

Exponents

Positive Exponents

A **power** consists of a **base** and an **exponent**. In the power 10^3, the number 10 represents the base, and the number 3 represents the exponent. To **evaluate** a power, factor the base the number of times indicated by the exponent. Then, complete the calculation.

$10^3 = (10)(10)(10) = 1\ 0$

A variable may be used as the base, with or without a leading numerical **coefficient**. A **variable** is any letter that represents a value that can change in an expression. For example, x is a variable. A numerical coefficient of 1 is always implied in front of any single variable. For example, in the power x^4, x is the base, 4 is the exponent, and the numerical coefficient is 1.

$x^4 = 1 \cdot x \cdot x \cdot x \cdot x$

In the power $-x^2$, x is the base, 2 is the exponent, and the coefficient is -1.

$-x^2 = -1 \cdot x \cdot x$

Negative Exponents

Powers can have exponents with a negative value. The base can be either positive or negative. To solve a power with a negative exponent, write the **reciprocal** of the base, and then change the sign of the exponent to positive. For example, to solve $\left(\frac{3}{4}\right)^{-2}$, start by changing the expression to $\left(\frac{4}{3}\right)^{2}$.

Substitution and Evaluation of Expressions with Exponents

Evaluate **algebraic expressions** with exponents by substituting a given value for the variable. For example, in $y^3 + y^2$, substitute $y = -2$. That is, $(-2)^3 + (-2)^2$.

1. If $x = -3$ and $y = -2$, then the expression $\frac{(x^3)^2(y^2)^3}{y^4}$ is equal to

A. $-\frac{186\ 624}{16}$

B. $\frac{186\ 624}{16}$

C. $-2\ 916$

D. 2916

2. The area of each face of a cube is 36 cm^2. What is the volume of the cube?

A. 466 565 cm^3 **B.** 2 116 cm^3

C. 216 cm^3 **D.** 16 cm^3

9NA1.02 describe the relationship between the algebraic and geometric representations of a single-variable term up to degree three

Relating Algebraic Terms to Geometric Representations

Degrees of a Term

In mathematics, an algebraic **term** can take on one of a number of different forms. The following chart outlines different examples of terms.

Term	Examples
Integer	2, −3, 4
Integer with a variable	$2x$, $3xy$, $3x4y$, $(12xy)$
Integer with a variable and positive exponent	$2x^2$, $4x^2y^3$
Positive or negative variable	$-x$, y, $-xy$

First-Degree Terms (One-Dimensional)

A **first-degree term** occurs when the **sum** of the exponents equals one, or when there are no exponents. Examples of first-degree terms include 2, $2x$, and x. To relate a first-degree term to a **geometric expression**, look to geometric expressions that are **one-dimensional**. Let the length of this line segment be x cm. The power, $x\left(x^{1}\right)$, is used to represent length, which is a one-dimensional quantity and is represented by a first-degree term.

x cm

Second-Degree Terms (Two-Dimensional)

When the sum of the exponents in a term equals two, the term is of the **second-degree**. Examples of second-degree terms include x^2, $2x^2$ and xy. Geometric expressions that have two dimensions can be related to second-degree terms.

Let x cm be the length of the sides of the given square. The **area** is equal to $l \times w$. The units are also multiplied and the result is cm^2 (cm × cm), a second-degree term.

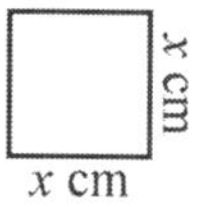

Third-Degree Terms (Three-Dimensional)

Third-degree terms have an exponent sum that equals three. The terms x^3, $3x^3$, $2xy^2$, $2xyz$, x^2y, and xyz are all third-degree terms. Third-degree terms can be related to geometric expressions that have three dimensions.

Let x cm be the side length of this cube. The **volume** can be found by multiplying $l \times w \times h$. The units are also multiplied, with a result of cm^3 (cm × cm × cm), which is a third-degree term.

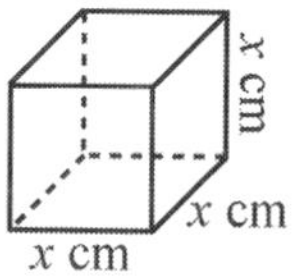

3. A cylindrical drinking bottle with a base radius of x centimetres is filled with a liquid up to a height of x centimetres. The volume of liquid in the bottle is

A. x^3 cm^3

B. πx^3 cm^2

C. πx^3 cm^3

D. $\pi r^2 h$ cm^2

Use the following information to answer the next question.

Todd's pencil case has a rectangular lid with a length of 25 cm and a width of 15 cm.

4. What is the perimeter of the lid?

A. 40 cm **B.** 40 cm^2

C. 80 cm **D.** 80 cm^2

9NA1.03 derive, through the investigation and examination of patterns, the exponent rules for multiplying and dividing monomials, and apply these rules in expressions involving one and two variables with positive exponents

9NA1.04 extend the multiplication rule to derive and understand the power of a power rule, and apply it to simplify expressions involving one and two variables with positive exponents

Exponent Laws

The exponent rules or laws explain how to deal with exponents in operations that contain powers.

Exponent of One Law

$x^1 = x$

When you have a power with an exponent of 1, it means factor the base once: $5^1 = 5$. Since 5^1 is equal to 5, the exponent is left off when **simplifying** expressions or equations.

Multiplying Powers Law

$x^m \cdot x^n = x^{m+n}$

The multiplying powers law states that you add the exponents when you multiply powers that have the same base.

Dividing Powers Law

$x^m \div x^n = x^{m-n}$

When dividing powers with the same base, subtract the exponents.

Exponent of Zero Law

$x^0 = 1$

A power with an exponent of zero has a value of 1. Any number divided by itself is equal to 1: $2 \div 2 = 1$. You also know that you can subtract exponents of powers with the same base $\frac{2^3}{2^3} = 2^{3-3} = 2^0$. Thus, any power with an exponent of zero is equal to 1.

Power of a Power Law

$(x^m)^n = x^{mn}$

When a base is raised to multiple exponents, keep the base the same and multiply the exponents.

Power of a Product Law

$(xy)^m = x^m y^m$

The exponent is equally applied to all bases in a set of brackets.

Copyright Protected

5. The simplified form of the expression $\dfrac{x^{20}y^{13}z^{14}}{x^{17}y^{12}z^{11}}$ is

A. x^3yz^3 B. x^2yz^4

C. $x^3y^2z^3$ D. $x^2y^2z^3$

6. What is the product of the expressions a^5b^3 and $(a + b + ab)$?

A. $a^6b^3 + a^5b^4 + a^6b^4$

B. $a^6b^3 + a^5b^3 + a^6b^4$

C. $a^6b^3 + a^5b^4 + a^5b^4$

D. $a^6b^3 + a^5b^3 + a^6b^3$

7. The **most** simplified form of the expression $\left(\dfrac{4x^3y^8}{2x^5y^6}\right)^3$ is

A. $\dfrac{8y^6}{x^6}$ B. $\dfrac{16x^9}{y^9}$

C. $\dfrac{8x^9}{y^9}$ D. $8x^6y^6$

8. What is the simplified form of the expression $-(-2x^3)^4$?

A. $8x^{12}$ B. $-8x^{12}$

C. $16x^{12}$ D. $-16x^{12}$

Open Response

a) Simplify the given expression.

$$\frac{(3xy^2)^3 \times (-4x^2y)}{(2x^2y^2)^2}$$

b) Solve the given expression for the values $x = 2$ and $y = 3$.

9NA2.01 simplify numerical expressions involving integers and rational numbers, with and without the use of technology

Operations with Integers

Integers include all positive and negative whole numbers.

Addition

When adding integers, pay attention to the signs attached to the integers and follow the rules below.

Rule 1: If the signs are the same (both positive or both negative), add the two absolute values (the number without its positive or negative sign) and keep the sign.

Rule 2: If the signs are different (one negative and one positive), subtract the smaller absolute value from the larger absolute value and take the sign of the larger **absolute value**.

Example

What is the result of $(+3) + (-6)$?

$6 - 3 = 3$

As 6 is the larger absolute value, the answer takes its sign (negative).

$(+3) + (-6) = -3$

Subtraction

To subtract integers, add the opposite. Rewrite the equation into an addition equation and change the sign on the number being subtracted to its opposite. Then, perform the addition. For example, $(-4) - (-5)$ is rewritten as $(-4) + 5$.

Multiplication and Division

There are four rules to follow when performing multiplication or division with integers.

Rule 1: If the signs are the same, the solution is positive.

Rule 2: If the signs are different, the solution is negative.

Rule 3: If there is an even number of negative signs, the answer will be positive.

Rule 4: If there is an odd number of negative signs, the answer will be negative.

Operations with Rational Numbers

A rational number is any number that can be written in the form $\frac{a}{b}$. Both a and b must be integers, and b cannot equal zero. When performing operations amongst rational numbers without a calculator, the majority of the work involves manipulating the **numerators** and **denominators**.

Addition and Subtraction

To add or subtract fractions with the same (common) denominator, the numerators are added or subtracted and placed over the **common denominator**. The resulting fraction is reduced to **lowest terms** if possible. When adding or subtracting fractions with different denominators, find the **lowest common denominator** (LCD) of the given fractions. Create new **equivalent fractions** of the original fractions using the LCD. Then, add or subtract the numerators and place the result over the LCD. If possible, reduce the resulting fraction to lowest terms. When adding or subtracting fractions that involve **mixed numbers** in the form of $c\frac{a}{b}$, follow the same process as above, except first convert the mixed number to an **improper fraction**.

$$c\frac{a}{b} = \frac{(c \times b) + a}{b}$$

Multiplication

When multiplying fractions, multiply the numerators together. Then, multiply the denominators. Reduce the resulting fraction to lowest terms if possible.

$$\frac{a}{b} \times \frac{c}{d} = \frac{ac}{bd}$$

Division

When dividing fractions, convert the division to multiplication. Multiply the first fraction (**dividend**) by the reciprocal of the second fraction (**divisor**). The reciprocal of a fraction is the flip of a fraction. Now, follow the same steps as for multiplication. If possible, reduce the resulting fraction to lowest terms, converting any improper fraction into a mixed number if required.

$$\frac{a}{b} \div \frac{c}{d} = \frac{a}{b} \times \frac{d}{c}$$

Order of Operations

When solving questions involving integers and rational numbers, the operations must be performed in a certain order to get the correct answer. Remember the word BEDMAS to help you with the correct **order of operations**.

Brackets

Exponents

Division

Multiplication

Addition

Subtraction

When there are brackets inside of brackets, start on the inside set first. For division and multiplication, and also addition and subtraction, perform the operations in order from left to right, similar to how you read from left to right.

Copyright Protected

10. A simplified form of the expression $\frac{5}{x}+\frac{7}{x^2+2}$ is

A. $\frac{12}{x^2+2}$

B. $\frac{5x+7}{x^2+2}$

C. $\frac{12}{x^3+2x}$

D. $\frac{5x^2+7x+10}{x^3+2x}$

9NA2.02 solve problems requiring the manipulation of expressions arising from applications of percent, ratio, rate, and proportion

Ratios

A ratio compares two quantities of the same unit. Ratios of two terms can be written in three different forms. For example, a ratio relating 3 apples to 5 bananas can be written in the following forms:

Ratio form → 3:5

Word form → three to five

Fraction form → $\frac{3}{5}$

When writing ratios, the order of the terms is important. Terms are written in the order that they are presented in a mathematical problem. Regardless of form, ratios should always be reduced to lowest terms. Before this can be done, the terms must be expressed in the same unit of measurement.

Example

Write 30 minutes to 2 hours as a ratio.

30 min:2 h

1 h = 60 min → 2 h = 120 min

30 min:120 min

Remove the units of measure and reduce the ratio to lowest terms by dividing both terms by 30.

3:120 → 1:4

Equivalent ratios, like equivalent fractions, are ratios that have the same value but contain different terms. Equivalent ratios are multiples of a ratio in lowest terms.

There are two strategies used to determine if two ratios are equivalent. You can either reduce each ratio to its lowest terms in fraction form and see if the fractions are equal, or you can find the **cross products**. If two ratios, $\frac{a}{b}=\frac{c}{d}$, are equal and b and d are not equal to zero, then the cross products will be equal: $a \times d = b \times c$.

Proportions

A **proportion** is another name for an equivalent ratio. When working with proportions, the goal is to make two equivalent ratios given one complete ratio and a part or portion of another ratio. To solve proportions, change any ratios in word or ratio form to fraction form and then set the fractions equal to each other. As a proportion is an equivalent ratio, you can use one of the given strategies to solve a proportion: equivalent fractions or cross products.

Rates

A **rate**, similar to a ratio, compares two or more quantities. However, rates contain quantities with different units. For example, 300 km in 5 h is a rate. The units are kilometres and hours. A rate is usually written as a **unit rate**, where the value of the second term is 1. To change a rate to a unit rate, divide the first term by the second term and add the units of measurement. Units for unit rates go behind the rate. An exception is monetary units in dollars, where the dollar sign goes in front of the unit rate. **Equivalent rates** are just multiples of a unit rate.

Percentages

A percentage represents a portion out of a whole. The word **percent** means "out of one hundred." The denominator of a percentage is always assumed to be 100. For example, 35% is equal to 35 out of 100, which is equal to $\frac{35}{100}$.

To find the percentage of a number, use the cross products or equivalent fractions strategy. The percentage can also be changed to decimal form. Multiply the decimal by the number given.

Not for Reproduction

Example
What is 25% of 800 g?

$25\% \rightarrow 25 \div 100 = 0.25$

$0.25 \times 800 = 200$ g

---

11. An illustrator who charges \$30.00 / h increases her hourly rate to \$45.00 / h. By what percentage does the illustrator increase her hourly rate?

A. 15% **B.** 30%

C. 45% **D.** 50%

12. An item with a price of \$118.98 is marked down by 50%. If the item is reduced by 50% two more times, what is the new price?

A. \$14.88 **B.** \$59.49

C. \$89.24 **D.** \$10412

9NA2.03 relate their understanding of inverse operations to squaring and taking the square root, and apply inverse operations to simplify expressions and solve equations

Understanding and Applying Inverse Operations

When solving **equations** to undo an operation, apply the opposite or **inverse** of that operation to both sides of the equation. Consider the following examples.

Subtraction and addition are the inverses of each other.	Division and multiplication are the inverses of each other.
$x + 6 = 15$ $x + 6 - 6 = 15 - 6$ $x = 9$	$3x = 51$ $\frac{3x}{3} = \frac{51}{3}$ $x = 17$

This same principle applies to solving an equation involving the square of a number (x^2) or a square root ($\sqrt{x}$).

When squaring a number, find the answer by multiplying the number by itself. For example, the square of 3 is 9 $(3 \times 3 = 3^2)$.

The inverse operation of **squaring a number** is finding the square root. Taking the **square root** of a number is expressed by writing a radical sign ($\sqrt{}$) over the **radicand**; the number (x) you are taking the root of with an **index** of 2. That is, you write $\sqrt[2]{x}$. By convention, the index is not written when it is 2. Instead, it is written as $\sqrt{x}$. Only the positive square root is given when the radical sign is by itself. When the radical sign is written as $\pm\sqrt{}$, both the positive and negative roots are given and are written as $\pm x$. To eliminate the square root sign, perform the opposite operation, which is squaring the radical $(\sqrt{x})^2 = x$

Use the following information to answer the next question.

The following model represents the inverse of $\sqrt{16}$.

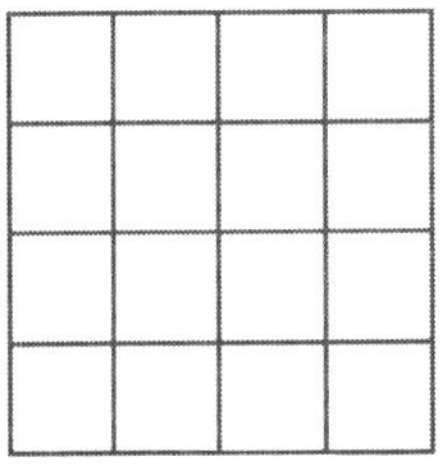

13. Which of the following arrangements represents the inverse of $\sqrt{64}$?

A. 8 rows of 8 squares

B. 8 rows of 16 squares

C. 8 rows of 64 squares

D. 16 rows of 8 squares

14. What is the expression $\sqrt{4a^8 \times 9b^4}$ in its **simplest** form?

A. $6a^4b^2$ **B.** $6a^8b^4$

C. $36a^4b^2$ **D.** $36a^8b^4$

Copyright Protected

9NA2.04 add and subtract polynomials with up to two variables, using a variety of tools

Addition and Subtraction of Polynomials

A **polynomial** has one or more terms connected with addition or subtraction operators. *Poly* means "many" and *nomial* means "term." In the polynomial $5x^2 + 4x + 6$, there are three terms: $5x^2$, $4x$, and 6. The variable is x. 6 is the constant (the value does not change). 5 and 4 are numerical coefficients.

To add or subtract polynomials, first gather like terms in descending order of degree with the constant being the last term. **Like terms** have the exact same variables with identical exponents in the term. For example, $2x^2$ and $5x^2$ are like terms because both have x^2 as a variable.

Then, perform the operation on the coefficients, keeping the variable the same. With subtraction, remember to apply the integer rule of adding the opposite first.

Example

$(2y^3 + 3y - y^2 - 12) - (5y + 3y^3 - y^2 + 6)$
$= (2y^3 + 3y - y^2 - 12) + (-5y - 3y^3 + y^2 - 6)$
$= (2y^3 - 3y^3) + (-y^2 + y^2) + (3y - 5y) + (-12 - 6)$
$= -y^3 + 0y^2 - 2y - 18$
$= -y^3 - 2y - 18$

---

15. What is the result of simplifying the expression $(3x^2 - 4xy + 2yz)$ $+(4xy + 5yz - 2x^2)$ $+(x^2 - 5xy - 3yz + x)$?

A. $2x^2 - 3yz + x$

B. $2x^2 - 5xy + 4yz + x$

C. $-5xy + 4yz + x$

D. $6x^2 - 5xy + 4yz + x$

9NA2.05 multiply a polynomial by a monomial involving the same variable, using a variety of tools

Multiplication of a Polynomial by a Monomial

When a polynomial inside of a set of brackets has a **monomial** (one term) immediately in front of it, multiply each term inside the brackets by the monomial. This process follows the **distributive property** because the term in front is being distributed to each term inside the brackets. When the multiplication is complete, collect like terms. The resulting terms are written in descending order of degree, with the **constant** being the last term.

Example

$3x(4x - 1) + 2x(2x + 6)$
$3x(4x) + 3x(-1) + 2x(2x) + 2x(6)$
$12x^2 - 3x + 4x^2 + 12x$
$16x^2 + 9x$

---

16. The expression $4a(2a + 3) - 2a(a + 2)$ in its **most** simplified form is

A. $6a^2 - 10a$ **B.** $6a^2 + 10a$

C. $6a^2 - 8a$ **D.** $6a^2 + 8a$

9NA2.06 expand and simplify polynomial expressions involving one variable using a variety of tools

Simplifying Polynomials

17. The expression $(4\sqrt{5} - 3\sqrt{2})^2$ is equivalent to

A. 62

B. 98

C. $98 - 24\sqrt{10}$

D. $16\sqrt{5} - 24\sqrt{10} + 9\sqrt{2}$

Not for Reproduction

18. The expression $(2x+7)(3x-4)$ is equal to

A. $6x^2+13x-28$

B. $5x^2+7x-4$

C. $6x^2+21x+3$

D. $5x^2+13x+3$

9NA2.07 solve first-degree equations, including equations with fractional coefficients, using a variety of tools and strategies

Solving First-Degree Equations

A **first-degree equation** has one variable in a mathematical statement containing an equal (=) sign. Each term in the polynomial can only have a degree of one. Remember, if there is no exponent, the implied exponent is 1. The following equation is an example of a first-degree equation.
$2x+7=6(x-1)+15$

Simple First-Degree Equations

Solve simple first-degree equations by adding or subtracting any constant from both sides of the equation, or by dividing each term on both sides of the equation by the coefficient. The purpose is to isolate the variable. It is important to remember that whatever operation you perform to one side of an equation, you must also perform that same operation to the other side.

Example

Solve the equation $x+5=13$ for x.

$x+5=13$

$x+5-5=13-5$

$x=8$

Multi-Step Equations

Example

Multi-step equations have variables on both sides of the equal sign. To solve these equations, use algebraic techniques to get all the variables together on one side and the constant on the other side. Then, solve like a simple first-degree equation.

Solve $2x=6+8x$ for x.

$$\begin{aligned} 2x-2x &= 6+8x-2x \\ 0 &= 6+6x \\ 0-6 &= 6-6+6x \\ -6 &= 6x \\ \frac{-6}{6} &= \frac{6x}{6} \\ -1 &= x \end{aligned}$$

Equations with Fractional Coefficients

When given an equation with a fraction in front of the variable or brackets, multiply both sides of the equation by the denominator of the fraction. This will eliminate the fraction by making its value 1. In the equation $8=\frac{1}{2}(x+4)$, $\frac{1}{2}$ is the **fractional coefficient**. To remove the fraction, multiply both sides of the equation by 2.

When solving an equation that has two fractional coefficients with different denominators, determine the lowest common denominator (LCD) of the two fractions and multiply both sides of the equation by this value.

Example

Solve for $\frac{1}{2}(x+2) = \frac{1}{3}(2x+4)$ for x.

The LCD of these two fractions is 6.

$6 \times \frac{1}{2}\left(x+2\right) = 6 \times \frac{1}{3}\left(2x+4\right)$

$3(x+2) = 2(2x+4)$

$3x+6 = 4x+8$

$3x+6-8 = 4x+8-8$

$3x-2 = 4x$

$3x-3x-2 = 4x-3x$

$-2 = x$

---

19. In the equation $3x+9 = 7x-19$, the value of x is

A. -1 **B.** 1

C. 4 **D.** 7

20. What is the value of x in the equation $\frac{1}{2}(x+1)+\frac{1}{3}(x+2)+\frac{1}{4}(x+3) = 16$?

A. -13 **B.** $-\frac{10}{3}$

C. $\frac{10}{3}$ **D.** 13

9NA2.08 rearrange formulas involving variables in the first degree, with and without substitution

Rearranging Formulas Involving Variables

Sometimes you are given a formula and asked to solve for a given variable. As mentioned previously, solving for a given variable means isolating the variable. This can be accomplished by using all of the same rules that have been applied in solving equations.

Example

Solve the equation $h(a-k) = y$ for a.

$ha - hk = y$

$ha - hk + hk = y + hk$

$ha = y + hk$

$\frac{ha}{h} = \frac{y+hk}{h}$

$a = \frac{y+hk}{h}$

---

21. What is the height of a cone that has a radius of 4 cm and a volume of 40 cm^3?

A. 2.05 cm **B.** 2.39 cm

C. 3.12 cm **D.** 4.16 cm

Not for Reproduction

Use the following information to answer the next question.

The following diagram represents the dimensions of a professional soccer field. The width of the field is $\frac{3}{4}$ the length and the radius of the centre circle is $\frac{1}{10}$ the width.

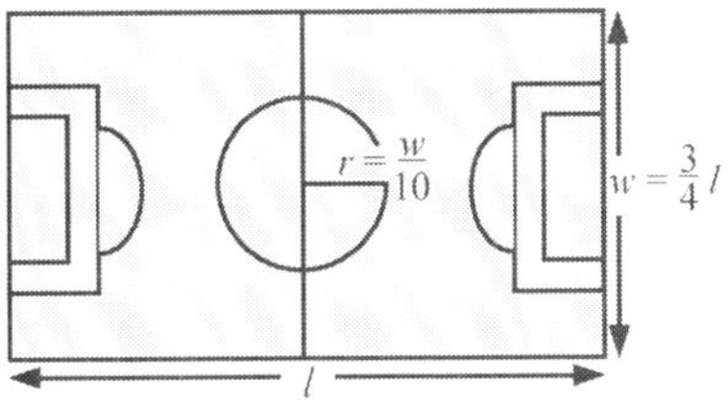

22. What are the dimensions of the soccer field, given that its perimeter is 420 m?

A. 152.7 m × 114.5

B. 120.0 m × 90.0 m

C. 85.4 m × 64.1 m

D. 60.0 m × 30.0 m

9NA2.09 solve problems that can be modelled with first-degree equations, and compare algebraic methods to other solution methods

Real-Life Problems Modelled on First-Degree Equations

Many real-life situations are represented as **algebraic models**, which are then solved using algebraic techniques. To solve the problems successfully, it is important to have an organized approach. A good approach follows the steps outlined below.

Step 1: Define the variable (what you need to solve for).

Step 2: Create an equation using the variable(s) to represent the situation.

Step 3: Solve the equation.

Step 4: Check your solution.

Example
Vivian has 14 fewer quarters than nickels. If the value of these coins is $8.80, find the number of each type of coin that Vivian has.

Let x = number of nickels.

$x - 14$ = number of quarters

(value of nickels) + (value of quarters) = $8.80

(value of one nickel)(number of nickels) + (value of one quarter)(number of quarters) = $8.80

$5x + 25(x - 14) = 880$

$5x + 25x - 350 = 880$

$30x - 350 = 880$

$30x - 350 + 350 = 880 + 350$

$30x = 1230$

$\frac{30x}{30} = \frac{1230}{30}$

$x = 41$

Note: When dealing with coins, decide whether you will treat everything as cents (as done here) or as dollars.

If she has 41 nickels, then she has
41 – 14 = 27 quarters.

Check:
41 nickels = 41 × $0.05 = $2.05
27 = 27 × $0.25 = $6.75

$2.05 + $6.75 = $8.80

Vivian has 41 nickels and 27 quarters.

---

23. It takes 25 people to build a house in 36 days. How long would it take 15 people to build the same house if they worked at the same rate?

A. 60 days **B.** 65 days

C. 70 days **D.** 75 days

24. Peter can build a fence in 12 days and Jason can build the same fence in 8 days. If they work together, how long will it take Peter and Jason to build the fence?

A. $4\frac{1}{5}$ days

B. $4\frac{1}{4}$ days

C. $4\frac{1}{2}$ days

D. $4\frac{4}{5}$ days

Use the following information to answer the next multipart question.

25. Tim and Eric are two brothers that started a fast food restaurant. After a few years of success, they sold the restaurant to Arthur, who developed it into a world famous franchise. The franchise agreement entitled Arthur 1.9% of the revenue from each restaurant and out of Arthur's share, 25% is paid to the brothers.

Open Response

a) If x is the revenue earned by a particular franchise, what expression models how much money Tim and Eric receive?

b) One of the locations that Arthur helped to start produced revenues of $2.3 million. What amount of money did the brothers receive from this location?

Not for Reproduction

ANSWERS AND SOLUTIONS
NUMBER SENSE AND ALGEBRA

1. D	7. A	12. A	18. A	24. D
2. C	8. D	13. A	19. D	25. a) OR
3. C	9. a) OR	14. A	20. D	b) OR
4. C	b) OR	15. B	21. B	
5. A	10. D	16. D	22. B	
6. A	11. D	17. C	23. A	

1. D

Rewrite the equation with $x = -3$ and $y = -2$.

$$\frac{((-3)^3)^2((-2)^2)^3}{(-2)^4}$$

An exponent outside the brackets means that you factor everything inside the brackets the number of times indicated by the exponent.

$$\frac{((-3)^3 \times (-3)^3)((-2)^2 \times (-2)^2 \times (-2)^2)}{(-2) \times (-2) \times (-2) \times (-2)}$$

Now factor each base the number of times indicated by the exponent inside the brackets.

$$\frac{(-3 \times -3 \times -3)(-3 \times -3 \times -3) \times (-2 \times -2)(-2 \times -2)(-2 \times -2)}{-2 \times -2 \times -2 \times -2}$$

Complete the operations.

$$= \frac{(-27)(-27)(4)(4)(4)}{16}$$

$$= \frac{46656}{16}$$

Divide by the denominator.

$= 2916$

2. C

All the sides of a cube have the same measure. The given area of each face is 36 cm^2.

side × side = 36 cm^2

$s^2 = 36 \text{ cm}^2$

$s = \sqrt{36 \text{ cm}^2}$

$s = 6 \text{ cm}$

$V = (\text{side length})^3$

$= 6 \text{ cm} \times 6 \text{ cm} \times 6 \text{ cm}$

$= 216 \text{ cm}^3$

3. C

The formula for the volume of a cylinder is $\pi r^2 h$. Three dimensions are being multiplied, so only answers with cubic units can be considered; therefore, only alternatives A and C can be considered.

Volume $= \pi r^2 h$

Substitute the given values:
radius $= x$
height $= x$

$V = \pi x^2 x$

$V = \pi x^3 \text{ cm}^3$

4. C

Perimeter measures one dimension: length. Therefore, the units are written with the implied exponent of 1. Alternatives B and D are immediately incorrect because they contain square units (two-dimensional quantities).

$P = l + w + l + w$ or $P = 2l + 2w$
$P = 25 + 15 + 25 + 15$ or $P = 2(25) + 2(15)$

$P = 50 \text{ cm} + 30 \text{ cm}$
$P = 80 \text{ cm}$

5. A

Break the expression up into its separate terms.

$$= \frac{x^{20}}{x^{17}} \times \frac{y^{13}}{y^{12}} \times \frac{z^{14}}{z^{11}}$$

Subtract the exponents with the same base and then simplify.

$= x^{20-17} \times y^{13-12} \times z^{14-11}$

$= x^3 y^1 z^3$

$= x^3 y z^3$

6. A

Recall that finding the product means completing the operation of multiplication.

$a^5b^3(a+b+ab)$

Distribute the term outside of the brackets to each term inside the brackets.

$(a^5b^3 \times a)+(a^5b^3 \times b)+(a^5b^3 \times ab)$

When multiplying powers with the same base, the exponents are added together. Recall that 1 is the implied exponent when there is no exponent given.

$(a^{5+1}b^3)+(a^5b^{3+1})+(a^{5+1}b^{3+1})$

$= a^6b^3 + a^5b^4 + a^6b^4$

7. A

Step 1
Use the quotient of powers law to simplify the expression in the brackets.

$$\left(\frac{4x^3y^8}{2x^5y^6}\right)^3 = \left(\frac{4}{2}x^{3-5}y^{8-6}\right)^3$$
$$= (2x^{-2}y^2)^3$$

Step 2
Use the power of a product law to simplify the expression further.

$$(2x^{-2}y^2)^3 = 2^3x^{-2\times3}y^{2\times3}$$
$$= 8x^{-6}y^6$$

Step 3
Rewrite the expression in terms of positive exponents applying the negative exponent principle.

$$8x^{-6}y^6 = \frac{8y^6}{x^6}$$

8. D

The exponent outside the brackets indicates how many times the content inside the brackets is factored. The negative sign outside the brackets remains where it is.

$-(-2x^3)(-2x^3)(-2x^3)(-2x^3)$

There are five negative signs being multiplied together $(-1 \times -2 \times -2 \times -2 \times -2)$. An odd number of negative signs being multiplied together results in a negative answer.

$-(-2x^3)(-2x^3)(-2x^3)(-2x^3)$

$= -(-2)(-2)(-2)(-2)(x^{3+3+3+3})$

$= -16x^{12}$

9. **a) OR**

Points	Sample Answer
4	Use the power of a power law to simplify the brackets. Therefore, each number or variable inside the brackets is multiplied three times (the number of the exponent outside the brackets). $\frac{(3xy^2)^3 \times (-4x^2y)}{(2x^2y^2)^2}$ $= \frac{(3\times3\times3)(x\times x\times x)(y^2\times y^2\times y^2)(-4x^2y)}{(2\times2)(x^2\times x^2)(y^2\times y^2)}$ Apply the exponent law for multiplying monomials to further simplify the brackets. Add the exponents of the bases that are the same. $= \frac{(27)(x^{1+1+1})(y^{2+2+2})\times(-4x^2y)}{(4)(x^{2+2})(y^{2+2})}$ $= \frac{27x^3y^6\times(-4x^2y)}{4x^4y^4}$ $= \frac{27\times(-4)x^{3+2}y^{6+1}}{4x^4y^4}$ $= \frac{(-108)x^5y^7}{4x^4y^4}$ Apply the exponent law for dividing monomials. Subtract the exponents of the bases that are the same. $= (-108 \div 4)x^{5-4}y^{7-4}$ $= (-27)xy^3$
Application of knowledge and skills involving simplifying expressions by applying the exponent and power of a power laws shows a high degree of effectiveness due to: • a thorough understanding of the concepts • an accurate application of the procedures (any minor errors and/or omissions do not detract from the demonstration of a thorough understanding)	

Not for Reproduction

<table>
<tr><th>Points</th><th>Sample Answer</th></tr>
<tr><td>3</td><td>When using the power of a power law, the exponent is applied to the variables, but is missing on the coefficient. Other exponent laws are applied correctly. An example showing an error in the procedure is:
$= \dfrac{(3x^3y^6)\times(-4x^2y)}{(2x^4y^4)}$
$= \dfrac{-12x^5y^7}{2x^4y^4}$
$= -6xy^3$</td></tr>
<tr><td colspan="2">Application of knowledge and skills involving simplifying expressions by applying the exponent and power of a power law shows considerable effectiveness due to:
• an understanding of most of the concepts
• minor errors and/or omissions in the application of the procedures</td></tr>
<tr><td>2</td><td>The power of a power laws is applied correctly, but the other exponent laws are applied incorrectly.
$= \dfrac{(3^3x^3y^6)\times(-4x^2y)}{2x^4y^4}$
$= \dfrac{27x^6y^6}{2x^4y^4}$</td></tr>
<tr><td colspan="2">Application of knowledge and skills involving simplfying expressions by applying the exponent and power of a power laws shows some effectiveness due to:
• a partial understanding of the concepts
• minor errors and/or omissions in the application of the procedures</td></tr>
<tr><td>1</td><td>The power of a power law and the other exponent laws are applied incorrectly.
$= \dfrac{(3x^5y^5)\times(-4x^2y)}{(2x^4y^4)}$</td></tr>
<tr><td colspan="2">Application of knowledge and skills involving simplifying expressions by applying the exponent and power of a power laws shows limited effectiveness due to:
• a misunderstanding of concepts
• an incorrect selection or misuse of procedures</td></tr>
</table>

b) OR

<table>
<tr><th>Points</th><th>Sample Answer</th></tr>
<tr><td>4</td><td>$-27xy^3 = (-27)(2)(3)^3$
$= (-27)(2)(27)$
$= -1\ 458$</td></tr>
<tr><td colspan="2">Application of knowledge and skills involving substitution and evaluation of algebraic expressions involving exponents shows a high degree of effectiveness due to:
• a thorough understanding of the concepts
• an accurate application of the procedures (any minor errors and/or omissions do not detract from the demonstration of a thorough understanding)</td></tr>
<tr><td>3</td><td>The values are substituted in correctly, but the negative sign is not included.</td></tr>
<tr><td colspan="2">Application of knowledge and skills involving substitution and evaluation of algebraic expressions involving exponents shows considerable effectiveness due to:
• an understanding of most of the concepts
• minor errors and/or omissions in the application of the procedures</td></tr>
<tr><td>2</td><td>The values are substituted in correctly, but the exponent is not evaluated first.</td></tr>
<tr><td colspan="2">Application of knowledge and skills involving substitution and evaluation of algebraic expressions involving exponents shows some effectiveness due to:
• a partial understanding of the concepts
• minor errors and/or omissions in the application of the procedures</td></tr>
<tr><td>1</td><td>The correct values are not substituted in for the variables.
The exponent is not completed as the first operation.</td></tr>
<tr><td colspan="2">Application of knowledge and skills involving substitution and evaluation of algebraic expressions involving exponents shows limited effectiveness due to:
• a misunderstanding of concepts
• an incorrect selection or misuse of procedures</td></tr>
</table>

10. D

When adding or subtracting fractions, the first thing to do if the denominators are different is to find a common denominator. Once you have found one (usually the lowest common denominator), multiply the numerators by whatever values you multiplied each denominator by to reach the common denominator. In this case, the LCD is $x(x^2+2)$.

Find each new fraction.

$$\frac{5}{x} \rightarrow \frac{5(x^2+2)}{x(x^2+2)}$$

$$\frac{7}{x^2+2} \rightarrow \frac{x(7)}{x(x^2+2)}$$

Put the expression together again.

$$\frac{5(x^2+2)}{x(x^2+2)} + \frac{x(7)}{x(x^2+2)}$$

Perform distribution.

$$\frac{5x^2+10}{x^3+2x} + \frac{7x}{x^3+2x}$$

Add the numerators and keep the denominator the same. In this case, all the variables have a different exponent so all that is left to do is rearrange the terms so they are in descending order of degree.

$$\frac{5x^2+7x+10}{x^3+2x}$$

11. D

The illustrator increases her rate by $\$45.00 - \$30.00 = \$15.00$.

Determine what percentage $15.00 is of $30.00. To do this, set up equivalent fractions. As you are looking for a percentage, make the second fraction out of 100.

$$\frac{15}{30} = \frac{x}{100}$$

Find the cross products to solve for x.

$15 \times 100 = 30x$

$1500 = 30x$

$$\frac{1500}{30} = \frac{30x}{30}$$

$x = 50$

The illustrator increases her rate by 50%.

12. A

The original price of the item was $118.98. The item is discounted by 50% on three consecutive occasions.

Convert the percentage to a decimal.

$$50\% = \frac{50}{100} = 50 \div 100 = 0.5$$

Price after the first discount is $\$118.98 \times 0.5 = \$59.49$

Price after the second discount is $\$59.49 \times 0.5 = \$29.75$

Price after the third discount is $\$29.75 \times 0.5 = \$14.88$

13. A

The given diagram is 4 rows of 4 squares. There are a total of 16 squares. This represents the inverse of $\sqrt{16}$.

$4 \times 4 = 4^2 = 16$

The square root of 16 is 4.

Similarly, the square root of 64 is 8, because $8 \times 8 = 8^2 = 64$.

Therefore, 8 rows of 8 squares represents the inverse of $\sqrt{64}$.

14. A

Start by completing the operation under the radical sign.

$\sqrt{4a^8 \times 9b^4} = \sqrt{36a^8b^4}$

Take the square root of 36.

$6^2 = 6 \times 6 = 36$

$\sqrt{36} = 6$

To calculate the square root of the exponents 8 and 4 divide each by the index of 2. This follows the exponent laws.

$8 \div 2 = 4$

$\sqrt{a^8} = a^4$

$4 \div 2 = 2$

$\sqrt{b^4} = b^2$

Put the terms back together.

$6a^4b^2$

15. B

Rewrite the polynomials grouping like terms.

$(3x^2 - 2x^2 + x^2) + (-4xy + 4xy - 5xy)$
$+ (2yz + 5yz - 3yz) + x$

Simplify by adding and / or subtracting the like terms.

$2x^2 - 5xy + 4yz + x$

16. D

Distribute the terms outside the brackets to each term inside the brackets that they are next to.

$= (4 \times 2a^{1+1}) + (4a \times 3) + (-2 \times 1a^{1+1}) + (-2a \times 2)$

Multiply the coefficients and add the exponents with like bases. Remember that a variable with no exponent has an implied exponent of 1.

$= 8a^2 + 12a - 2a^2 - 4a$

Group the like terms. Then, complete the operations.

$= (8a^2 - 2a^2) + (12a - 4a)$

$= 6a^2 + 8a$

17. C

Rewrite the expression as two binomials.

$(4\sqrt{5} - 3\sqrt{2})^2$

$= (4\sqrt{5} - 3\sqrt{2})(4\sqrt{5} - 3\sqrt{2})$

Use the FOIL strategy to multiply each term of the first binomial by each term of the second binomial.

Recall that when you are multiplying radicals, multiply the two radicands under the radical sign.

$\sqrt{2} \times \sqrt{5} = \sqrt{2 \times 5} = \sqrt{10}$

If you are multiplying two radicals that are the same, the radical is simplified by taking the square root.

$\sqrt{2} \times \sqrt{2} = \sqrt{2 \times 2} = \sqrt{4} = 2$

$4\sqrt{5} \times 4\sqrt{5} = 4 \times 4\sqrt{5 \times 5} = 16 \times 5 = 80$

$4\sqrt{5} \times -3\sqrt{2} = 4 \times -3\sqrt{5 \times 2} = -12\sqrt{10}$

$-3\sqrt{2} \times 4\sqrt{5} = -3 \times 4\sqrt{2 \times 5} = -12\sqrt{10}$

$-3\sqrt{2} \times -3\sqrt{2} = -3 \times -3\sqrt{2 \times 2} = 9 \times 2 = 18$

$= 80 - 12\sqrt{10} - 12\sqrt{10} + 18$

Group the like terms and simplify.

$= (80 + 18) + (-12\sqrt{10} - 12\sqrt{10})$

$= 98 - 24\sqrt{10}$

18. A

Write the two binomials on top of each other and use the vertical multiplication strategy.

Multiply $3x$ by each term in the top row. Then, multiply -4 by each term in the top row. Finally, combine the like terms together.

$2x + 7$

$\underline{3x - 4}$

$6x^2 + 21x$

$\underline{\quad - 8x - 28}$

$6x^2 + 13x - 28$

19. D

$3x + 9 = 7x - 19$

Move $3x$ to the other side of the equation by subtracting it from both sides.

$3x - 3x + 9 = 7x - 3x - 19$

$9 = 4x - 19$

Move 19 to the other side of the equation by adding it to both sides.

$9 + 19 = 4x - 19 + 19$

$28 = 4x$

Divide both sides of the equation by 4 to isolate the variable.

$\frac{28}{4} = \frac{4x}{4}$

$7 = x$

20. D

Find the lowest common denominator (LCD) of all the fractions.

2: 2, 4, 6, 8, 10, 12
3: 3, 6, 9,12
4: 4, 8, 12

The LCD is 12.

Multiply both sides of the equation by 12.

$6(x + 1) + 4(x + 2) + 3(x + 3) = 16 \times 12$

Distribute the coefficients through the brackets.

$6x + 6 + 4x + 8 + 3x + 9 = 192$

Group like terms and simplify.

$(6x + 4x + 3x) + (6 + 8 + 9) = 192$

$13x + 23 = 192$

Move the 23 to the other side of the equation by subtracting it from both sides.

$13x + 23 - 23 = 192 - 23$

$13x = 169$

Divide both sides by 13 to isolate x.

$\frac{13x}{13} = \frac{169}{13}$

$x = 13$

21. B

Recall the formula for the volume of a cone.

$V = \frac{1}{3}\pi r^2 h$

Substitute the given values into the formula.

$40 = \frac{1}{3}\pi 4^2 h$

Multiply both sides of the equation by 3 to eliminate the fractional coefficient.

$40 \times 3 = \frac{1}{3} \times 3\pi 4^2 h$

$120 = \pi 4^2 h$

Simplify the exponent and then multiply by π.

$120 = \pi 16h$

$120 = 50.24h$

Divide both sides by 50.24 to isolate h.

$\frac{120}{50.24} = \frac{50.24h}{50.24}$

$2.388\ 535\ 32 = h$

Round the answer to the hundredths place.

$h = 2.39$ cm

22. B

The perimeter of the rectangular soccer field is 420 m, and its width is $\frac{3}{4}$ its length. The perimeter of a rectangle $= 2l + 2w$.

Substitute $w = \frac{3}{4}l$ for w.

$420 = 2l + 2w$

$= 2l + 2\left(\frac{3}{4}l\right)$

Create equivalent fractions and simplify.

$420 = \frac{8}{4}l + \frac{6}{4}l$

$= \frac{14}{4}l$

$= \frac{7}{2}l$

Multiply both sides by the inverse fractional coefficient of $\frac{7}{2}$ to isolate l.

$\frac{2}{7} \times 420 = \frac{2}{7} \times \frac{7}{2}l$

$120 = l$

Therefore, the length of the soccer field is 120 m.

Substituting in 120 m, you can calculate the value of w as follows:

$w = \frac{3}{4}l$

$= \frac{3}{4}(120)$

$= 90$ m

Therefore, the width of the soccer field is 90 m.

Thus, the dimensions of the soccer field are 120.0 m × 90.0 m.

23. A

Define the variable.
Let x be the number of days.
If 25 people can build a house in 36 days, 15 people can build the same house in x days.

Write the equation.

$25 \times 36 = 15x$

Solve for x.

$900 = 15x$

$\frac{900}{15} = \frac{15x}{15}$

$60 = x$

It would take 60 days for 15 people to build the same house at the same rate.

Not for Reproduction

24. D

Peter can build the fence in 12 days. Jason can build the fence in 8 days.

In 1 day, Peter can build $\frac{1}{12}$ of the fence. In 1 day, Jason can build $\frac{1}{8}$ of the fence.

In 1 day, Peter and Jason working together can build the following portion of the fence.

$$\frac{1}{12}+\frac{1}{8}=\frac{2}{24}+\frac{3}{24}=\frac{5}{24}$$

Find how long it will take the boys to build the fence together.

$$1\div\frac{5}{24}=1\times\frac{24}{5}=\frac{24}{5}=4\frac{4}{5}$$

Therefore, Peter and Jason together can build the fence in $4\frac{4}{5}$ days.

25. a) OR

Arthur receives 1.9% of an owner's revenue, of which 25% goes to Tim and Eric. Let the owner's revenue be x.

Then, the value that Arthur receives is $0.019x$ (since 1.9% = 0.019 in decimal notation).

Tim and Eric receive 25% of what Arthur receives. In algebraic form, this is
25% of $0.019x = 0.25(0.019x)$.

This expression represents the amount of money that Tim and Eric receive from a franchise.

b) OR

Points	Sample Answer
4	Arthur takes 1.9 % of the owner's revenue, and of that, he gives 25 % to the brothers. Determine the dollar value of the 1.9% that Arthur takes of the \$2.3 million. 1.9% = 0.019 in decimal notation The amount Arthur receives from the given location is 0.019 × \$23 000.000 = \$43 700.00 If the brothers get 25% of what Arthur receives, then you have to find 25% of the \$43 700.00. 25% = 0.25 in decimal notation 0.25 × \$43 700.00 = \$10 925.00 The brothers receive \$10 925.00 from a location with \$2.3 million of revenue.
	Application of knowledge and skills in solving problems that can be modelled with first-degree equations shows a high degree of effectiveness due to: • a thorough understanding of the concepts • an accurate application of the procedures (any minor errors and/or omissions do not detract from the demonstration of a thorough understanding)
3	Substitutes the correct number into the expression and has a minor calculation error.
	Application of knowledge and skills in solving problems that can be modelled with first-degree equations shows considerable effectiveness due to: • minor errors and/or omissions in the application of the procedures • an understanding of most of the concepts
2	Substitutes the correct value into the expression, but performs calculations in the wrong order.
	Application of knowledge and skills in solving problems that can be modelled with first-degree equations shows some effectiveness due to: • a partial understanding of the concepts • minor errors and/or omissions in the application of the procedures
1	Substitutes the wrong value into the expression, but the calculations are done correctly.
	Application of knowledge and skills in solving problems that can be modeled with first-degree equations shows limited effectiveness due to: • a misunderstanding of concepts • an incorrect selection or misuse of procedures

Copyright Protected

UNIT TEST — NUMBER SENSE AND ALGEBRA

Use the following information to answer the next question.

$3p^3 + 14q^2 + r^3 - 2p^3$

1. What is the value of this expression, given that $p = 1$, $q = -2$, and $r = -3$?

A. −59 **B.** 30

C. 65 **D.** 66

Open Response

2. What is the value of the expression $\frac{1}{2}x^4 + 3x^3 - 2x + 2$ when $x = 2$?

Show your work.

Use the following information to answer the next question.

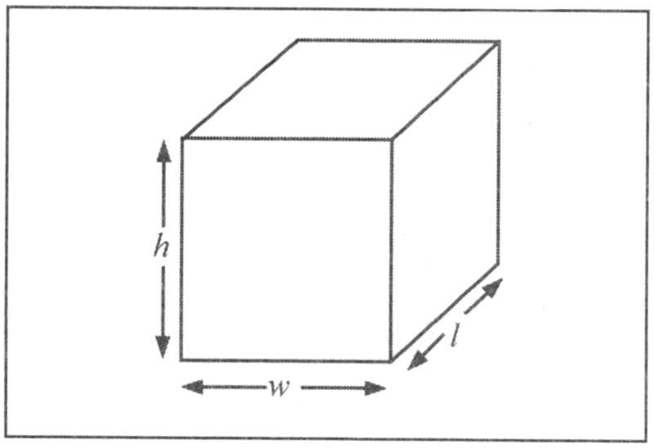

Open Response

3. The formula for finding the surface area (A) of a rectangular prism (shown above) is $A = 2lw + 2wh + 2lh$. If the length is 4 cm, the width is 5 cm, and the height is 6 cm, what is the surface area of the rectangular prism?

Use the following information to answer the next question.

The lengths of the parallel sides of a trapezoid are 15 m and 25 m. The perpendicular distance between the parallel sides is 10 m.

4. What is the area of the trapezoid?

A. 200 m^2 **B.** 200 m^3

C. 400 m^2 **D.** 400 m^3

5. If the side length of a cube is x metres, then the volume can be expressed as

A. x m **B.** $3x$ m^2

C. x^3 m^3 **D.** $3x^3$ m^3

Not for Reproduction

6. What is the quotient when $a^3b^3 + ab^5 + a^4b^3$ is divided by ab^3?

A. $a^3 + b^2 + a^4$

B. $a^2 + b^2 + a^3$

C. $a^3 + b^3 + a^4$

D. $a^2 + b + a^3$

7. What is the simplified form of the expression $\left(\frac{2x^2}{3y^3}\right)^3$?

A. $\frac{5x^5}{6y^6}$ **B.** $\frac{5x^6}{6y^9}$

C. $\frac{8x^5}{27y^6}$ **D.** $\frac{8x^6}{27y^9}$

8. What is the **most** simplified form of the expression $\frac{(2x^2y^3)\left(\frac{1}{2x^2y^3}\right)}{((3x \times y^6)(4x^4y^{-1}))^0(xy)^0}$?

A. $\frac{1}{3xy^6}$

B. $\frac{1}{12x^5y^5}$

C. undefined

D. 1

9. What is the value of $(-4) \times (-2) + (-10) - (-1)$?

A. -3 **B.** -1

C. 17 **D.** 79

Use the following information to answer the next multipart question.

10. A recipe for chocolate-chip cookies is based on the requirement of 50 mL of sugar for every 250 mL of flour.

Open Response

a) If a batch of these cookies is made with 750 mL of flour, how much sugar is needed?

b) What is the ratio of flour to sugar in the given recipe?

Show your work.

11. A web designer who charges $30.00/h decreases his hourly rate by 40% for a friend. How much money will he now earn after working 5 hours?

A. $12.00 **B.** $18.00

C. $60.00 **D.** $90.00

12. A clothing retailer adds a 20% markup to the wholesale cost of his merchandise. If the retail price of a jacket is $330.00, what is the wholesale cost?

A. $235.00 **B.** $275.00

C. $300.00 **D.** $575.00

Open Response

13. A car's rate of fuel consumption is based on the number of kilometres travelled per litre. Fred filled his car's 35 L gas tank to its full capacity before a long drive. He travelled 455 km before the tank was empty. What is his car's rate of fuel consumption?

Show your work.

14. The expression $\sqrt{c^4 \div c^2}$ in its **simplest** form is

A. c^3 **B.** c^2

C. c **D.** $\frac{1}{c^2}$

15. The area of a square is 142.7 m^2. The **best** estimate of the length of each side of the square is

A. 12 m **B.** 15 m

C. 18 m **D.** 30 m

16. Which of the following polynomials is equivalent to $(7x^2 - 2x - 4) - (-2x^2 - 2x + 6)$?

A. $5x^2 - 4x + 2$

B. $9x^2 - 10$

C. $9x^2 - 4x - 10$

D. $9x^2 + 2$

17. When the expression $4x^3(6x^2 - 4x + 3)$ is simplified, the result is

A. $24x^5 - 16x^4 + 12x^3$

B. $24x - 16x^4 + 12x^3$

C. $24x^6 - 16x^4 + 12^3$

D. $24x^5 - 16x^4 + 12x$

18. An equivalent form of the expression $2(4x - 3)(4x + 3)$ is

A. $64x^2 - 96x - 36$

B. $64x^2 - 36$

C. $32x^2 + 48x - 18$

D. $32x^2 - 18$

19. The expression $(3x - 2)(x + 5)$ is represented by which of the following algebra tile grids?

A.
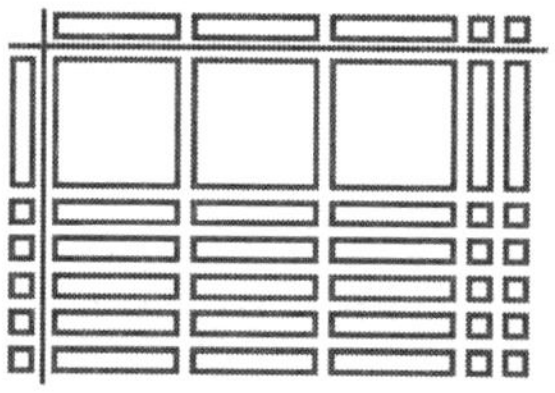

B.
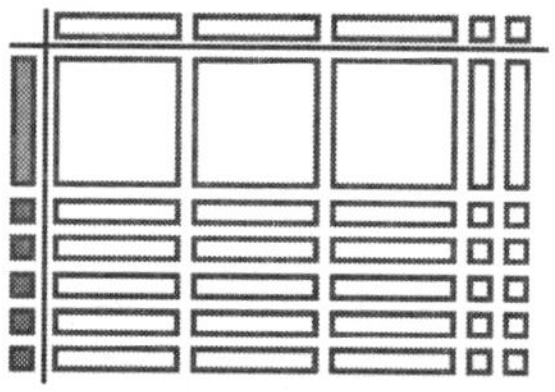

C.
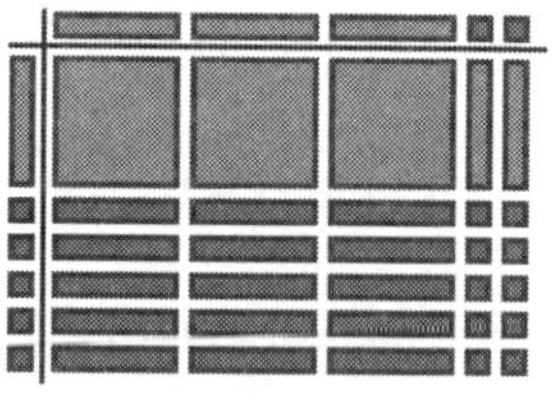

D.
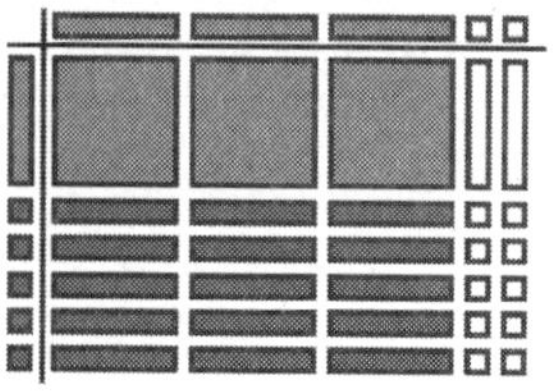

Not for Reproduction

Use the following information to answer the next question.

A square with a side length of $(2x + 3)$ m is mounted along the width of a rectangle whose length is $(4x + 1)$ m. The width of the rectangle is equal to the side length of the square.

Open Response

20. What is the combined area of the square and the rectangle?

Show your work.

21. What is the value of x in the equation $12x = 50x - 20$?

A. 38 **B.** $\frac{10}{19}$

C. $-\frac{10}{19}$ **D.** -38

22. The area of a rectangle is 240 cm^2. If the width of the rectangle is 6 cm, then what is its length?

A. 40 cm **B.** 116 cm

C. 232 cm **D.** 1 440 cm

Use the following information to answer the next question.

The owners of a hotel decide to renovate. The hotel has 189 rooms for guests to stay in, of which 9 are specialty suites. The owners spend $7 000 000 on refurbishing the rooms. An equal amount was spent on each specialty suite and an equal amount was spent on each regular suite.

23. Twice as much money is spent on each specialty suite than on each regular suite. Rounded to the nearest dollar, how much do the owners spend to refurbish each specialty suite?

A. $33 354.00 **B.** $65 421.00

C. $69 815.00 **D.** $70 707.00

24. A particular rectangle is 3 times longer than it is wide, and its perimeter is 20 cm. What is the width of the rectangle?

A. 2.5 cm **B.** 10 cm

C. 15 cm **D.** 18.75 cm

Open Response

25. Alex lives on an acreage. Alex can cut and trim the grass in 2 hours. Alex's son can cut and trim the grass in 3 hours. Working together, what is the time it will take Alex and his son to cut and trim the grass?

Show your work.

ANSWERS AND SOLUTIONS — UNIT TEST

1. B	7. D	12. B	18. D	24. A
2. OR	8. D	13. OR	19. D	25. OR
3. OR	9. B	14. C	20. OR	
4. A	10. a) OR	15. A	21. B	
5. C	b) OR	16. B	22. A	
6. B	11. D	17. A	23. D	

1. B

Replace the p with 1, the q with −2, and the r with −3.

$3p^3 + 14q^2 + r^3 - 2p^3$

$= 3(1)^3 + 14(-2)^2 + (-3)^3 - 2(1)^3$

Factor the base the number of times indicated by the exponent.

$= \begin{pmatrix} 3(1 \times 1 \times 1) + 14(-2 \times -2) \\ +(-3 \times -3 \times -3) - 2(1 \times 1 \times 1) \end{pmatrix}$

Perform the multiplication first and then the addition and subtraction in order from left to right.

$= 3(1) + 14(4) + (-27) - 2(1)$
$= 3 + 56 + (-27) - 2$
$= 30$

2. OR

If $x = 2$, start by substituting 2 into the equation at every place there is an x.

Solve according to the order of operations (BEDMAS).

$\frac{1}{2}(2)^4 + 3(2)^3 - 2(2) + 2$

Calculate the exponents first.

$= \frac{1}{2}(16) + 3(8) - 2(2) + 2$

Perform multiplication and division in order from left to right.

$= 8 + 24 - 4 + 2$

Perform addition and subtraction in order from left to right.

$= 32 - 4 + 2$
$= 28 + 2$
$= 30$

3. OR

Points	Sample Answer
4	In the equation $A = 2lw + 2wh + 2lh$, substitute 4 cm for l, 5 cm for w, and 6 cm for h. $A = 2(4)(5) + 2(5)(6) + 2(4)(6)$ Simplify by following the order of operations, completing the multiplication operations first. $A = 2(20) + 2(30) + 2(24)$ $A = 40 + 60 + 48$ Complete the addition. $A = 148$ Recall that the question is asking for surface area. You are multiplying two dimensions when calculating area, so the units are squared. $A = 148\ \text{cm}^2$
Application of knowledge and skills involving algebraic and geometric representations shows a high degree of effectiveness due to: • a thorough understanding of the concepts • an accurate application of the procedures (any minor errors and/or omissions do not detract from the demonstration of a thorough understanding)	
3	The units in the final answer are cubed instead of squared. The wrong values are substituted in, but the calculations and units are correct.
Application of knowledge and skills involving algebraic and geometric representations shows considerable effectiveness due to: • an understanding of most of the concepts • minor errors and/or omissions in the application of the procedures	

Points	Sample Answer
2	The values are substituted in correctly, but the order of operations is completed incorrectly. The units are written with an exponent of one.
Application of knowledge and skills involving algebraic and geometric representations shows some effectiveness due to: • minor errors and/or omissions in the application of the procedures • an understanding of most of the concepts	
1	The values are substituted incorrectly and calculations are incomplete. Units are not included in the answer.
Application of knowledge and skills involving algebraic and geometric representations shows limited effectiveness due to: • a misunderstanding of concepts • an incorrect selection or misuse of procedures	

4. A

Lengths of the parallel sides $= 15$ m and 25 m
Height of trapezoid $= 10$ m

$\therefore$ Area of the trapezoid $= \frac{1}{2}$(sum of parallel sides) × height

$= \left[\frac{1}{2}(15+25) \times 10\right] \text{m}^2$

$= 200 \text{ m}^2$

Because area is measuring two dimensions, length times width, the units are squared.

Therefore, the area of the trapezoid is 200 m^2.

5. C

Volume of a cube $=$ side × side × side.

Three dimensions are being multiplied, so only answers with cubic units can be considered correct.

$\text{m} \times \text{m} \times \text{m} = \text{m}^3$

Volume $= (\text{side})^3 = x^3$

Volume $= x^3 \text{ m}^3$

6. B

Break the question up into its separate terms.

$$\frac{a^3b^3}{ab^3} + \frac{ab^5}{ab^3} + \frac{a^4b^3}{ab^3}$$

Subtract the exponents that have the same base and then simplify.

$$\begin{aligned}&\left(a^{3-1}b^{3-3}\right) + \left(a^{1-1}b^{5-3}\right) + \left(a^{4-1}b^{3-3}\right)\\ &= \left(a^2b^0\right) + \left(a^0b^2\right) + \left(a^3b^0\right)\\ &= \left(a^2 1\right) + \left(1b^2\right) + \left(a^3 1\right)\\ &= a^2 + b^2 + a^3\end{aligned}$$

7. D

The exponent is applied to everything in the brackets, as outlined in the exponent laws.

$$\begin{aligned}&\left(\frac{2x^2}{3y^3}\right)^3\\ &= \left(\frac{2x^2}{3y^3}\right)\left(\frac{2^x2}{3y^3}\right)\left(\frac{2x^2}{3y^3}\right)\\ &= \frac{(2 \times 2 \times 2)\left(x^{2+2+2}\right)}{(3 \times 3 \times 3)\left(y^{3+3+3}\right)}\\ &= \frac{8x^6}{27y^9}\end{aligned}$$

8. D

Simplify the numerator first.

$$\frac{2x^2y^3}{1} \times \frac{1}{2x^2y^3} = \frac{2x^2y^3}{2x^2y^3}$$

$$\begin{aligned}&= 2 \div 2x^{2-2}y^{3-3}\\ &= 1\end{aligned}$$

Then, simplify the denominator. The terms $\left(3xy^6\right)\left(4x^4y^{-1}\right)$ and (xy) are both raised to the power of 0. According to the exponent laws, we know that any number raised to 0 equals 1.

Therefore, the expression reduces to $\frac{1}{1} = 1$.

9. B

Start by rewriting the subtraction operation. Remember to add the opposite.

$= (-4) \times (-2) + (-10) + (+1)$

Now, follow the order of operations (BEDMAS). First, complete multiplication and division from left to right. As two negatives are being multiplied, the product is positive.

$= (-4) \times (-2) = (+8)$

$= 8 + (-10) + (+1)$

Complete the addition and subtraction in order from left to right. When adding a positive and negative number together, subtract the two absolute values and take the sign of the larger absolute value.

$= 10 - 8 = 2$

The larger absolute value is 10, so its sign is given to the result.

$= -2$

$= (-2) + (+1)$

Because 2 is the larger absolute value, the result is negative.

$= 2 - 1 = 1$
$= -1$

10. a) OR

Points	Sample Answer
4	Even with a larger batch of cookies than what can be made with the original recipe, the ratio of sugar to flour must be kept the same. The original recipe requires 50 mL of sugar for every 250 mL of flour. The amount of flour increases to 750 mL. To determine how much sugar is needed, set up equivalent ratios. $\frac{50\text{ mL}}{250\text{ mL}} = \frac{x\text{ mL}}{750\text{ mL}}$ Now, use either cross products or equivalent fractions to solve for the missing value. Cross products strategy: multiply the numerator of each fraction by the denominator of the other fraction. $50 \times 750 = 250x$ $37\ 500 = 250x$ Divide by 250 to solve for x. $\frac{37\ 500}{250} = \frac{250x}{250}$ $150 = x$ Equivalent fractions strategy: determine what 250 is multiplied by to get a value of 750. Then, multiply the sugar amount by this number. $\frac{50}{250 \times 3} = \frac{x}{750}$ $\frac{50 \times 3}{250 \times 3} = \frac{150}{750}$ Therefore, 150 mL of sugar would be required to make the larger batch of cookies.

Points	Sample Answer
	Application of knowledge and skills involving solving problems requiring the manipulation of expressions arising from applications of ratios and proportion shows a high degree of effectiveness due to: • a thorough understanding of the concepts • an accurate application of the procedures (any minor errors and/or omissions do not detract from the demonstration of a thorough understanding)
3	The ratios are set up incorrectly in that 250 mL flour does not equal 50 mL sugar. However, solving for x is completed correctly and the solution is 150 mL. $\frac{250\text{ mL flour}}{750\text{ mL flour}} = \frac{50\text{ mL sugar}}{x\text{ mL sugar}}$
	Application of knowledge and skills involving solving problems requiring the manipulation of expressions arising from applications of ratios and proportion shows considerable effectiveness due to: • minor errors and/or omissions in the application of the procedures • an understanding of most of the concepts
2	There is no connection with the ratios, but the cross products strategy is applied correctly. $\frac{250\text{ mL flour}}{750\text{ mL flour}} = \frac{x\text{ mL sugar}}{50\text{ mL sugar}}$ $50 \times 250 = 750x$ $12\ 500 = 750x$ $\frac{12\ 500}{750} = \frac{750x}{750}$
	Application of knowledge and skills involving solving problems requiring the manipulation of expressions arising from applications of ratios and proportion shows some effectiveness due to: • a partial understanding of the concepts • minor errors and/or omissions in the application of the procedures
1	Ratios are set up incorrectly. There is no solution for x. $\frac{250\text{ mL flour}}{750\text{ mL flour}} = \frac{50\text{ mL sugar}}{x\text{ mL sugar}}$
	Application of knowledge and skills involving solving problems requiring the manipulation of expressions arising from applications of ratios and proportion shows limited effectiveness due to:

Not for Reproduction

Points	Sample Answer
	• a misunderstanding of concepts • an incorrect selection or misuse of procedures

b) OR

Points	Sample Answer
4	Application of knowledge and skills involving solving problems requiring the manipulation of expressions arising from applications of ratios and proportion shows a high degree of effectiveness due to: • a thorough understanding of the concepts • an accurate application of the procedures (any minor errors and/or omissions do not detract from the demonstration of a thorough understanding) Solution Set up the original ratio. Remember to keep the order of the measurements correct with how they are listed in the question. $\frac{250}{50}$ Reduce the ratio to lowest terms by dividing both numbers by 50. $\frac{250 \div 50}{50 \div 50} = \frac{5}{1}$ The ratio of flour to sugar is $\frac{5}{1}$, 5:1, or five to one.
3	Application of knowledge and skills involving solving problems requiring the manipulation of expressions arising from applications of ratios and proportion shows considerable effectiveness due to: • minor errors and/or omissions in the application of the procedures • an understanding of most of the concepts Example The ratio is set up correctly. The calculations are done correctly, but not reduced to lowest terms. $\frac{250 \div 25}{50 \div 25} = \frac{10}{2}$

Points	Sample Answer
2	Application of knowledge and skills involving solving problems requiring the manipulation of expressions arising from applications of ratios and proportion shows some effectiveness due to: • a partial understanding of the concepts • minor errors and/or omissions in the application of the procedures Example The ratio is set up in reverse. The calculations are done correctly, but not reduced to lowest terms. $\frac{50 \div 25}{250 \div 25} = \frac{2}{10}$
1	Application of knowledge and skills involving solving problems requiring the manipulation of expressions arising from applications of ratios and proportion shows limited effectiveness due to: • a misunderstanding of concepts • an incorrect selection or misuse of procedures Example The ratio is set up correctly, but not reduced.

11. D

To calculate the percentage of a rate, multiply the rate by the percentage.

First change the percentage to a decimal.

$40\% = \frac{40}{100} = 40 \div 100 = 0.4$

Multiply the rate by the decimal to get the decrease in rate.
$\$30.00/\text{h} \times 0.4 = \$12.00/\text{h}$

Subtract $12.00 from the original rate to get the reduced rate.
$\$30.00 - \$12.00 = \$18.00$

He worked 5 hours at the lower rate. Multiply 5 by the rate of $18.00 / h.
$5 \times \$18.00/\text{h} = \$90.00$

12. B

The retail price of the jacket is the wholesale cost plus 20%. Work backward to find the wholesale cost.

Let x = wholesale cost.
$0.2x$ = 20% of wholesale cost.

Retail = wholeale + mark up
$330 = x + 0.2x$
$330 = 1.2x$
$\frac{330}{1.2} = \frac{1.2}{1.2}x$
$275 = x$

The wholesale cost is \$ 275.00

13. OR

Set up the rate comparing kilometres travelled to litres of fuel consumed.
$\frac{455 \text{ km}}{35 \text{ L}}$

To calculate the unit rate, divide the first term by the second term.
$455 \div 35 = 13$

Now, add the units of measurement behind the quotient.

13 km/L

14. C

To simplify $\sqrt{c^4 \div c^2}$, use the exponent laws to reduce the expression under the radical.

$c^4 \div c^2 = c^{4-2} = c^2$

Therefore, $\sqrt{c^2} = \sqrt{c \times c} = c$.

15. A

The area, A, of a square is $s \times s$, where s is the length of each side of the square.
$s = \sqrt{A}$

Round 142.7 to the closest number whose square root is a whole number.

$142.7 \rightarrow 144$

$s = \sqrt{144}$
$s = 12$ m (since $12 \times 12 = 144$)

The best estimate is 12 m.

16. B

Rewrite the subtraction by adding the opposite, as with integers.
$(7x^2 - 2x - 4) - (-2x^2 - 2x + 6)$
$= (7x^2 - 2x - 4) + (+2x^2 + 2x - 6)$

Group the like terms together.
$= (7x^2 + 2x^2) + (-2x + 2x) + (-4 - 6)$

Complete the operations.
$= 9x^2 + 0 - 10$
$= 9x^2 - 10$

17. A

Distribute $4x^3$ through each term inside the brackets.
$= [4x^3 \times 6x^2] + [4x^3 \times (-4x)] + [4x^3 \times 3]$

Multiply the coefficients and add the exponents of the like bases. Remember, a variable with no exponent has an implied exponent of 1.
$= (24x^{3+2}) + (-16x^{3+1}) + (12x^3)$
$= 24x^5 - 16x^4 + 12x^3$

18. D

Use the distributive property to distribute the 2 through the first set of brackets.
$= [(2 \times 4x) - (2 \times 3)](4x + 3)$
$= (8x - 6)(4x + 3)$

Use the FOIL strategy to multiply each term within the first brackets by each term within the second brackets.
$= (8x \times 4x) + (8x \times 3) + (-6 \times 4x) + (-6 \times 3)$
$= 32x^2 + 24x - 24x - 18$

Collect like terms.
$= 32x^2 + (24x - 24x) - 18$
$= 32x^2 + 0 - 18$

Simplify.
$= 32x^2 - 18$

19. D

Step 1
Use the FOIL strategy to expand the polynomial.
$(3x - 2)(x + 5)$
$= 3x^2 + 15x - 2x - 10$
$= 3x^2 + 13x - 10$

Not for Reproduction

Step 2

Eliminate the algebra tiles that do not include a mix of positive and negative tiles.

Positive tiles are shaded and negative tiles are white.

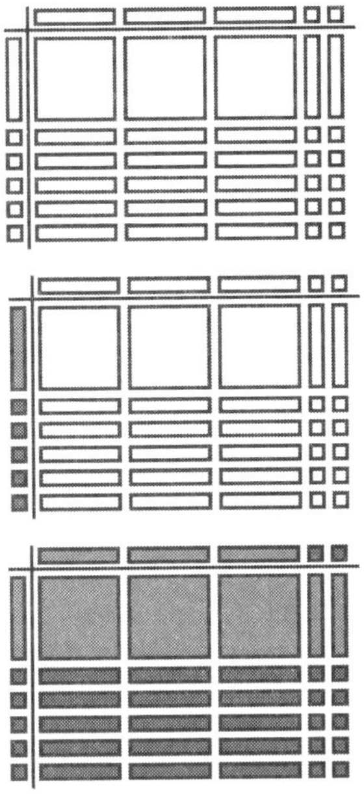

are not correct because they do not include a mix of positive and negative tiles.

Step 3

The correct grid will represent $3x$ as three shaded rectangles and -2 as two white squares.

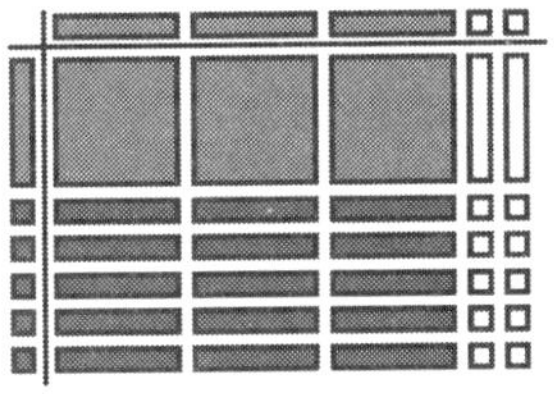

20. OR

$s_{\text{square}} = (2x+3)$ m

Total area

$A_{\text{square}} = (2x+3)(2x+3)$ m^2

$l_{\text{rectangle}} = (4x+1)$ m

Width of the rectangle

$w_{\text{rectangle}} = s_{\text{square}} = (2x+3)$ m

$A_{\text{rectangle}} = [(2x+3)(4x+1)]$ m^2

$$A_{\text{total}} = \begin{bmatrix} (2x+3)(2x+3) \\ +(2x+3)(4x+1) \end{bmatrix} \text{m}^2$$

Use the FOIL strategy to expand the polynomials.

$$= \begin{pmatrix} 4x^2+6x+6x+9 \\ +8x^2+2x+12x+3 \end{pmatrix} \text{m}^2$$

$$= \begin{pmatrix} 4x^2+12x+9 \\ +8x^2+14x+3 \end{pmatrix} \text{m}^2$$

Collect like terms and simplify.

$= (12x^2+26x+12)$ m^2

21. B

$12x = 50x - 20$

Move the constant (20) to the other side of the equal sign.

$12x + 20 = 50x - 20 + 20$

$12x + 20 = 50x$

Group the terms with the variables together.

$12x - 12x + 20 = 50x - 12x$

$20 = 38x$

Isolate x by dividing both sides by 38.

$$\frac{20}{38} = \frac{38x}{38}$$

$$\frac{20}{38} = x$$

Reduce the fraction to lowest terms.

$$\frac{20 \div 2}{38 \div 2} = \frac{10}{19}$$

$$x = \frac{10}{19}$$

22. A

Recall the formula for area is $A = l \times w$.

To solve for length, the formula will have to be adjusted using algebraic techniques.

$$\frac{A}{w} = \frac{l \times w}{w}$$

$$\frac{A}{w} = l$$

Substitute the given values into the formula and perform division.

$$\frac{240}{6} = l$$

$l = 40$ cm

23. D

Define the variable.
Let x be the cost of a regular room.
Specialty suites are twice as expensive $\rightarrow 2x$

Write the equation.
$7,0,0 = 180x + 9(2x)$

Solve for x.
$700 = 180x + 18x$
$700 = 198x$
$\frac{700}{198} = \frac{198x}{198}$
$35353.54 = x$

Specialty suite $= 2x = 2 \times 35353.54 = 70707.07$

The owners spend $70 707.07 on each specialty suite.

24. A

Define the variable.
Let x be the width.
Length is 3 times longer $\rightarrow 3x$

Perimeter $= 2(l + w)$

Write the equation.
$2(x + 3x) = 20$

Solve for x.
Distribute the 2 to the terms inside the brackets.

$2(x + 3x) = 20$

$2x + 6x = 20$

$8x = 20$

Divide both sides by 8 to isolate the variable.

$\frac{8x}{8} = \frac{20}{8}$

$x = 2.5$

Check your answer.
$2(2.5 + 3 \times 2.5) = 20$

$2(2.5 + 7.5) = 20$

$2(10) = 20$

$20 = 20$

The width is 2.5 cm.

25. OR

Define the variable.

	Time to Complete Job	Part of Job Completed in 1 h
Alex	2 h	$\frac{1}{2}$
Son	3 h	$\frac{1}{3}$
Together	t h	$\frac{1}{t}$

Write the equation.

The word "together" implies addition.

$\frac{1}{2} + \frac{1}{3} = \frac{1}{t}$

Multiply each term by the lowest common denominator, which is $6t$.

$6t \cdot \frac{1}{2} + 6t \cdot \frac{1}{3} = 6t \cdot \frac{1}{t}$

Simplify.

$3t + 2t = 6$

$5t = 6$

$t = \frac{6}{5} = 1.2$ hours

Linear Relations

Copyright Protected

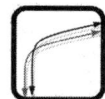

LINEAR RELATIONS

Table of Correlations

	Specific Expectation	Practice Questions	Unit Test Questions	Practice Test 1	Practice Test 2
9LRV.01	Using Data Management to Investigate Relationships				
9LR1.01	*interpret the meanings of points on scatter plots or graphs that represent linear relations, including scatter plots or graphs in more than one quadrant*	1, 2	32, 33	31	
9LR1.02	*pose problems, identify variables, and formulate hypotheses associated with relationships between two variables*	3, 4	34, 35		
9LR1.03	*design and carry out an investigation or experiment involving relationships between two variables, including the collection and organization of data, using appropriate methods, equipment, and/or technology and techniques*	5, 6	36, 37		
9LR1.04	*describe trends and relationships observed in data, make inferences from data, compare the inferences with hypotheses about the data, and explain any differences between the inferences and the hypotheses*	7, 8, 9	38, 39, 40, 41		31
9LRV.02	Understanding Characteristics of Linear Relations				
9LR2.01	*construct tables of values, graphs, and equations, using a variety of tools to represent linear relations derived from descriptions of realistic situations*	10, 11	1, 2, 3, 4	1	
9LR2.02	*construct tables of values, scatter plots, and lines or curves of best fit as appropriate, using a variety of tools for linearly related and non-linearly related data collected from a variety of sources*	12, 13	5, 6, 7, 8		1
9LR2.03	*identify, through investigation, some properties of linear relations, and apply these properties to determine whether a relation is linear or non-linear*	14, 15	9, 10, 11	2	2
9LR2.04	*compare the properties of direct variation and partial variation in applications, and identify the initial value*	16, 17	12, 13, 14, 15	3	3
9LR2.05	*determine the equation of a line of best fit for a scatter plot, using an informal process*	18, 19, 20	16, 17, 18	4	4
9LRV.03	Connecting Various Representations of Linear Relations				
9LR3.01	*determine values of a linear relation by using a table of values, by using the equation of the relation, and by interpolating or extrapolating from the graph of the relation*	21, 22	19, 20, 21, 22	5	
9LR3.02	*describe a situation that would explain the events illustrated by a given graph of a relationship between two variables*	23, 24	23, 24, 25		5
9LR3.03	*determine other representations of a linear relation, given one representation*	25, 26	26, 27	6	6
9LR3.04	*describe the effects on a linear graph and make the corresponding changes to the linear equation when the conditions of the situation they represent are varied*	27, 28	28, 29, 30, 31	7	7

Not for Reproduction

9LR1.01 interpret the meanings of points on scatter plots or graphs that represent linear relations, including scatter plots or graphs in more than one quadrant

Interpreting Points on a Scatter Plot

A **scatter plot** represents data that displays the relationship or correlation between two variables. The x-axis represents the independent variable and the y-axis represents the dependent variable. An **independent variable** (x) is a variable that you can change. For example, if you conduct an experiment to see how long it will take for different volumes of water to boil on the stove, the independent variable could be the various volumes of water used. The **dependent variable** (y) responds to the independent variable. In the given example, the dependent variable is the time it takes for the various volumes of water to boil.

The variables are plotted as points on a **coordinate plane**. The location of each point is represented as an **ordered pair**. Each ordered pair (x, y) contains an x- and y-value, according to where the point is situated on each axis.

To interpret any point (x, y) on a scatter plot, begin at the **origin** (0, 0). Follow along the x-axis to the position of the point and note its value. Then follow the y-axis to the point and note its value. These two values are the ordered pair for the particular point.

Example
What does point (3, 2) mean on the following graph?

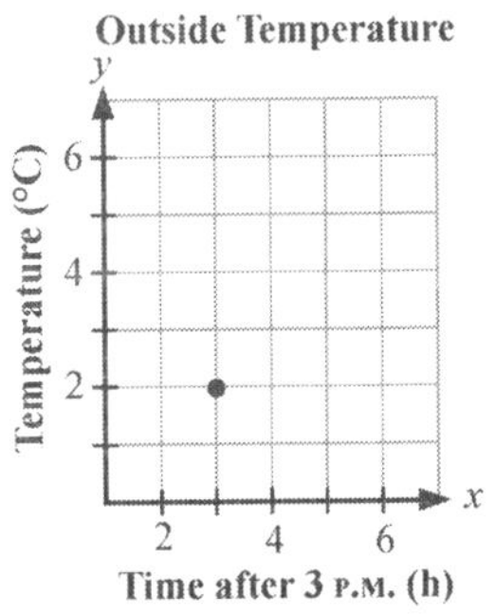

The 3 indicates 3 hours after 3:00 P.M., or 6:00 P.M. The 2 indicates an outside temperature of 2°C.

Use the following information to answer the next question.

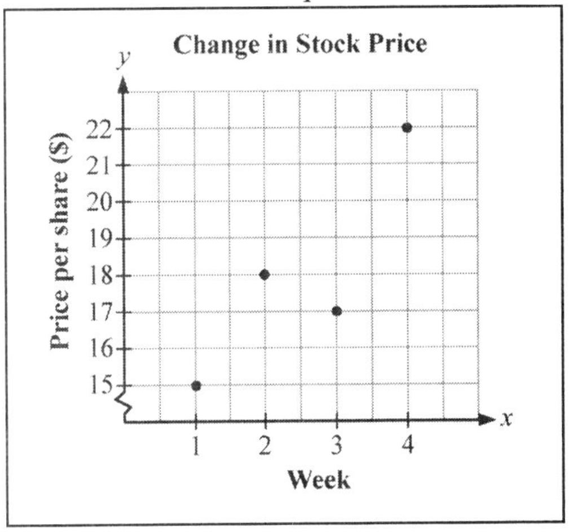

1. Leslie bought 1 0 shares of the stock during week 1 and sold these shares at the end of week 4. What was the value of Leslie's profit or loss?

   A. $1 500 **B.** $7 000
   C. $22 000 **D.** $37 000

Use the following information to answer the next question.

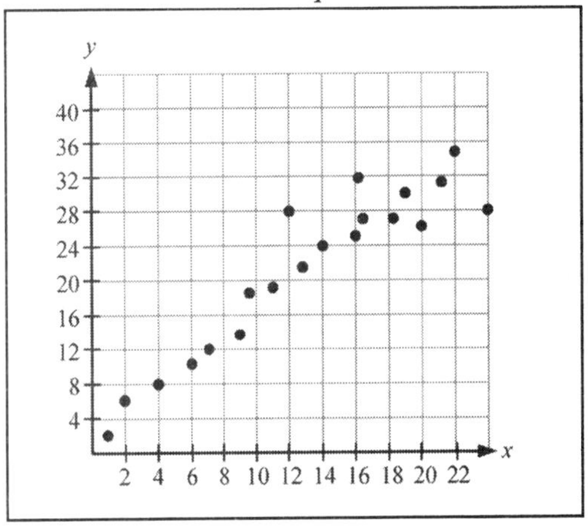

2. When $x = 20$, the value of y is

   A. 24
   B. 26
   C. 29
   D. 31

Copyright Protected

9LR1.02 pose problems, identify variables, and formulate hypotheses associated with relationships between two variables

Identifying Variables and Formulating Hypotheses

When a question is presented about an event, understanding the relationship between the two variables is important. Before the question can be solved, the variables are identified and one or more hypotheses are formulated. A **hypothesis** is an educated guess or statement about the relationship between the two variables. The information gathered to make the hypothesis can come from statistics (primary data) that you gather directly or from other sources you find through research (secondary data).

Example

Does the rebound height of a ball depend upon the height from which it was dropped?

Before you carry out the experiment, identify the variables and formulate hypotheses.

Independent variable – height from which the ball is dropped
Dependent variable – height to which the ball rebounds
Hypotheses:

1. The rebound height of a ball increases as the height from which it was dropped increases.
2. The rebound height of a ball is directly proportional to the height from which it was dropped.
3. The rebound height of a ball decreases as the height from which it was dropped increases.

Use the following information to answer the next question.

John wanted to determine if there was any correlation between the number of car accidents and the age of the driver.

3. What is the independent variable in this relationship?

A. Type of car

B. Age of the driver

C. Gender of the driver

D. Number of accidents

4. Which of the following statements is the **best** hypothesis about attendance and a student's final mark?

A. A student who has very good attendance will get a high final mark.

B. A student who has very good attendance will get a low final mark.

C. A student who has very poor attendance will get a low final mark.

D. A student who has very poor attendance will get a high final mark.

9LR1.03 design and carry out an investigation or experiment involving relationships between two variables, including the collection and organization of data, using appropriate methods, equipment, and/or technology and techniques

Designing an Investigation

To carry out an investigation involving the relationship between two variables, you need to answer the following questions before you can begin:

- What two variables are you going to examine?
- How will you measure the **data**?
- How will you organize and present your findings?

Not for Reproduction

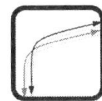

After you have determined the variables, decide on how to measure the data. This may involve tools such as metre sticks or thermometers. When your data is presented, consider what method best represents the relationship between the variables. For instance, one type of relationship might be best represented with a line graph, another type might suit a circle graph.

Use the following information to answer the next question.

Josette plans to carry out an experiment. She wants to investigate the temperature of ice water in a container and the time it takes for the temperature to change.

5. Which of the following lists contains all the necessary items for Josette's experiment?

A. 500 mL plastic cup, water at room temperature, a metre stick, a clock, and a thermometer

B. 500 mL plastic cup, water at room temperature, a clock, and a thermometer

C. 500 mL plastic cup, ice water, a metre stick, a clock, and a thermometer

D. 500 mL plastic cup, ice water, a clock, and a thermometer

Use the following information to answer the next question.

The following table shows data taken from the attendance register of a class for a particular month.

Number of days absent	2	3	4	5	6
Number of students	4	5	2	1	3

6. Which of the following scatter plots **correctly** represents the given data?

A.

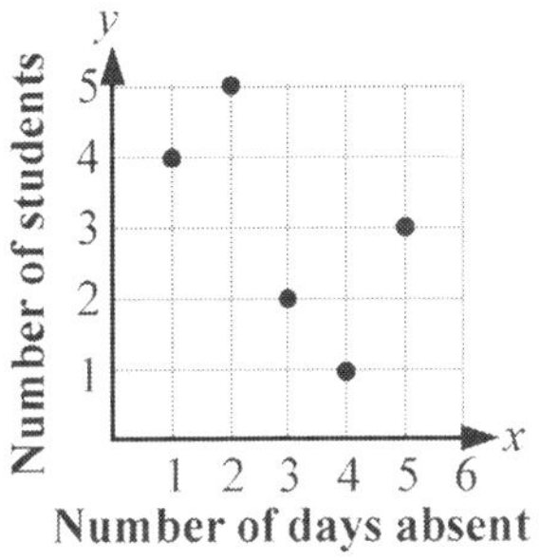

B.

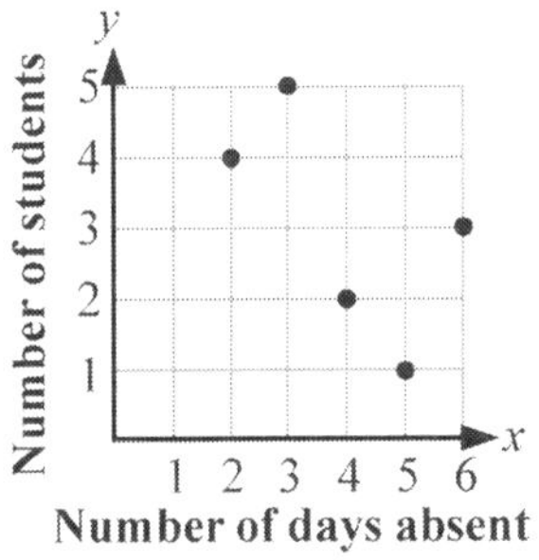

C.

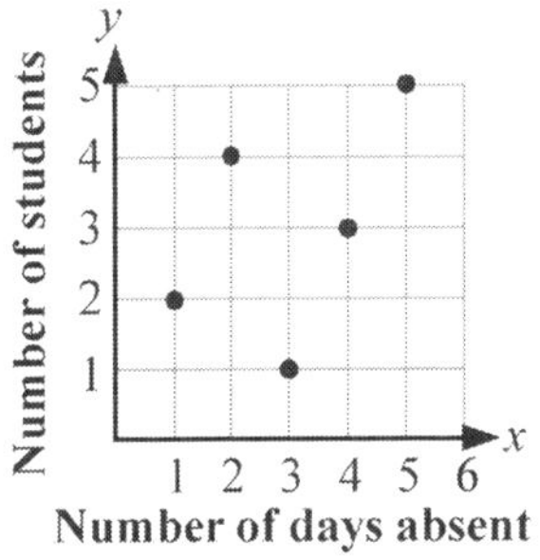

D.

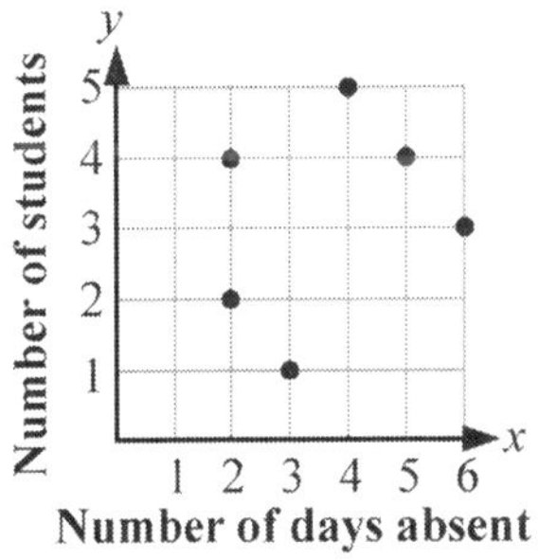

Copyright Protected

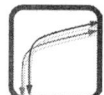

9LR1.04 describe trends and relationships observed in data, make inferences from data, compare the inferences with hypotheses about the data, and explain any differences between the inferences and the hypotheses

Describing Trends and Relationships in Scatter Plots

Once the data has been collected and graphed as a scatter plot, the next step involves describing the trends and relationship between the two variables. The closer the points come to making a straight line, the stronger the relationship between the two variables. If one set of data consistently changes in a linear pattern while the other set of data increases or decreases, a **proportional relationship** is represented. **Inferences** or conclusions can be made about the data in a proportional relationship. These inferences can then be compared with the original hypothesis.

Types of Trends

- If both variables increase, the relationship displays an **upward trend**. The points will follow a fairly straight line and the relationship is a direct proportion.
- If one variable increases while the other decreases, the resulting graph displays a **downward trend**. The relationship also displays a proportional relationship.
- If the points are scattered randomly on the graph, the inference would be that there is no relationship. The variables are independent of each other. Therefore, there is no trend.

You can quickly check whether a scatter plot has a positive (upward trend), negative (downward trend), or no relationship by drawing a line around the majority of the points. The direction in which the oval is leaning suggests what type of trend is displayed.

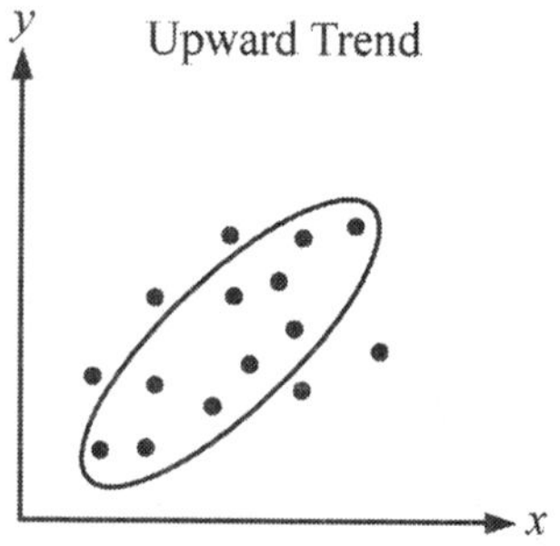

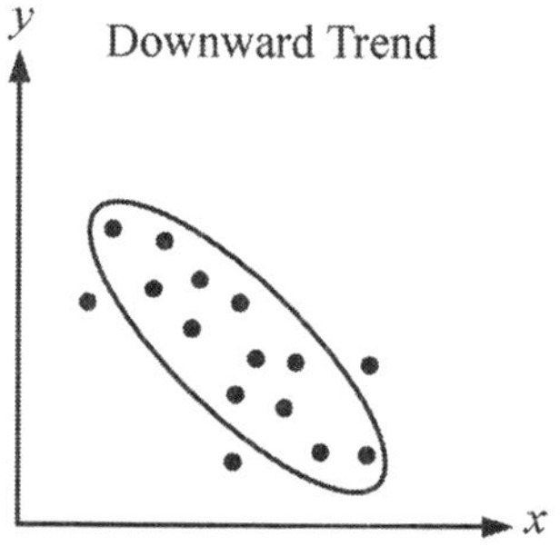

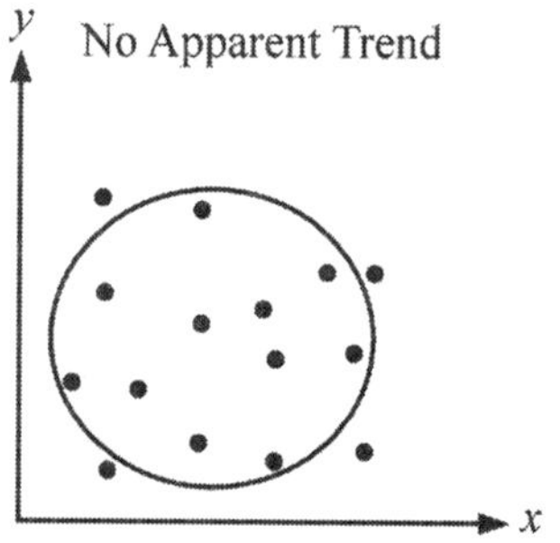

Not for Reproduction

Use the following information to answer the next question.

A pizza restaurant uses the following price structure.

Number of Slices	Price ($)
1	3.25
4	13.00
8	26.00

Open Response

7. Plot the data on the grid below. Describe the relationship and trend of the data set.

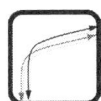

8. Which of the following scatter plots represents two variables that are independent of each other?

A. 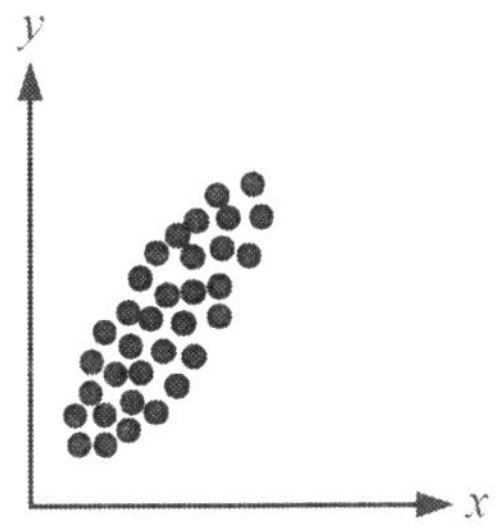

B. 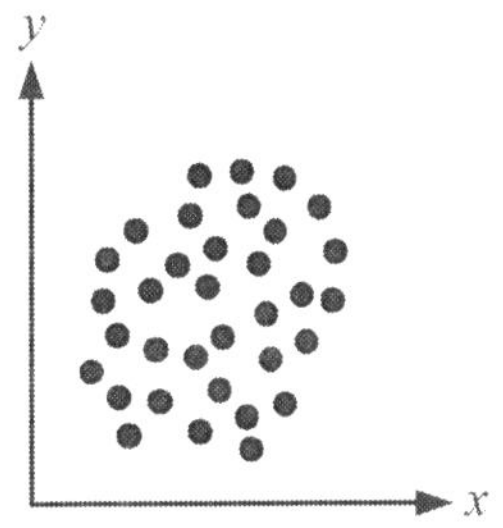

C. 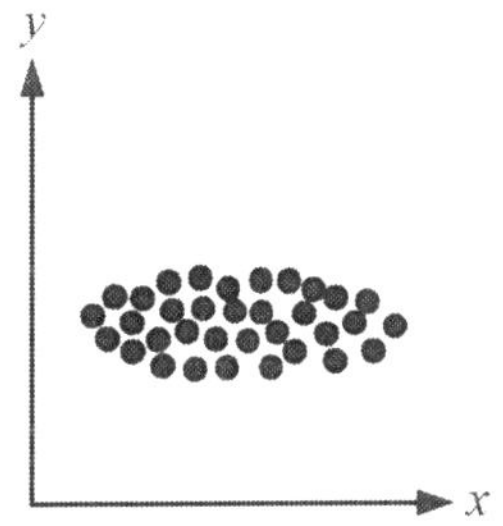

D. 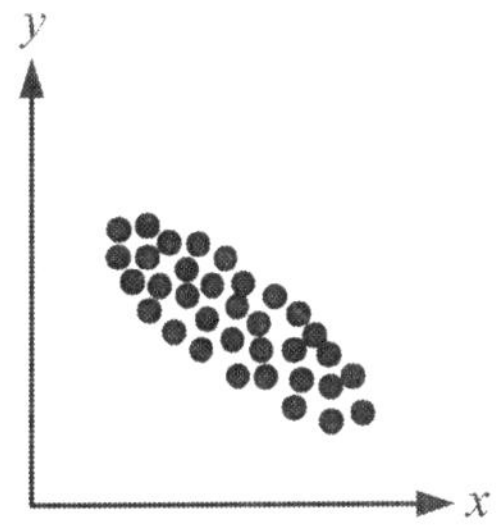

Copyright Protected

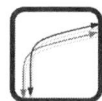

Use the following information to answer the next question.

Pairs of Shoes Sold		
Month	**Recreation World**	**Mackey's**
1	34	9
2	31	10
3	25	13
4	22	16
5	18	18
6	10	25

This table compares the number of shoes sold at Recreation World with the number of shoes sold at Mackey's over a six-month period.

9. Which of the following statements about the given data is **false**?

A. Recreation World's sales show an upward trend.

B. Recreation World's sales show a trend.

C. Mackey's sales show an upward trend.

D. Mackey's sales show a trend.

9LR2.01 construct tables of values, graphs, and equations, using a variety of tools to represent linear relations derived from descriptions of realistic situations

Representing Linear Relations

A **relation** is any set of ordered pairs. The expression (x, y) represents an ordered pair.

A **linear relation** occurs when the ordered pairs make a straight line on a scatter plot. A non-linear relation occurs when the ordered pairs make a curved line, or the direction of the line changes.

Relations can be further described as positive (upward trend) or negative (downward trend). These descriptions depend on which direction the line travels.

Representing a linear relation first requires constructing a **table of values**. This table consists of two columns. The first column contains a number of different x-values and the second column contains the corresponding y-values. You then plot these values on a scatter plot.

Example

A telephone company has a monthly cell phone plan that costs \$25.00 a month, plus \$0.10 per minute of airtime. Represent this relation for a number of different airtime minutes.

First, construct the table of values relating the number of airtime minutes, x, and the monthly cost, y, in dollars. For every value of x, calculate the corresponding y-value. The total monthly cost is the number of airtime minutes multiplied by \$0.10, plus the \$25.00 basic charge.

x-value Airtime (min)	y-value Total monthly cost (\$)
0	$25 + 0(0.10) = 25.00$
5	$25 + 5(0.10) = 25.50$
10	$25 + 10(0.10) = 26.00$
15	$25 + 15(0.10) = 26.50$
20	$25 + 20(0.10) = 27.00$
25	$25 + 25(0.10) = 27.50$
30	$25 + 30(0.10) = 28.00$
35	$25 + 35(0.10) = 28.50$

Not for Reproduction

Now, graph this data to create a scatter plot.

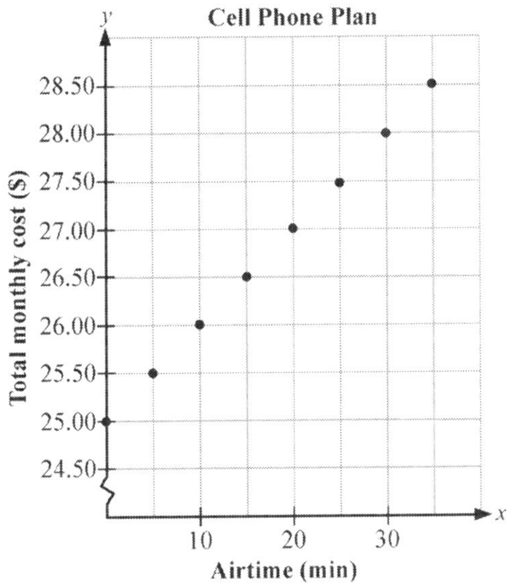

The scatter plot shows that this relationship is a positive linear relation, since the graphed points form a straight line in an upward direction.

10. Which of the following graphs represents a linear relation?

A.

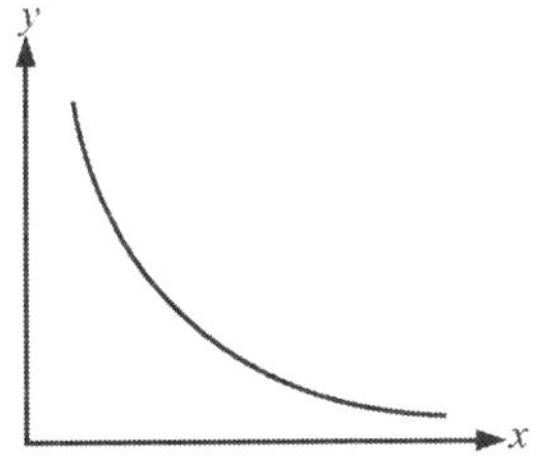

B.

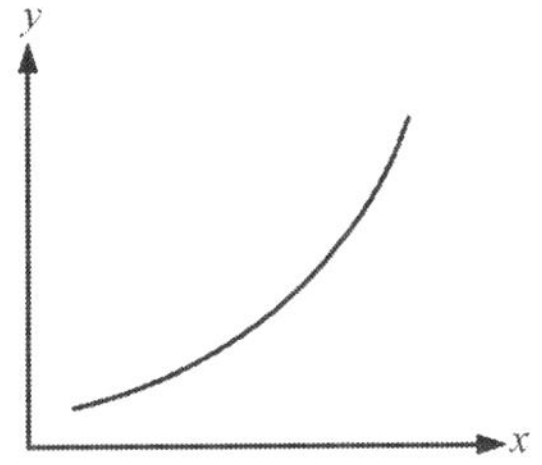

C.

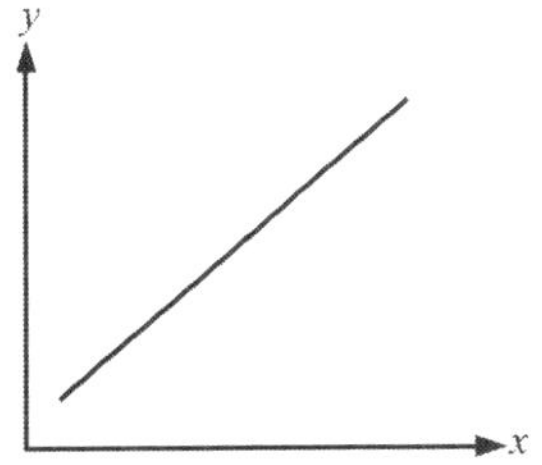

D.

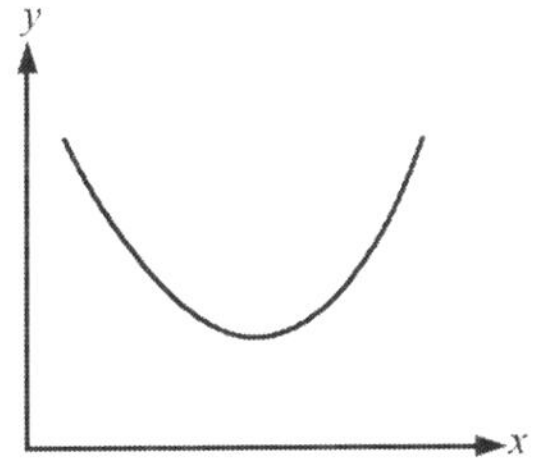

Copyright Protected

Use the following information to answer the next question.

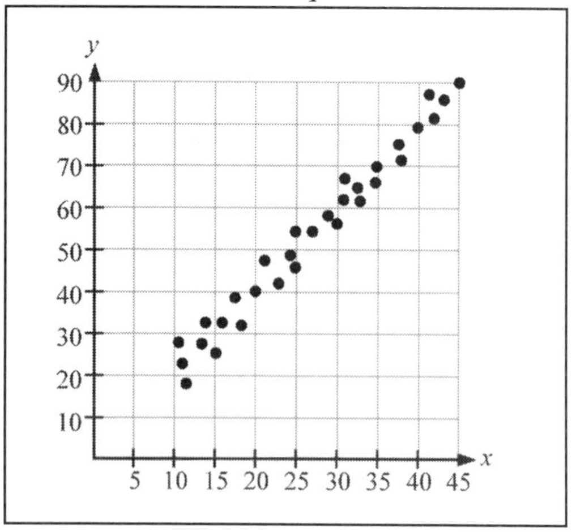

11. This scatter plot is **best** described as a

A. linear relation

B. positive linear relation

C. non-linear relation

D. negative non-linear relation

9LR2.02 construct tables of values, scatter plots, and lines or curves of best fit as appropriate, using a variety of tools for linearly related and non-linearly related data collected from a variety of sources

Constructing Lines and Curves of Best Fit

Linear Relations

Sometimes, the points of a linear relation do not form a perfect straight line. You can draw a **line of best fit** on a scatter plot to represent the average of the data as you follow the pattern. Draw a line of best fit by setting your ruler such that it goes through the middle of the pattern formed by the points. An even number of points will ideally be above and below the line drawn.

The following scatter plot contains a line of best fit.

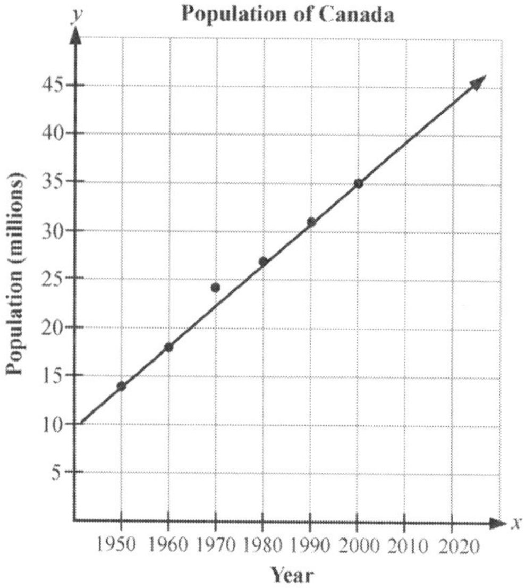

Non-Linear Relations

As non-linear relations form curves, a line of best fit cannot be drawn. Instead, a **curve of best fit** is drawn. Again, not all the points must lie directly on the curve, but the curve should reflect the trend of the data.

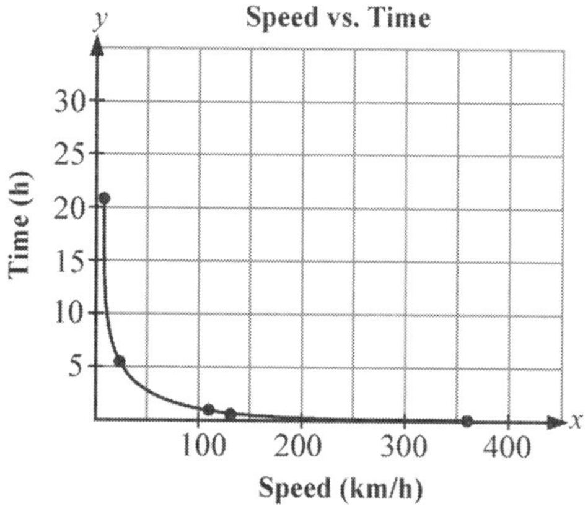

This graph represents points on a scatter plot and the curve of best fit that is drawn to connect them.

Not for Reproduction

Use the following information to answer the next question.

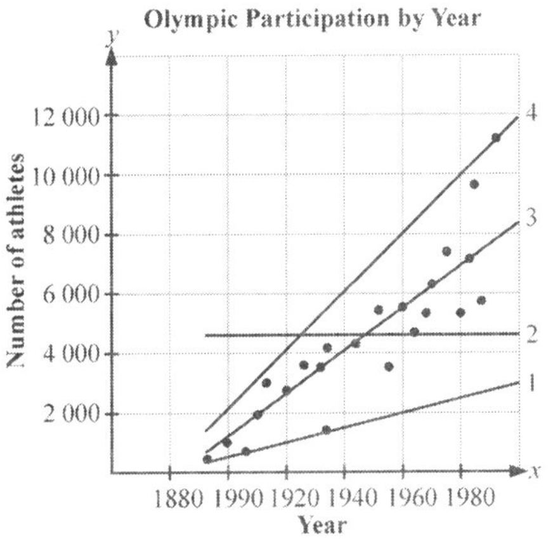

12. Which of the labelled lines **best** represents the data?

A. 1 **B.** 2

C. 3 **D.** 4

Use the following information to answer the next question.

The city of Guelph wants to determine how frequently a certain road is used. The scatter plot below shows the number of vehicles spotted at various times of the day. Each dot represents a certain number of vehicles.

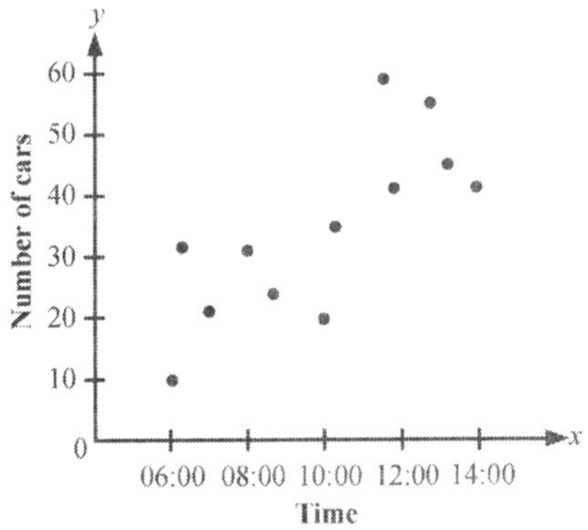

13. The point that lies **closest** to the line of best fit is the point plotted at time

A. 06:00 **B.** 08:40

C. 10:00 **D.** 13:00

9LR2.03 identify, through investigation, some properties of linear relations, and apply these properties to determine whether a relation is linear or non-linear

Identifying Properties of Relations

First differences are differences between successive y-values in tables with evenly spaced x-values.

The two tables that follow represent different cases of first differences.

Table 1

x	$y = x + 5$	**First Differences**
2	$y = 2 + 5 = 7$	
		$9 - 7 = 2$
4	$y = 4 + 5 = 9$	
		$11 - 9 = 2$
6	$y = 6 + 5 = 11$	
		$13 - 11 = 2$
8	$y = 8 + 5 = 13$	

Notice:
The x-values are evenly spaced in increments of two.
The first difference is found by subtracting one y-value from the next y-value that follows. The first differences in this table are all the same.

Table 2

x	$y = x^2$	**First Differences**
−3	$y = -3^2 = 9$	
		$4 - 9 = -5$
−2	$y = -2^2 = 4$	
		$1 - 4 = -3$
−1	$y = -1^2 = 1$	
		$0 - 1 = -1$
0	$y = 0^2 = 0$	
		$1 - 0 = 1$
1	$y = 1^2 = 1$	
		$4 - 1 = 3$
2	$y = 2^2 = 4$	
		$9 - 4 = 5$
3	$y = 3^2 = 9$	

Notice:
The x-values are evenly spaced in increments of one. The first differences in this case are all different, but there still is a pattern.

First differences and the degree of an equation indicate whether a relation is linear or non-linear. Linear relations have the same first differences and the degree of the expression is always one. For example, $y = x + 5$.

Copyright Protected

Graph 1

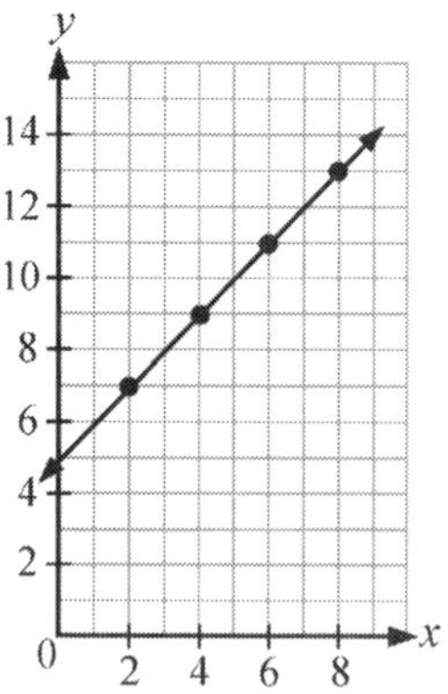

Non-linear relations have different first differences, such as in the second table above. Notice that the degree of the equation is greater than one. This is true of all non-linear relations, such as $y = x^2$.

Graph 2

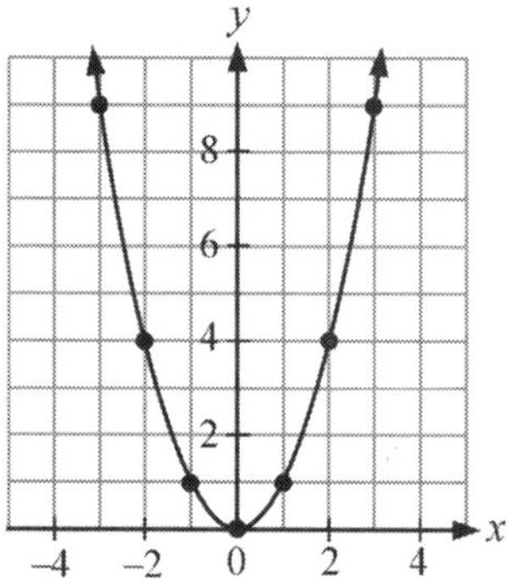

14. Which of the following tables represents a linear relationship between the variables x and y?

A.

x	y
2	6
3	11
4	17

B.

x	y
2	6
3	9
4	12

C.

x	y
2	8
3	27
4	64

D.

x	y
2	2
3	7
4	14

15. Which of the following equations represents a non-linear relationship between x and y?

A. $y = \frac{5}{2}x + 7$ **B.** $x = y - \frac{2}{3}$

C. $y = \frac{x}{y} + 6$ **D.** $x = \frac{y}{2} - \frac{1}{2}$

9LR2.04 compare the properties of direct variation and partial variation in applications, and identify the initial value

Comparing Direct and Partial Variation

When the first differences are the same, create a ratio of the y- to x-value differences to represent the **rate of change** in the points on a scatter plot.

$$\text{Rate of change} = \frac{\text{value of first difference}}{\text{difference between } x\text{-values}}$$

This ratio is also referred to as the **slope** of the line and it is the coefficient of the x-value in the equation of a line. For example, in $y = 2x + 4$, the slope is 2.

Not for Reproduction

Direct Variation

In a **direct variation**, the linear relation has a constant rate of change between the variables x and y. The graph of a linear relation passes through the origin (0, 0). Some examples of linear relations are below.

Yoga costs $14.00 per class.
Rate of change is 14; initial value of 0 (passes through the origin).

$y = -4x$
Rate of change is -4; initial value of 0.

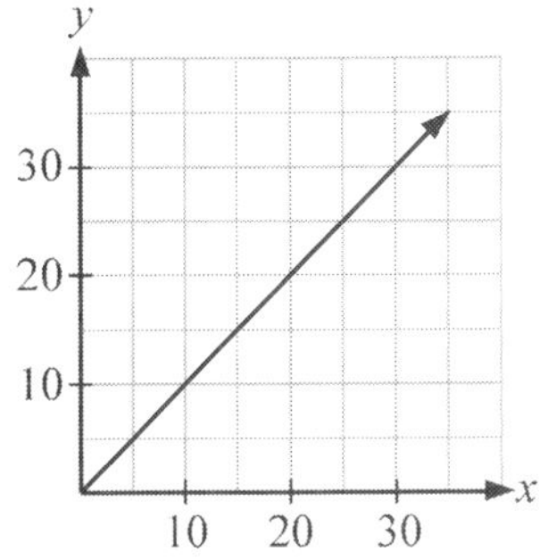

Rate of change is 1; initial value of 0.

Partial Variation

With a **partial variation**, the equation takes the form $y = mx + b$, where m equals the rate of change between the x-and y-values, and b represents the **initial value**. The graph of this relation does not pass through the origin.

Kung Fu costs $30.00 for registration plus $10.00 per class.
Constant rate of change is 10 (m); initial value of 30 (b).

$y = 2x + 9$
Constant rate of change is 2 (m); initial value of 9 (b).

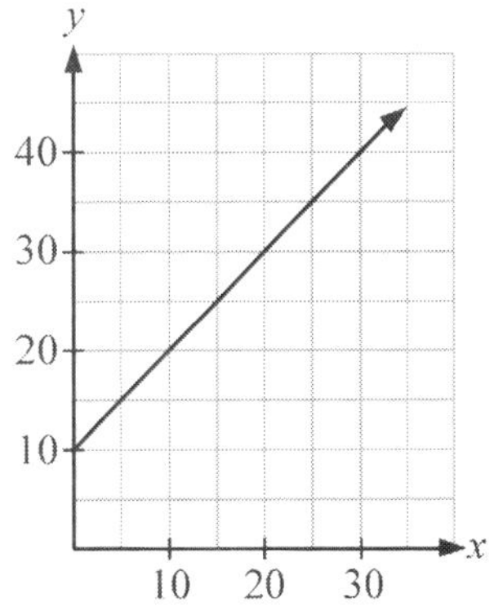

Constant rate of change is1 (m); initial value of 10 (b).

16. Which of the following situations **best** describes direct variation?

A. The price of soup at a restaurant is $5.

B. A kickboxing school charges $30 for registration and $10 for each class.

C. An Internet service provider charges $10 for installation and a monthly fee of $20.

D. The entry fee at an amusement park is $10, and the cost for each ride is $5.

Copyright Protected

Use the following information to answer the next question.

The exports of country A to country B are \$10 billion when the difference between their currencies is zero. For every unit increase in the difference between their currencies, the exports of country A to country B rise by \$5 billion.

17. Which of the following equations correctly depicts the variation in the given situation?

A. $y = 10 + 5x$, where $y =$ exports value in billions of dollars and $x =$ currency rate difference

B. $y = 5 + 10x$, where $y =$ exports value in billions of dollars and $x =$ currency rate difference

C. $y = 10 + 5x$, where $y =$ currency rate difference and $x =$ exports value in billions of dollars

D. $y = 5 + 10x$, where $y =$ currency rate difference and $x =$ exports value in billions of dollars

9LR2.05 determine the equation of a line of best fit for a scatter plot, using an informal process

Determining the Equation of a Line

Two common methods for determining the **equation of a line** involve using the graph of the line or two known points on the line.

Determining the Equation from a Graph

When there is a line of best fit for a scatter plot, an equation can be created that represents the line.

Example

What is the equation for the given line of best fit?

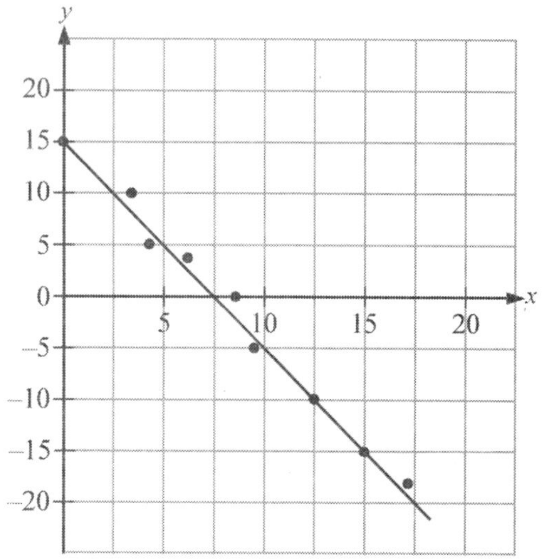

Step 1: Note the ***y*-intercept**.
The graph crosses the y-axis at 15. This is the initial value.

Step 2: Note two points that fall on the line.
The line appears to go through (0, 15) and (15, –15).

Step 3: Determine the **vertical separation** $(y_2 - y_1)$.
The two y-values are 15 and –15.
$15 - (-15) = 15 + 15 = 30$

Step 4: Determine the **horizontal separation** $(x_2 - x_1)$
The two x-values are 0 and 15.
$0 - 15 = -15$

Step 5: Insert these values into the formula as follows:

$$y = \left(\frac{\text{vertical separation}}{\text{horizontal separation}}\right)x + (\text{initial value})$$

The equation of this line is $y = \frac{30}{-15}x + 15$, or when simplified, $y = -2x + 15$.

Not for Reproduction

Notice the rate of change uses vertical and horizontal separation instead of first differences, but the same answer results. The rate of change is negative and the line has a downward trend.

Determining the Equation from Points

If given two points on a line and the y-intercept, follow the procedure as above to write the equation of a line.

Example

What is the equation of a line with the points (2, −2) and (8, 16), and a y-intercept of −8?

Vertical separation $(y_2 - y_1)$:

$(-2) - 16 = (-2) + (-16) = (-18)$

Horizontal separation $(x_2 - x_1)$:

$2 - 8 = 2 + (-8) = (-6)$

The equation of this line is $y = \frac{-18}{-6}x + (-8)$ or

$y = 3x - 8$ when simplified.

Use the following information to answer the next question.

A multi-lane track is created with parallel lines so that runners stay within their lane during a race. The following graph shows a portion of its length.

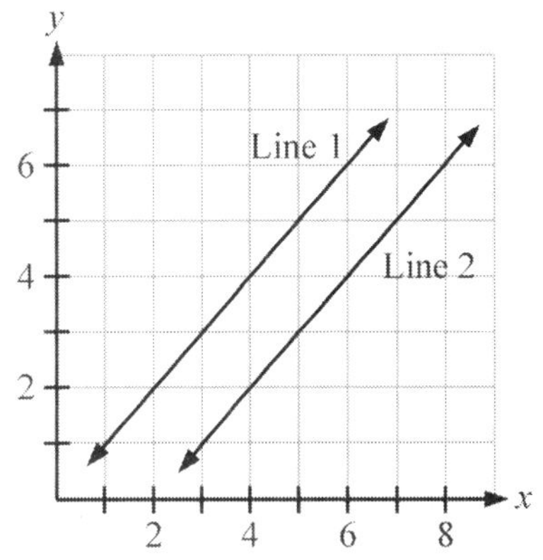

18. Which of the following equations represents Line 1 and Line 2 respectively?

A. $x + y = 0,\ x - y = 2$

B. $x - y = 0,\ x + y = 2$

C. $x - y = 0,\ x - y = 2$

D. $x + y = 0,\ x + y = 2$

Use the following information to answer the next question.

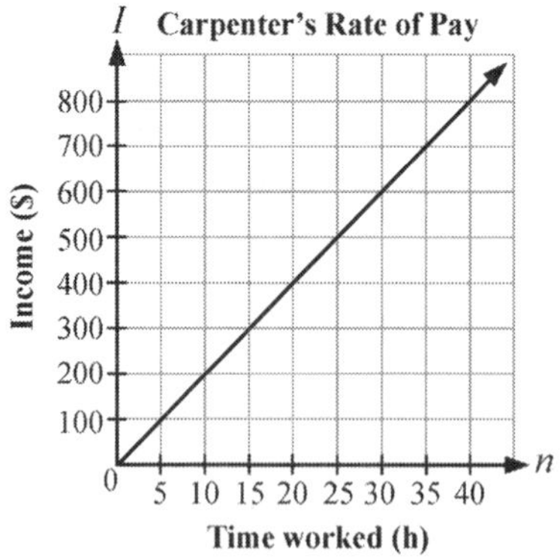

19. If S represents the salary of the carpenter and n represents the number of hours worked by the carpenter, then a linear equation that could show the relationship between salary and the number of hours worked is

A. $S = 100n$ **B.** $S = 20n$

C. $S = n + 100$ **D.** $S = n + 20$

Use the following information to answer the next question.

This scatter plot shows the profits for a computer software company during its first five years of operation.

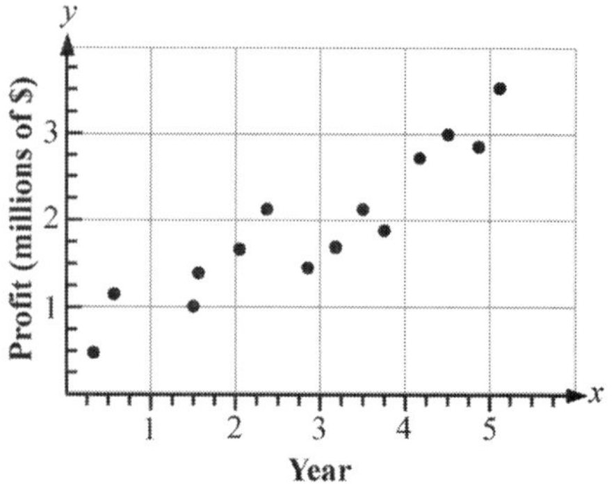

Open Response

20. Add the line of best fit to the scatter plot and then determine the equation of this line.

Show your work.

9LR3.01 determine values of a linear relation by using a table of values, by using the equation of the relation, and by interpolating or extrapolating from the graph of the relation

Finding Values of a Linear Relation

When trying to determine the values of a linear relation, two of the easiest methods are creating a graph of the relation and using the equation of the relation to solve for the values algebraically.

Not for Reproduction

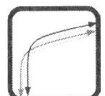

Using a Graph

To find the missing values of a relation, create a scatter plot of the known data, and then use the graph to help complete the table of values. Consider the example of temperature conversion between Celsius and Fahrenheit.

Celsius (°C)	Fahrenheit (°F)
0	32
100	212
25	77
32	?
?	100
40	?

Temperature Conversion

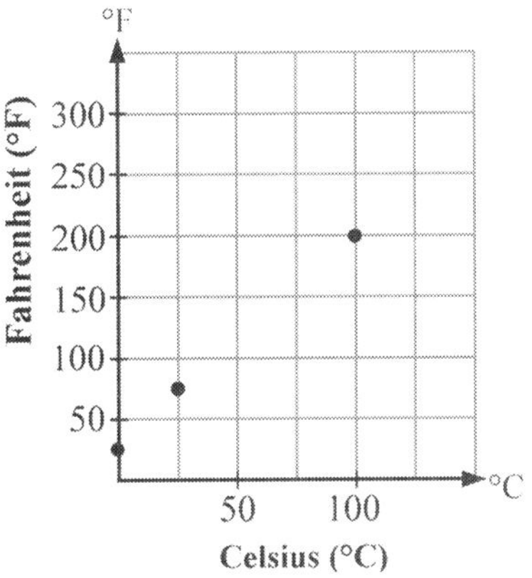

A line of best fit can be drawn to **interpolate**. Interpolation means finding values that correspond to points between the known points. Notice that 32°C corresponds to a temperature around 90°F and 40°C is slightly more than 100°F.

Temperature Conversion

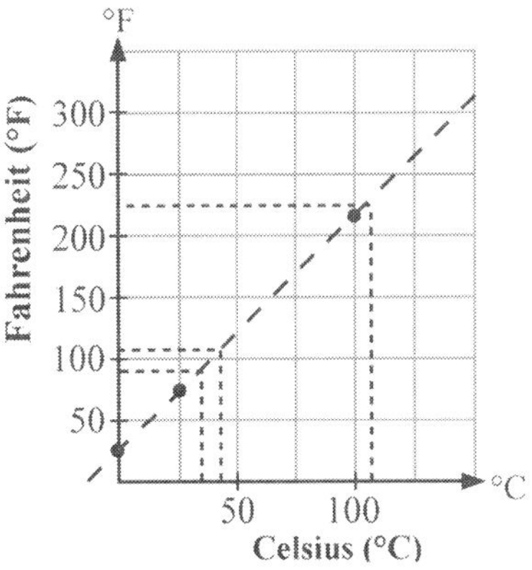

The line can also be used to **extrapolate** values. This means to find values that correspond to points beyond the known points. At 225°F, the temperature is about 105°C.

Using the Equation of the Line

If you have two known points and the y-intercept, you can find missing values algebraically because this information gives you the equation of the line. In the temperature example, the y-intercept is 32.

Rate of change $= \dfrac{212-77}{100-25} = \dfrac{135}{75}$

Simplify $\dfrac{135 \div 15}{75 \div 15} = \dfrac{9}{5}$

The equation of this line is $°F = \dfrac{9}{5}°C + 32$

Substitute one of the known values into the equation to determine some of the missing values.

$°C = 32,\ °F = ?$	$°C = ?,\ °F = 100$
$°F = \frac{9}{5}(32) + 32$ $°F = 57.6 + 32$ $°F = 89.6$	$100 = \frac{9}{5}C + 32$ $100 - 32 = \frac{9}{5}C + 32 - 32$ $\left(\frac{5}{9}\right)68 = \frac{9}{5}\left(\frac{5}{9}\right)C$ $37.\bar{7} = °C$

Use the following information to answer the next question.

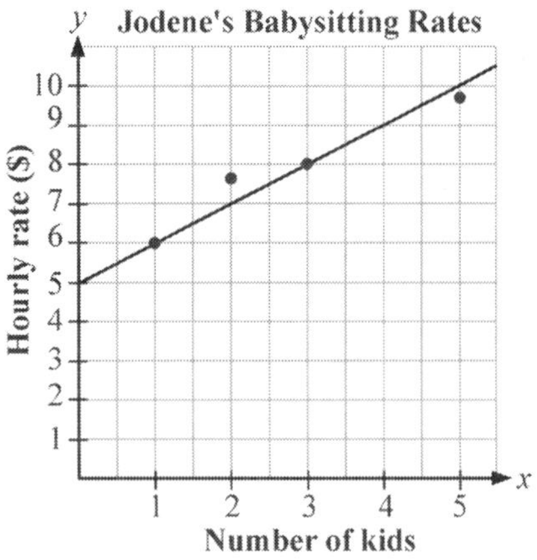

This graph shows the hourly rate that Jodene earns when she babysits. Her hourly rate depends on how many kids she is babysitting.

21. What is Jodene's hourly rate when she babysits 4 kids?

A. \$9.00 **B.** \$9.25

C. \$9.50 **D.** \$10.00

Use the following information to answer the next question.

In the equation $R = \frac{I}{50} + 20$, R represents the revenue earned after one year on a company's investment, I (in millions of dollars).

22. If the revenue after one year was \$21 million, what was the original investment?

A. \$20 million **B.** \$30 million

C. \$50 million **D.** \$60 million

9LR3.02 describe a situation that would explain the events illustrated by a given graph of a relationship between two variables

Illustrating Events with Graphs

A graph provides a picture of a relationship between two variables. To describe a situation that reflects each part of a graph, follow the steps below:

1. Identify the labelling on the axis.
2. Look at the trend of the line (increasing or decreasing).
3. See where the line crosses the axis (both vertical and horizontal).
4. Think of a situation that might satisfy all of the conditions.

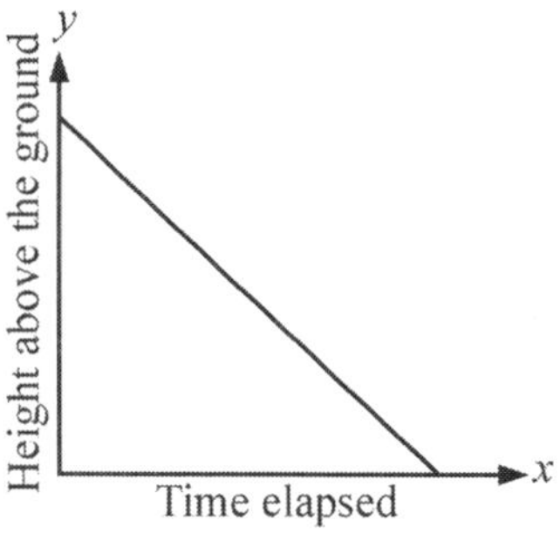

The given graph does not offer a lot of information. There are no real heights or times given. What can be observed is that something starts above the ground and ends at ground level some time later. Think of a situation where this might happen:

- Someone taking an escalator to another floor
- An airplane coming in for a landing
- The height of a ball falling from the top of a tall building

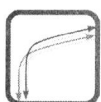

Use the following information to answer the next question.

While skateboarding, Dan goes down and then up the side of a halfpipe.

23. Which of the following graphs **best** shows the relationship between his speed and the elapsed time?

A.
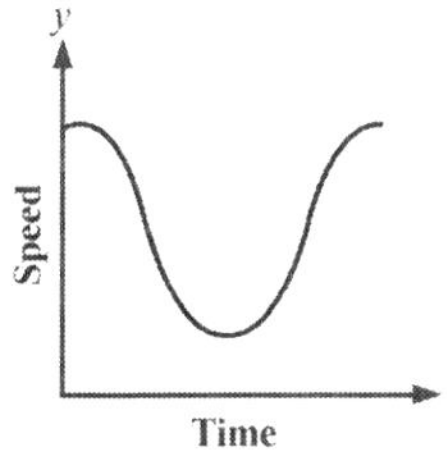

B.
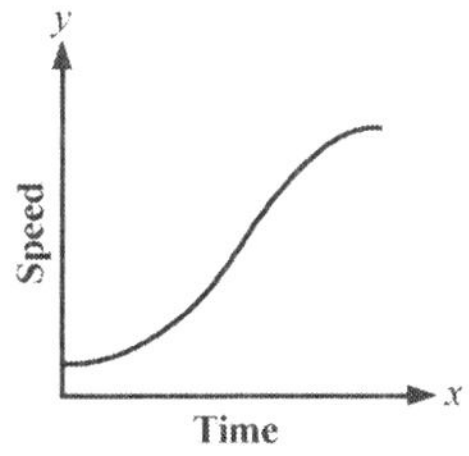

C.
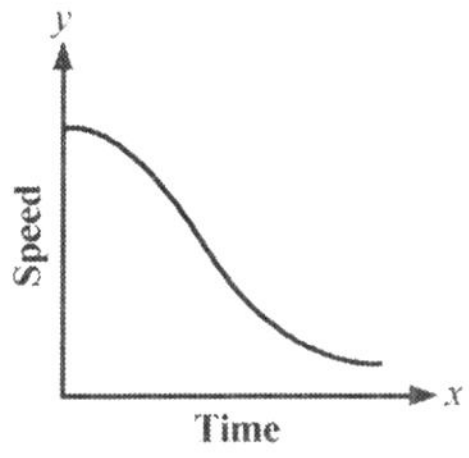

D.
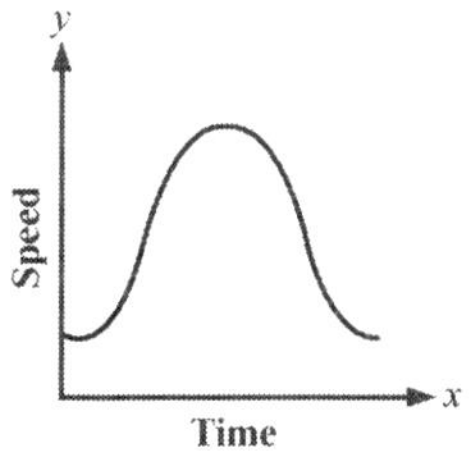

Use the following information to answer the next question.

A woman takes an elevator from the main floor of an office tower to the top floor. The elevator makes two stops on its way to the top.

24. Which of the following graphs **best** represents this scenario?

A.
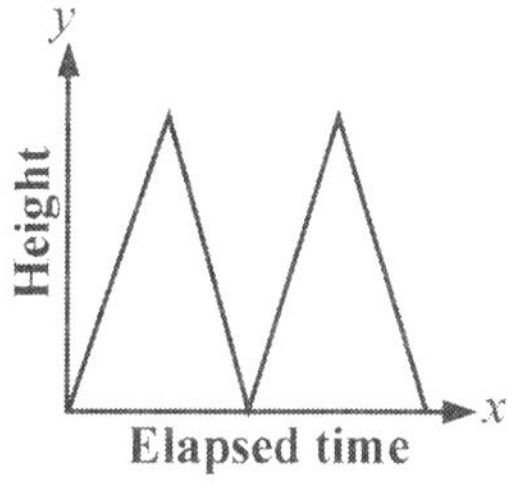

B.
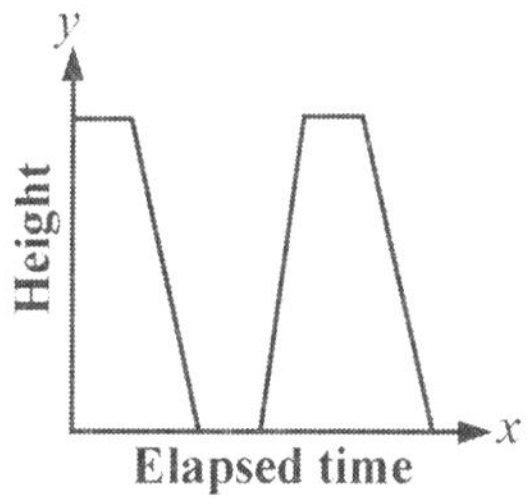

C.
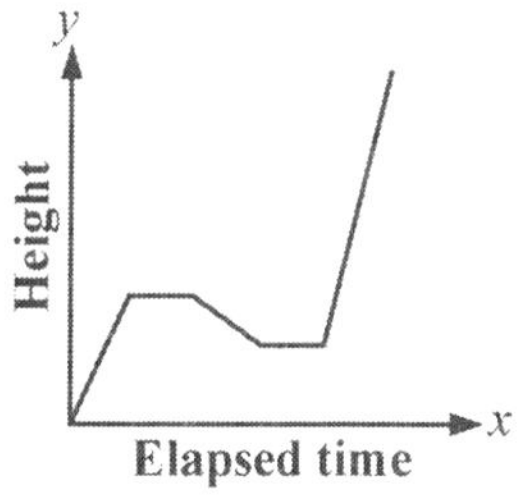

D.
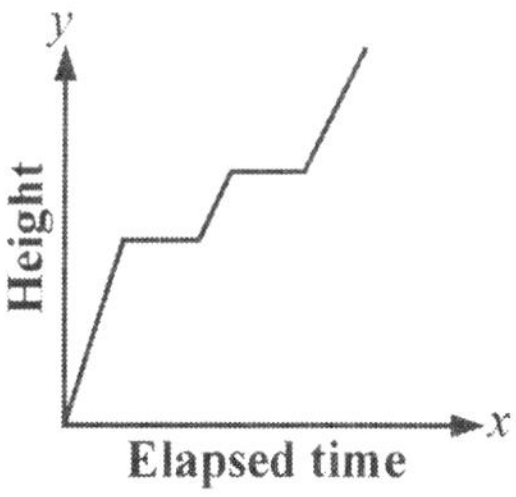

9LR3.03 determine other representations of a linear relation, given one representation

Determining other Representations of a Linear Relation

When you are given a relation in a table of values, as a graph, or as an algebraic expression, you can present the relation in one of the other two forms.

For example, the table of values below represents the distance, *d*, from a lightning flash, to the time, *t*, between seeing the lightning and hearing the thunder.

Time (s)	3	6	9	12	15
Distance (km)	1	2	3	4	5

This linear relation can then be represented graphically.

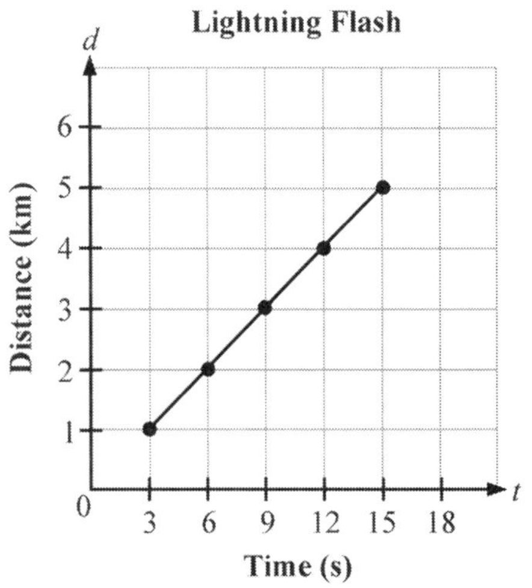

Recall that the rate of change is the ratio of the y-value to its x-value, also known as the slope of the line.

It is clear that the constant rate of change is $\frac{1}{3}$, since the distance increases 1 km (y-value) for every 3 s (x-value). If the line is extended back, it passes through the origin (0, 0). This means the initial value is (0, 0).

This linear relation can be represented algebraically in the form $y = mx + b$:

$$d = \frac{1}{3}t + 0 \rightarrow d = \frac{1}{3}t$$

Use the following information to answer the next question.

Kilograms (x)	10	15	20	25
Pounds (y)	22	33	44	55

25. Which equation may be used to convert kilograms to pounds?

A. $y = x + 2.2$ **B.** $x = y + 2.2$

C. $y = 2.2x$ **D.** $x = 2.2y$

Not for Reproduction

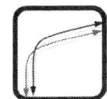

Use the following information to answer the next question.

Kilograms (x)	10	15	20	25
Pounds (y)	22	33	44	55

26. Which of the following graphs represents the data given in the table?

A.

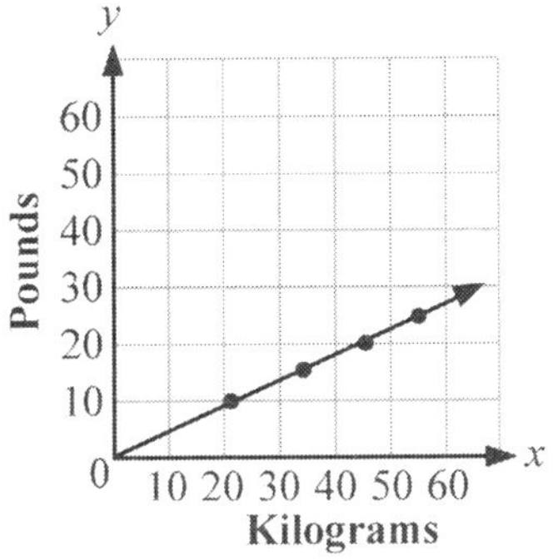

B.

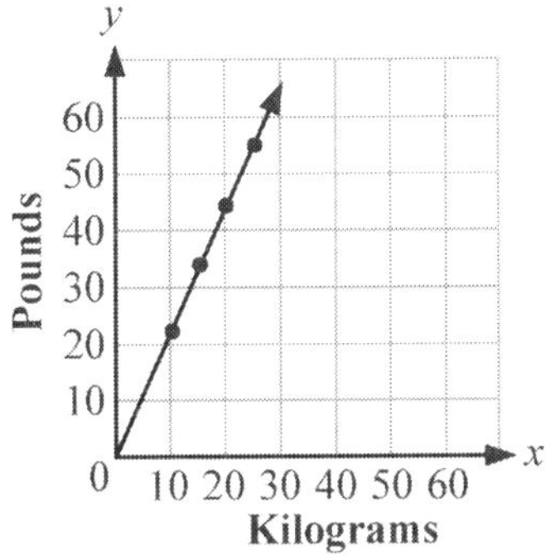

C.

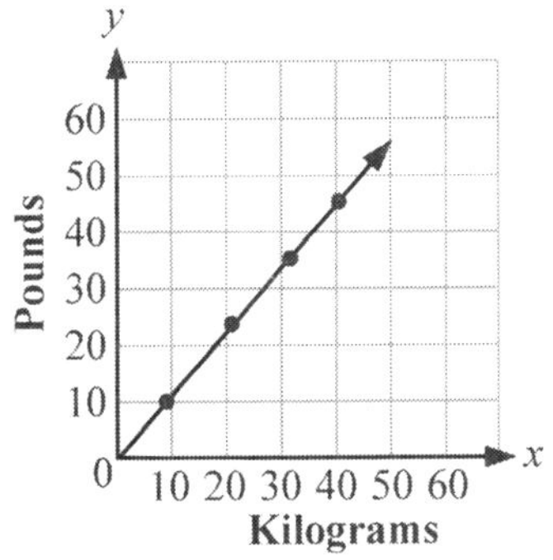

D.

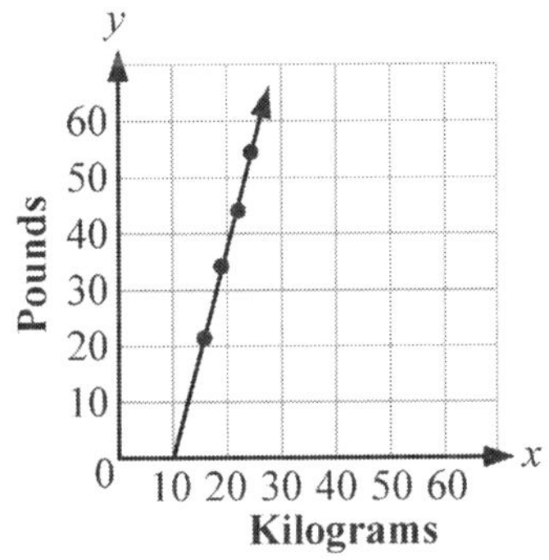

9LR3.04 describe the effects on a linear graph and make the corresponding changes to the linear equation when the conditions of the situation they represent are varied

When the rate of change $\left(\text{slope} = \frac{y}{x}\right)$ and the initial fixed value (y-intercept) are altered for a situation, the graph and equation are also altered.

For example, a phone company offers two plans:
Plan A: \$20.00 per month (fixed value) and \$0.10 per minute $\left(\text{slope} = \frac{\$0.10}{1 \text{ min}}\right)$

This plan represented algebraically is
$C = 0.1x + 20$

Plan B: \$30.00 per month and \$0.05 per minute
$C = 0.05x + 30$

The following graph represents these two relations.

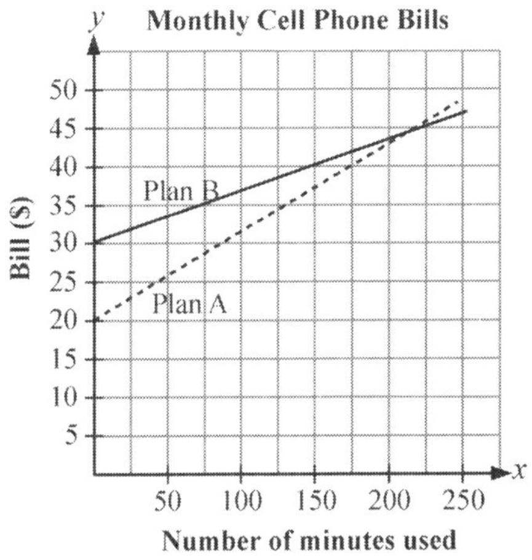

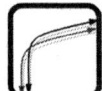

Copyright Protected

Use the following information to answer the next question.

Graphs I and II represent the distances that two different cars travelled over time. The equation $d = 40 + 100t$ depicts the relationship in Graph I, where d is the distance travelled and t is the time travelled.

Graph I

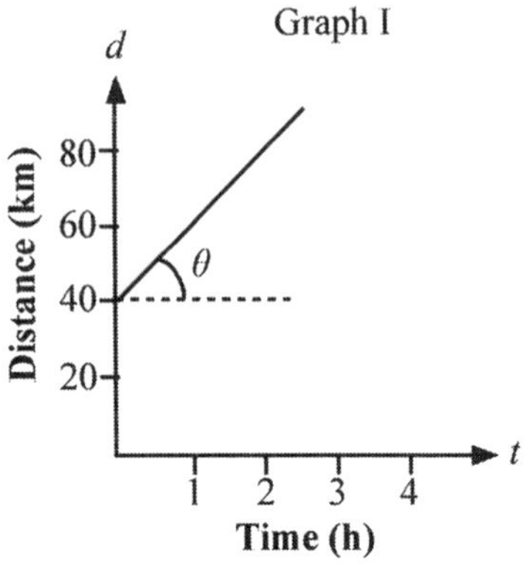

Graph II

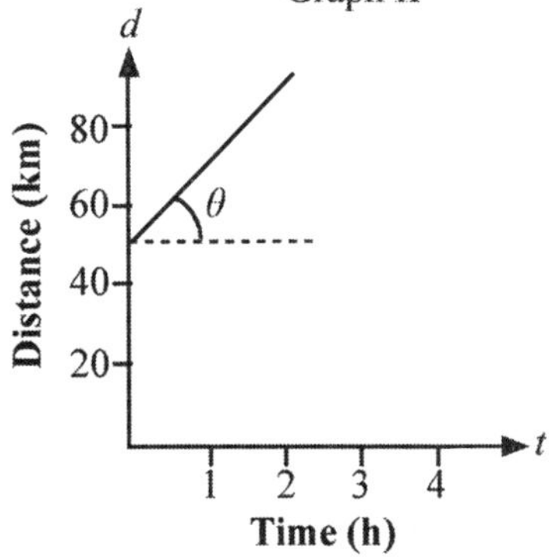

27. What is the equation of the line in Graph II?

A. $d = 50 + 200t$

B. $d = 40 + 100t$

C. $d = 50 + 100t$

D. $d = 40 + 200t$

Use the following information to answer the next question.

The equation $C = 200 + 3n$ is displayed in the graph below.

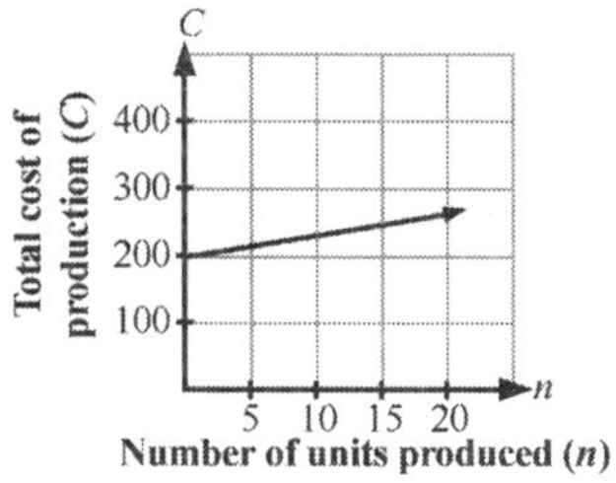

As a result of some labour problems, the ratio of production cost to the number of units produced changes to 5, and the fixed cost increases by \$100.

Not for Reproduction

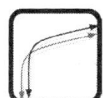

28. Which of the following graphs represents the new relationship between the cost of production and the number of units produced?

A.

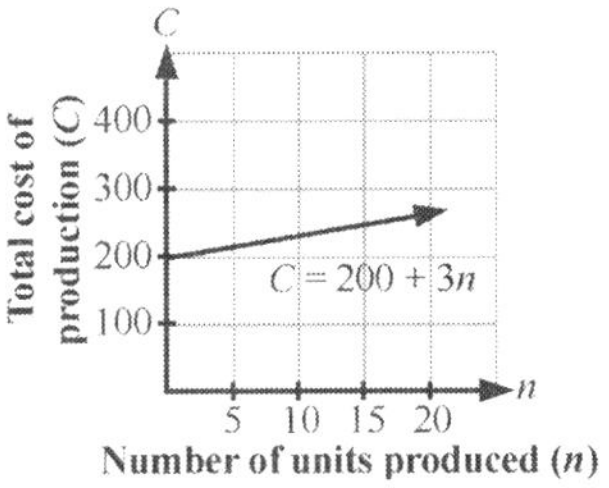

B.

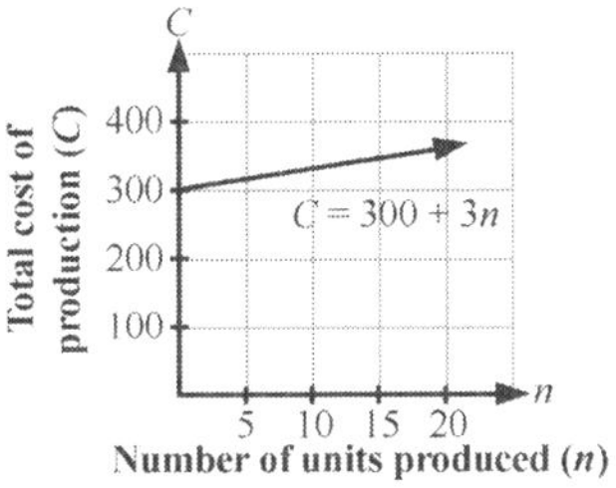

C.

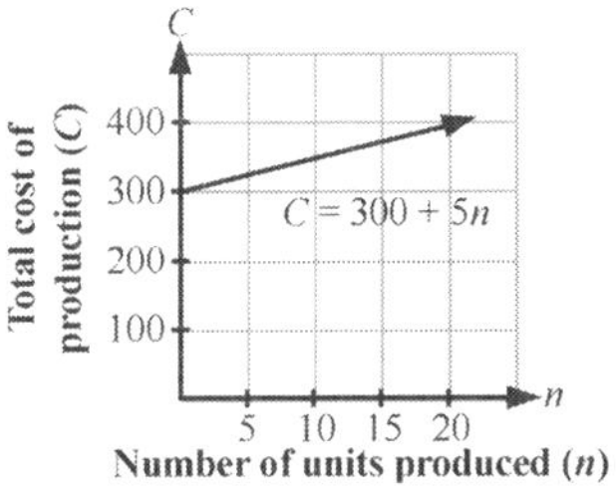

D.

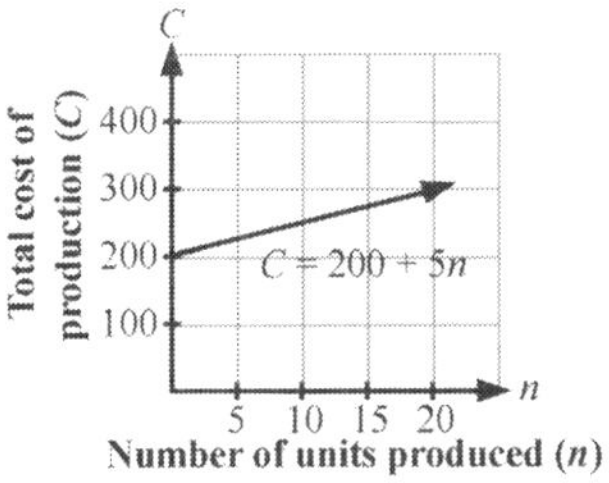

Copyright Protected

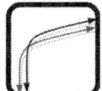

ANSWERS AND SOLUTIONS
LINEAR RELATIONS

1. B	7. OR	13. B	19. B	25. C
2. B	8. C	14. B	20. OR	26. B
3. B	9. A	15. C	21. A	27. C
4. C	10. C	16. A	22. C	28. C
5. D	11. B	17. A	23. D	
6. B	12. C	18. C	24. D	

1. B

Start by finding the purchase price of the stock. Go to week 1 on the x-axis. Move up the y-axis until you reach the point. Move left to determine its value on the y-axis. The purchase price of the stock is \$15.
Week 1 = 1 0 × \$15 = \$150

Follow the same process for calculating the price of the stock at week 4.
Week 4 = 1 0 × \$22 = \$220

Now subtract the purchase price from the selling price.
\$220 – \$150 = \$7 0

Leslie made a profit of \$7 000.

2. B

Move along the x-axis until you reach 20. Then travel up the y-axis until you reach the point. From that point, move left to the y-axis to determine the y-value.

It can be seen that when $x = 20$, $y = 26$.

3. B

The relationship is looking at age and the number of accidents. Therefore, alternatives A and C are immediately eliminated. John is looking at how age (independent variable) affects the number of accidents (dependent variable).

4. C

Alternative A: Good attendance does not guarantee a high mark. The work put into studying also affects the final mark.

Alternative B: Students with very good attendance can get low marks if they do not pay attention or study.

Alternative C: A student who has poor attendance is likely to miss instruction and assignments and therefore, will most likely have a lower mark. This statement is the best hypothesis.

Alternative D: Based on the rationale of alternative C, a student with poor attendance is unlikely to have a high final mark.

5. D

Since it is an experiment involving ice water, room temperature water should not be used. This eliminates alternatives A and B

A metre stick is not needed to measure temperature or time, so this eliminates alternative C

Alternative D is correct because it uses ice water and has all the other necessary tools: 500 mL plastic container, thermometer to measure the change in temperature, and a clock to record the time.

6. B

There were no students absent for only one day. As a result, there should be no points with an x-value of 1. This eliminates alternatives A and C

There were 4 students who were absent for 2 days. Move across the x-axis to 2 and then up the y-axis to 4. Alternative D has points plotted at 2 and 4 on the y-axis, which is not correct.

Alternative B correctly represents the given values.

Not for Reproduction

7. OR

<table>
<tr><th>Points</th><th>Sample Answer</th></tr>
<tr><td>4</td><td>Plot the points on the graph with the independent variable (number of slices) on the x-axis and the dependent variable (price) on the y-axis.
1 slice costs $3.25 = $3.25 / slice
4 slices cost $13.00 = 13 ÷ 4
= $3.25 / slice
8 slices cost $26.00 = 26 ÷ 8
= $3.25 / slice
The cost of pizza per slice is constant at $3.25 / slice.
Therefore, the data is a proportional relationship with an upward trend.
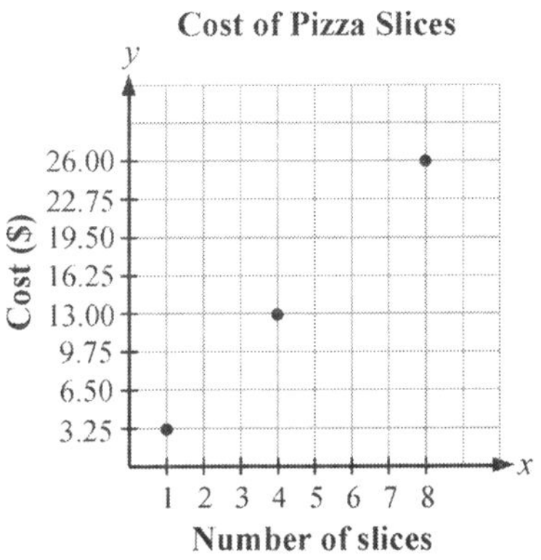
</td></tr>
<tr><td colspan="2">Application of knowledge and skills involving variables, scatter plots, trends, and relationships shows a high degree of effectiveness due to:
• a thorough understanding of the concepts
• an accurate application of the procedures (any minor errors and/or omissions do not detract from the demonstration of a thorough understanding)</td></tr>
<tr><td>3</td><td>Application of knowledge and skills involving variables, scatter plots, trends, and relationships shows considerable effectiveness due to:
• an understanding of most of the concepts
• minor errors and/or omissions in the application of the procedures
Example
Variables on the graph are correct, with minor errors on labels. A label may be missing.
Identifies the relationship or trend correctly.</td></tr>
</table>

<table>
<tr><th>Points</th><th>Sample Answer</th></tr>
<tr><td>2</td><td>Puts the variables on the wrong axes, but graphs them correctly.
Identifies the relationship or trend correctly with how the graph was labelled (proportional relationship with a downward trend).</td></tr>
<tr><td colspan="2">Application of knowledge and skills involving variables, scatter plots, trends, and relationships shows some effectiveness due to:
• a partial understanding of the concepts
• minor errors and/or omissions in the application of the procedures</td></tr>
<tr><td>1</td><td>Puts the variables on the wrong axes, but graphs them correctly.
Identifies the relationship or trend incorrectly.</td></tr>
<tr><td colspan="2">Application of knowledge and skills involving variables, scatter plots, trends, and relationships shows limited effectiveness due to:
• a misunderstanding of concepts
• an incorrect selection or misuse of procedures</td></tr>
</table>

8. C

The relationship described has no apparent trend. When the points of this relationship are plotted, no clear upward or downward trend appears.

9. A

Alternatives A and B: The relationship of months to pairs sold for Recreation World is a negative relationship, so the trend is downward.

Alternatives C and D: The relationship of months to pairs sold at Mackey's is a positive relationship, so the trend is upward.

Recreation World's sales do not show an upward trend.

10. C

The graph of a linear relation is always a straight line. Alternative C is the only graph that is a straight line.

11. B

The values in the scatter plot follow a linear pattern and increase along that pattern. Therefore, the scatter plot represents a positive linear relation.

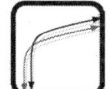

12. C

A line of best fit is a line as close as possible to all the data points with about as many points above the line as below. By doing so, it best represents given data. Of the four lines given, line 3 is the line of best fit as it satisfies the criteria better than the others.

Line 1 is below every data point and so likely would underestimate the data. Although about as many points appear to be above line 2 as below, the line is not as close as possible to all the points. Line 4 is above all the data points and so likely would overestimate the data.

13. B

A line of best fit is a line as close as possible to all the data points with about as many points above the line as below. When the line is drawn, one can see that 08:40 is on the line, while the remaining points are either above or below the line.

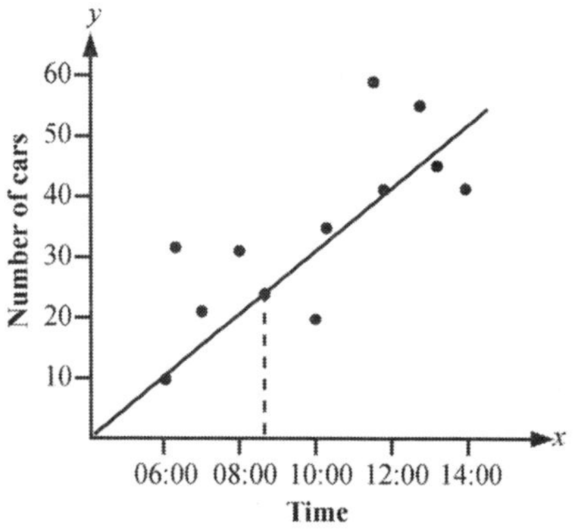

14. B

Calculate the first differences for each of the table of values. If the values of x and y change at constant rates, then their relationship is said to be linear. In the given tables, the value of x always increases by 1. However, only in alternative B does the value of y change at a constant rate. This table represents a linear relationship between x and y.

Alternative A: $11 - 6 = 5$, $17 - 11 = 6$
Alternative B: $9 - 6 = 3$, $12 - 9 = 3$
Alternative C: $27 - 8 = 19$, $64 - 27 = 37$
Alternative D: $7 - 2 = 5$, $14 - 7 = 7$

15. C

The equations in alternatives A and B have a degree of one and are, therefore, linear.

The equations in alternatives C and D need to be simplified before the equations can evaluated.

Alternative C

Multiply the equation by y to remove the denominator.

$$y \times y = y \times \frac{x}{y} + y \times 6$$

$y^2 = x + 6y$

This equation has a degree of two, which indicates that it is non-linear.

Alternative D

Using the same process to simplify, multiply the equation by 2.

The result is $2x = y - 1$.

Alternative D is also of the first degree.

16. A

Direct variation means that only a rate of change exists between the variables. For every x-value, a y-value changes in response. There is no initial value. Alternative A has a rate of change of $5, with no initial value.

Alternatives B, C, and D all have initial values and rates of change in their descriptions.

17. A

When the currency difference (x) is 0, the exports value (y) is 10 (billions of dollars). When there is a difference in the currencies (x), the rate of change is 5 (billions of dollars) for each unit increase. Therefore, the equation that correctly depicts the variation is $y = 10 + 5x$.

18. C

Line 1 shows direct variation, meaning that $y = x + 0$. It goes through the origin if you extrapolate. However, the alternatives are not given in this form. Use algebraic techniques to rearrange the equation.

$y = x + 0$

$y - y = x - y + 0.$

$0 = x - y$

Not for Reproduction

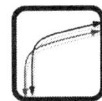

Only alternatives B and C have this as an equation for Line 1.

Write the equation of Line 2 in the form $y = mx + b$.
Extrapolating from the line shows that the y-intercept (b) is -2.

To calculate the rate of change, use any two points on the second line, such as (3, 1) and (4, 2).

$$\frac{y_2 - y_1}{x_2 - x_1} = \frac{2 - 1}{4 - 3} = \frac{1}{1} = 1$$

Therefore, the equation of Line 2 is $y = x - 2$.

Use algebraic techniques to rearrange the equation.

$y = x - 2$

$y + 2 = x - 2 + 2$

$y - y + 2 = x - y$

$2 = x - y$

The two equations are $x - y = 0$ and $x - y = 2$.

19. B

Slope y-intercept form indicates that the rate of change is the coefficient of x.

The rate of change is calculated with the following formula.

$m = \frac{\Delta y}{\Delta x} = \frac{y_2 - y_1}{x_2 - x_1}$. Take any two points from the graph and substitute them into the equation.

$(x_1, y_1) = (5, 100)$

$(x_2, y_2) = (10, 200)$

$$m = \frac{200 - 100}{10 - 5} = \frac{100}{5} = 20$$

The correct equation is $S = 20n$.

20. OR

Points	Sample Answer
4	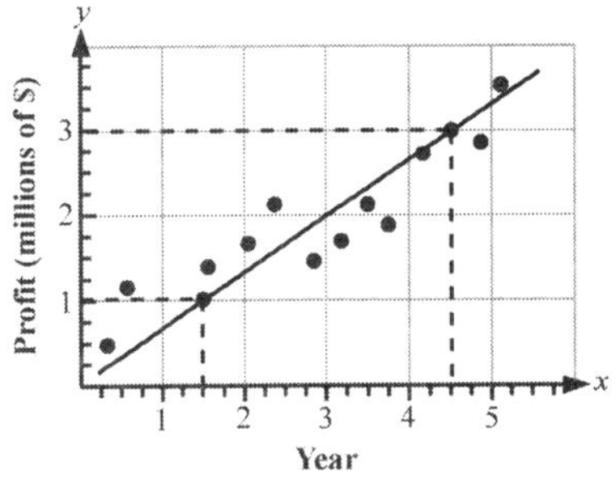 From the line of best fit, use two points on the line to calculate the equation:(4.5, 3) and (1.5, 1). There is no initial value because no profit was made when the company first started up. Equation of the line: $y = \left(\frac{\text{vertical separation}}{\text{horizontal separation}}\right)x + \text{initial value}$ $y = \left(\frac{3 - 1}{4.5 - 1.5}\right)x + 0$ $y = \frac{2}{3}x$
Application of knowledge and skills involving the line of best fit and the equation of a line shows a high degree of effectiveness due to: • a thorough understanding of the concepts • an accurate application of the procedures (any minor errors and/or omissions do not detract from the demonstration of a thorough understanding)	
3	The line of best fit is drawn slightly off. Calculations are done correctly using the chosen points and the equation of the line is correct in accordance with the drawn line.
Application of knowledge and skills involving the line of best fit and the equation of a line shows considerable effectiveness due to: • an understanding of most of the concepts • minor errors and/or omissions in the application of the procedures	
2	The line of best fit is drawn correctly. There are some calculation errors in the equation of the line.

Points	Sample Answer
Application of knowledge and skills involving the line of best fit and the equation of a line shows some effectiveness due to: • a partial understanding of the concepts • minor errors and/or omissions in the application of the procedures	
1	The line of best fit is drawn correctly, but the equation of the line is not determined.
Application of knowledge and skills involving the line of best fit and the equation of a line shows limited effectiveness due to: • a misunderstanding of concepts • an incorrect selection or misuse of procedures	

21. A

Find the amount that Jodene charges by locating the number of kids on the x-axis and then finding the corresponding value of the y-axis by tracing a line straight upward until it intercepts the line.

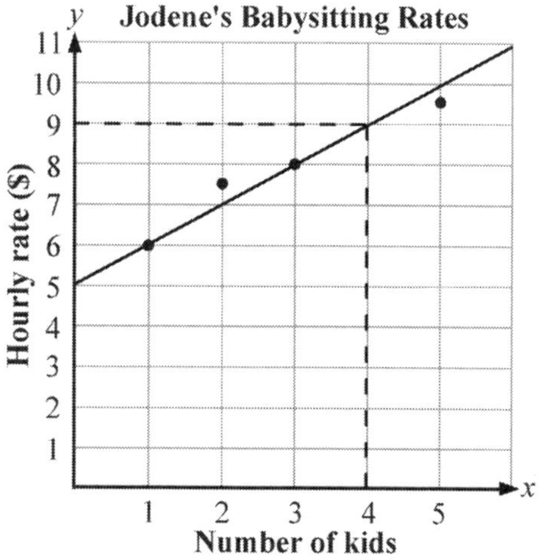

An hourly charge of \$9.00 corresponds to 4 kids.

22. C

Rearrange the equation to isolate I.

$$R = \frac{I}{50} + 20$$

$$I = 50(R - 20)$$

Substitute 21 for R.

$$I = 50(21 - 20) = 50$$

Therefore, the company originally invested \$50 million.

23. D

Since he is already skateboarding, his speed cannot start at zero. He gains speed as he goes down the halfpipe. The graph must progress in the positive direction. After peaking, he then slows down as he goes up the other side of the halfpipe. The graph has to then move in a negative direction, ending with a slower speed as he continues skateboarding.

The following graph shows this situation the best.

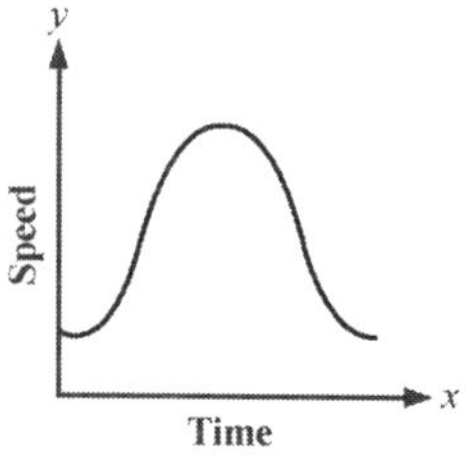

24. D

You must assume that a height of 0 is the main floor and the maximum height is the top floor of the office tower.

Alternative A: In this graph, the height goes from the main floor to the top floor, back to the main level, back up, and then returns to the main floor. This is not the situation described.

Alternative B: In this graph, the height that the elevator starts at is the top floor, which is not described in the given information.

Alternative C: In this graph, the height increases, remains constant for a time, then decreases before going up again. This could be the situation, but it is unlikely that the second stop would be at a lower floor.

Alternative D: The height of the elevator continues to increase in this graph, with two flat spots that represent the two stops. This graph best represents the scenario described.

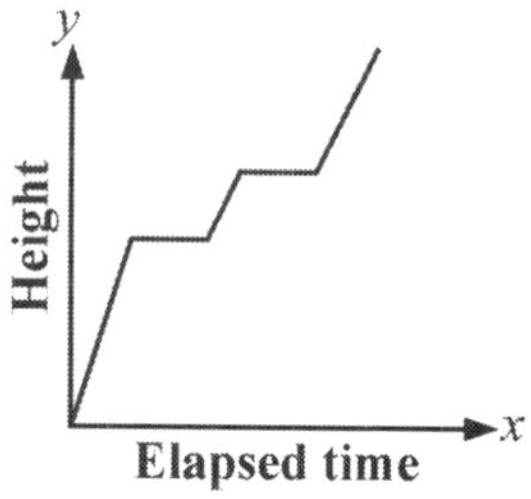

25. C

Rate of change is the ratio of a y-value to an x-value. Dividing the number of pounds (y) by the number of kilograms (x) results in:

$$\frac{22}{10} = \frac{33}{15} = \frac{44}{20} = \ldots = 2.2$$

1 kg = 2.2 lbs

In the form of an equation, the rate of change between pounds (y) and kilograms (x) is $y = 2.2x$.

26. B

The graph of the relationship between kilograms (x) and pounds (y) must have x- and y-values that are the same as those given in the table.

When pounds equal 0, so do kilograms. Therefore, the graph must go through the origin. Graph D is eliminated.

The first x-value in the table is 10. Graph A has the first x-value at 22. Graph A is eliminated. The first y-value of Graph C is 10, which eliminates it as the correct answer.

The first y-value is 22. Graph B has the first y-value at 22 and it goes through the origin.

27. C

The y-intercept in Graph II is 50 km. So, alternatives B and D can be eliminated.

The slope of the line (θ) is the same in both graphs, so the rate of change ($100t$) must also be the same.

The equation for Graph II is $d = 50 + 100t$.

28. C

The initial value increases by \$100, so the y-intercept shifts up to 300. This eliminates alternatives A and D.

The rate of change goes from 3 to 5, so the slope of the line will be steeper.

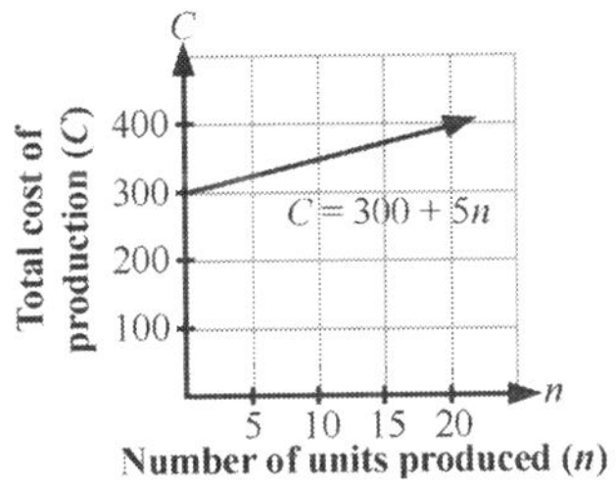

Copyright Protected

UNIT TEST — LINEAR RELATIONS

Use the following information to answer the next question.

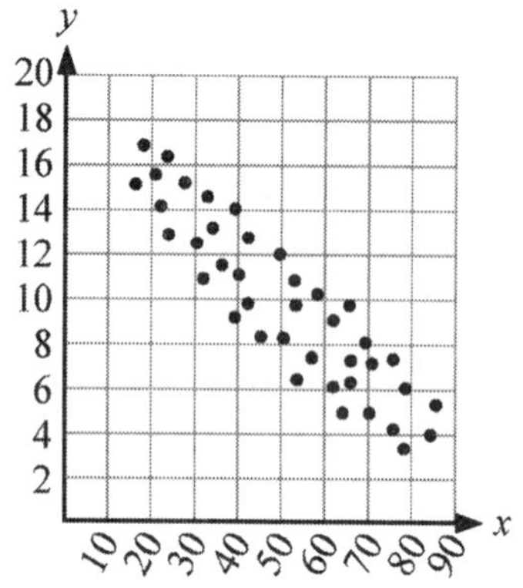

1. Which type of relation is represented by the data in the given scatter plot?

A. Positive linear relation

B. Negative linear relation

C. Positive non-linear relation

D. Negative non-linear relation

2. Which of the following graphs does **not** represent a linear relationship?

A.

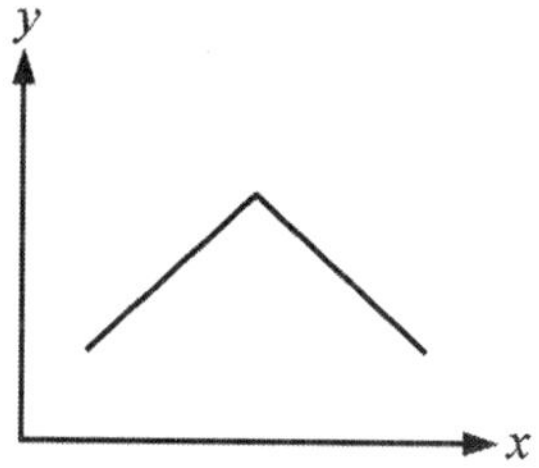

B.

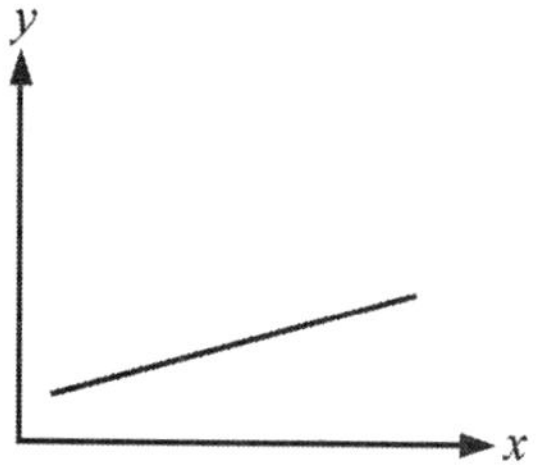

C.

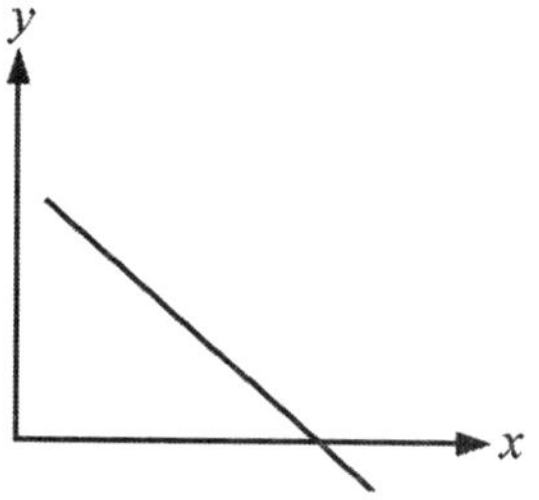

D.

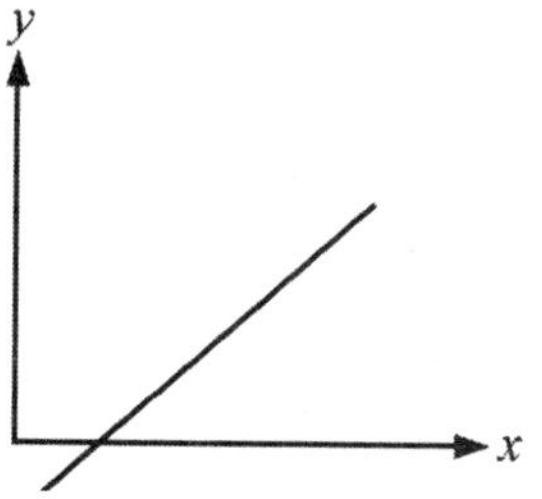

Not for Reproduction

Use the following information to answer the next question.

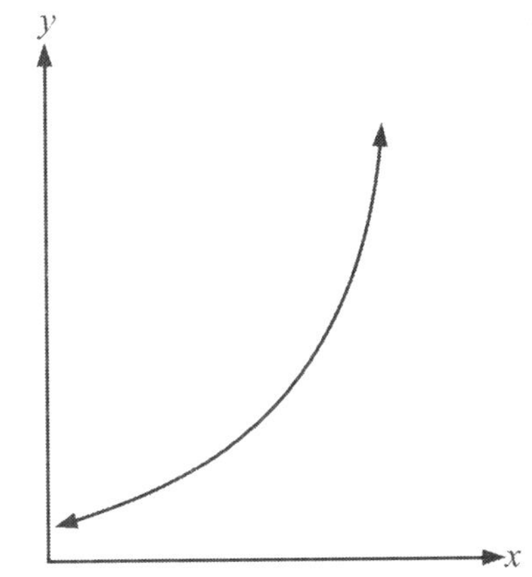

Open Response

3. The given graph can be described as what type of relation?

Justify your answer.

Use the following information to answer the next question.

Max's Yearly Expenditure on Sports Equipment					
Year	2002	2003	2004	2005	2006
Money Spent	750	850	950	1 050	1 150

Open Response

4. If the given data is represented graphically, what type of trend appears?

Use the following information to answer the next question.

The following graph shows the effect of the amount of spring rainfall on crop yield for fifteen different farms.

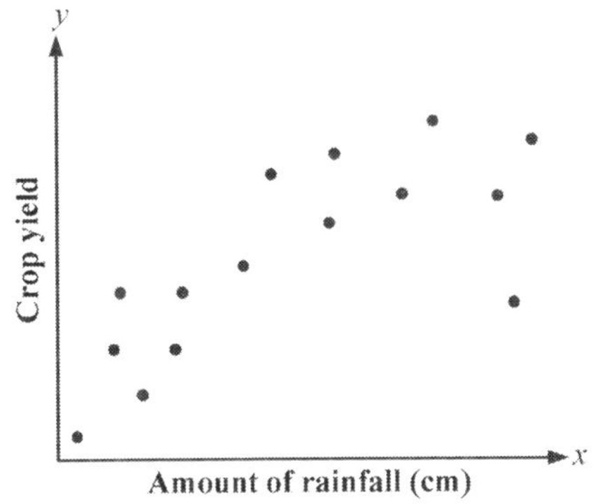

5. Which of the following statements regarding the line of best fit for the scatterplot shown is **true**?

A. No line of best fit exists.

B. The line of best fit is perfectly horizontal.

C. The line of best fit steadily rises as the x-values increase.

D. The line of best fit steadily declines as the x-values increase.

Copyright Protected

6. Which of the following scatter plots has a line of best fit that represents a negative relationship?

A.

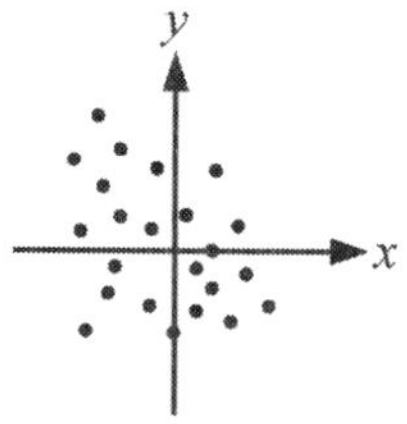

B.

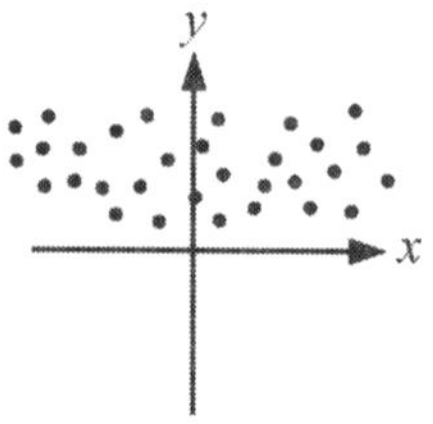

C.

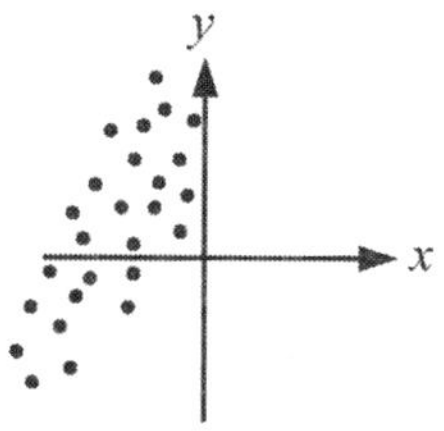

D.

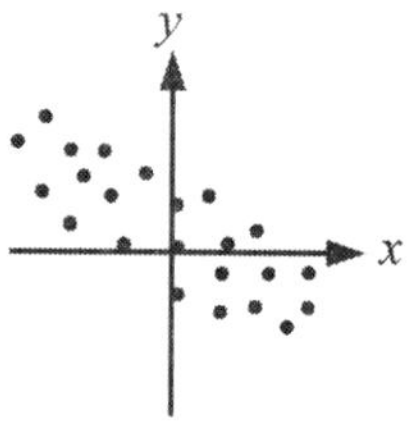

Open Response

7. If the line of best fit on a scatter plot is parallel to the y-axis, what is the relationship between the two variables?

Use the following information to answer the next question.

The following table compares certain physical properties of bodies in our solar system. The values have been given in terms of Earth units. The distance between the sun and Earth is 1 astronomical unit.

Planet	Distance from the Sun	Radius	Surface Gravity
Mercury	0.39	0.38	0.38
Venus	0.72	0.95	0.91
Earth	1.00	1.00	1.00
Mars	1.52	0.53	0.39
Jupiter	5.20	11.20	2.74
Saturn	9.54	9.42	1.17
Uranus	19.18	4.10	0.94
Neptune	30.06	3.88	1.15
Pluto	39.44	0.18	0.03

Open Response

8. Plot the data. Draw a line or curve of best fit. Describe the correlation that results.

Not for Reproduction

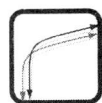

Show your work and justify your answer.

9. Which of the following tables represents a non-linear relationship between x and y?

A.

x	2	3	4
y	8	11	14

B.

x	3	4	5
y	10	14	18

C.

x	1	2	3
y	3	6	11

D.

x	4	5	6
y	7	8	9

10. Which of the following equations represents a linear relationship between x and y?

A. $y = x^2 + 3$ **B.** $y^2 = 2x + 5$

C. $y^2 = x^2$ **D.** $y^2 = 5x + 2$

Use the following information to answer the next question.

A student determined the volume, V, of a cube by changing the length, l, of each side.

Volume of Cube Related to Length of its Sides

l (cm)	2	3	4	5	6	7
v (cm^3)	8	27	64	125	216	343

11. Which of the following statements correctly describes the relation between l and V?

A. This is a linear relation because as l increases, V increases at a constant rate.

B. This is a linear relation because as l increases, V decreases at a constant rate.

C. This is a non-linear relation because as l increases, V increases at a varying rate.

D. This is a non-linear relation because as l increases, V decreases at a varying rate.

12. Which of the following graphs represents direct variation?

A.

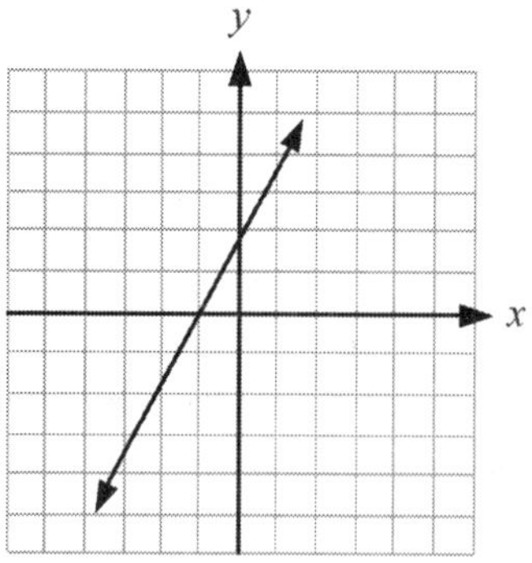

B.

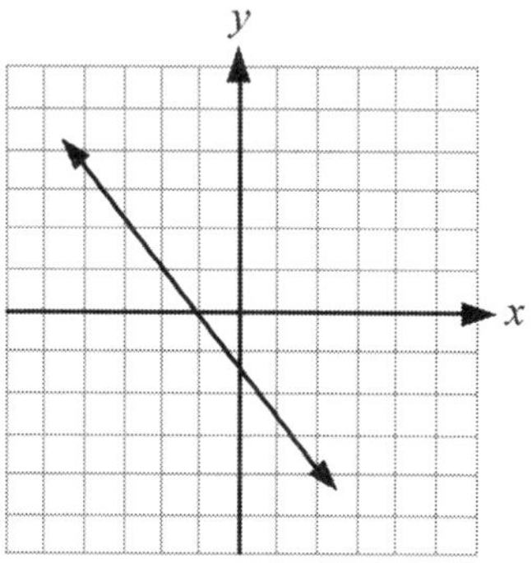

C.

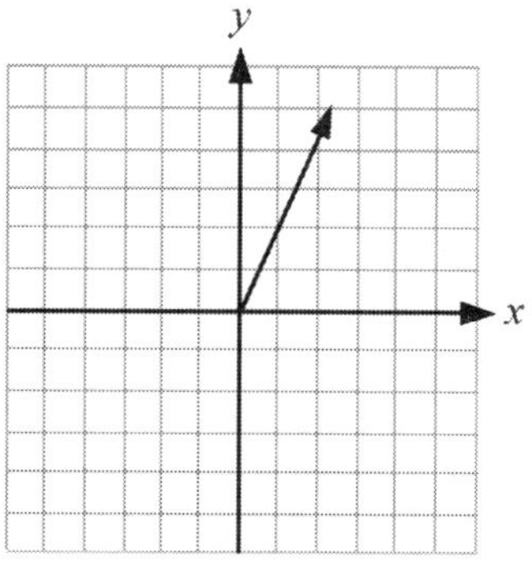

D.

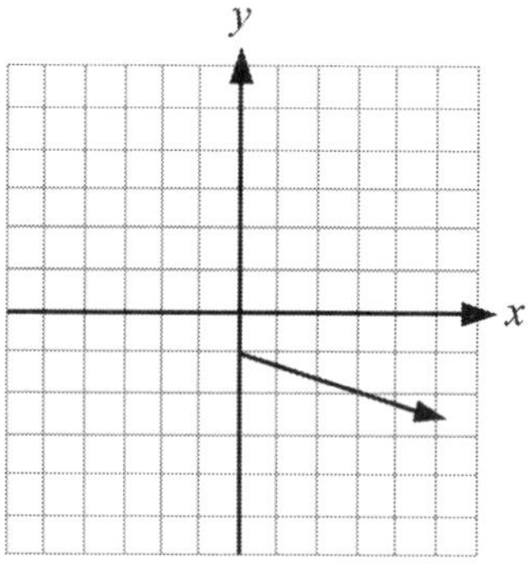

Use the following information to answer the next question.

Jessica's dad bought a car for \$35 000. The value of the car depreciates by \$200 each year.

13. Which of the following graphs correctly shows the depreciation of the value of the car?

A.

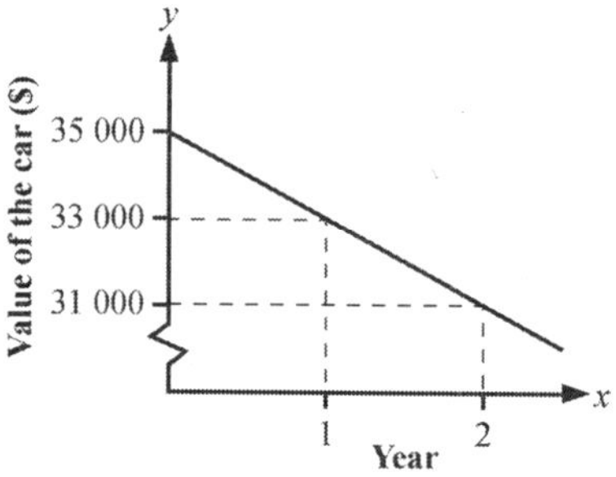

B.

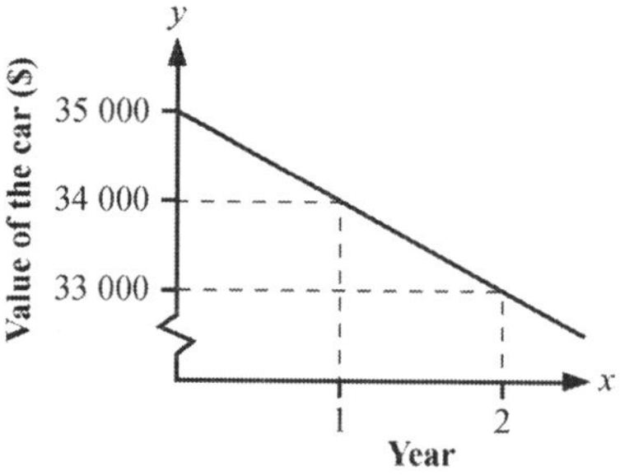

C.

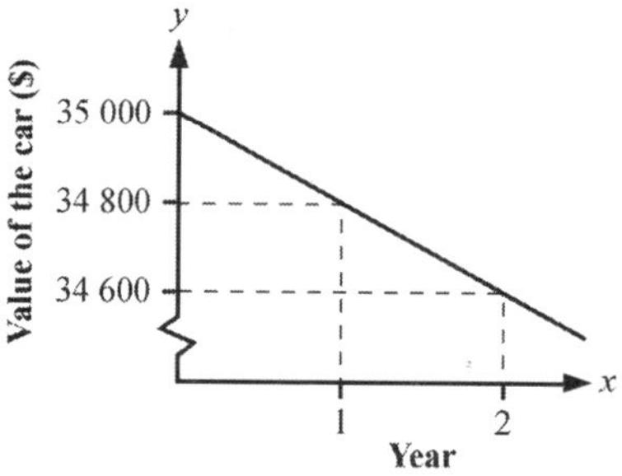

D.

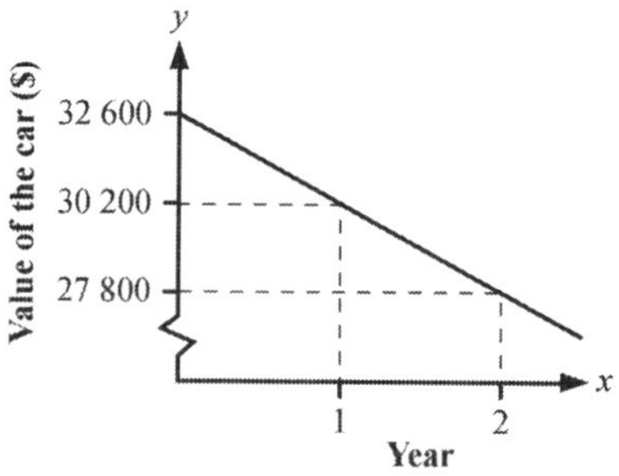

Not for Reproduction

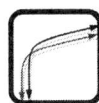

Use the following information to answer the next question.

The given graph represents the height of a projectile at various intervals after it is launched from Earth.

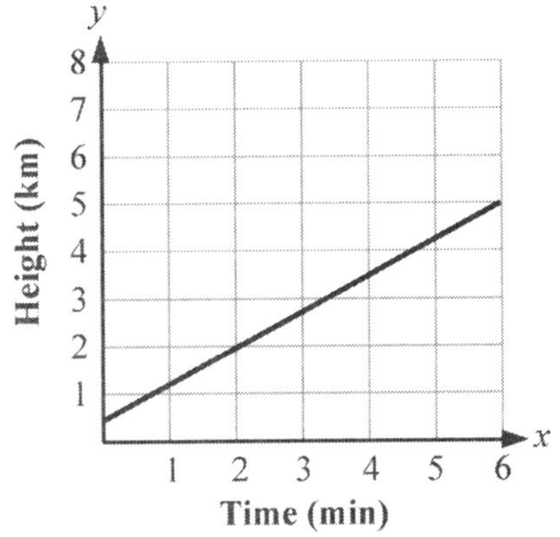

14. At what height was the projectile launched?

A. 0 km **B.** 0.5 km

C. 1.0 km **D.** 1.5 km

Use the following information to answer the next question.

The full cost (in dollars) of manufacturing a product in a factory is given by the equation $y = 100 + 2x$.

Open Response

15. Explain what each number and variable represents in the given equation.

Use the following information to answer the next question.

x	y
−8	−6
−4	−3
0	0
4	3

16. The points in the given table of values are on which line?

A. $y = \frac{3}{4}x$ **B.** $y = -\frac{3}{4}x$

C. $y = \frac{4}{3}x$ **D.** $y = -\frac{4}{3}x$

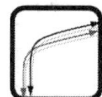

Copyright Protected

17. The equation $x = y - 2$ is represented by which of the following graphs?

A.

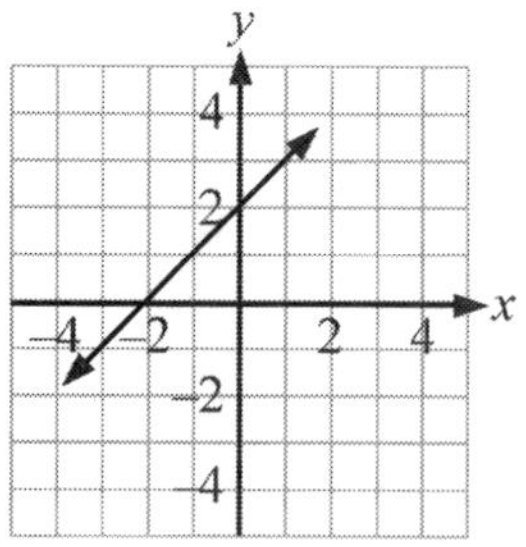

B.

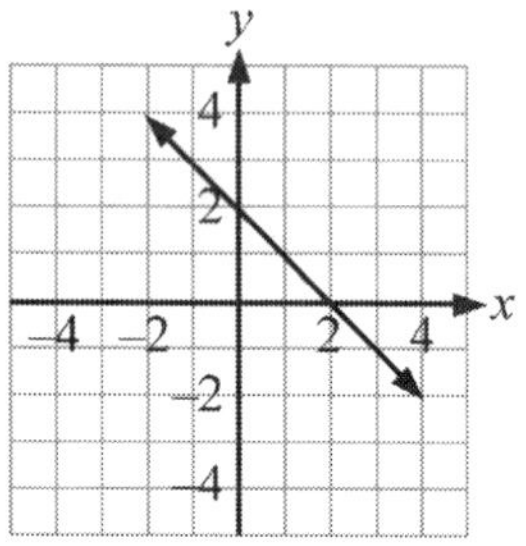

C.

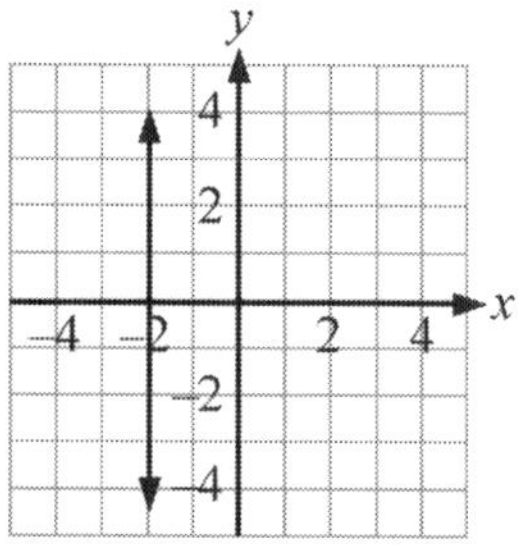

D.

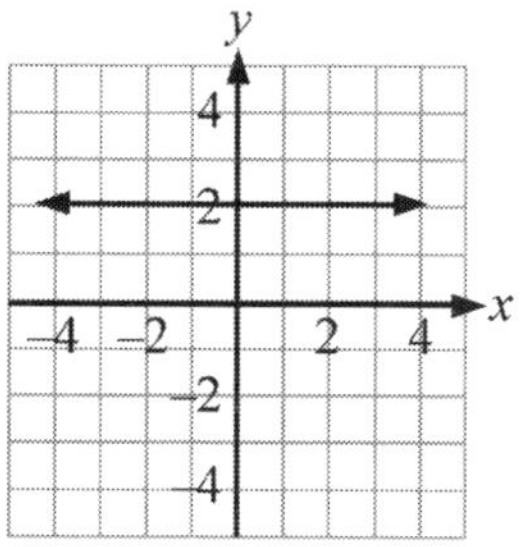

Use the following information to answer the next question.

The given graph represents the number of doctors required in a hospital in relation to the number of patients that visit the hospital each day.

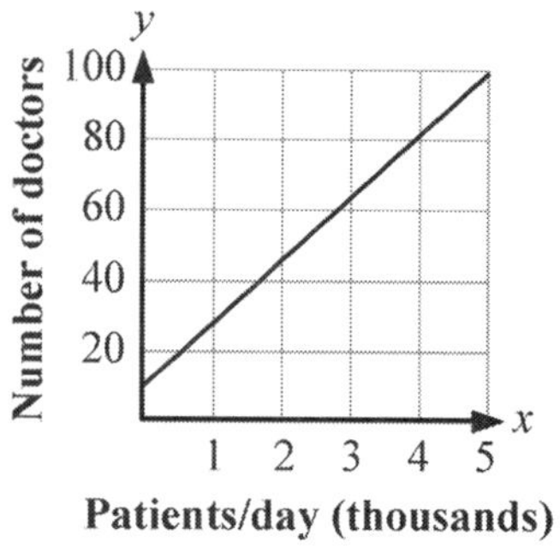

18. What is the equation of the given line?

A. $y = \frac{9}{500} + 10x$

B. $y = 10 + \frac{9}{500}x$

C. $x = \frac{9}{500} + 10y$

D. $x = 10 + \frac{9}{500}y$

Not for Reproduction

Use the following information to answer the next question.

The following scatter plot shows the quarterly profits for a pharmaceutical company.

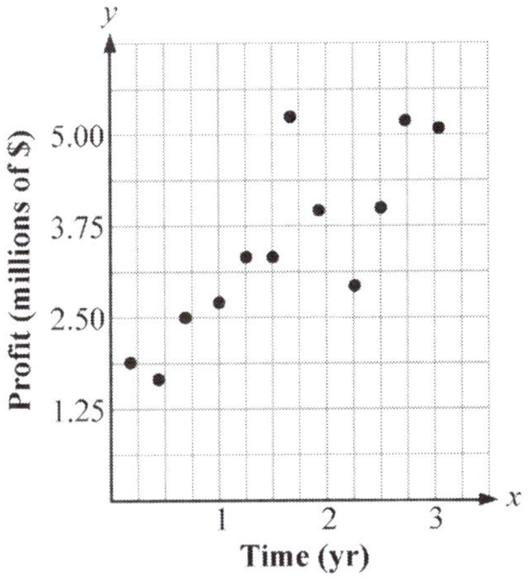

19. If the given trend continues, what will the company's profit be by the second quarter of the fourth year?

A. \$3.95 M **B.** \$4.38 M

C. \$4.69 M **D.** \$5.52 M

Use the following information to answer the next question.

Year	Number of Dentists in Canada
1980	10 325
1985	12 075
1990	13 025

20. What is the **best** estimate for the number of dentists in Canada in 1995?

A. 12 800 **B.** 13 550

C. 13 975 **D.** 14 975

Use the following information to answer the next question.

At the end of each month, Maria records the number of visitors to her website about kittens. She keeps a running tally, which means the value for April represents the number of visitors since January 1.

Month	Number of Visitors to Date
January	500
February	?
March	?
April	2 000
May	?
June	?

Open Response

21. Determine the equation of the line that represents Maria's data and complete the table. Predict how many visitors will be recorded by the end of December.

Show your work.

Open Response

22. Calculate the rate of change of the line passing through the points (–2, 4) and (1, –5).

Show your work.

Copyright Protected

Use the following information to answer the next question.

> An airplane flies at a constant acceleration of 200 km/h^2 for the first four hours of a flight. It then has zero acceleration for the next four hours and a deceleration of 200 km/h^2 for the last four hours.

23. Which of the following velocity-time graphs represents the flight of this airplane?

A.

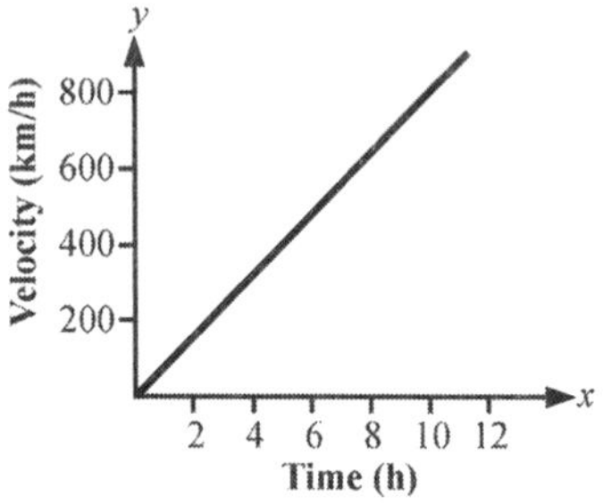

B.

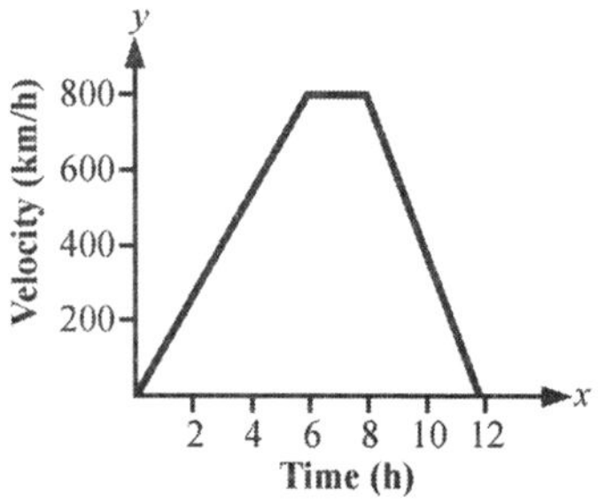

C.

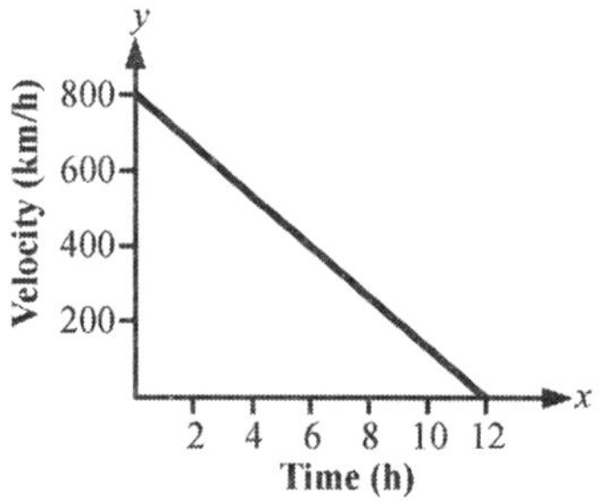

D.

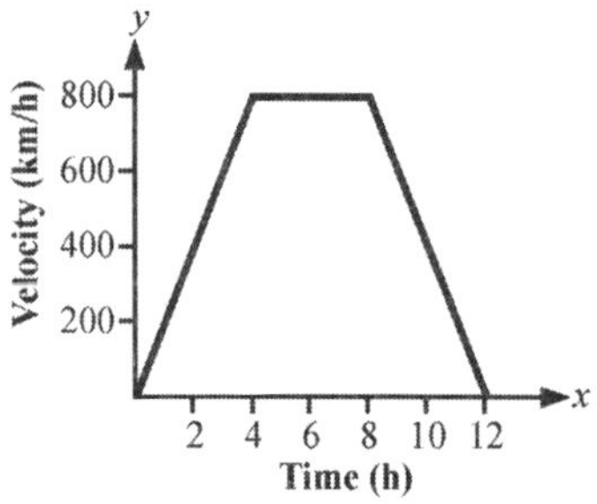

Use the following information to answer the next question.

> David jogs home from work. The route David chooses is not a direct route, but it is relatively free of traffic.

24. Which of the following graphs **best** represents the distance David is from home relative to the time he spends jogging?

A.

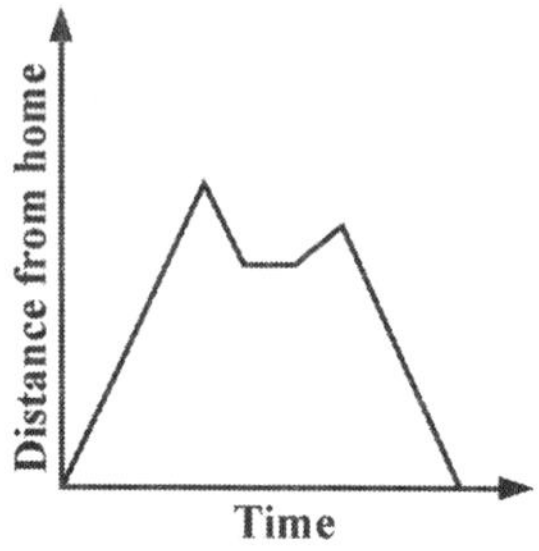

B.

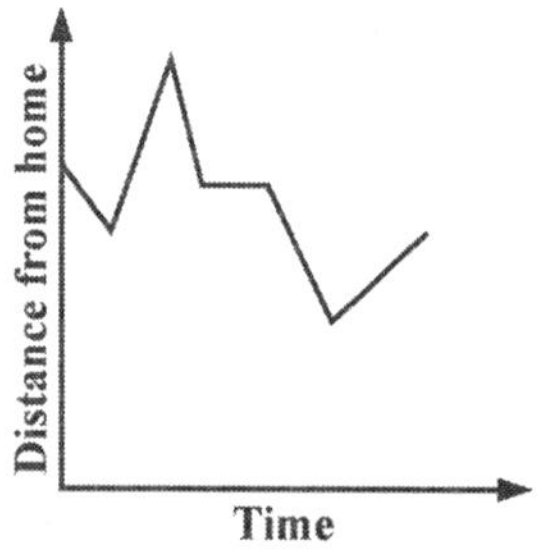

C.

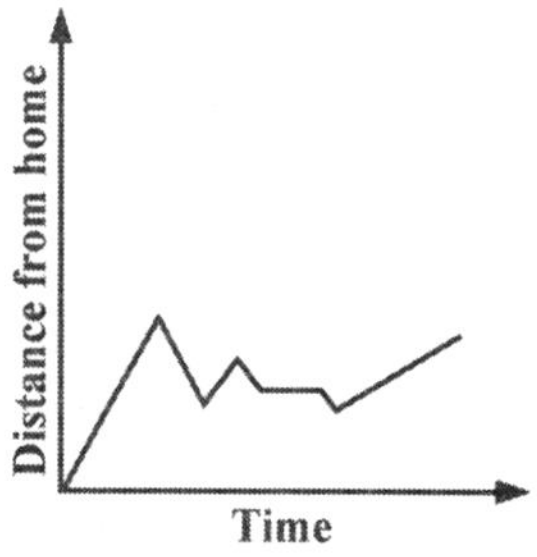

D.

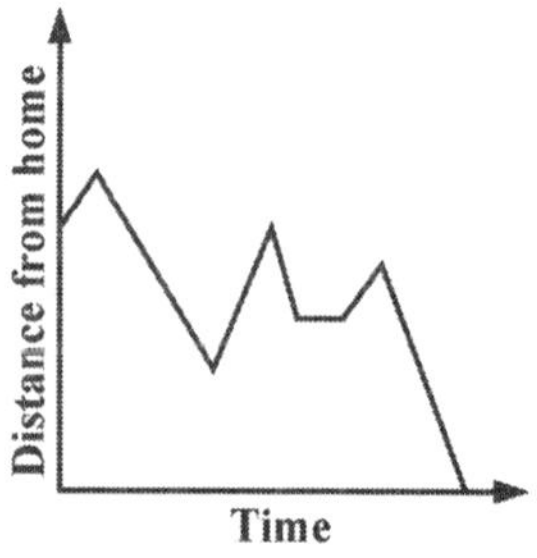

Not for Reproduction

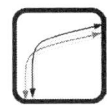

Use the following information to answer the next question.

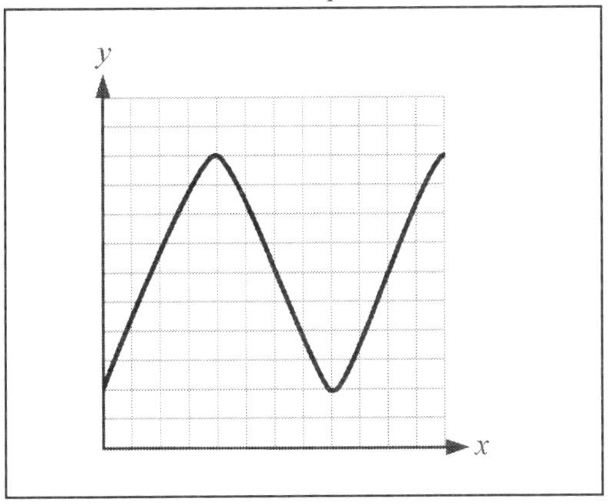

25. The given graph **best** represents which of the following situations?

A. A basketball repeatedly bounces on the ground.

B. The height of a chair on a ferris wheel changes as the wheel rotates.

C. The distance between a commuter's home and work as she bicycles to work.

D. The speed of a child starting on a skateboard, as she goes up and down one hill, and then up the next hill.

Use the following information to answer the next question.

x	–5	–3	–1	0	1	3	5
y	y_1	5	1	–1	y_2	y_3	–11

Open Response

26. What are the values of y_1, y_2, and y_3, respectively?

Show your work.

Use the following information to answer the next question.

Sarah works at the store Zedmans. The amount of money she earns varies directly with the number of hours she works. During the last pay period, Sarah worked 35 hours and earned \$323.75. This pay period, she worked 50 hours and earned \$462.50.

27. The constant rate of change in the relationship between the amount of money Sarah earns and the number of hours she works is

A. \$6.48 / h

B. \$9.25 / h

C. \$13.21 / h

D. \$13.88 / h

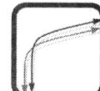

Copyright Protected

Use the following information to answer the next question.

The given velocity-time graph represents the journey of a particular train. In order to reduce the travel time, a high-powered engine is used to double the train's acceleration.

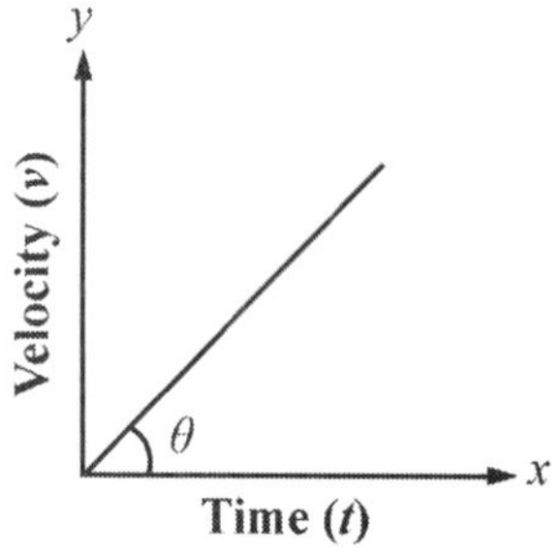

28. What is the new velocity-time graph for the train?

A.
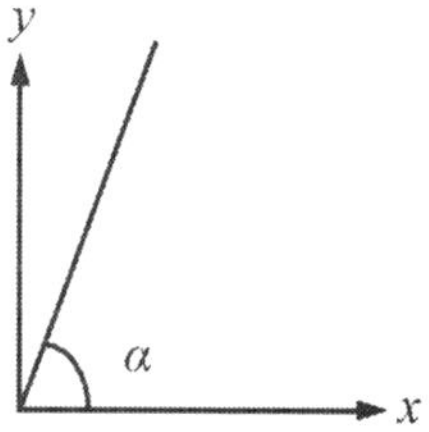

B.
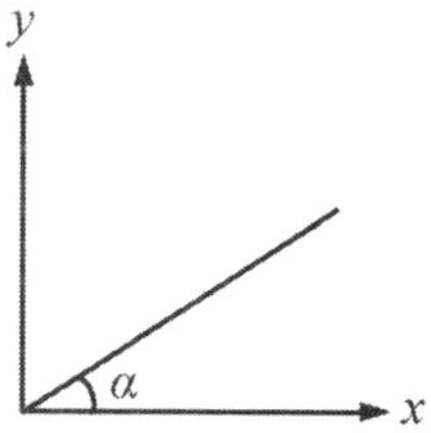

C.
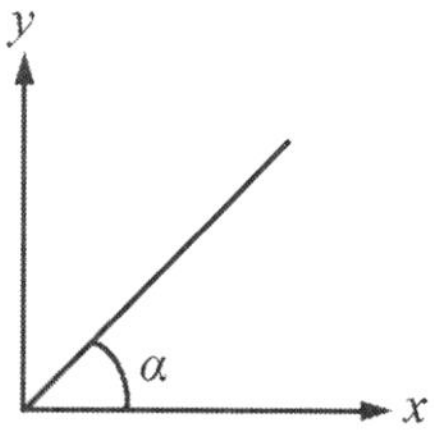

D.
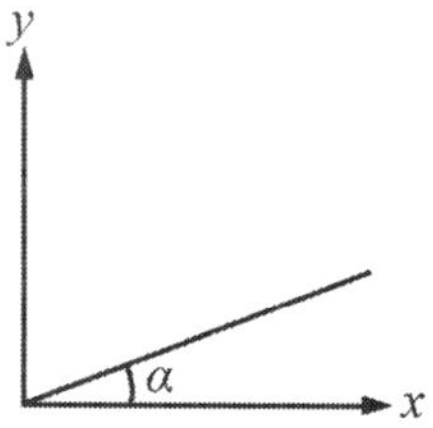

29. The membership fee at a particular health club switched from $50 per month plus $5 per day of use to a flat fee of $10 per day of use. Which graph represents the new monthly fees?

A.
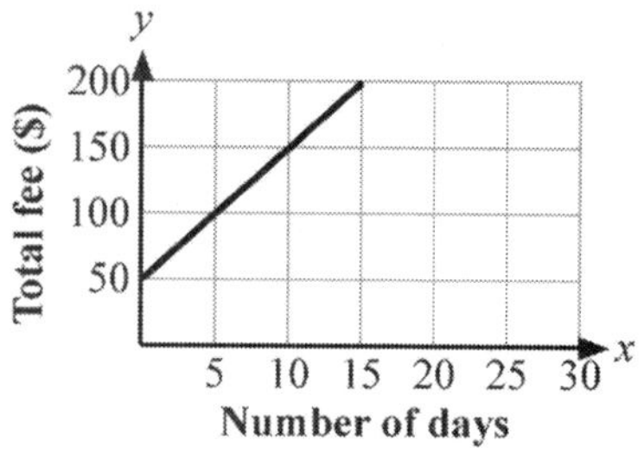

B.
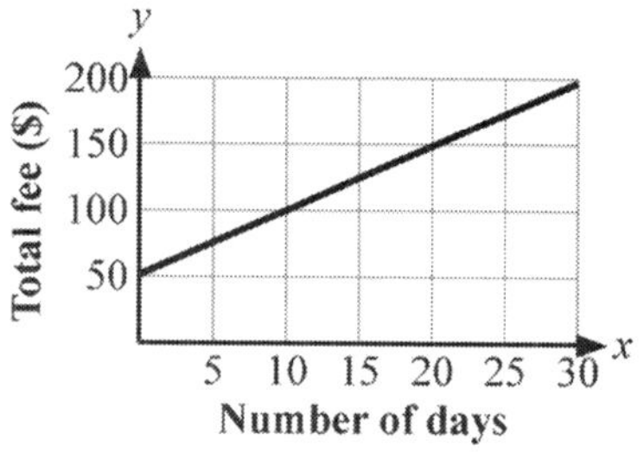

C.
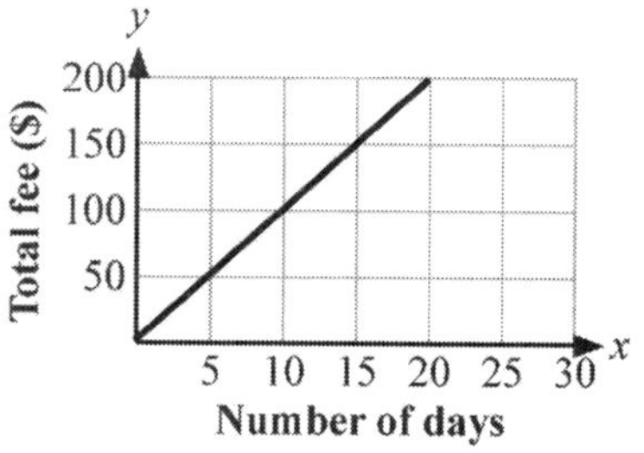

D.
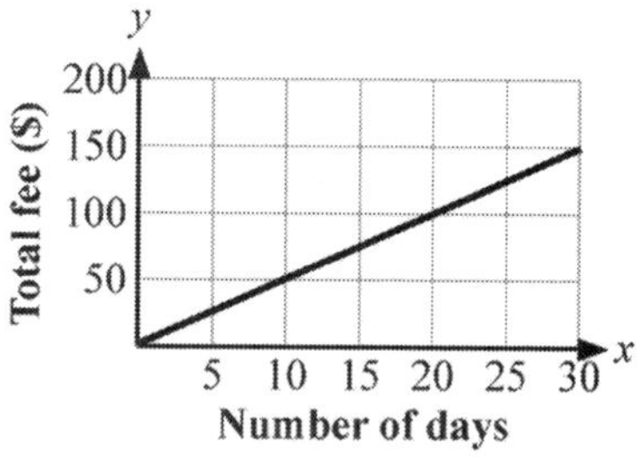

Not for Reproduction

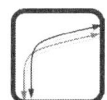

Use the following information to answer the next question.

The given graph represents the relationship between Brad's monthly Internet bill and his corresponding monthly Internet usage.

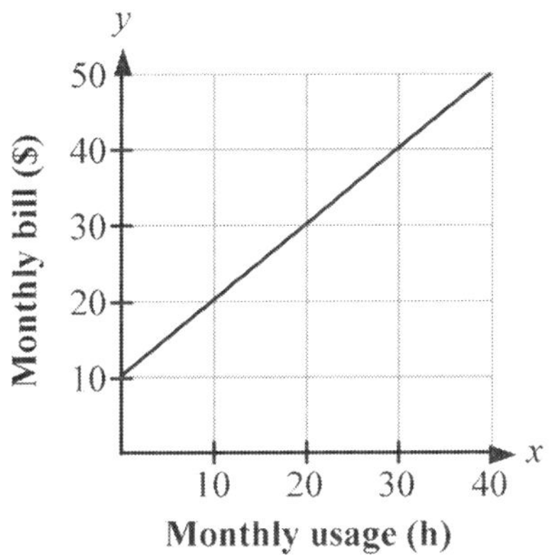

Open Response

30. If the monthly charge increases by $5 and the hourly charge increases to $2, how would the line of the graph change?

Show your work.

Use the following information to answer the next question.

Each of the following four relations are modelled on the equation $C = an + b$, where C is the total cost of producing n items.

Relation 1: The cost of producing n stuffed toys is $200 plus an additional $4 for each stuffed toy that is produced.

Relation 2: The cost of producing n plates is $300 plus an additional $4 for each plate that is produced.

Relation 3: The cost of producing n cups is $200 plus an additional $6 for each cup that is produced.

Relation 4: The cost of producing n vases is $8 plus an additional $8 for each vase that is produced.

Open Response

31. Which of the given relations have the same a-value?

Show your work.

Copyright Protected

Use the following information to answer the next question.

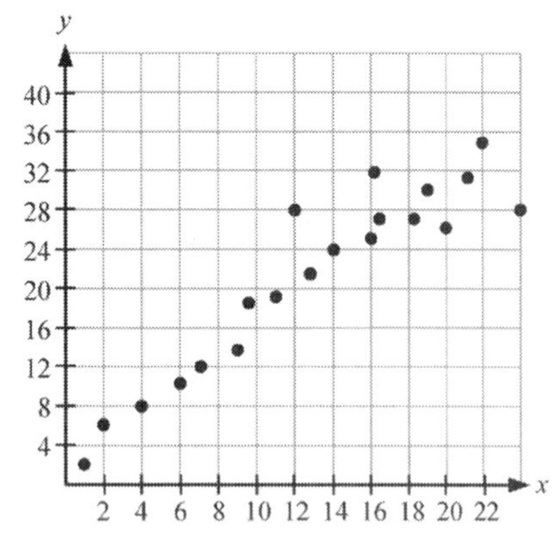

32. In the scatter plot, what y-value **most likely** corresponds to $x = 13$?

A. 20 **B.** 22

C. 24 **D.** 26

Use the following information to answer the next question.

The given graph indicates the variation in temperature of a particular city over the period of one week.

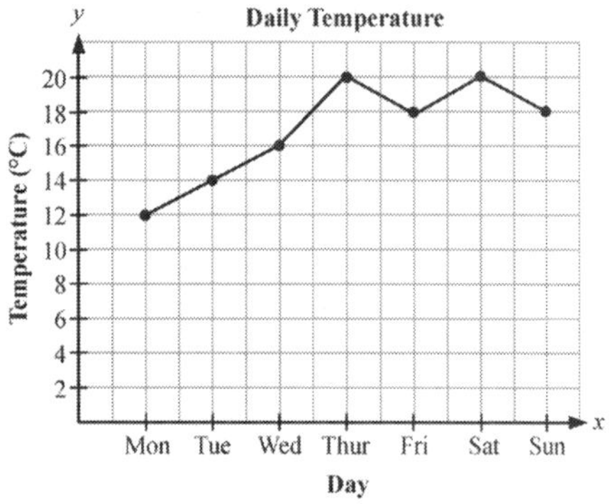

Open Response

33. What do the coordinates (Thur, 20) represent about the given temperatures?

Show your work.

Use the following information to answer the next question.

In an investigation, Mavis is trying to find out whether or not the age of a person affects his or her ability to float in water.

34. Which of the following statements about her investigation is **true**?

A. The person's age is the dependent variable.

B. The person's height is the independent variable.

C. The person's ability to float is the dependent variable.

D. The person's ability to float is the independent variable.

35. Which of the following hypotheses about the age and height of children under 12 years of age is **most unlikely**?

A. As a child gets taller, his or her age increases.

B. As a child gets older, his or her height increases.

C. For every year that a child gets older, his or her height increases by a greater amount.

D. For every year that a child gets older, his or her height increases by a similar amount.

Not for Reproduction

Use the following information to answer the next question.

In an experiment designed to understand the growth of a certain kind of bacteria, it was found that the bacteria count doubled each day. The bacteria count on the first day was 1.

36. If x represents the number of days and y represents the bacteria count, then which of the following tables correctly shows the relationship between x and y?

A.

x	1	2	3
y	1	2	3

B.

x	1	2	3
y	2	4	8

C.

x	1	2	3
y	1	2	4

D.

x	1	2	3
y	2	3	5

37. One chocolate bar costs $0.50. Which of the following graphs correctly displays the relationship between the cost and the number of chocolate bars?

A.

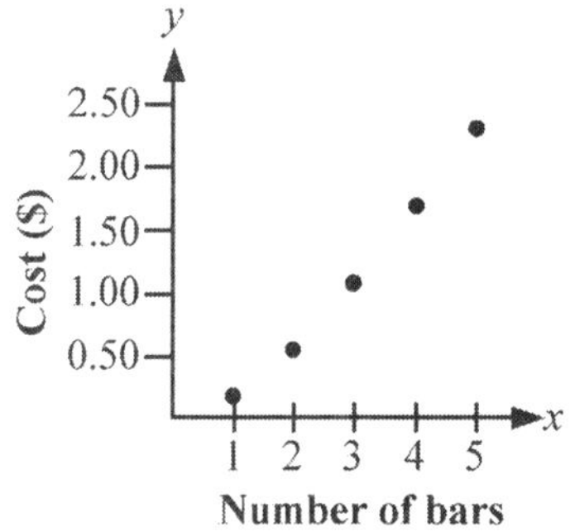

B.

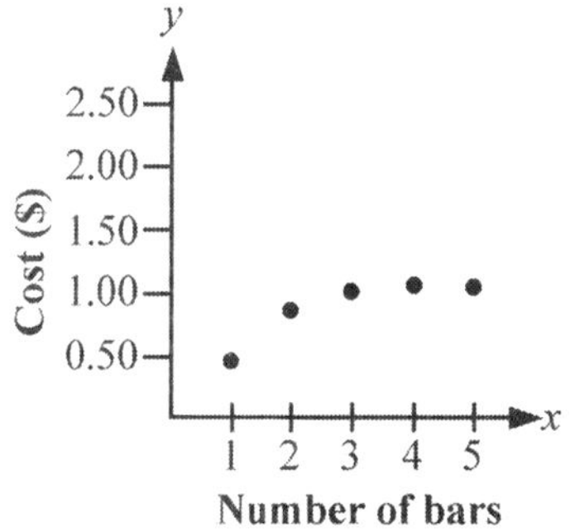

C.

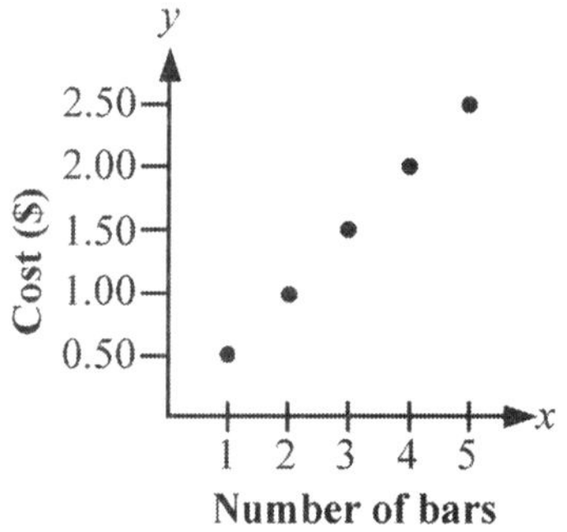

D.

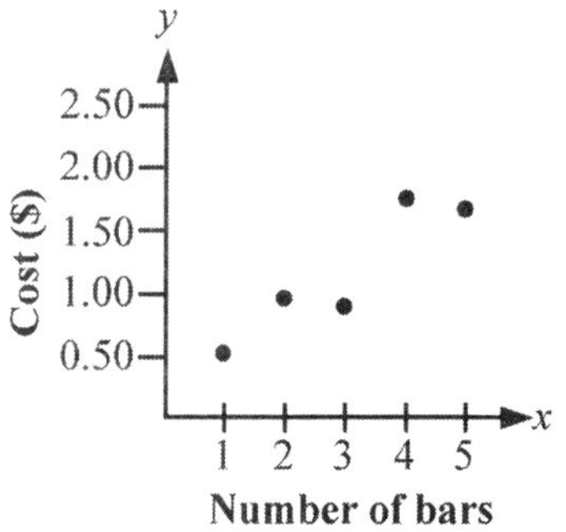

38. The trend line for any given scatter plot

A. connects all the points of a scatter plot

B. connects the most important points of a scatter plot

C. determines the positive correlation in the data

D. determines whether there is a positive, negative, or no correlation in the data

39. Two variables are related such that an increase in one results in a decrease in the other. Which of the following scatter plots represents these two variables?

A.

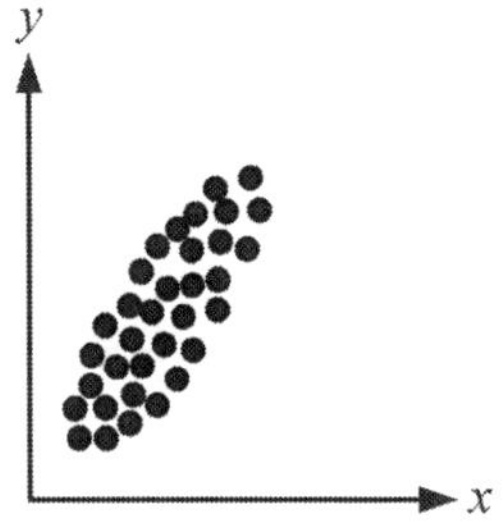

B.

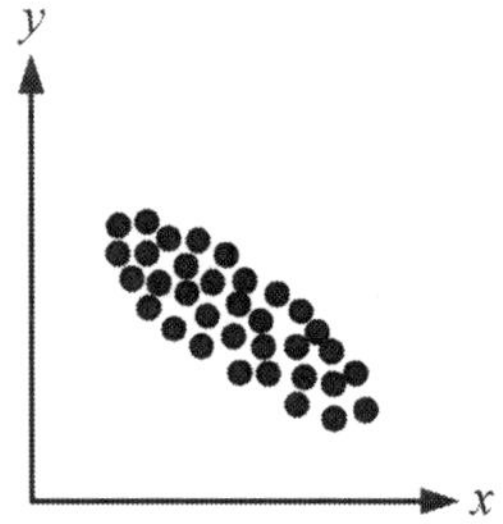

C.

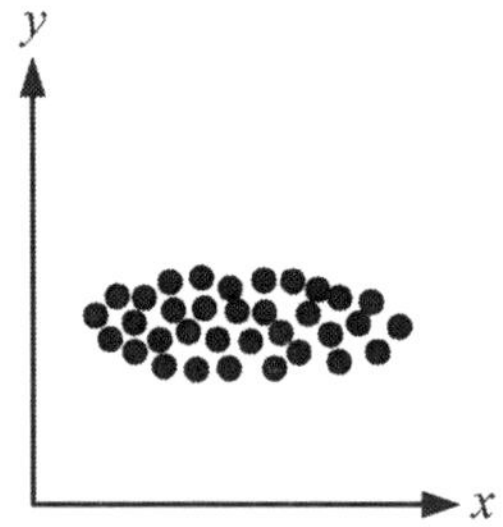

D.

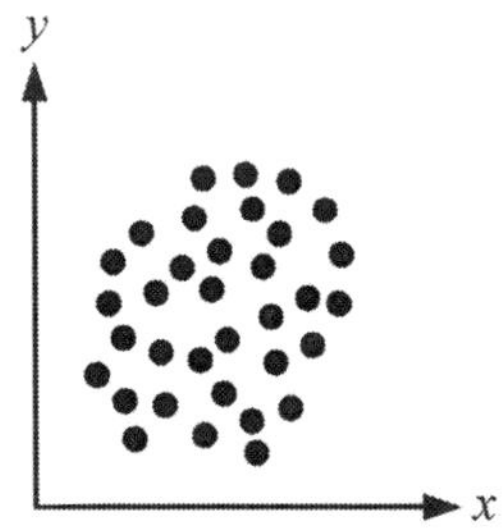

Use the following information to answer the next question.

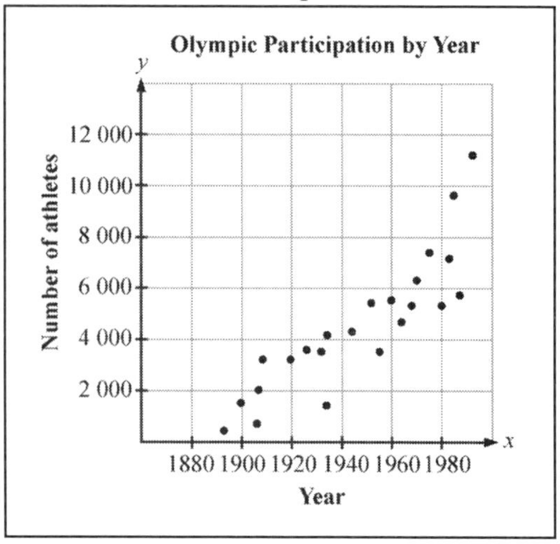

40. The trend indicated by the scatter plot above can be reasonably attributed to each of the following factors **except** for an increase in the

A. number of events

B. number of participating nations

C. number of athletes for each event

D. frequency of the Olympic Games

Not for Reproduction

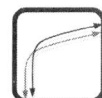

Use the following information to answer the next question.

Average Annual Precipitation in a Town

Year	Precipitation (cm)
1998	18.5
1999	18.8
2000	20.4
2001	19.6
2002	20.0
2003	20.6

Open Response

41. If the given data were represented graphically, what trend would be displayed?

Justify your answer.

Copyright Protected

ANSWERS AND SOLUTIONS — UNIT TEST

1.	B	10.	C	19.	D	28.	A	37.	C
2.	A	11.	C	20.	B	29.	C	38.	D
3.	OR	12.	C	21.	OR	30.	OR	39.	B
4.	OR	13.	C	22.	OR	31.	OR	40.	D
5.	C	14.	B	23.	D	32.	B	41.	OR
6.	D	15.	OR	24.	D	33.	OR		
7.	OR	16.	A	25.	B	34.	C		
8.	OR	17.	A	26.	OR	35.	C		
9.	C	18.	B	27.	B	36.	C		

1. B

The values in the scatter plot follow the pattern of a straight line and decrease along that pattern. Therefore, the data represents a negative linear relationship.

2. A

The graph of a linear function is always a straight line. The graph in alternative A begins as an upward line but then changes direction and continues downward. The change in direction means the entire graph is not linear.

3. OR

The given graph rises, so it must be a positive relation. The line is curved; therefore, it is non-linear.

The relation can be described as positive and non-linear.

4. OR

As the years increase, the amount of money spent also increases in regular intervals. This is an example of a positive linear relation.

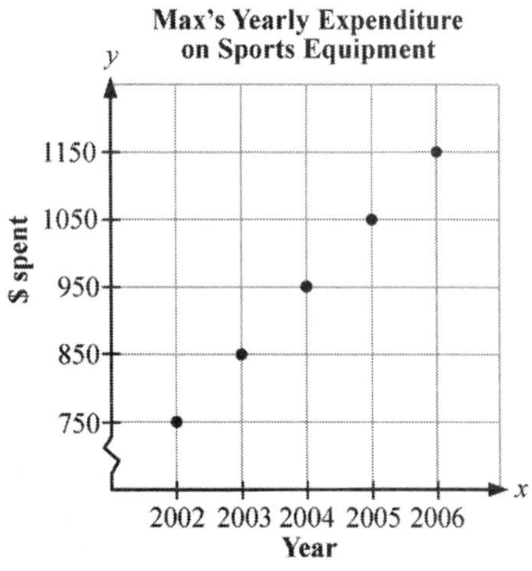

5. C

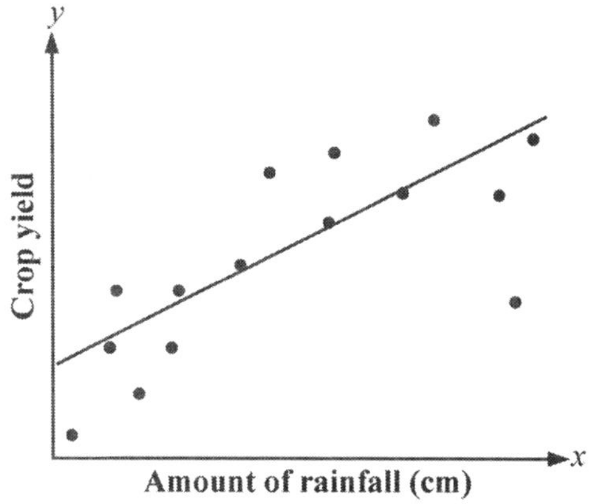

When the line of best fit is drawn, it can be seen that the line steadily rises.

6. D

A negative relationship means that as the x-values increase, the y-values decrease. The line of best fit would have to start at the upper left and go down toward the right, as shown in alternative D.

In alternative A, there is no line of best fit that could be marked. In alternative B, the line would be horizontal. In alternative C, the line would be positive.

7. OR

If the scatter plot is parallel to the y-axis, the line of best fit is straight up and down on the graph. This line indicates that the y-variable is changing and the x-variable is not changing. There is no relationship between the two variables.

8. OR

Points	Sample Answer
4	Plot the points on a graph. 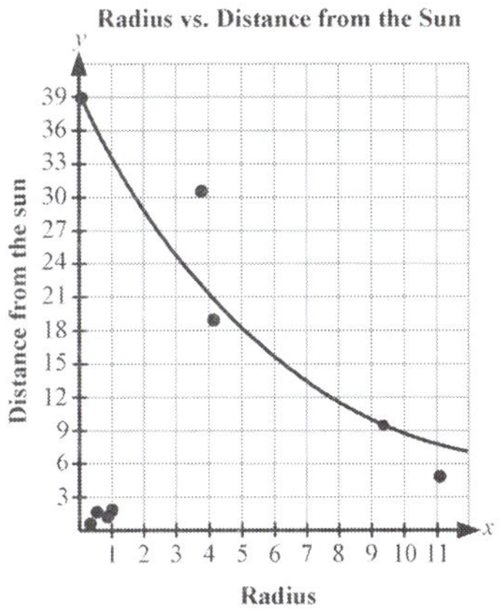 A non-linear relationship results. Not all points have to lie on the curve of best fit.
Application of knowledge and skills involving scatter plots and curves of best fit shows a high degree of effectiveness due to: • a thorough understanding of the concepts • an accurate application of the procedures (any minor errors and/or omissions do not detract from the demonstration of a thorough understanding)	
3	Plots one or two points incorrectly or makes a small error in labelling the axes. Identifies the relationship correctly.
Application of knowledge and skills involving scatter plots and curves of best fit shows considerable effectiveness due to: • an understanding of most of the concepts • minor errors and/or omissions in the application of the procedures	
2	Plots one or two points incorrectly and makes a small error in the labelling of the axes. Does not identify the relationship correctly.
Application of knowledge and skills involving scatter plots and curves of best fit shows some effectiveness due to: • a partial understanding of the concepts • minor errors and/or omissions in the application of the procedures	
1	Plots the wrong data set, but does so correctly. Does not identify the relationship correctly.
Application of knowledge and skills involving scatter plots and curves of best fit shows limited effectiveness due to: • a misunderstanding of concepts • an incorrect selection or misuse of procedures	

9. C

Calculate the first differences of the values given in the tables. If the values of x and y change at constant rates, their relationship is linear. If the values of x and y do not change at constant rates, their relationship is non-linear. In the given tables, the value of x always increases by 1. However, only the table in alternative C has y-values that change at different rates.

Alternative A: $11 - 8 = 3$, $14 - 11 = 3$
Alternative B: $14 - 10 = 4$, $18 - 14 = 4$
Alternative C: $6 - 3 = 3$, $11 - 6 = 5$
Alternative D: $8 - 7 = 1$, $9 - 8 = 1$

10. C

An equation that represents a linear relationship has a degree of one. The square root of the equation in alternative C can be taken.

$$y^2 = x^2$$
$$\sqrt{y^2} = \sqrt{x^2}$$
$$y = x$$

A linear relationship exists between x and y because it is now of the first degree.

11. C

The first differences are not the same for each increment.

$27 - 8 = 19$

$64 - 27 = 37$

$125 - 64 = 61$

$216 - 125 = 91$

$343 - 216 = 127$

Therefore, this is a non-linear relation. As l increases, V increases at a varying rate.

12. C

A graph that represents direct variation must go through the origin (0, 0). Only the graph in alternative C goes through this point.

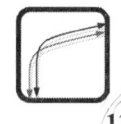

13. C

The initial value of the car = \$350. Depreciation is the rate of change. The rate of change = −\$200 / year.

The graph must start at 35 000 on the y-axis and then proceed downward 200 dollars each year since the rate of change is negative. The graph in alternative C displays this correct rate of change.

14. B

The line in the graph meets the y-axis at 0.5 when x is 0. This x-value corresponds to the time of the launch. Therefore, the projectile was launched 0.5 km above ground.

15. OR

In the given equation, $y = 100 + 2x$, y is the total cost and x is the number of products the factory manufactures. The coefficient of x is always the rate of change, which is \$2 in this equation. The initial value is \$10 000. 10 000 = 100 + 2x

9 900 = 2x / 2 / 2 x = 4950

16. A

To write the equation of the line, use the form $y = mx + b$.

The line passes through the origin. Therefore, b equals 0, so it will not be included in the equation.

To calculate the rate of change, use any two points from the table. In this case, use (4, 3) and (−4, −3).

$$\frac{y_2 - y_1}{x_2 - x_1} = \frac{3 - (-3)}{4 - (-4)} = \frac{6}{8} = \frac{3}{4}$$

$$y = \frac{3}{4}x$$

17. A

First, use algebraic techniques to put the equation of the line in the form $y = mx + b$.

$$x = y - 2$$
$$x + 2 = y - 2 + 2$$
$$x + 2 = y \rightarrow y = x + 2$$

The y-intercept is 2. This eliminates alternative C.

The rate of change is 1, so the line must rise up toward the right. This eliminates alternatives B and D.

The graph in alternative A displays the correct line for the given equation.

18. B

Write the equation in the form

$$y = \left(\frac{\text{vertical separation}}{\text{horizontal separation}}\right)x + (\text{initial value}).$$

The line meets the y-axis at $y = 10$ (the y-intercept).

$\therefore b = 10$

To calculate the rate of change (m), use the coordinates (0, 10) and (5 000, 100).

$$m = \frac{y_2y2 - y_1y1}{x_2x2 - x_1x1} = \frac{100 - 10}{50 - 0} = \frac{90}{50} = \frac{9}{500}$$

The equation that represents the given line is

$$y = 10 + \frac{9}{500}x.$$

19. D

You are required to find a value past the given points. Draw the line of best fit and then extrapolate. Where the second quarter of the fourth year is indicated on the x-axis, travel upward until you hit the line of best fit. Move left to the y-axis to determine the value.

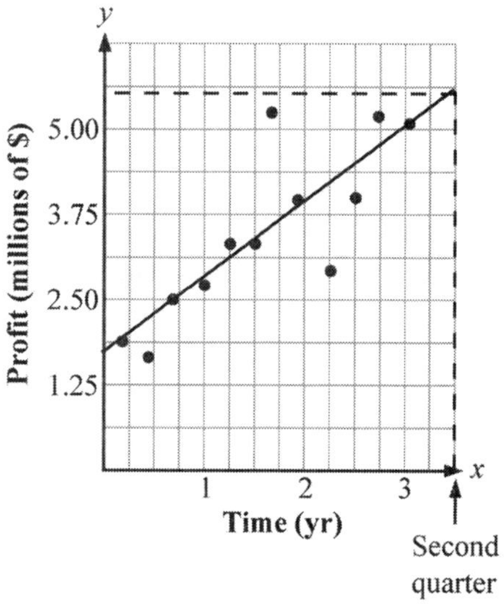

Of the alternatives given, 5.52 is the best-matched value to the point on the line.

The profit will be \$5.52 million.

20. B

The numbers of dentists are given for the years 1980, 1985, and 1990. The following table gives the change in the number of dentists (first differences) in the two five-year periods: 1980–85 and 1985–90.

Not for Reproduction

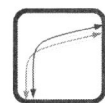

Time Period	First Difference
1980-85	1 750
1985-90	950

Although the number of dentists increased, the rate of increase decreased. Assuming this trend continued, the number of dentists in 1995 should be more than in 1990, but the increase should be smaller than 950, which was the change in the period 1985-90.

Find the first differences of the given alternatives.

Alternative A: 12 800 – 1325 = –225
Alternative B: 13 550 – 1325 = 525
Alternative C: 13 975 – 1325 = 950
Alternative D: 14 975 – 1325 = 1950

The most reasonable amount is 525.

1325 + 535 = 13 550

21. OR

<table>
<tr><th>Points</th><th>Sample Answer</th></tr>
<tr><td>4</td><td>

Start by calculating the rate of change. Assign each month a number, making January equal to 1, February equal to 2, and so on. Two points are given: (1, 500) and (4, 2 000).

$y = \left(\dfrac{\text{vertical separation}}{\text{horizontal separation}}\right)x + \text{initial value}$

$y = \left(\dfrac{2\ 0 - 500}{4 - 1}\right)x + 0$

$y = \dfrac{1500}{3}x$

$y = 500x$

Use the equation of the line to fill in the table and make a prediction for December (month 12).

Month	Number of Visitors to Date
January (1)	500
February (2)	$y = 500(2)$ $= 1\ 0$
March (3)	$y = 500(3)$ $= 1500$
April (4)	$y = 500(4)$ $= 2\ 000$
May (5)	$y = 500(5)$ $= 2500$
June (6)	$y = 500(6)$ $= 3\ 0$
December (12)	$y = 500(12)$ $= 6\ 0$

By December, the website will have had 6 000 visitors.

</td></tr>
<tr><td colspan="2">

Application of knowledge and skills involving values of a linear relation and extrapolation shows a high degree of effectiveness due to:

- a thorough understanding of the concepts
- an accurate application of the procedures (any minor errors and/or omissions do not detract from the demonstration of a thorough understanding)

</td></tr>
</table>

Copyright Protected

Points	Sample Answer
3	The equation of the line is calculated incorrectly, but the values put into the chart are correct based on the equation found.
Application of knowledge and skills involving values of a linear relation and extrapolation shows considerable effectiveness due to: • an understanding of most of the concepts • minor errors and/or omissions in the application of the procedures	
2	The equation of the line is shown with no work to demonstrate the process. The chart is filled in correctly, including December.
Application of knowledge and skills involving values of a linear relation and extrapolation shows some effectiveness due to: • a partial understanding of the concepts • minor errors and/or omissions in the application of the procedures	
1	Chart is filled in only from January through June. No value is calculated for December. No equation of the line is shown.
Application of knowledge and skills involving values of a linear relation and extrapolation shows limited effectiveness due to: • a misunderstanding of concepts • an incorrect selection or misuse of procedures	

22. OR

The line passes through the following points: (–2, 4) and (1, –5)

$$= \frac{y_2 - y_1}{x_2 - x_1}$$

$$\text{Rate of change} = \text{slope} = \frac{\text{vertical separation}}{\text{horizontal separation}}$$

$$\begin{aligned} &= \frac{y_2 - y_1}{x_2 - x_1} \\ &= \frac{-5-4}{1-(-2)} \\ &= \frac{-9}{1+2} \\ &= \frac{-9}{3} \\ &= -3 \end{aligned}$$

23. D

The acceleration is equal to the rate of change. Because the plane accelerates for the first four hours, the first part of the line should move upward. The plane then travels with zero acceleration for the next four hours, which corresponds to a straight, horizontal line on the graph. Finally, the plane decelerates for the last four hours. This is represented by a downward rate of change.

Alternative B is close but has zero acceleration occurring for two hours, not four. The only graph that correctly represents the flight is given in alternative D.

24. D

Because David jogs from work, his distance from home is greater than zero. Alternatives A and C can be eliminated. The point at which he reaches home would have a y-value of zero. Alternative B is eliminated because it does not show David reaching home.

25. B

Alternative A: The graph would start as it does, but it would go down first to indicate the bounce before the rebound. This answer is not correct.

Alternative B: The graph shows the chair going up in the air, peaking, returning to the ground level, and then peaking again.

Alternative C: The graph shows the commuter going to work from some other place than home, returning to that place, and then going back to work. This is not the correct answer.

Alternative D: The graph shows the skateboard starting in motion, not at rest. This answer is not correct.

26. OR

Write the equation of the line first by calculating the rate of change and the y-intercept.

$$\begin{aligned} \text{Rate of change} &= \frac{\text{vertical separation}}{\text{horizontal separation}} \\ &= \frac{y_2 - y_1}{x_2 - x_1} \\ &= \frac{5-1}{(-3)-(-1)} \\ &= \frac{4}{-2} \\ &= -2 \end{aligned}$$

According to the table the y-intercept is –1, which means the equation is $y = -2x - 1$.

Not for Reproduction

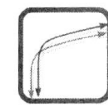

To complete the table, substitute the values of x into the equation $y = -2x - 1$ and solve for y.

- For $x = -5$: $y = -2(-5) - 1 = 9$
- For $x = 1$: $y = -3$
- For $x = 3$: $y = -2(3) - 1 = -7$

x	-5	-3	-1	0	1	3	5
y	9	5	1	-1	-3	-7	-11

Therefore, $y_1 = 9$, $y_2 = -3$, and $y_3 = -7$.

27. B

The two variables of the relation are the number of hours Sarah works and the amount she earns. You are given two ordered pairs of this relation from which you can determine the rate of change: (50, 462.5) and (35, 323.75)

$$\text{rate of change} = \frac{\text{vertical separation}}{\text{horizontal separation}} = \frac{y_2 - y_1}{x_2 - x_1}$$

$$\frac{462.50 - 323.75}{50 - 35} = \frac{\$138.75}{15\text{ h}}$$

$$= \$9.25/\text{h}$$

28. A

As the acceleration of the train doubles, the rate of change (slope) also doubles. Therefore, the slope of the line is much steeper.

The graph in alternative A is the only one that shows a steeper slope.

29. C

If there is no initial value (flat monthly fee), the graph must start at the origin. Only the graphs in alternatives C and D represent this.

The cost per day is $10. The equation that represents this relation is $y = 10x$. Create a table of values to verify the points.

x	$y = 10x$
5	50
10	100
15	150
20	200

30. OR

The monthly charge refers to the initial value. If the initial value increases, then the y-intercept shifts up.

The use per hour refers to the rate of change. From the graph it can be determined that the rate of change is 1. If it increases to $2, then the line will be steeper.

31. OR

Relations 1 and 2 have the same rate of change ($4). Using the equation $C = an + b$, $a = 4$ for both relations.

32. B

Move along the x-axis until you reach 13. Then, move up the y-axis until you reach the corresponding point. Move left to the y-axis to determine the value. It can be seen that when $x = 13$, the y-value is most likely 22.

33. OR

The coordinates (Thur, 20) represent one of the days when the temperature was at a maximum (20°C). The other day it reached this temperature was on the Saturday.

34. C

Alternative A: The person's age is not dependent on his or her ability to float; therefore, it is the independent variable.

Alternative B: Height is not part of the relationship.

Alternative C: The person's ability to float cannot be controlled; therefore, it is the dependent variable. This statement is true.

Alternative D: The person's ability to float cannot be controlled; therefore, it is the dependent variable.

35. C

Generally, as a child gets older, she or he gets taller. Heights increase, but not by a greater amount from one year to the next. A child does not grow two inches one year, four inches the next, six inches the next, and so on. That is not realistic. Therefore, alternative C is the most unlikely hypothesis.

36. C

The independent variable x, represents the number of days. The dependent variable y, represents the bacteria count.

Initially, the bacteria count was 1, and every day the bacteria count doubles. On day 2 (x), the count would be $1 \times 2 = 2$ (y), and on day 3, the count would be $2 \times 2 = 4$. The table in alternative C accurately represents the relationship between x and y.

37. C

The price of chocolate bars increases uniformly at \$0.50 per bar. So, 2 bars cost twice as much (\$0.50 × 2 = \$1.00), and 3 bars cost triple the amount (\$0.50 × 3 = \$1.50). When these points are plotted, the graph shows a linear relationship.

Alternatives A, B, and D do not form a straight line. As the price increases uniformly, a linear relationship is being discussed.

38. D

A scatter plot is a collection of points on a graph that represents data. It displays relationships between data presented on the x- and y-axes. A trend line is used to determine whether there is a positive, negative, or no correlation in the data.

39. B

The relationship described has a downward trend; meaning that as the x-value increases, the y-value decreases. This leads to points that start high and then are plotted lower as you move to the right.

40. D

The trend indicated in the scatter plot is that the number of athletes participating in the Olympics is increasing over time. This can reasonably be attributed to an increase in the number of athletes for each event, an increase in the number of participating nations, and an increase in the number of events. In 1992, the Olympic Winter Games and Summer Games were split up, but this change did not contribute to the trend that had been already established.

41. OR

By observing the data, one can see that as the years increase, the precipitation also increases for most years. There is a slight decrease in the year 2001, but this is not enough of a change to upset the trend. This is an example of a positive relationship. It would display as an upward trend on a scatter plot.

Analytic Geometry

Copyright Protected

ANALYTIC GEOMETRY

Table of Correlations

Specific Expectation		Practice Questions	Unit Test Questions	Practice Test 1	Practice Test 2
9AGV.01	Investigating the Relationship Between the Equation of a Relation and the Shape of Its Graph				
9AG1.01	*determine, through investigation, the characteristics that distinguish the equation of a straight line from the equations of nonlinear relations*	1, 2, 3, 4	14, 15, 16	10	
9AG1.02	*identify, through investigation, the equation of a line in any of the forms* $y = mx + b$, $Ax + By + C = 0$, $x = a$, $y = b$	5, 6, 7	17, 18, 19, 20		11
9AG1.03	*express the equation of a line in the form* $y = mx + b$, *given the form* $Ax + By + C = 0$	8, 9, 10	21, 22, 23	11	12
9AGV.02	Investigating the Properties of Slope				
9AG2.01	*determine, through investigation, various formulas for the slope of a line segment or a line*	11, 12, 13	1, 2, 3		
9AG2.02	*identify, through investigation with technology, the geometric significance of m and b in the equation* $y = mx + b$	14, 15, 16, 17	4, 5, 6		8
9AG2.03	*determine, through investigation, connections among the representations of a constant rate of change of a linear relation*	18, 19, 20	7, 8, 9, 10	8	9
9AG2.04	*identify, through investigation, properties of the slopes of lines and line segments using graphing technology to facilitate investigations, where appropriate*	21, 22, 23	11, 12, 13	9	10
9AGV.03	Using the Properties of Linear Relations to Solve Problems				
9AG3.01	*graph lines by hand, using a variety of techniques*	24, 25, 26	24, 25, 26	21	
9AG3.02	*determine the equation of a line from information about the line*	27, 28, 29	27, 28, 29, 30	22, 23	23
9AG3.03	*describe the meaning of the slope and y-intercept for a linear relation arising from a realistic situation, and describe a situation that could be modelled by a given linear equation*	30, 31, 32	31, 32, 33, 34	24	
9AG3.04	*identify and explain any restrictions on the variables in a linear relation arising from a realistic situation*	33, 34, 35	35, 36, 37		24
9AG3.05	*determine graphically the point of intersection of two linear relations, and interpret the intersection point in the context of an application*	36, 37, 38	38, 39, 40	25	25, 26

Not for Reproduction

9AG1.01 determine, through investigation, the characteristics that distinguish the equation of a straight line from the equations of nonlinear relations

Determining the Characteristics of Linear and Non-Linear Equations

A table of values looks at the relationship between x- and y-values. Thus, the data in a table of values represents a relation. There are two types of relations.

Linear Relations

The equation of a linear relation has one exponent (of the first degree) or root signs on the variables. The graph of a linear relation is a straight line. The following table of values and graph represent the linear relation $y = 3x - 7$.

x	$y = 3x - 7$
2	$3(2) - 7 = -1$
4	$3(4) - 7 = 5$
6	$3(6) - 7 = 11$

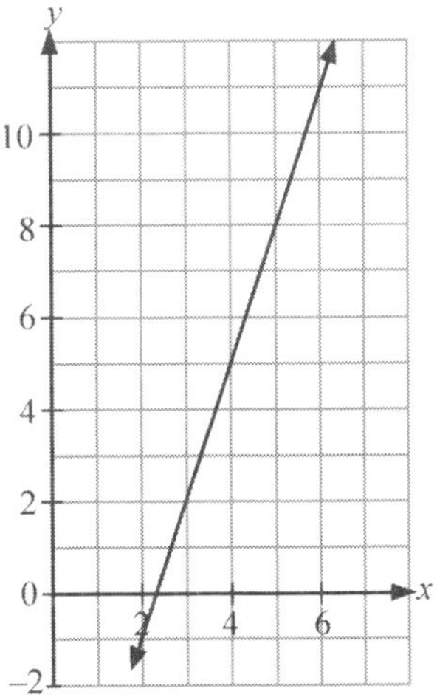

Non-Linear Relations

The equation of a non-linear relation is of the second degree or greater or has root signs on the variables. The graph of a non-linear relation is not a straight line. The following table of values and graph represent the non-linear relation $y = x^2 - 1$.

x	$y = x^2 - 1$
−3	$(-3)^2 - 1 = 8$
−2	$(-2)^2 - 1 = 3$
−1	$(-1)^2 - 1 = 0$
0	$(0)^2 - 1 = -1$
1	$(1)^2 - 1 = 0$
2	$(2)^2 - 1 = 3$
3	$(3)^2 - 1 = 8$

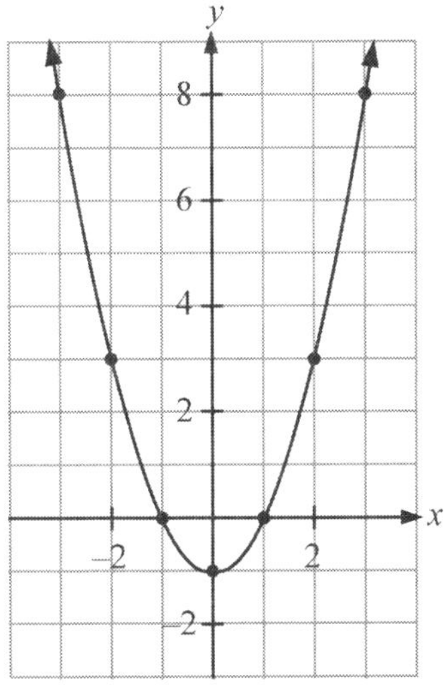

1. Which of the following equations represents a linear relationship when plotted on a coordinate grid?

A. $x^2 = xy + 6$ **B.** $x^2 = y^2 + 9$
C. $y = 6x + 3$ **D.** $y = xy - 4$

Use the following information to answer the next question.

> $y = x$
> $y = x + 3$
> $y = x^2 + 3$
> $y = 3x + 3$
> $y = x^3 - 6$

2. How many of the given equations have a graph of a straight line?

A. Two **B.** Three
C. Four **D.** Five

Copyright Protected

3. A first-degree equation always graphs

A. a curved line

B. a straight line

C. parallel lines

D. perpendicular lines

Use the following information to answer the next question.

$y = -2x + 5$

Open Response

4. Determine whether the given equation is a linear or non-linear relation. Justify your answer by describing the characteristics of the equation and graph.
Show your work.

9AG1.02 identify, through investigation, the equation of a line in any of the forms $y = mx + b$, $Ax + By + C = 0$, $x = a$, $y = b$

Identifying the Equation of a Line

The equation of a line is most often written in one of two forms: slope y-intercept form or standard form.

The **slope y-intercept form** is written as $y = mx + b$, where the variable m represents the slope of the line and b is the y-intercept. In **standard form**, all terms are collected on one side and are made equal to zero. The coefficient of x is always positive. Standard form is written as
$Ax + By + C = 0$,
where $A \neq 0$, $B \neq 0$. Here, A is the slope of the line and C represents the y-intercept.

Both forms display the characteristics of a linear relation: the equation is of the first degree and there is no root on the variable. When graphed, the line is straight.

The equation $y = 3x - 7$ is shown in both forms in the table of values below. A partial graph of the line follows.

	Slope y-intercept Form	**Standard Form**
x	$y = 3x - 7$	$3x - y - 7 = 0$
2	$3(2) - 7 = -1$	$3(2) - y - 7 = 0$ $6 - y - 7 = 0$ $-1 - y = 0$ $-1 = y$
6	$3(6) - 7 = 11$	$3(6) - y - 7 = 0$ $18 - y - 7 = 0$ $11 - y = 0$ $11 = y$

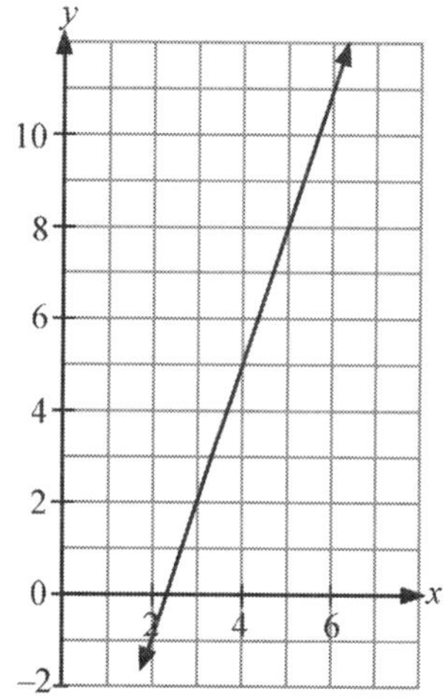

Linear relations can also be horizontal or vertical lines. The equation of a **horizontal line** containing the points (a, b) is $y = b$.

Not for Reproduction

The line $y = 2$ is represented below.

b	$y = b$
2	2

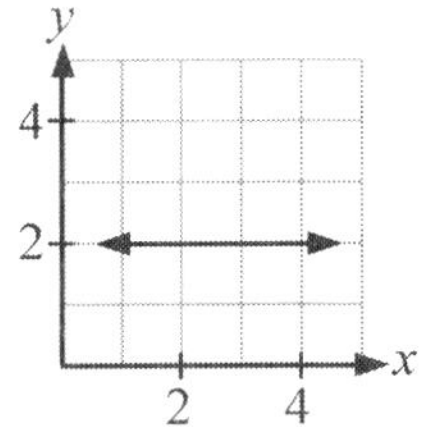

The equation of a **vertical line** containing points (a, b) is $x = a$. The line $x = 3$ is represented below.

a	$x = a$
3	3

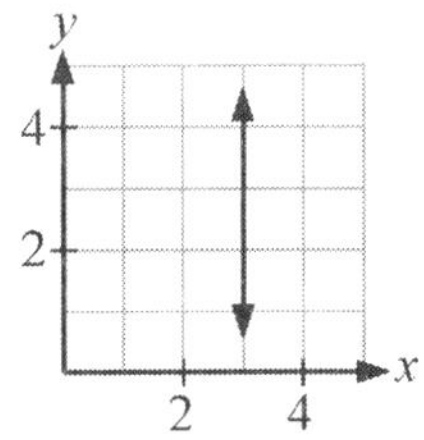

5. Which of the following equations is written in standard form?

A. $y = 3$

B. $y = 3x + 2$

C. $y = 3x$

D. $2x + \frac{y}{3} - 3 = 0$

Use the following information to answer the next question.

> The slope of a line is $\frac{2}{3}$ and the y-intercept is -2.

6. What is the equation of this line in slope y-intercept form?

A. $y = 2x - 6$ **B.** $y = 2x - 3$

C. $y = \frac{3}{2}x - 2$ **D.** $y = \frac{2}{3}x - 2$

7. The equation of the horizontal line passing through point $(-2, 7)$ is

A. $y = -7$ **B.** $x = -2$

C. $x = 2$ **D.** $y = 7$

9AG1.03 express the equation of a line in the form $y = mx + b$, given the form $Ax + By + C = 0$

Converting Standard Form to Slope y-Intercept Form

Using the inverse operation is one method for isolating a variable in an algebraic expression. It is also a method that you can use to convert equations in standard form to slope y-intercept form.

Example

Write the equation $3x + 5y + 15 = 0$ in slope y-intercept form.

The equation is currently in standard form $(Ax + By + C = 0)$. Slope y-intercept form is $y = mx + b$.
$3x + 5y + 15 = 0$ (standard form).

Use the inverse operation of subtraction to move $3x$ and 15.

$3x - 3x + 5y + 15 - 15 = 0 - 3x - 15$

$5y = -3x - 15$

Divide both sides by 5 to isolate y.

$\frac{5y}{5} = \frac{-3x}{5} - \frac{15}{5}$

$y = \frac{-3x}{5} - 3$ (slope y-intercept form)

---

8. The equation $y = \frac{4}{5}x - 7$ in standard form is

A. $4x - 5y + 7 = 0$

B. $4x - 5y - 7 = 0$

C. $4x - 5y + 35 = 0$

D. $4x - 5y - 35 = 0$

9. Which of the following equations represents $5x - 3y = -6$ in slope y-intercept form?

A. $5x - 3y + 6 = 0$

B. $y = -\frac{5}{3}x + 2$

C. $y = \frac{5}{3}x + 2$

D. $-\frac{5}{3}x + y - 2 = 0$

10. What is the equation of the line $2x - 6y = 12$ expressed in slope y-intercept form?

A. $y = -\frac{1}{3}x - 2$

B. $y = -\frac{1}{3}x + 2$

C. $y = \frac{1}{3}x - 2$

D. $y = \frac{1}{3}x + 2$

9AG2.01 determine, through investigation, various formulas for the slope of a line segment or a line

Determining Formulas for Slope

When you talk about the slope of a line (m), you are referring to its steepness. Steepness is the ratio of the line's rise (vertical separation of two points on the y-axis) to its run (horizontal separation of the same two points on the x-axis).

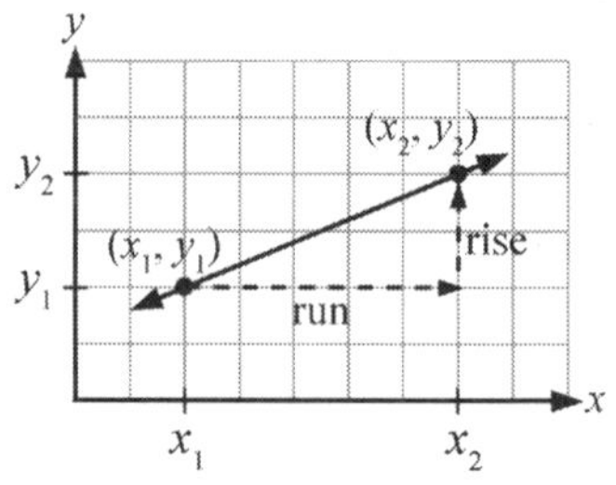

Rise is the change (indicated by the Greek letter delta, Δ) in the y-values. **Run** is the change in the x-values.

$$m = \frac{\Delta y}{\Delta x} \text{ or } m = \frac{\text{rise}}{\text{run}}$$

The change in the x- and y-values can be found by finding the difference between two sets of ordered pairs. Therefore, the following **slope formula** can also be used.

$$m = \frac{y_2 - y_1}{x_2 - x_1}$$

For example, if you are finding the slope of the line joining points (3, 1) and (−4, −3), you would label the points and find the slope as follows.

$y_2 = -3,\ y_1 = 1$

$x_2 = -4,\ x_1 = 3$

$$m = \frac{y_2 - y_1}{x_2 - x_1}$$

$$= \frac{-3 - 1}{-4 - 3}$$

$$m = \frac{-4}{-7}$$

$$= \frac{4}{7}$$

Use the following information to answer the next question.

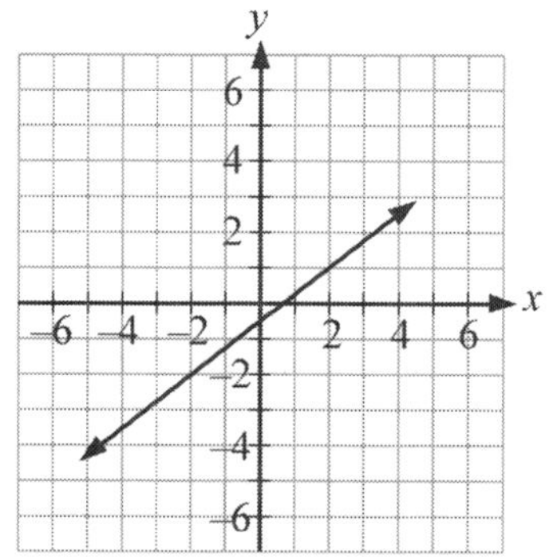

11. What is the slope of the given line?

A. $-\frac{4}{3}$ **B.** $-\frac{3}{4}$

C. $\frac{3}{4}$ **D.** $\frac{4}{3}$

12. The slope of the line passing through points (4, 6) and (2, 12) is

A. -3 **B.** -2

C. 2 **D.** 3

Not for Reproduction

Use the following information to answer the next question.

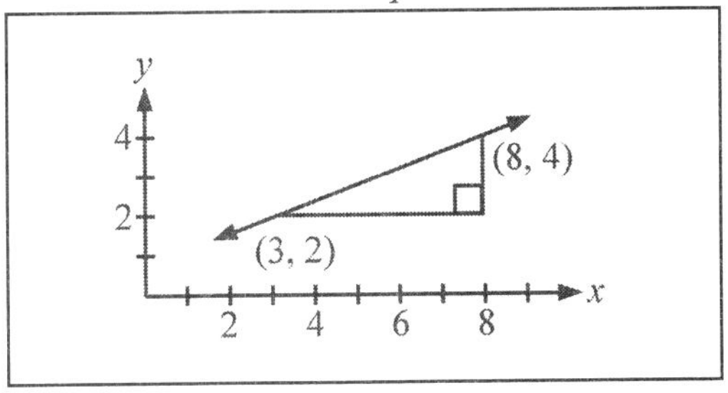

13. What is the slope of the line in the diagram?

A. $-\frac{2}{3}$ **B.** $-\frac{2}{5}$

C. $\frac{2}{5}$ **D.** $\frac{2}{3}$

9AG2.02 identify, through investigation with technology, the geometric significance of m and b in the equation y = mx + b

Identifying the Significance of *m* and *b*

If given a graph, the slope (m) and y-intercept (b) are determined through inspection of the points.

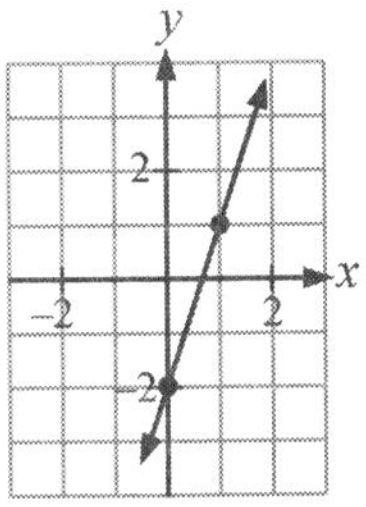

The y-intercept (b) is the y-value that sits on the y-axis when x is 0: $(0, -2)$. That is, $b = -2$

To find the slope, use two points from the graph and apply the slope formula.

$$m = \frac{y_2 - y_1}{x_2 - x_1}$$

$$m = \frac{1-(-2)}{1-0}$$

$$m = 3$$

Given m and b, it is possible to plot the points and write the equation of the line.

Example

What is the equation of the line where $m = -\frac{3}{4}$ and $b = 2$?

Start by plotting the y-intercept. Then, use the slope to rise and run to the next point. Because the slope is negative, you can either fall 3 units and run four units right, or rise 3 units and run 4 units left.

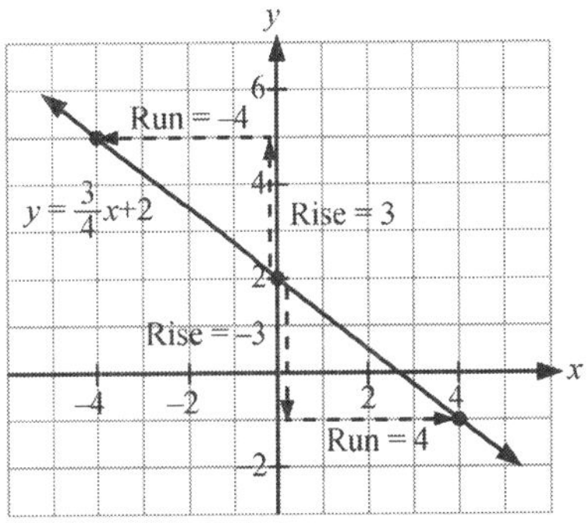

Both movements follow the same line.

Substitute the values into the slope y-intercept form to express the equation of the line.

$$y = -\frac{3}{4}x + 2$$

Copyright Protected

Use the following information to answer the next question.

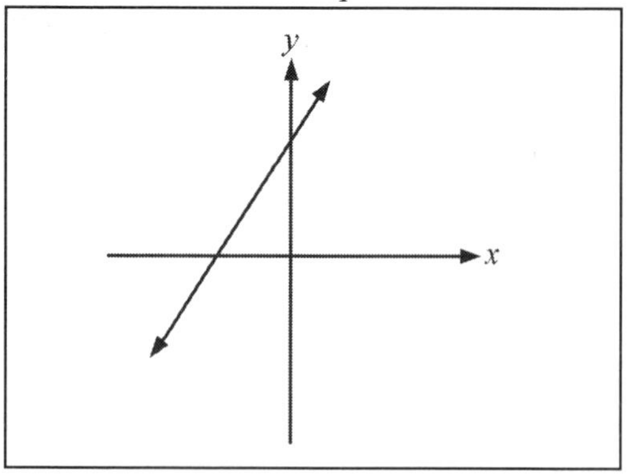

14. What are the coordinates of this graph's y-intercept?

A. (3, 0) **B.** (0, 3)

C. (–2, 0) **D.** (0, –2)

Use the following information to answer the next question.

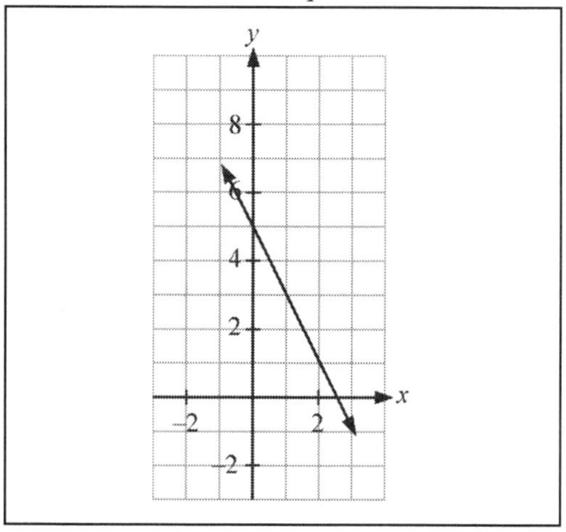

15. What is the **most likely** equation of this line?

A. $y - 2x - 4 = 0$

B. $y - 2x - 5 = 0$

C. $y = -2x + 5$

D. $y = -2x + 4$

16. Which of the following diagrams represents the graphs of the line $y = x$ and line PQ that has a slope of $\frac{7}{4}$?

A.

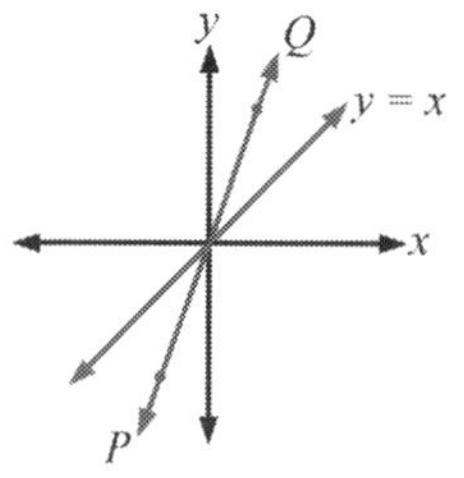

B.

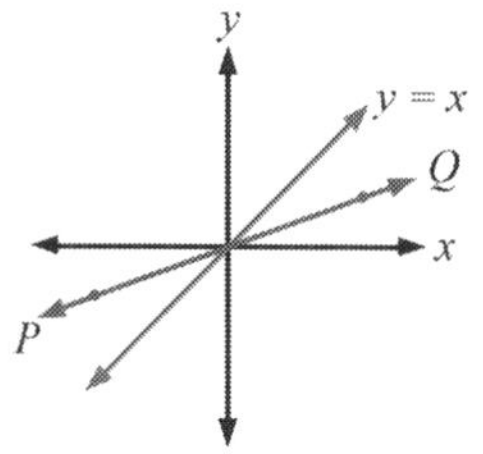

C.

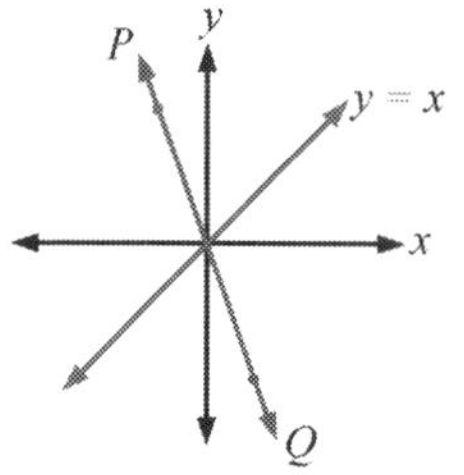

D.

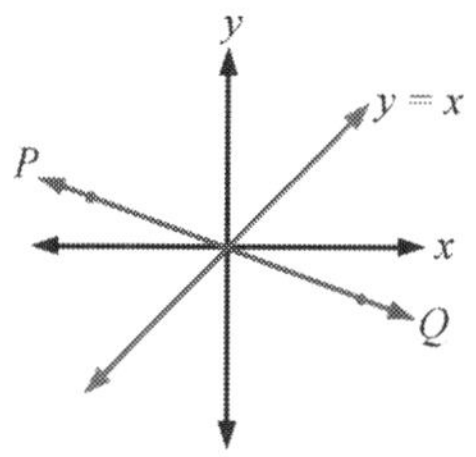

Not for Reproduction

Use the following information to answer the next question.

Points (0, –2) and (3, 4) lie on the same line.

Open Response

17. Graph these two points and indicate the slope and the y-intercept of the line. Determine the equation of the line in slope y-intercept form.
Show your work.

9AG2.03 determine, through investigation, connections among the representations of a constant rate of change of a linear relation

Determining Connections Between Constant Rates of Change

The cost of producing a book of photos is \$50.00 plus \$5.00 per photo. The equation $C = 50 + 5b$, where b is the number of photos, represents this relation. There are a number of different methods that can be used to determine a relation's rate of change.

First Differences

b	$C = 50 + 5b$	First difference
1	$C = 50 + 5(1)$ $= 55$	
2	$C = 50 + 5(2)$ $= 60$	$60 - 55 = 5$
3	$C = 50 + 5(3)$ $= 65$	$65 - 60 = 5$
4	$C = 50 + 5(4)$ $= 70$	$70 - 65 = 5$

The consistent first difference indicates that the constant rate of change is 5.

Graphically

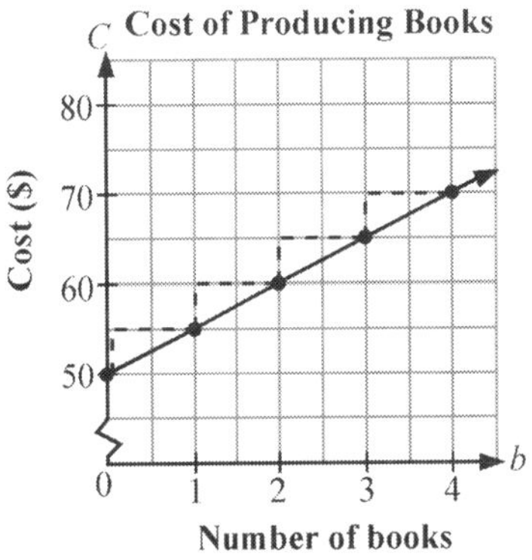

Notice the line rises 5 units and runs 1 unit between each point $\left(\frac{5}{1} = 5\right)$.

Slope Y-Intercept Form

This equation rewritten in slope y-intercept form is $C = 5b + 50$, where 5 is the constant rate of change or slope of the line.

Use the following information to answer the next question.

The relationship between the mass of a gas and its density is given by this graph.

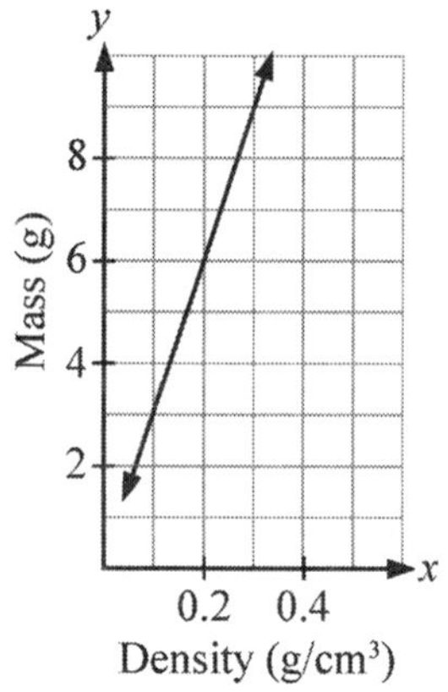

18. As the density of a gas changes, the rate of change of its volume is

A. 60 cm^3 **B.** 45 cm^3

C. 30 cm^3 **D.** 15 cm^3

19. A new company earns $10 000 on its first day of business. Every day after that, the company's income grows by $2 000. Which of the following expressions calculates the company's total income after x number of days?

A. $100 + x$

B. $100x$

C. $100 + 2\ 0x$

D. $2\ 0x$

Use the following information to answer the next question.

A submarine once reached a depth of 6 060 m. The dive rate is shown below.

Time (s)	Depth (m)
10	41
20	54
30	67
40	80

20. The rate of descent for the submarine during each 10-second interval is

A. 1.3 m / s **B.** 2.0 m / s

C. 13 m / s **D.** 20 m / s

9AG2.04 identify, through investigation, properties of the slopes of lines and line segments using graphing technology to facilitate investigations, where appropriate

Identifying the Properties of Slope

The properties of a line's slope can often be identified simply by investigating the line's graph.

Direction

The direction of the line can tell you if the slope is positive or negative. You "read" the line from left to right. A positive slope rises toward the right, and a negative slope falls toward the right.

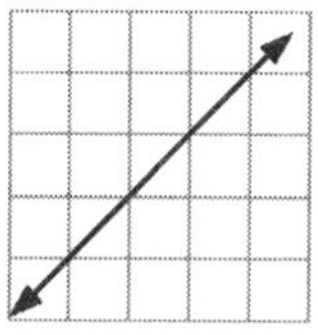
Positive slope

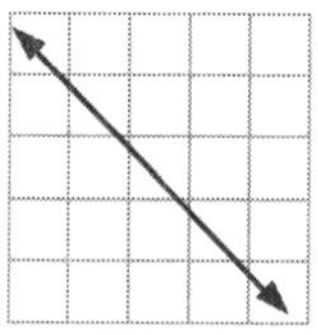
Negative slope

Not for Reproduction

STEEPNESS

The larger the slope value, the steeper the line. For example, a line with a slope of 4 is steeper than a line with a slope of 2.

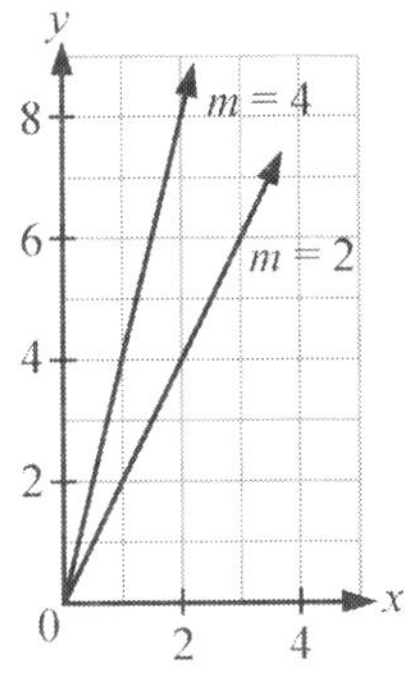

A horizontal line ($y = c$) has no rise, so the slope formula becomes $m = \frac{\text{rise}}{\text{run}} = \frac{0}{\text{run}} = 0$.

A vertical line ($x = a$) has no run, so the formula becomes $m = \frac{\text{rise}}{\text{run}} = \frac{\text{rise}}{0}$. Since division by 0 is undefined, $m =$ undefined. A vertical line cannot be written in slope y-intercept form.

PARALLELISM AND PERPENDICULARITY

Parallel lines have the same slope with a different y-intercept. For example, the two lines below both have a slope of 2.

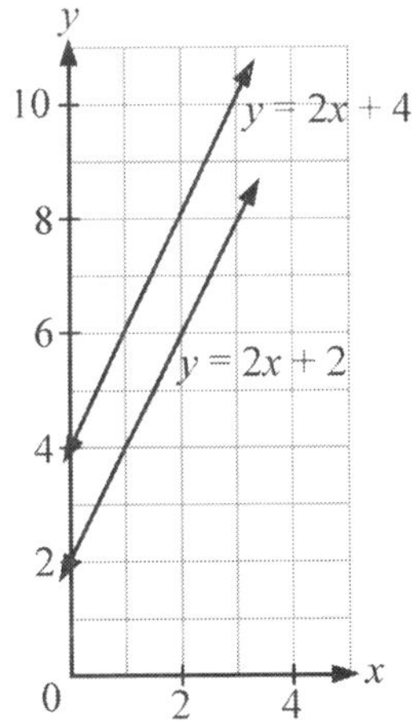

Perpendicular lines have opposite signs—if one line goes up, the other must go down. The product of their slopes is −1. Also, rise and run are negative reciprocals of each other with perpendicular lines.

For example, if the slope of one line is $\frac{2}{3}$, the perpendicular line has a slope of $\frac{-3}{2}$. These two slopes multiplied together equal −1.

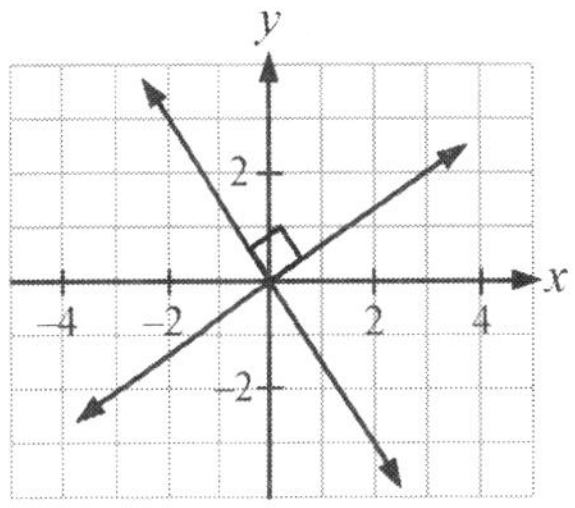

21. A line segment that has an undefined slope

A. is vertical

B. is horizontal

C. has an undefined length

D. passes through the origin

Use the following information to answer the next question.

The vertices of triangle PQR are $P(-6, -4)$, $Q(6, 2)$ and $R(-2, 8)$.

22. The equation of the line that is parallel to side PQ and that passes through point R is

A. $y = \frac{1}{2}x - 1$

B. $y = \frac{1}{2}x + 9$

C. $y = -2x + 4$

D. $y = -\frac{1}{6}x + \frac{23}{3}$

23. The lines defined by the equations $2x + 5y = 10$ and $2x + 5y = 5$

A. are parallel

B. intersect at right angles

C. intersect at oblique angles

D. are identical to each other in all respects

9AG3.01 graph lines by hand, using a variety of techniques

Graphing Lines

Often you will have to draw a line by hand. There are a few methods to choose from.

Slope and y-Intercept Method

Use this method when given the equation in the form $y = mx + b$. To graph a line according to this method, start by plotting the y-intercept (b). Then, use the slope (m) to plot other points from the intercept. This means using the rise and run values. Finish by connecting the points with a straight edge. Extend the line and place arrowheads on either end.

Intercepts Method

Use this method when the equation of the line is in either slope y-intercept or standard form. To draw the line, first determine the x- and y-intercepts. This involves making x or y equal to zero. Make x equal to zero when finding the y-intercept, and make y equal to zero when finding the x-intercept. Plot these two points and then connect them with a straight edge.

Example

Find the intercepts of the line $2x - 5y - 10 = 0$.

y-intercept	x-intercept
$2x - 5y - 10 = 0$	$2x - 5y - 10 = 0$
$2(0) - 5y - 10 = 0$	$2x - 5(0) - 10 = 0$
$y = -2$	$x = 5$

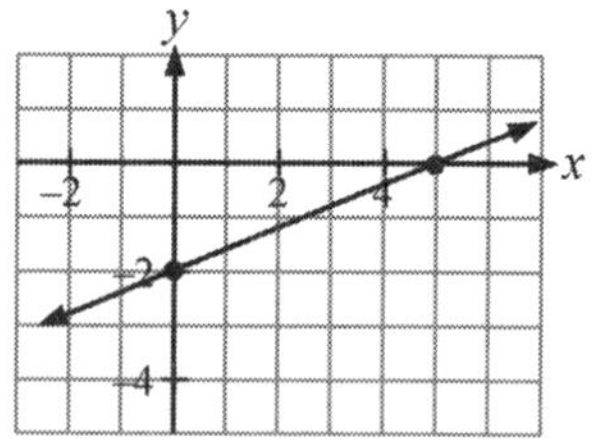

Horizontal and Vertical Lines

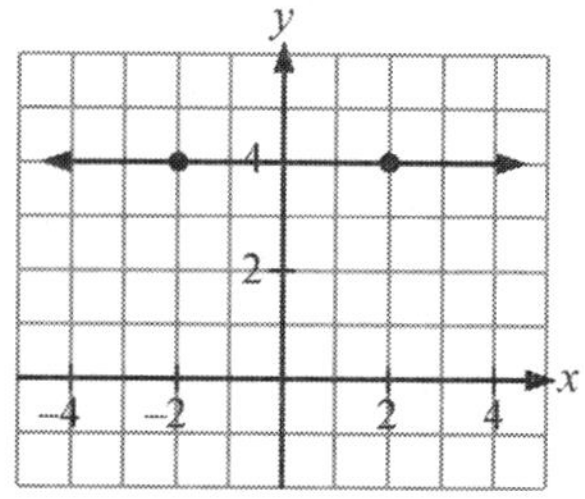

When the equation of a line only has one variable, it indicates that the line goes through that particular axis indefinitely. For example, the equation $y = 4$ means that the line only has a y-value of 4. That is, when $x = 2$, $y = 4$, when $x = -2$, $y = 4$, and so on. The graph is a horizontal line at $y = 4$. Use a straight edge to create this line.

An equation where $x = a$ indicates a vertical line at a.

24. Which of the following graphs represents the line $4x - 3y = 24$?

A.

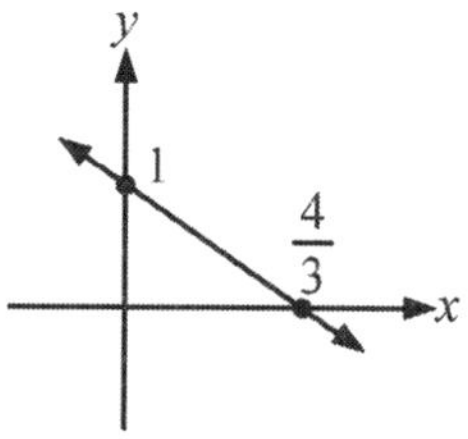

B.

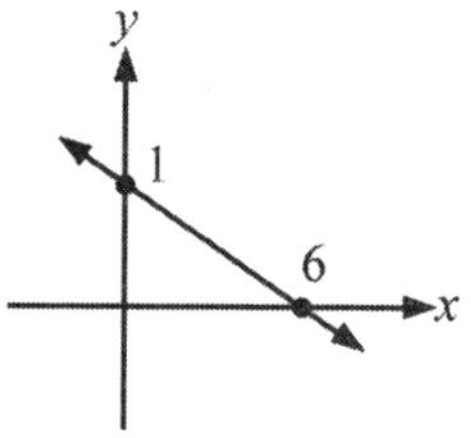

C.

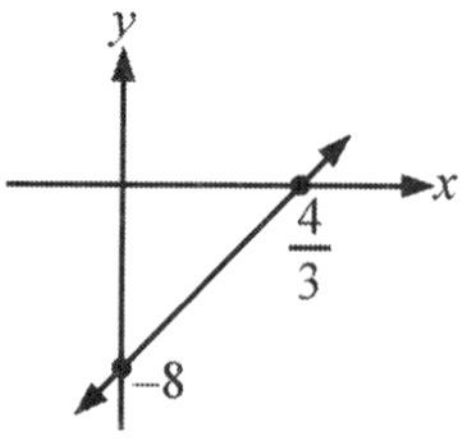

D.

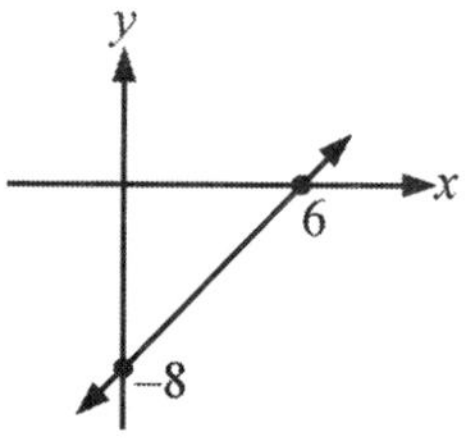

25. Which of the following graphs represents the linear equation $y = -\frac{1}{2}x + 2$?

A.

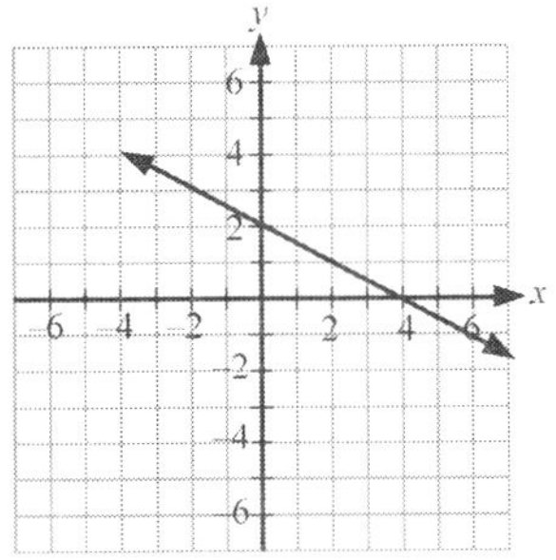

B.

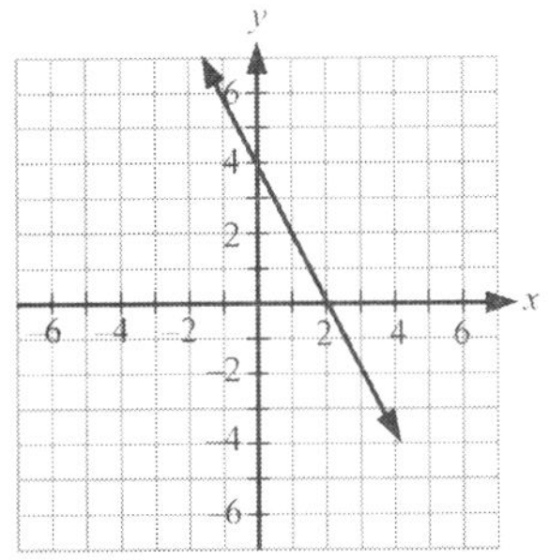

C.

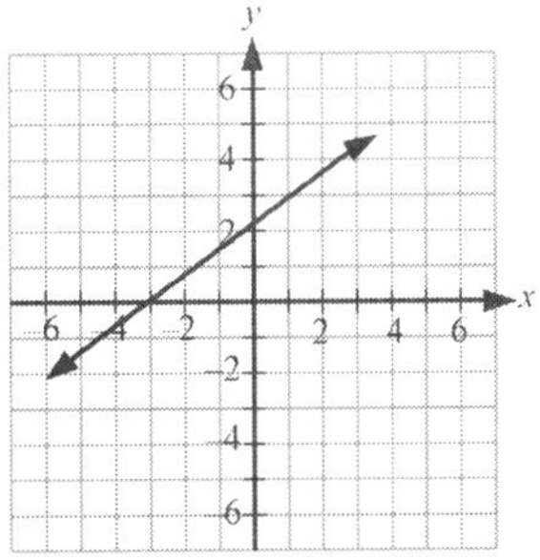

D.

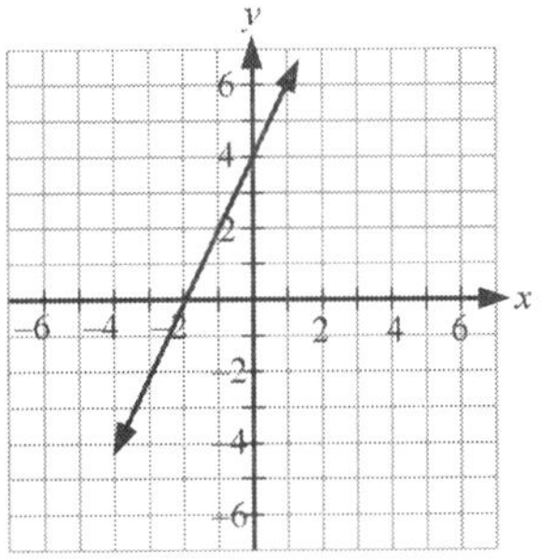

26. Which of the following graphs represents the line that has an x-intercept of 1 and a slope of $\frac{1}{2}$?

A.

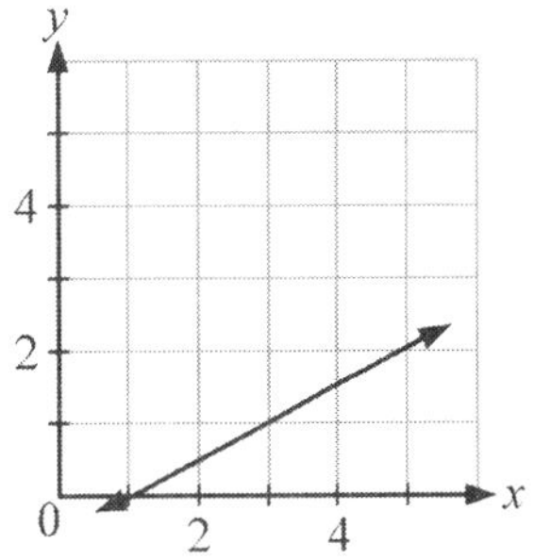

B.

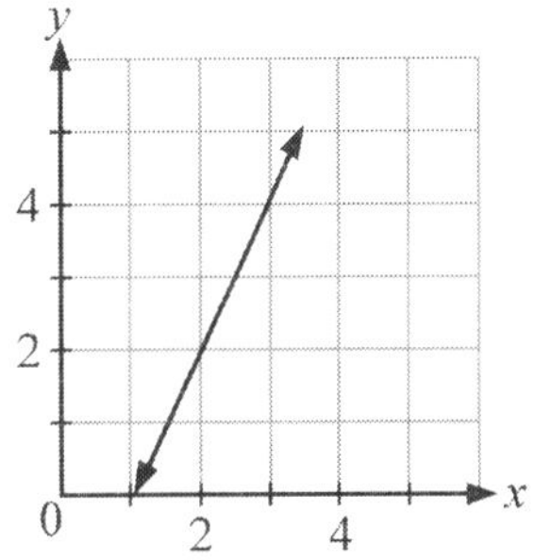

C.

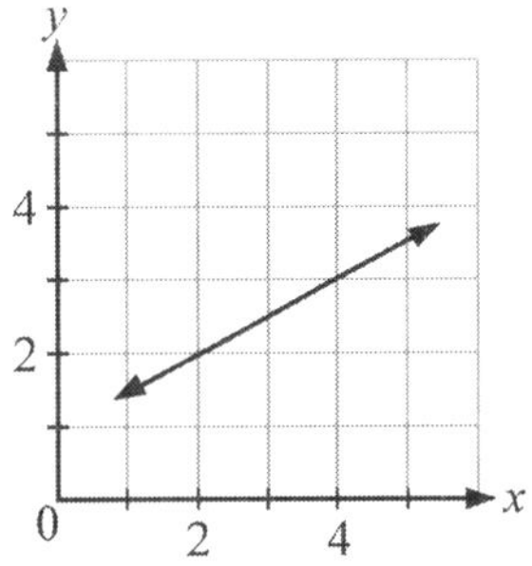

D.

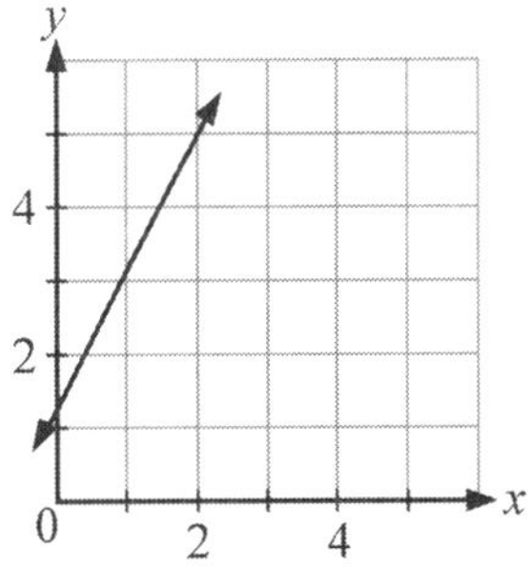

Copyright Protected

9AG3.02 determine the equation of a line from information about the line

Determining the Equation of a Line from Specific Information

The equation of a line can be determined if you know certain characteristics. If you are given the slope and the y-intercept, two points on the line, or the slope and one point, you can determine the equation.

Slope and y-Intercept

If given the slope and y-intercept, substitute these values into the slope y-intercept form of an equation, $y = mx + b$, or standard form, $Ax + By + C = O$.

Example

Find the equation of the line with the slope $m = 2$ and y-intercept $b = -4$.

Slope y-intercept form:

$y = mx + b$

$y = 2x - 4$

Standard form:

$Ax + By + C = 0$

$2x - y - 4 = 0$

Two Points

The equation of a line passing through two points, (x_1, y_1) and (x_2, y_2), is found using the formula $\frac{y - y_1}{x - x_1} = \frac{y_2 - y_1}{x_2 - x_1}$. Substitute given values into the formula.

Example

Determine the equation of the line that goes through points $(-1, 4)$ and $(2, 3)$.

$$\frac{y - y_1}{x - x_1} = \frac{y_2 - y_1}{x_2 - x_1}$$

$$\frac{y - 4}{x - (-1)} = \frac{3 - 4}{2 - (-1)}$$

$$\frac{y - 4}{x - (-1)} = \frac{-1}{3}$$

$$3y - 12 = -x - 1$$

$$x + 3y - 11 = 0$$

$$y = -\frac{1}{3}x + \frac{11}{3}$$

Slope and One Point

When given one point on a line and the line's slope, substitute the x- and y-values and the slope (m) into the **point slope formula**:

$y - y_1 = m(x - x_1)$.

Use the following information to answer the next question.

> A line runs parallel to the line defined by the equation $3x + 4y + 5 = 0$. It has the same x-intercept as the line defined by the equation $4x + 5y - 6 = 0$.

27. What is the equation of the parallel line in general form?

A. $-6x - 8y - 9 = 0$

B. $-6x + 8y + 9 = 0$

C. $6x + 8y - 9 = 0$

D. $6x + 8y + 9 = 0$

28. What is the slope y-intercept form of the equation of the line that passes through point $(3, 4.5)$ and has a slope of 2.5?

A. $y = 2.5x + 1.5$

B. $y = 2.5x - 7.5$

C. $y = 2.5x - 3$

D. $y = 2.5x - 12$

29. Two lines, l_1 and l_2, are perpendicular. They intersect at the point (4, −5). The slope of l_1 is $\frac{3}{2}$. The equation of l_2 is

A. $2x + 3y - 7 = 0$

B. $2x + 3y + 7 = 0$

C. $2x - 3y + 7 = 0$

D. $3x + 2y + 7 = 0$

9AG3.03 describe the meaning of the slope and y-intercept for a linear relation arising from a realistic situation, and describe a situation that could be modelled by a given linear equation

Meaning of y-intercept and Slope in Graphs of Real Situations

The slope and variables in the equation $y = mx + b$ can be used to represent a rate and quantities, respectively, in realistic situations. Doing so does not affect the linear relationship. For example, a local plumber charges $100.00 to come to your home plus $65.00 / h for the time that he spends fixing the problem. The equation to calculate his total cost is $C = 100 + 65h$. The equation rewritten in slope y-intercept form is $C = 65h + 100$. In this equation, the following substitutions are made:

- C replaces y (dependent variable)
- 100 replaces b (y-intercept)
- 65 replaces m (slope or constant rate of change)
- h replaces x (independent variable)

Because no variable has an exponent greater than 1, the equation is linear. This equation represents partial variation, where the y-intercept (100) represents the initial cost.

You can also be faced with problems where you have to come up with a realistic situation for a given linear relation.

For example, consider $C = 500 + 28n$.
One possible interpretation of the equation could be that it costs $500.00 plus $28.00 / person to rent a hall for a wedding reception.

Use the following information to answer the next question.

The cost of producing a car depends on both a fixed cost and a variable cost. The total cost to produce 40 cars is $600 000, while the total cost to produce 80 cars is $1 000 000.

30. Which of the following equations relates the total production cost (C) to the number of cars produced (n)?

A. $C = 100n + 2000$

B. $C = 200n + 2000$

C. $C = 80n + 100$

D. $C = 40n + 60$

Use the following information to answer the next question.

A local high school is hosting an athletic banquet at a community centre. The graph below shows how the total cost relates to the number of tickets sold.

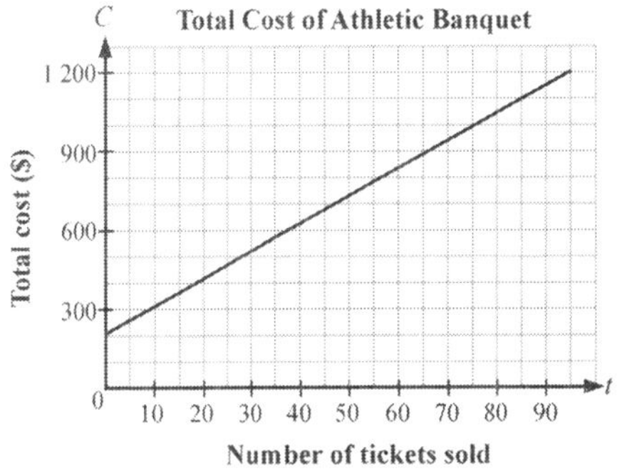

31. The slope of this graph represents the

A. cost of food

B. cost per ticket

C. profit per ticket

D. banquet hall cost

32. The equation $p = 50n - 250$ **most likely** models which of the following situations?

A. 50 represents the cost to manufacture each pair of sunglasses. -250 represents an upfront manufacturing cost.

B. 50 represents the profit earned on each pair of sunglasses. -250 indicates that a profit is not made until at least 5 pairs of sunglasses are sold.

C. 50 represents the cost to manufacture each pair of sunglasses. -250 indicates that a profit is not made until at least 5 pairs of sunglasses are sold.

D. 50 represents the profit earned on each pair of sunglasses. -250 represents an upfront manufacturing cost.

9AG3.04 identify and explain any restrictions on the variables in a linear relation arising from a realistic situation

Identifying Restrictions on Variables in a Linear Relation

Linear relations based on realistic situations often require that restrictions be placed on the variables. This is because the possible values for the variables are not infinite. For example, if one of the variables in an equation represents hours, the value can never be negative because time cannot be negative.

There are also times when there is a lower restriction and an upper restriction. The equation $C = 50 + 25n$ represents a linear relation, where C is the cost of holding a party in a hall and n is the number of guests. The number of guests must be a whole number, but it cannot be more than the number of people the hall can hold. If the capacity is 125, then n is restricted to whole numbers less than or equal to 125. This is the lower restriction. This in turn puts an upper restriction on C. If the restriction on n is 125, then the upper restriction on C is found by substituting 125 into the equation.

$C = 50 + 25n$

$C = 50 + 25(125) = 3175$

The upper restriction is \$3175.00.

33. If the value of h is restricted to whole numbers of 100 or less, in which of the following relations is the value of H restricted to values between 10 and 5 510?

A. $H = 10 + 100h$

B. $H = 100 + 10h$

C. $H = 55 + 10h$

D. $H = 10 + 55h$

Use the following information to answer the next question.

> In the relation $B = 40 + 6m$, B is the total number of heavy vehicles that drive through a city in a particular month, and m is the number of months that have passed since the city started recording these numbers. The number of heavy vehicles in the city cannot exceed 400. The date for January, 2000 is $m = 0$.

34. In which month did the **maximum** number of vehicles drive through the city?

A. January, 2003 **B.** January, 2004

C. January, 2005 **D.** January, 2006

Use the following information to answer the next question.

> A high school graduation committee is planning a year-end banquet. The chosen caterer charges \$15 per person plus a setup fee of \$250. The equation $C = 15n + 250$ represents the cost, C, in dollars, of the banquet. The number of people attending the banquet is represented by n.

35. If the total cost of the graduation banquet cannot be more than \$2 900, then the maximum number of people who can attend the banquet is

A. 176 **B.** 177

C. 209 **D.** 210

Not for Reproduction

9AG3.05 determine graphically the point of intersection of two linear relations, and interpret the intersection point in the context of an application

Determining the Point of Intersection

A **linear system** contains two or more linear equations representing different conditions for the same context. The two equations are graphed on the same coordinate plane. Two lines that are not parallel will eventually intersect at a point.

The **point of intersection** occurs where the two lines have the same x- and y-values. It is also the solution when the values are put into a system of equations. Points before and beyond the point of intersection can provide information about the differences in the conditions of a given realistic situation.

Example

A cellphone company offers two different plans. Plan A is $20.00 per month and $0.10 per minute. Plan B is $30.00 per month and $0.05 per minute. How many minutes per month would a person need to talk in order for Plan B to be the better option?

The equation for Plan A is $C = 20 + .1\text{min}$.

The equation for Plan B is $C = 30 + .5\text{min}$.

The point of intersection represents where the monthly cost of both plans is the same. It can be seen on the graph that Plan B is the better option if a person talks more than 200 minutes per month.

Monthly Charges of Two Cellphone Plans

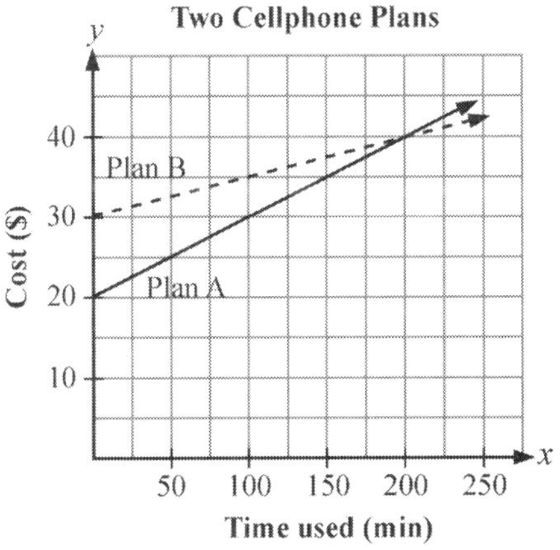

Use the following information to answer the next question.

Astrid is asked to solve a linear system of equations. She uses a graphical approach to solve the given system. One of the equations that Astrid graphs correctly is shown below.

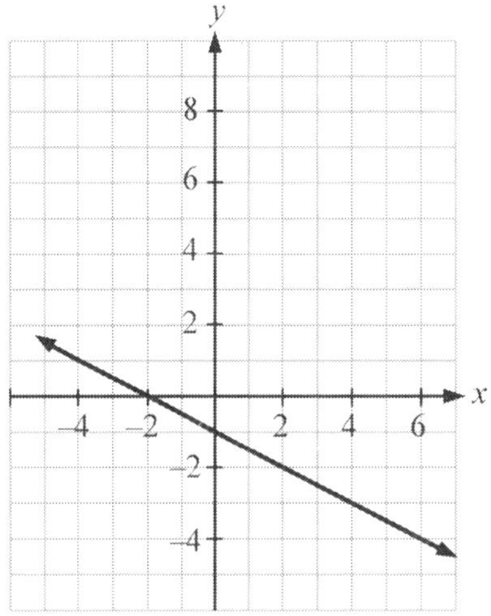

36. If the other equation in the system is $y = 2x + 9$, then the solution to the system is

A. $(-4, 1)$ **B.** $(2, 5)$

C. $(1, 11)$ **D.** $(3, 15)$

Copyright Protected

37. Which of the following graphs shows the solution to the system of equations $2x - y = -1$ and $3x + y = -9$?

A.

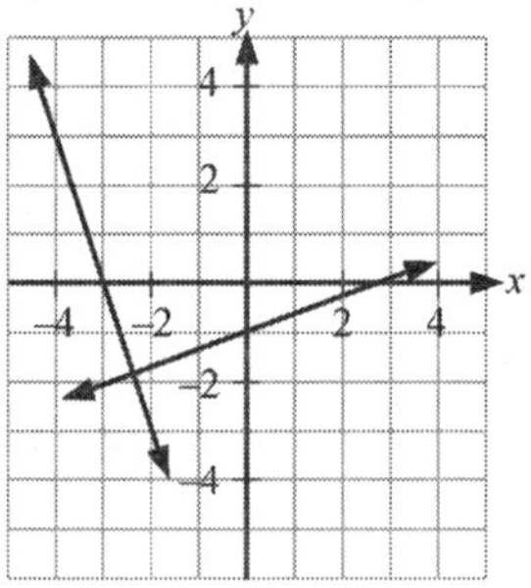

B.

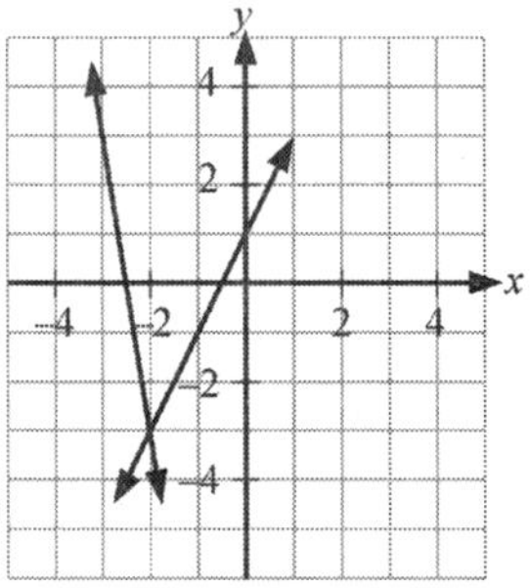

C.

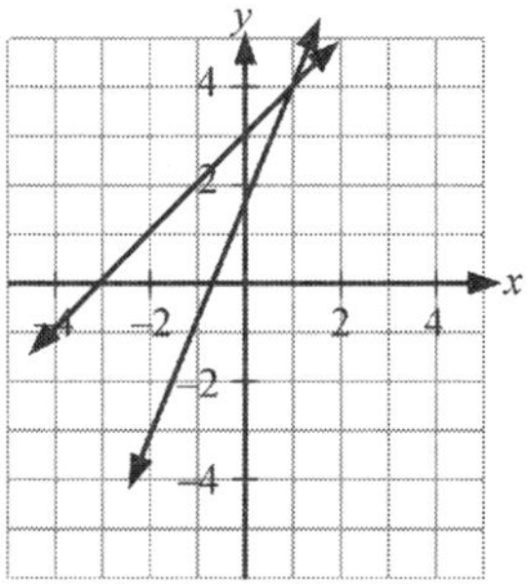

D.

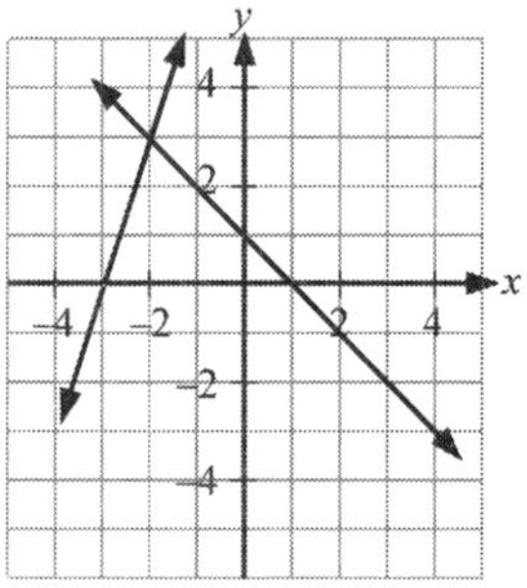

Use the following information to answer the next question.

A telephone company offers two long distance plans. Plan A: \$40 per month with unlimited calling Plan B: \$5 per month plus \$0.50 per minute.

38. Which of the following statements is **true**?

A. Plan A is the better value if a person talks less than 70 minutes per month.

B. Plan A is the better value if a person talks more than 70 minutes per month.

C. Plan B is the better value if a person talks more than 70 minutes per month.

D. Plan B is the better value no matter how many minutes a person talks per month.

Not for Reproduction

ANSWERS AND SOLUTIONS
ANALYTIC GEOMETRY

1. C	9. C	17. OR	25. A	33. D
2. B	10. C	18. C	26. A	34. C
3. B	11. C	19. C	27. C	35. A
4. OR	12. A	20. A	28. C	36. A
5. D	13. C	21. A	29. B	37. B
6. D	14. B	22. B	30. A	38. B
7. D	15. C	23. A	31. B	
8. D	16. A	24. D	32. B	

1. C

Linear equations are of the first degree (exponent of 1).

Alternative A: The exponent of x^2 is 2.

Alternative B: The exponent of both x^2 and y^2 is 2.

Alternative C: The exponent of both x and y is 1.

Alternative D: Adding the exponents of $xy(1 + 1)$ means that it is of the second degree.

2. B

Any equation of the first degree will graph a straight line. The equations $y = x^2 + 3$ and $y = x^3 - 6$ are of the second and third degree, respectively. The remaining three equations have graphs of straight lines.

3. B

The graph of a linear equation is always a straight line. To achieve this, the equation can only be of the first degree.

4. OR

Points	Sample Answer
4	The equation is linear. The equation has a degree of one. There are no root signs on the variable. Create a table of values.

x	$y = -2x + 5$
−3	$y = -2(-3)$ $+5 = 11$
−2	$y = -2(-2)$ $+5 = 9$
−1	$y = -2(-1)$ $+5 = 7$
0	$y = -2(0)$ $+5 = 5$
1	$y = -2(1)$ $+5 = 3$
2	$y = -2(2)$ $+5 = 1$
3	$y = -2(3)$ $+5 = -1$

Points	Sample Answer
	Plot the points on the given grid. 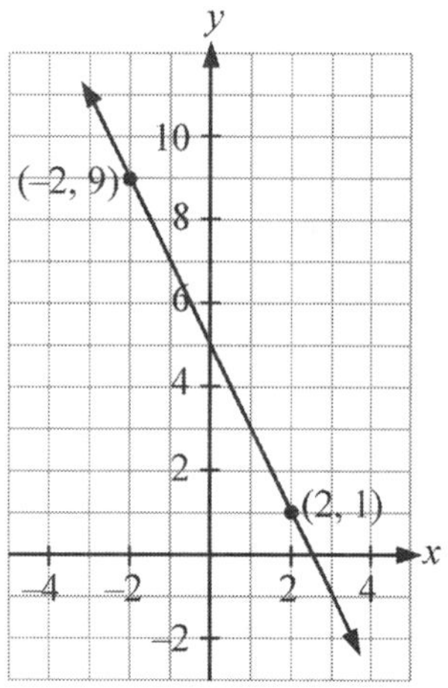
Application of knowledge and skills involving characteristics of a linear equation shows a high degree of effectiveness due to • a thorough understanding of the concepts • an accurate application of the procedures (any minor errors and/or omissions do not detract from the demonstration of a thorough understanding)	
3	Missing one of the two characteristics listed. A minimal table of values is included. As a result, a minimal, but correct line is shown. Graph is missing labels on the axes or grid.
Application of knowledge and skills involving characteristics of a linear equation shows considerable effectiveness due to • an understanding of most of the concepts • minor errors and/or omissions in the application of the procedures	
2	Missing one of the two characteristics listed. No table of values is included. A minimal, but correct, line is shown.
Application of knowledge and skills involving characteristics of a linear equation shows some effectiveness due to • minor errors and/or omissions in the application of the procedures • an understanding of most of the concepts	

Points	Sample Answer
1	Missing one of the two characteristics listed. No table of values is included. Graph is incorrectly drawn.
Application of knowledge and skills involving characteristics of a linear equation shows limited effectiveness due to • a misunderstanding of concepts • an incorrect selection or misuse of procedures	

5. D

Standard form is $Ax + By + C = 0$. The equation $2x + \frac{y}{3} - 3 = 0$ is in standard form.

6. D

slope $= m = \frac{2}{3}$

y-intercept $= b = -2$

$y = mx + b$

$y = \frac{2}{3}x + (-2)$

The correct equation is $y = \frac{2}{3}x - 2$.

7. D

A horizontal line has the equation $y = b$, where b is the vertical height of the line above the x-axis.

As the given horizontal line passes through $(-2, 7)$, its vertical height above the x-axis is 7 units.

So, the equation of the line is $y = 7$.

8. D

The equation $y = \frac{4}{5}x - 7$ is in slope y-intercept form. Standard form has all the terms equal to zero $(Ax + By + C = 0)$. The coefficient of x must be positive.

$y = \frac{4}{5}x - 7$

Multiply each of the terms by 5 to eliminate the fractional coefficient.

$5y = 4x - 35$

Use inverse operations to move $5y$ to the other side of the equation.

$$5y - 5y = 4x - 5y - 35$$
$$0 = 4x - 5y - 35$$
$$4x - 5y - 35 = 0$$

Not for Reproduction

9. C

Slope y-intercept form is $y = mx + b$.

Isolate y in the given equation.

$5x - 3y = -6$

Subtract $5x$ from both sides of the equation.

$$5x - 5x - 3y = -5x - 6$$
$$-3y = -5x - 6$$

Divide both sides of the equation by -3.

$$\frac{-3y}{-3} = \frac{-5x}{-3} + \frac{-6}{-3}$$
$$y = \frac{5}{3}x + 2$$

10. C

Slope y-intercept form is $y = mx + b$. Isolate y in the given equation.

$2x - 6y = 12$

Subtract $2x$ from both sides of the equation.

$$2x - 2x - 6y = -2x + 12$$
$$-6y = -2x + 12$$

Divide both sides of the equation by -6.

$$\frac{-6y}{-6} = \frac{-2x + 12}{-6}$$
$$y = \frac{1}{3}x - 2$$

11. C

A slope (m) that rises to the right is always positive. Thus, the alternatives with negative slopes are eliminated.

Method 1 - Graphically

$$m = \frac{\text{rise}}{\text{run}}$$

Using the graph only, count the number of units that the line rises and then runs.

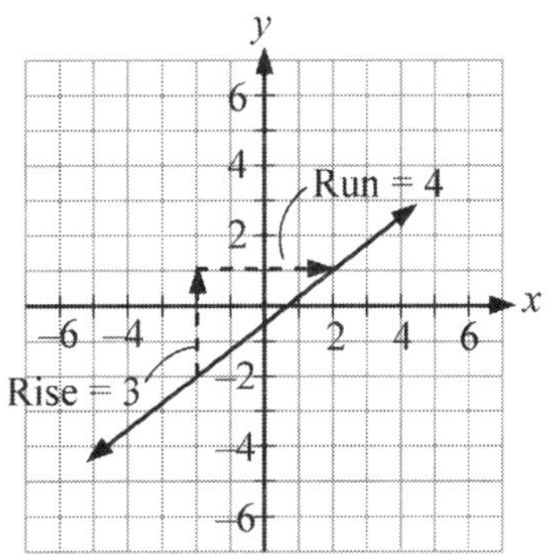

$$m = \frac{\text{rise}}{\text{run}} = \frac{3}{4}$$

Method 2 – Using the slope formula

$$m = \frac{y_2 - y_1}{x_2 - x_1}.$$

Pick two points on the graph, such as (2, 1) and (–2, –2).

Substitute the values into the slope formula and then solve.

$$m = \frac{y_2 - y_1}{x_2 - x_1} = \frac{1 - (-2)}{2 - (-2)} = \frac{1 + 2}{2 + 2} = \frac{3}{4}$$

12. A

Let the two points be (x_1, y_1) and (x_2, y_2).

$(x_1, y_1) = (4, 6)$
$(x_2, y_2) = (2, 12)$

$$\begin{aligned}\text{slope} &= m \\ &= \frac{y_2 - y_1}{x_2 - x_1} \\ &= \frac{12 - 6}{2 - 4} \\ &= \frac{6}{-2} \\ &= -3\end{aligned}$$

13. C

The line of the graph rises to the right indicating a positive slope. Alternatives A and B can be eliminated.

You are given two points on the line (3, 2) and (8, 4). With this information, use the slope formula.

$$m = \frac{\text{rise}}{\text{run}} = \frac{y_2 - y_1}{x_2 - x_1}$$

Substitute in the given values.

$$m = \frac{4 - 2}{8 - 3} = \frac{2}{5}$$

14. B

The y-intercept of a linear relation is located at the point where the graph crosses the y-axis and the x-value is 0. The y-value on this graph is positive. Of the given points, the only point that satisfies these two conditions is (0, 3).

15. C

The slope, $m = \frac{\text{rise}}{\text{run}} = \frac{-2}{1} = -2$. The y-intercept is 5. Substitute these values into the slope y-intercept form of the equation of the line.

$y = -2x + 5$

16. A

The slope of line PQ is given as $\frac{7}{4}$, which is a positive value. Since the slope is positive, the graph of the line PQ must rise to the right. Only the graphs given in alternatives A and B fulfill this requirement. The slope of the line $y = x$ is 1. The slope of PQ is greater than $1\left(\frac{7}{4} > 1\right)$. Thus, the graph of line PQ must be steeper than the graph of line $y = x$. The graph given in alternative A fulfills this requirement as well.

17. OR

Points	Sample Answer
4	Solution Mark the two given points on the graph. Connect the points with a line. The y-intercept is at $(0, -2)$. This is where the line crosses the y-axis because the x-value is zero. To indicate slope, draw a dotted line rising up from the y-intercept. Then, run across to meet the second point. The line rises up 6 units and runs across 3 units. 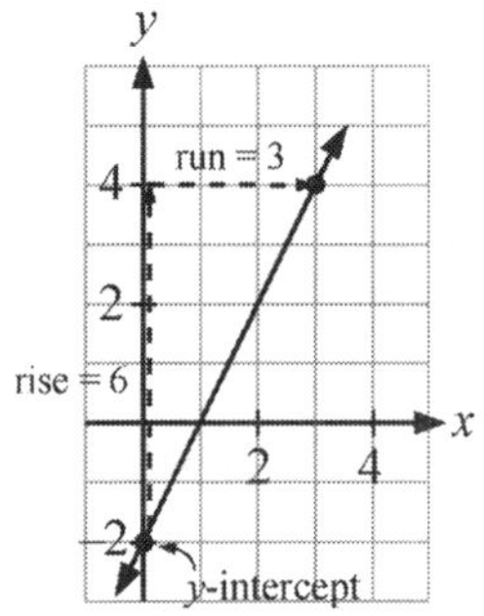 $m = \frac{6}{3} = 2$ Substitute the values into the slope y-intercept form of the equation, $y = mx + b$. $y = 2x - 2$
Application of knowledge and skills involving the slope, y-intercept, and equation of a line shows a high degree of effectiveness due to: • a thorough understanding of the concepts • an accurate application of the procedures (any minor errors and/or omissions do not detract from the demonstration of a thorough understanding)	

Points	Sample Answer
3	Graph is drawn correctly, indicating the points, y-intercept, and slope. Missing proper labels on the axes. Equation of the line is written correctly.
Application of knowledge and skills involving the slope, y-intercept, and equation of a line shows considerable effectiveness due to • an understanding of most of the concepts • minor errors and/or omissions in the application of the procedures	
2	Only one of the components (points, y-intercept, slope) on the graph is drawn incorrectly. Missing proper labels on the axes. Equation of the line is written correctly.
Application of knowledge and skills involving the slope, y-intercept, and equation of a line shows some effectiveness due to • minor errors and/or omissions in the application of the procedures • an understanding of most of the concepts	
1	Two or more of the components (points, y-intercept, slope) on the graph are drawn incorrectly. Missing proper labels on the axes. Equation of the line is written incorrectly.
Application of knowledge and skills involving the slope, y-intercept, and equation of a line shows limited effectiveness due to: • a misunderstanding of concepts • an incorrect selection or misuse of procedures	

Not for Reproduction

18. C

The rate of change of the volume is the slope of the line. Pick two points on the line, such as (0.1, 3) and (0.3, 9).

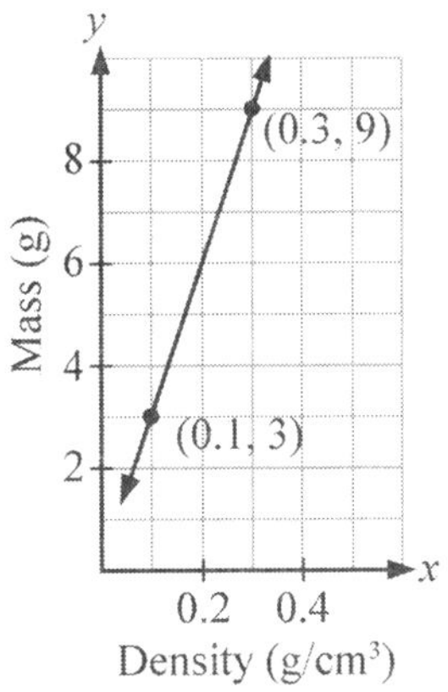

Rate of change of volume = slope = $\frac{\Delta y}{\Delta x}$

$= \frac{\Delta \text{mass}}{\Delta \text{density}} = \frac{9-3}{0.3-0.1} = 30 \text{ cm}^3$

19. C

The profit on the first day is \$10 000. It is a fixed amount and is therefore the constant in the equation. This eliminates the alternatives that do not have this value as a constant.

The daily growth or rate of change is the \$2 000. The number of days multiplied by the rate of change is 2 0x.

The correct expression is 100 + 2 0x.

20. A

Use first differences to calculate the rate of change.

x	y	First difference
10	41	54 – 41 = 13
20	54	
30	67	67 – 54 = 13
40	80	80 – 67 = 13

Rate of change = $\frac{\text{first difference}}{\Delta x}$

Rate of change = $\frac{13}{20-10} = \frac{13}{10} = 1.3$

The rate of descent is 1.3 m / s.

21. A

The slope formula is $m = \frac{\text{rise}}{\text{run}}$. A vertical line has no run and only rise. The formula becomes $m = \frac{\text{rise}}{\text{run}} = \frac{\text{rise}}{0}$. Division by 0 is undefined.

A vertical line segment has an undefined slope.

22. B

Determine the slope of line segment PQ.

$$m = \frac{y_2 - y_1}{x_2 - x_1} = \frac{-4-2}{-6-6} = \frac{-6}{-12} \xrightarrow{\text{reduce}} \frac{1}{2}$$

There are only two alternatives that have a slope of $\frac{1}{2}$.

The line passes through point $R(-2, 8)$. If you rise 1 unit and run 2 units across from point R, you arrive at the y-intercept, which is (0, 9).

Slope $= \frac{1}{2}$

y-intercept $= 9$

The equation of the line is $y = \frac{1}{2}x + 9$.

23. A

Rewrite the equations in slope y-intercept form.

$2x + 5y = 10$ $5y = -2x + 10$ Divide all the terms by 5. $y = -\frac{2}{5}x + 2$	$2x + 5y = 5$ $5y = -2x + 5$ Divide all the terms by 5. $y = -\frac{2}{5}x + 1$

The slope of both lines is equal to $-\frac{2}{5}$. Parallel lines have the same slope but different y-intercepts. The line $2x + 5y = 10$ is above $2x + 5y = 5$.

24. D

Rewrite the equation in slope y-intercept form ($y = mx + b$).

$4x - 3y = 24$

$4x - 24 = 3y$

Divide all the terms by 3.

$\frac{4}{3}x - 8 = y$

The y-intercept is -8.

To determine the x-intercept, substitute 0 for y.

$$\frac{4}{3}x - 8 = 0$$

$$\frac{4}{3}x = 8$$

Multiply all the terms by $\frac{3}{4}$.

$$x = \frac{24}{4} \xrightarrow{\text{reduce}} 6$$

The correct graph has an x-intercept of 6 and a y-intercept of -8.

25. A

A negative slope $\left(-\frac{1}{2}\right)$ falls toward the right.

Only two graphs have negative slopes.

When the equation of the line is written in slope y-intercept form, $y = mx + b$, b represents the y-intercept. The y-intercept is 2.

The graph in alternative A is correct.

26. A

First, eliminate the alternatives that do not have an x-intercept of 1. That is, the lines do not cross the x-axis at 1: alternatives C and D.

Since the line has an x-intercept of 1, it passes through the point (1, 0). Use the slope to rise 1 unit and run 2 units to plot the next point on the line (3, 1).

The line passes through the points (1, 0) and (3, 1).

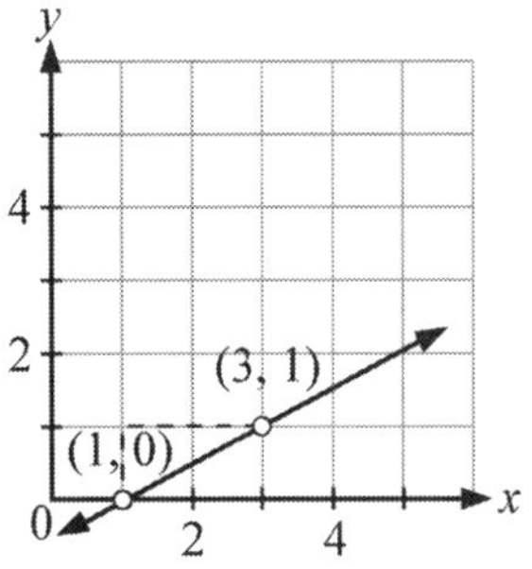

27. C

Step 1

Determine the slope of the parallel line.

Since the required line is parallel to the line defined by the equation $3x + 4y + 5 = 0$, both lines have the same slope.

Rewrite the equation in the form $y = mx + b$ to find the slope of the line defined by the equation $3x + 4y + 5 = 0$.

$$3x + 4y + 5 = 0$$
$$4y = -3x - 5$$
$$y = \frac{-3x}{4} - \frac{5}{4}$$
$$y = -\frac{3}{4}x - \frac{5}{4}$$

The slope of the parallel line is $-\frac{3}{4}$.

Step 2

Determine the x-intercept of the line defined by the equation $4x + 5y - 6 = 0$.

Substitute 0 for y in the equation $4x + 5y - 6 = 0$, and solve for x.

$$4x + 5y - 6 = 0$$
$$4x + 5(0) - 6 = 0$$
$$4x - 6 = 0$$
$$4x = 6$$
$$\frac{4x}{4} = \frac{6}{4}$$
$$x = \frac{3}{2}$$
$$x = 1.5$$

Step 3

Determine the equation of the parallel line.

The parallel line passes through the point (1.5, 0). Substitute the values of the x-intercept and slope into the slope-point form of the equation of a line, and convert it to general form.

$$y - y_1 = m(x - x_1)$$
$$y - 0 = -\frac{3}{4}(x - 1.5)$$
$$y = \frac{-3x}{4} + \frac{4.5}{4}$$
$$8(y) = 8\left[\frac{-3x}{4} + \frac{4.5}{4}\right]$$
$$8y = -6x + 9$$
$$6x + 8y - 9 = 0$$

The equation of the parallel line is $6x + 8y - 9 = 0$.

28. C

When given one point and the slope, use the formula $y - y_1 = m(x - x_1)$.

Substitute the values into the formula.

$(y - 4.5) = 2.5(x - 3)$

Distribute 2.5 through the brackets.
$y - 4.5 = 2.5x - 7.5$

Simplify.
$y - 4.5 + 4.5 = 2.5x - 7.5 + 4.5$
$y = 2.5x - 3$

29. B

The slope of l_1 is $\frac{3}{2}$, and l_1 and l_2 are perpendicular.

The slope of line $l_2 = -1 \times \frac{2}{3} = -\frac{2}{3}$.

The equation of the line is $y = -\frac{2}{3}x + b$, where b is the y-intercept of the line.

The line passes through the point (4, –5).

Substitute the values into the equation.

$-5 = -\frac{2}{3} \times 4 + b$

Rearrange the equation to solve for b.

$b = -5 + \frac{8}{3} = -\frac{7}{3}$

The equation of the line is $y = -\frac{2}{3}x - \frac{7}{3}$.

Multiply each term by 3 to eliminate the denominators.

$$3y = -2x - 7$$
$$2x + 3y = -7$$
$$2x + 3y + 7 = 0$$

30. A

Write the equation in the form $y = mx + b$, where x is the number of the cars produced and y is the total production cost.

The rate of change, $m = \frac{\Delta y}{\Delta x} = \frac{y_2 - y_1}{x_2 - x_1}$.

$(x_1, y_1) = (40, 6000)$

$(x_2, y_2) = (80, 100)$

$$m = \frac{100 - 6000}{80 - 40}$$
$$= \frac{4000}{40} = 100$$

Substitute the first set of values into the equation to solve for the y-intercept.
$6000 = 100 \times 40 + b$
$b = 2000$
The equation is $C = 100n + 2000$.

31. B

Slope is given by the $\frac{\text{rise}}{\text{run}}$, where rise is represents the total cost and the run represents the number of tickets sold. So, the slope represents the cost per ticket.

32. B

Because the equation represents profit (p), $50n$ represents the profit (not cost) earned on sales of n pairs of sunglasses.

The –250 indicates that if 0 pairs were sold, a loss of $250 would occur. At a $50 profit per pair, 5 pairs need to be sold before a profit is seen.

33. D

Obtain the minimum and maximum values of H when the values of h are 0 and 100, respectively. Solve for each alternative:

Alternative A: $H = 10 + 100h$

Minimum value: $H = 10 + 100 \times 0 = 10$

Maximum value:
$H = 10 + 100 \times 100 = 10 + 100 = 1010$

Not the required range.

Alternative B: $H = 100 + 10h$

Minimum value: $H = 100 + 10 \times 0 = 100$

Not the required range.

Alternative C: $H = 55 + 10h$

Minimum value: $H = 55 + 10 \times 0 = 55$

Not the required range.

Alternative D: $H = 10 + 55h$

Minimum value: $H = 10 + 55 \times 0 = 10$

Maximum value: $H = 10 + 55 \times 100 = 5510$

This is the required range.

Copyright Protected

34. C

The maximum value of B is 400. Substitute this value into the equation and then solve for m.

$$B = 40 + 6m$$
$$400 = 40 + 6m$$
$$360 = 6m$$
$$60 = m$$

The maximum number of vehicles drove through the city 60 months after January, 2000. Therefore the month the maximum of vehicle drove through the city is January, 2005.

35. A

Substitute the maximum total cost into the given equation.
$2900 = 15n + 250$

Solve for n, which is the maximum number of people that can attend at the total cost.
$2900 - 250 = 15n + 250 - 250$

$2650 \div 15 = 15n \div 15$

$176.67 = n$

Since there is no such thing as a partial person, 176, not 177, people can attend the graduation.

36. A

The equation is given in slope y-intercept form ($y = mx + b$).

Use the y-intercept to plot (0, 9). Use the slope (2) to determine second and third points, such as (−1, 7) and (−2, 5). Join the points and extend the line through that of the first equation.

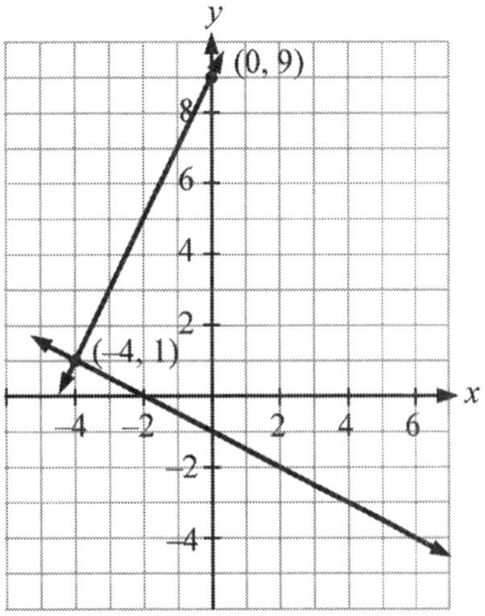

The intersection point or solution is (−4, 1).

37. B

Rewrite both equations in slope y-intercept form ($y = mx + b$).

$2x - y = -1$	$3x + y = -9$
$2x - y + y = -1 + y$	$3x - 3x + y = -3x - 9$
$2x + 1 = -1 + 1 + y$	$y = -3x - 9$
$2x + 1 = y$	

Looking at the slopes, one line will have a positive slope and one will have a negative slope.

The line with a positive slope must intersect at (0, 1). The only graph with a line intersecting at (0, 1) is shown in alternative B. Verify that this is the correct graph by checking that the slope rises 2 units up and runs 1 unit across. Check the line with the negative slope to verify that it descends 3 units and runs across 1 unit.

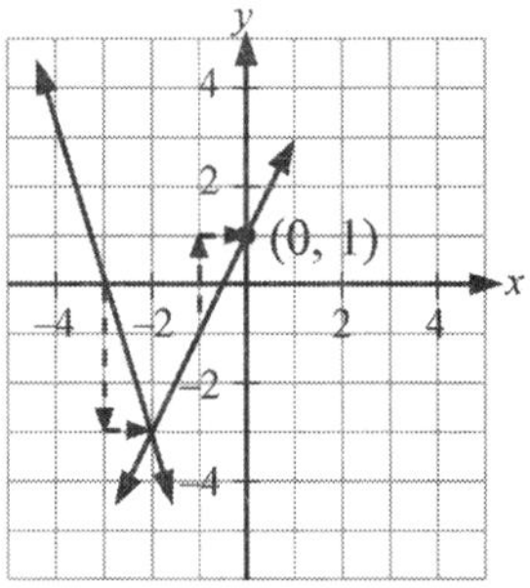

38. B

Since Plan A is $40 per month, the line of the equation is horizontal at the y-intercept.

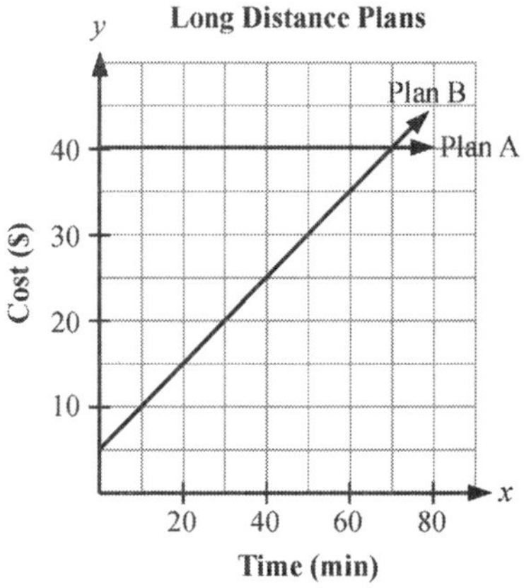

When $x < 70$ minutes, Plan B is the better value as its line is lower than that of Plan A.
When $x > 70$ minutes, Plan A's line is lower and is therefore the better value.
At $x = 70$ minutes, both plans cost the same.

The correct statement is given in alternative B.

Not for Reproduction

UNIT TEST — ANALYTIC GEOMETRY

1. The slope of the line that passes through points (5, 3) and (−1, −4) is

A. $\frac{3}{2}$ **B.** $\frac{7}{6}$

C. $\frac{6}{7}$ **D.** $\frac{2}{3}$

Use the following information to answer the next question.

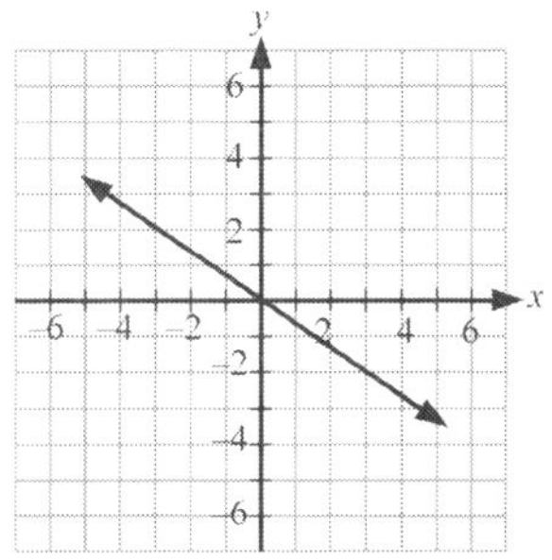

2. What is the slope of the given line?

A. $\frac{3}{2}$ **B.** $\frac{2}{3}$

C. $-\frac{3}{2}$ **D.** $-\frac{2}{3}$

Open Response

3. A line is plotted on a coordinate plane such that when its y-coordinate increases by 5, its x-coordinate decreases by 3. What is the slope of this line?

Show your work.

4. Which of the following equations represents a line with a slope of $-\frac{1}{2}$ and that passes through point (2, −3)?

A. $2x - 3y = -\frac{1}{2}$

B. $y = -\frac{1}{2}x - 3$

C. $x + 2y - 4 = 0$

D. $x + 2y + 4 = 0$

5. Which of the following graphs could be the graph of a linear relation that has a slope of −1?

A.

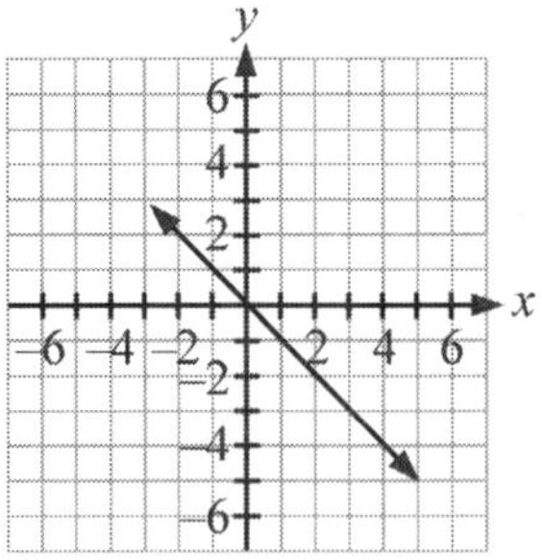

B.

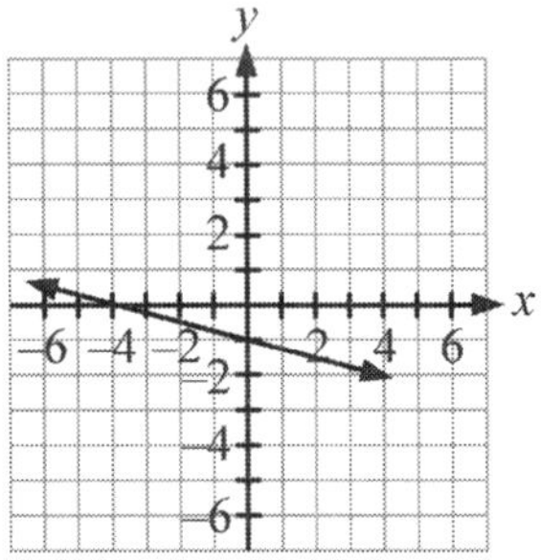

C.

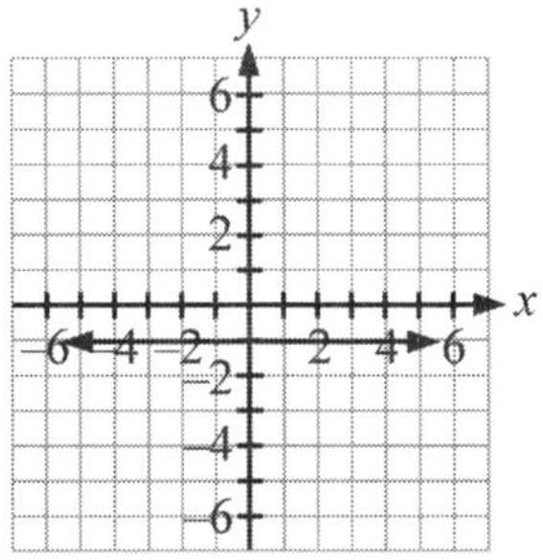

D.

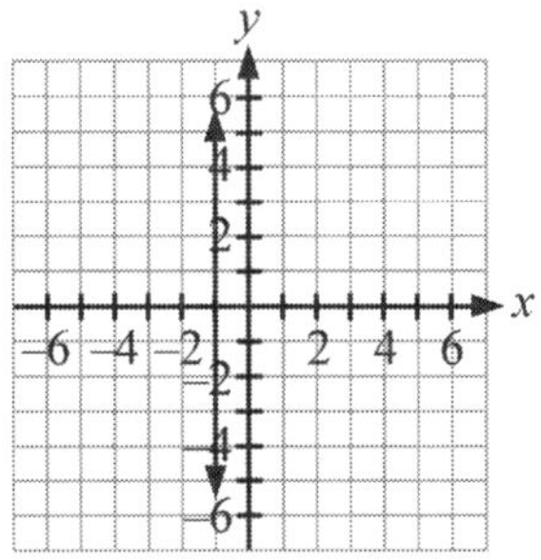

Use the following information to answer the next question.

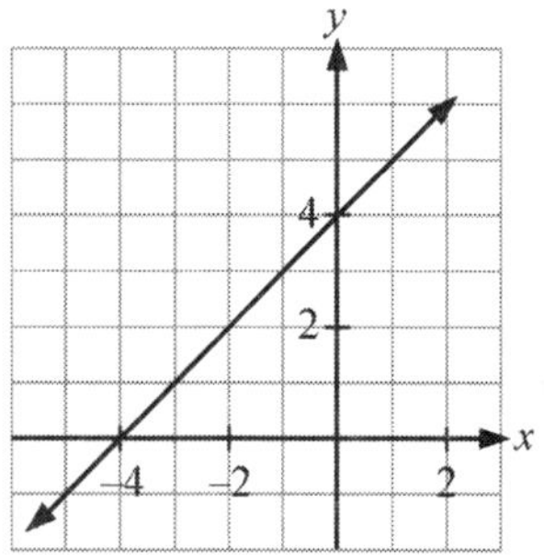

Open Response

6. What is the slope of this line?

Show your work.

Use the following information to answer the next question.

A glass box in a laboratory contains 150 fruit flies. After 25 days, the population of the fruit flies increases to 340.

7. The constant rate of change of the fruit fly population during this period is

A. 7.6 flies/day **B.** 8.6 flies/day

C. 9.6 flies/day **D.** 10.6 flies/day

Not for Reproduction

Use the following information to answer the next question.

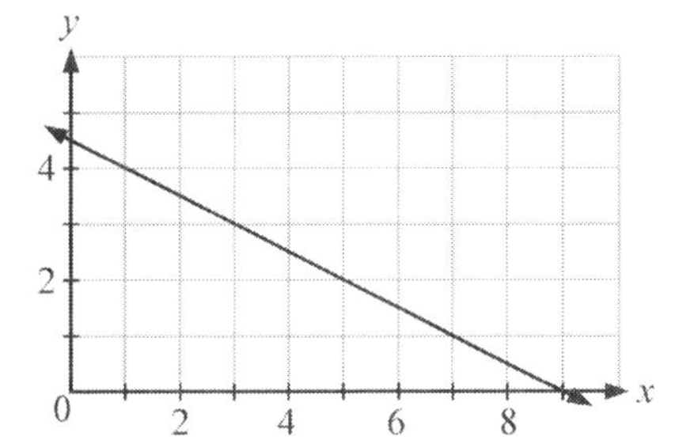

8. What is the rate of change of this graph?

A. $-\frac{1}{2}$ **B.** 0

C. $\frac{1}{2}$ **D.** 2

Use the following information to answer the next question.

Laura made this chart to show how much her plant grew each week.

Week	Plant Growth (cm)
1	3
2	6
3	9
4	12
5	15

9. What is the plant's rate of growth?

A. –3 cm / week

B. $-\frac{1}{3}$ cm / week

C. $\frac{1}{3}$ cm / week

D. 3 cm / week

Use the following information to answer the next question.

The cost of hiring a taxi is $3.00 plus $1.25 for every kilometre travelled.

Open Response

10. Demonstrate the constant rate of change using the equation of the line in slope y-intercept form, first differences, and a graph.

11. Which of the following lines is perpendicular to the line given by the equation $4y = 5x$?

A. $12x + 15y = 15$

B. $10x - 8y = -3$

C. $8x + 4y = 5$

D. $2x - 6y = -7$

Copyright Protected

12. Which of the following pairs of slopes represents two parallel lines?

A. $-\frac{1}{2}$ and $\frac{1}{2}$

B. $\frac{2}{5}$ and $\frac{10}{25}$

C. $\frac{2}{1}$ and $\frac{1}{2}$

D. $-\frac{2}{5}$ and $\frac{25}{10}$

Open Response

13. What is the equation of the horizontal line passing through point (3, 1)?

Show your work.

14. Which of the following equations is linear?

A. $x^2 + xy = 2$ **B.** $2x = y - 4$

C. $xy = y + 2$ **D.** $x^2 - y = 3$

15. It is **true** to state that linear relations have a degree of

A. one **B.** two

C. three **D.** four

Use the following information to answer the next question.

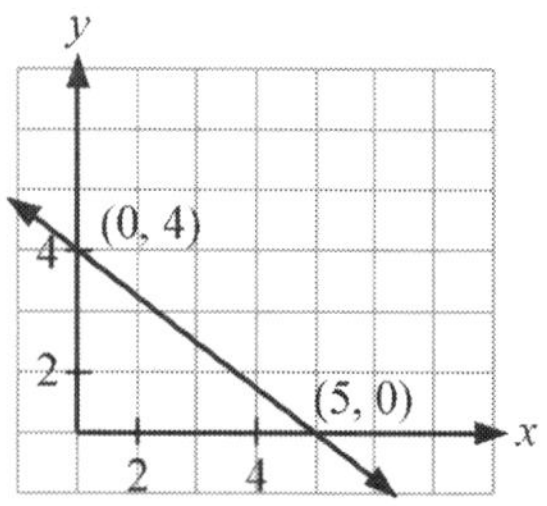

16. Which of the following equations represents the plotted line?

A. $x = 3$

B. $y = x^2$

C. $x^3 + 1 = y$

D. $5y + 4x = 20$

17. Which of the following linear equations is correctly written in slope y-intercept form?

A. $x + y - 2 = 0$ **B.** $y = 2x^2 + 1$

C. $y = 3x + \frac{1}{3}$ **D.** $x = \frac{y-1}{2}$

Use the following information to answer the next question.

> The slope of a line is $-\frac{3}{2}$, and the y-intercept is -3.

18. What is the equation of the line in standard form?

A. $3x - 2y - 6 = 0$

B. $3x - 2y + 6 = 0$

C. $3x + 2y - 6 = 0$

D. $3x + 2y + 6 = 0$

Not for Reproduction

Use the following information to answer the next question.

The slope of a line is –3 and the y-intercept is –2.

19. The equation of this line written in standard form is

A. $3x + y + 2 = 0$

B. $-3x - y - 2 = 0$

C. $y = 3x - 2$

D. $y = -3x - 2$

Use the following information to answer the next question.

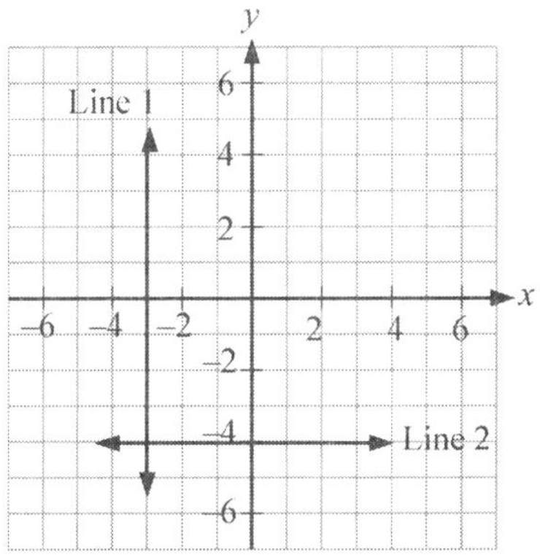

Open Response

20. What are the equations of Line 1 and Line 2, respectively?

21. The equation of the line $4y - 2x - 6 = 0$ can be expressed in slope y-intercept form as

A. $y = \frac{x}{2} - \frac{3}{2}$

B. $y = \frac{x}{2} + \frac{3}{2}$

C. $y = -\frac{x}{2} - \frac{3}{2}$

D. $y = -\frac{x}{2} + \frac{3}{2}$

22. What is the standard form of the equation $y = \frac{3}{4}x + \frac{2}{3}$?

A. $9x - y + 8 = 0$

B. $36x - 12y + 24 = 0$

C. $9x - 12y + 8 = 0$

D. $9x + 12y - 8 = 0$

Open Response

23. What is the equation of the line $x + 3y = 7$ expressed in slope y-intercept form?

Show your work.

24. Which graph represents the line that is parallel to $2x + y = 3$ and passes through point (1, 3)?

A.

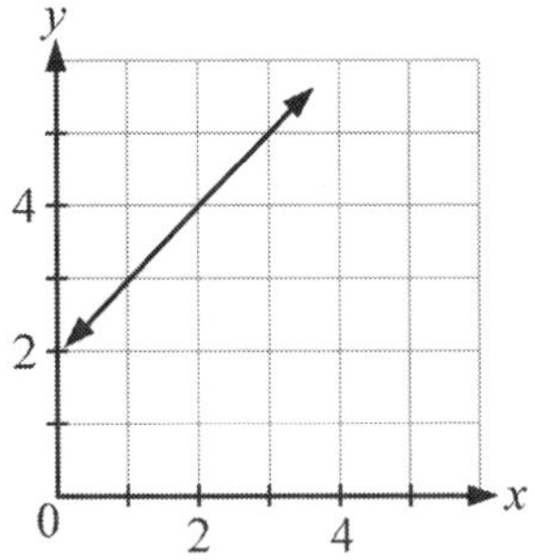

B.

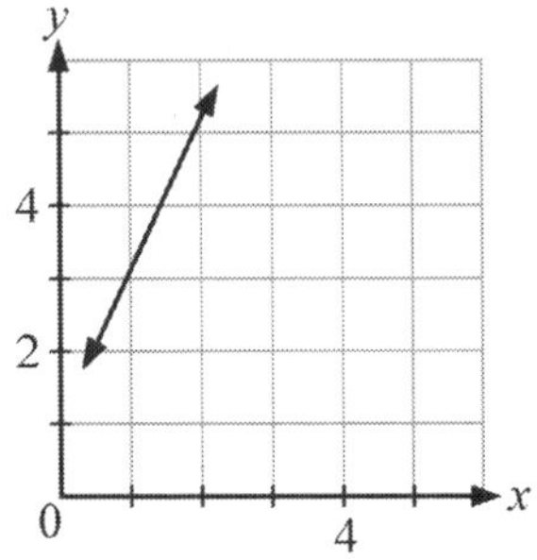

C.

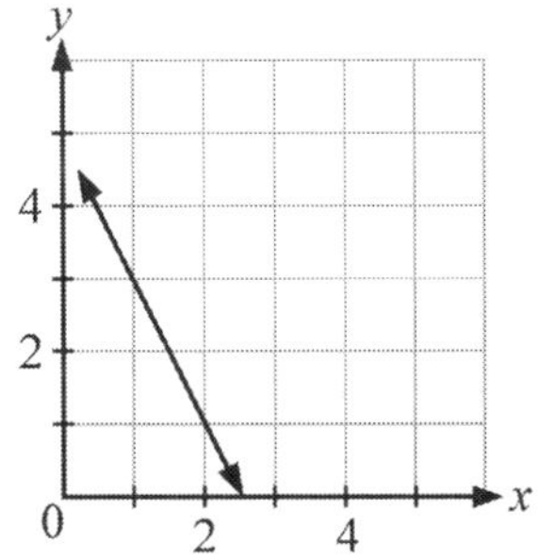

D.

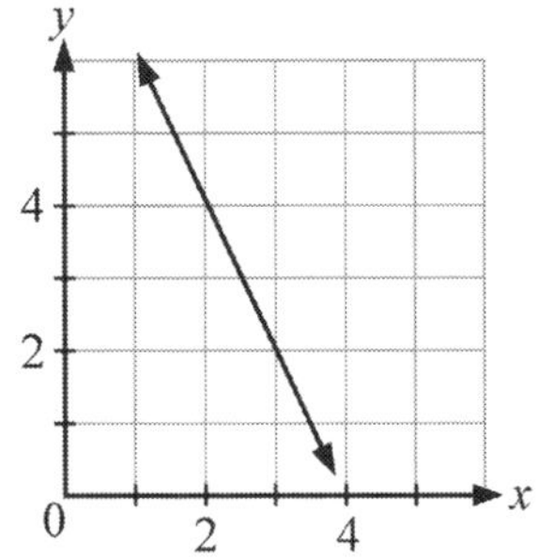

25. The graph of the equation $x - y = 0$ passes through the point

A. (–1, 0) **B.** (0, 0)

C. (1, 0) **D.** (2, 0)

26. Which of the following graphs represents the equation $2x - 5 = y$?

A.

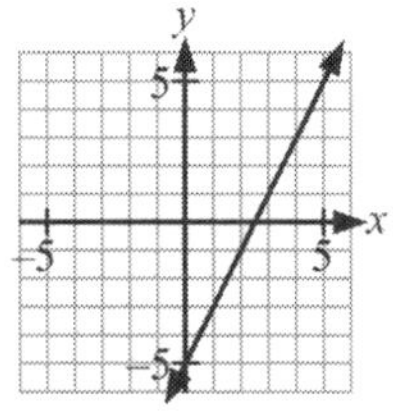

B.

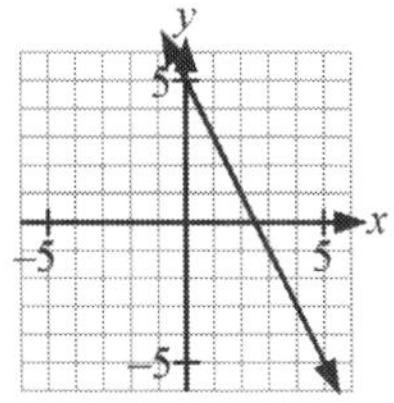

C.

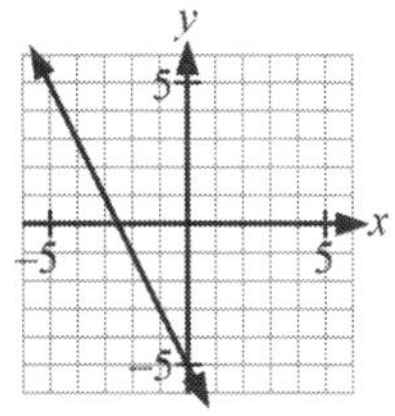

D.

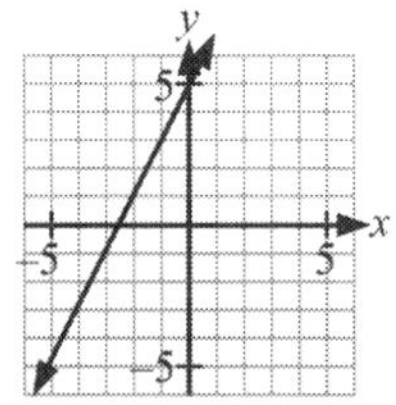

27. A line is parallel to the line $y = 5x + 3$ and has a y-intercept of –2. The equation of the line is

A. $y = 5x - 2$ **B.** $y = 5x + 2$

C. $y = 9x - 5$ **D.** $y = 9x + 5$

28. Which of the following equations represents a line that is perpendicular to the line $y = \frac{1}{3}x - 6$?

A. $x + 3y = 12$

B. $2x + 5y = 10$

C. $3x + 6y = 8$

D. $6x + 2y = 9$

Not for Reproduction

29. The equation of the line with a slope of $\frac{3}{4}$ and a y-intercept of $\frac{1}{2}$ is

A. $3x - 4y + 2 = 0$

B. $3x + 4y + 2 = 0$

C. $6x - 8y + 16 = 0$

D. $6x - 8y - 16 = 0$

Open Response

30. What is the equation of the line that passes through points (4, 5) and (3, 2)?

Show your work.

31. A library charges 50 cents for the first day that a book is overdue and 25 cents for each day after that. Which of the following equations relates the total cost to the number of days the book is overdue?

A. $C = n + 25$

B. $C = 25n + 50n$

C. $C = 50 \times 25n$

D. $C = 50 + 25n$

Use the following information to answer the next question.

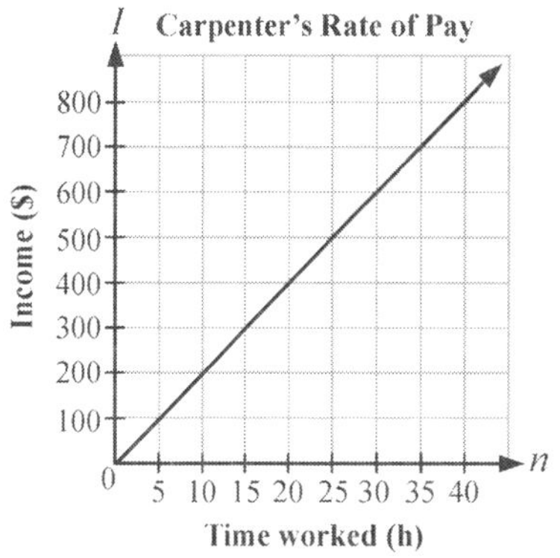

32. If I represents the income of the carpenter and n represents the number of hours worked, then a linear equation that could show the relationship between the two variables is

A. $I = 100n$ **B.** $I = 20n$

C. $I = n + 100$ **D.** $I = n + 20$

Use the following information to answer the next question.

A school club sells bags of popcorn for \$1.00 each as a fundraiser. The equation of the relation is $P = B - 25$, where P represents the profit in dollars and B represents the number of bags sold.

33. What does the P-intercept represent?

A. Cost of 25 bags of popcorn

B. Number of bags of popcorn that must be sold to recover the start-up cost of \$25.00

C. Start-up cost of \$25.00

D. Profit of \$25.00

Use the following information to answer the next question.

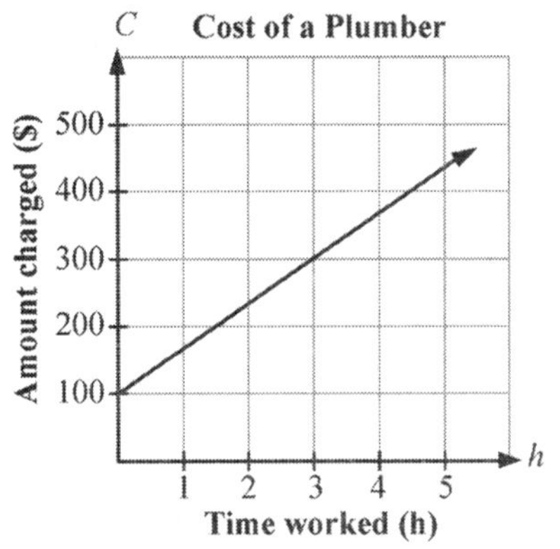

Open Response

34. Write the equation of the given relation in slope y-intercept form and describe the meaning of the slope and y-intercept for this linear relation.

Show your work.

Use the following information to answer the next question.

In the relation $N = 15 + 4p$, N represents the number of people who watch a car race, and p represents the number of participants in the race.

35. If p is restricted to whole numbers of 20 or less because of the size of the track, then the **maximum** number of people who can watch the race is

A. 20 **B.** 95

C. 215 **D.** 760

36. A 21 cm candle burns down 1.4 cm every hour. For how long can the candle burn?

A. 10 hours **B.** 15 hours

C. 21 hours **D.** 42 hours

37. A satellite approximately 12 0 km from Earth sends a signal to Earth at the speed of light. Given that the speed of light is approximately 3×10^8 m/s, the approximate value of the time required for the signal to travel from the satellite to Earth is

A. 0.000 04 s **B.** 0.0004 s

C. 0.004 s **D.** 0.04 s

Use the following information to answer the next question.

Akhil is asked to solve a system of linear equations. He uses a graphical approach for solving. Akhil's correct partial solution is below.

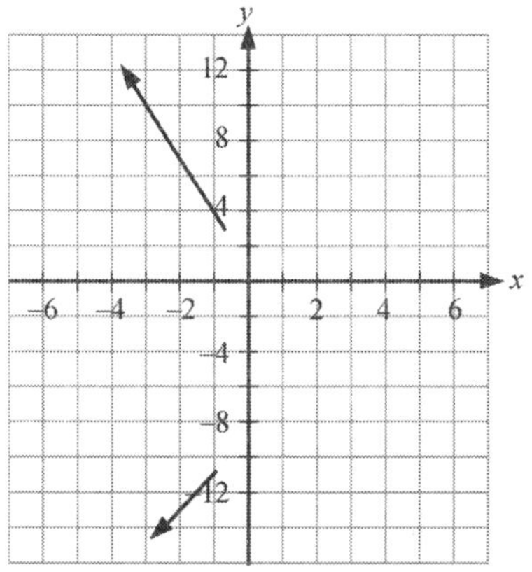

38. If Akhil correctly completes his solution, he will determine that the solution is

A. (3, –4) **B.** (3, –5)

C. (2, –4) **D.** (2, –5)

Not for Reproduction

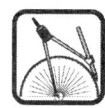

Use the following information to answer the next question.

The Wong family is planning to go to an all-inclusive resort for a vacation. The rates for two resorts are graphed.

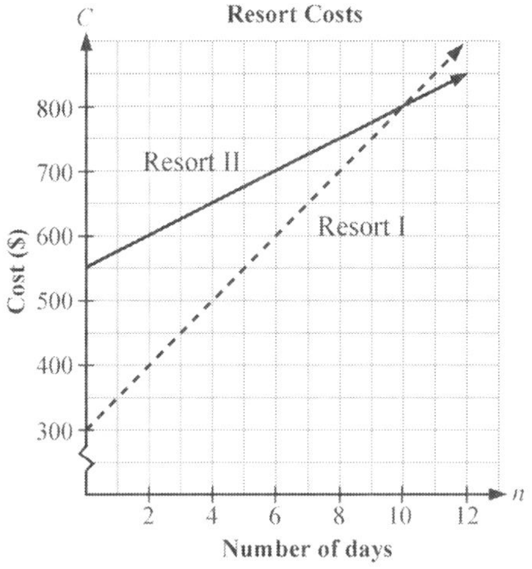

39. Which of the following statements is **true**?

A. Resort I is the better value if the family stays for 10 days.

B. Resort II is the better value if the family stays for 10 days.

C. Resort I is the better value if the family stays for 14 days.

D. Resort II is the better value if the family stays for 14 days.

Use the following information to answer the next question.

Krishna challenges Bill to a 5-km race. He gives Bill a 5-min head start.

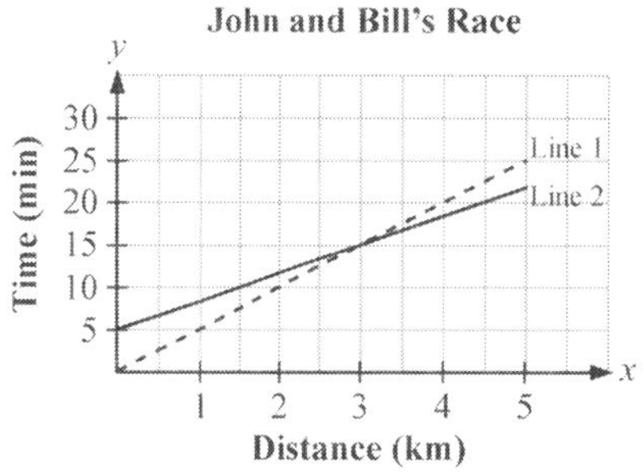

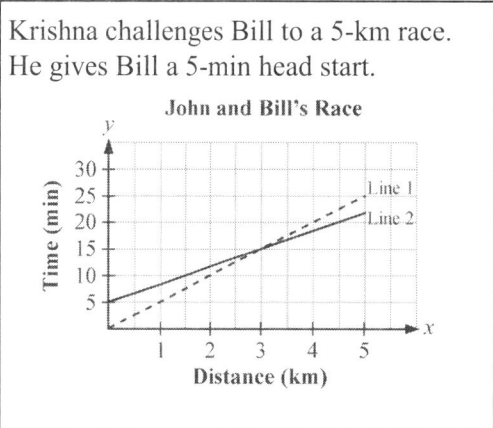

Open Response

40. Which line represents Krishna?

Copyright Protected

ANSWERS AND SOLUTIONS — UNIT TEST

1. B	9. D	17. C	25. B	33. C
2. D	10. OR	18. D	26. A	34. OR
3. OR	11. A	19. A	27. A	35. B
4. D	12. B	20. OR	28. D	36. B
5. A	13. OR	21. B	29. A	37. D
6. OR	14. B	22. C	30. OR	38. D
7. A	15. A	23. OR	31. D	39. D
8. A	16. D	24. C	32. B	40. OR

1. B

Let the two points be (x_1, y_1) and (x_2, y_2).

$(x_1, y_1) = (5, 3)$

$(x_2, y_2) = (-1, -4)$

Substitute the values into the slope formula.

$$m = \frac{y_2 - y_1}{x_2 - x_1}$$

$$= \frac{-4-3}{-1-5} = \frac{-7}{-6} = \frac{7}{6}$$

2. D

A slope (m) that rises to the left (or falls to the right) is always negative. Thus, the alternatives with positive slopes are eliminated.

Method 1 - Graphically

$$m = \frac{\text{rise}}{\text{run}}$$

Using the graph, count the number of units that the line rises and then runs.

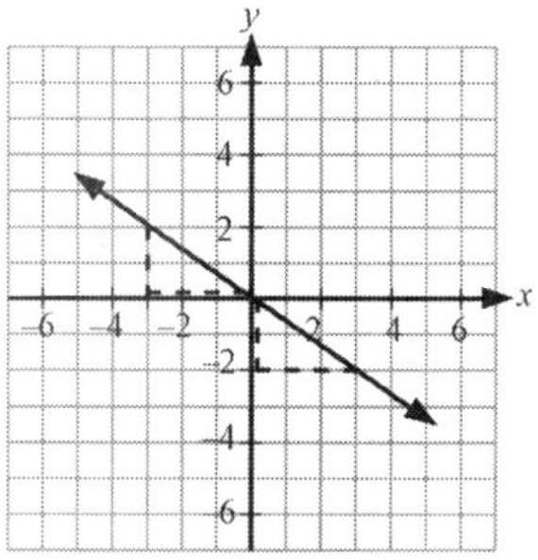

$$m = \frac{\text{rise}}{\text{run}} = \frac{-2}{3}$$

Method 2 – Using the slope formula

$$m = \frac{y_2 - y_1}{x_2 - x_1}$$

Pick two points on the graph, such as (3, −2) and (−3, 2).

Substitute the values into the formula and then solve.

$$m = \frac{(-2)-2}{3-(-3)} = = \frac{(-2)+(-2)}{3+3} = \frac{(-4)}{6} = -\frac{2}{3}$$

3. OR

$$\text{Slope} = \frac{\Delta y}{\Delta x} = \frac{5}{-3} = -\frac{5}{3}$$

4. D

Start at the point given (2, −3) and use the slope (rise of 1 and run of −2) to move to the y-intercept (b) of −2.

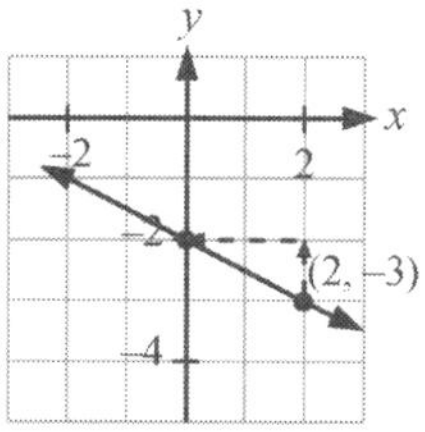

Not for Reproduction

Substitute the slope (m) and y-intercept (b) into the slope y-intercept formula.

$$y = -\frac{1}{2}x - 2$$

This equation does not match the equations in alternatives A or B.

Write the equation in standard form, as given in alternatives C and D.
Multiply both sides of the equation by 2 to remove the fractional coefficient.

$$2 \times y = 2 \times -\frac{1}{2}x - 2 \times 2$$

$$2y = -x - 4$$

Add x and 4 to both sides to make the equation equal to 0.

$$2y + x + 4 = -x + x - 4 + 4$$

$$x + 2y + 4 = 0$$

5. A

A line falling from left to right has a negative slope. Alternatives C and D can be eliminated.

Since the slope is -1, for every rise of -1 (fall of 1 unit), there should be a run of 1. Only the graph of alternative A displays this slope.

6. OR

Method 1 - Graphically

Pick any point on the line. Count how many units rise to the next point (1) and how many run (1).

$$m = \frac{\text{rise}}{\text{run}} = \frac{1}{1}$$

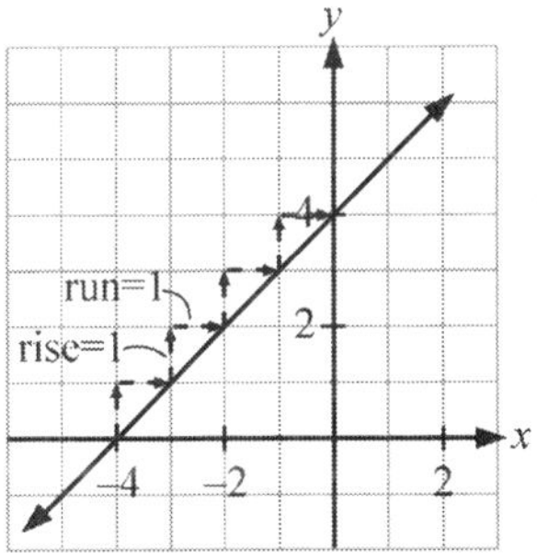

Method 2 – Using the slope formula

$$m = \frac{\text{rise}}{\text{run}} = \frac{y_2 - y_1}{x_2 - x_1}$$

Pick two points on the graph, such as (1, 5) and (0, 4). Substitute these values into the formula and solve.

$$m = \frac{5-4}{1-0} = \frac{1}{1} = 1$$

7. A

Let p represent the population and t the time.
Constant rate of change

$$= \frac{\Delta p}{\Delta t}$$

$$= \frac{340 - 150}{25 - 0}$$

$$= \frac{190}{25}$$

$= 7.6$ flies/day

8. A

$$\text{Rate of change} = \frac{\text{rise}}{\text{run}} = \frac{\Delta y}{\Delta x}$$

Choose two points that lie on the line, such as (0, 4.5) and (9, 0).

$$\text{Rate of change} = \frac{4.5 - 0}{0 - 9} = \frac{4.5}{-9} = -\frac{1}{2}$$

As the line falls to the right, you know that your negative slope is correct.

9. D

Use first differences to find the rate of change.

Week (x)	Growth (y)	First differences
1	3	$6 - 3 = 3$
2	6	
3	9	$9 - 6 = 3$
4	12	$12 - 9 = 3$
5	15	$15 - 12 = 3$

$$\text{Rate of change} = \frac{\text{first difference}}{\Delta x} = \frac{3}{2-1} = \frac{3}{1} = 3$$

The rate of growth is 3 cm / week.

10. OR

<table>
<tr><th>Points</th><th>Sample Answer</th></tr>
<tr><td>4</td><td>Slope formula:
The fixed cost is $3.00, meaning the y-intercept is +3.
The rate of change is $1.25 for each kilometre travelled (1.25k).
The equation of a line in slope y-intercept form is $y = mx + b$.
Substitute these values into the equation:
$C = 1.25k + 3$
First differences:
<table>
<tr><th>x</th><th>$C = 1.25k + 3$</th><th>First Difference</th></tr>
<tr><td>1</td><td>$C = 1.25(1)+3 = 4.25$</td><td></td></tr>
<tr><td>2</td><td>$C = 1.25(2)+3 = 5.50$</td><td>$5.50 - 4.25 = 1.25$</td></tr>
<tr><td>3</td><td>$C = 1.25(3)+3 = 6.75$</td><td>$6.75 - 5.50 = 1.25$</td></tr>
<tr><td>4</td><td>$C = 1.25(4)+3 = 8.00$</td><td>$8.00 - 6.75 = 1.25$</td></tr>
</table></td></tr>
</table>

Points	Sample Answer
	The first differences are the same. The coefficient of k is the constant rate of change, which is 1.25. Choose any of the points from the chart above to plot. Connect the points to create a line. Indicate the y-intercept. From one point draw a dotted line that rises 1.25 units and runs across 1 unit. 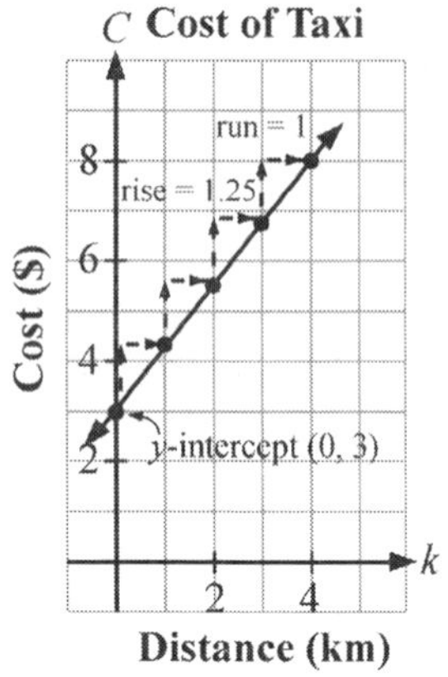
Application of knowledge and skills involving the constant rate of change shows a high degree of effectiveness due to • a thorough understanding of the concepts • an accurate application of the procedures (any minor errors and/or omissions do not detract from the demonstration of a thorough understanding)	
3	Slope formula: The terms are correct but are not in slope y-intercept form. First differences: The table of values is completed correctly, but the values are calculated incorrectly. Graph: The labels are left off, but the graph is correct according to data in the table of values.
Application of knowledge and skills involving the constant rate of change shows considerable effectiveness due to • an understanding of most of the concepts • minor errors and/or omissions in the application of the procedures	
2	Slope formula: The terms are correct but are not in slope y-intercept form. First differences: The table of values is completed correctly, but the values are calculated incorrectly. Graph: The labels are left off, and the graph is incorrect according to data in the table of values.
Application of knowledge and skills involving the constant rate of change shows some effectiveness due to • minor errors and/or omissions in the application of the procedures • an understanding of most of the concepts	
1	Slope formula: The equation does not represent the relation in the question. First differences: The table of values is completed correctly according to the equation written. Graph: The labels are left off, and the graph is incorrect according to data in the table of values.
Application of knowledge and skills involving the constant rate of change shows limited effectiveness due to:	

Points	Sample Answer
• a misunderstanding of concepts • an incorrect selection or misuse of procedures	

11. A

The given line is $4y = 5x$.

Rewrite it in slope y-intercept form. $y = \frac{5}{4}x$

The slope (m_1) is $\frac{5}{4}$.

The product of the slopes of two perpendicular lines equals -1.

$$m_1 m_2 = \frac{5}{4} \times m_2 = -1$$

$$m_2 = -1 \div \frac{5}{4} = -1 \times \frac{4}{5} = -\frac{4}{5}$$

Rewrite the equations of the alternatives in slope y-intercept form to determine which equation has a negative reciprocal starting with alternative A.
$15y = -12x + 15$

$$\frac{15y}{15} = \frac{-12x}{15} + \frac{15}{15}$$

$$y = -\frac{12 \div 3}{15 \div 3}x + 1$$

$$y = -\frac{4}{5}x + 1$$

This equation has the reciprocal slope. You could go on to rewrite the equations of the following three alternatives to verify you have the correct answer.

The line $12x + 15y = 15$ is perpendicular to the given line.

12. B

Parallel lines have the same slope but different y-intercepts.

Alternatives A and D have a positive and negative slope. The lines would intersect.

Alternative B has equivalent slopes.

$$\frac{10}{25} = \frac{10 \div 5}{25 \div 5} = \frac{2}{5}$$

$$\frac{2}{5} = \frac{2}{5}$$

Alternative C has two different slopes; the first being steeper than the second.

13. OR

A horizontal line has the equation $y = c$, where c is the vertical position of the line. The line must pass through point (3, 1); therefore, the equation of the line is $y = 1$.

14. B

Linear equations are of the first degree.

Alternative A: The exponents of x^2 and xy give the equation a degree of 2.

Alternative B: Both variables have an implied exponent of 1.

Alternative C: The exponents of xy added together $(1 + 1)$ give the equation a degree of 2.

Alternative D: The equation is of the second degree.

The equation $2x = y - 4$ is linear.

15. A

Linear relations can only be of the first degree. If the relation has a degree of two or more, it will not graph a straight line.

16. D

The plotted line is straight, so its equation is linear. This rules out alternatives B and C because they are second-degree equations. The line also meets both the x-axis and the y-axis, so the equation must involve both x and y. This rules out alternative A as it graphs a horizontal line.

Verify that $5y + 4x = 20$ is the correct equation by finding the x- and y-intercepts.

x-intercept:

$$5(0) + 4x = 20$$
$$4x = 20$$
$$x = 5$$

y-intercept:

$$5y + 4(0) = 20$$
$$5y = 20$$
$$y = 4$$

The graph crosses the x-axis at 5 and the y-axis at 4.

17. C

Slope y-intercept form is $y = mx + b$. The only equation in this form is $y = 3x + \frac{1}{3}$.

Alternative A is in standard form, alternative B is not a linear equation, and alternative D is not in any particular form.

18. D

Standard form is $Ax + By + C = 0$.

You can first put the equation in slope y-intercept form and then change it to standard form.

The slope (m) is $-\frac{3}{2}$ and the y-intercept is -3.

$y = mx + b$

Substitute the values in for the variables.

$y = -\frac{3}{2}x - 3$

Distribute 2 through the terms in the equation to eliminate the denominator in the fractional coefficient.$2(y) = 2\left(-\frac{3}{2}x\right) + 2(-3)$

$2y = -3x - 6$

Move the terms to one side making the equation equal to 0. Ensure that the coefficient of x is positive and the variables are in the correct order.

$$2y + 3x + 6 = 3x - 3x + 6 - 6$$
$$3x + 2y + 6 = 0$$

19. A

Standard form is $Ax + By + C = 0$, where A represents the slope and C represents the y-intercept. Alternatives A and B follow this form.

The equation in slope y-intercept is $y = -3x - 2$.

Rearrange the equation into standard form.

$$y - y = -3x - y - 2$$
$$0 = -3x - y - 2$$

The coefficient of x can not be negative by convention. Distribute -1 through the equation.

$$-1(0) = -1(-3x - y - 2)$$
$$0 = 3x + y + 2$$

20. OR

Line 1 is a vertical line. Its equation is $x = -3$.

Line 2 is a horizontal line. Its equation is $y = -4$.

21. B

Isolate y in the given equation.

$4y - 2x - 6 = 0$

Add $2x$ and 6 to both sides of the equation (inverse operations).

$$4y - 2x + 2x - 6 + 6 = 0 + 2x + 6$$
$$4y = 2x + 6$$

Divide both sides of the equation by 4 to isolate y.

$$\frac{4y}{4} = \frac{2x}{4} + \frac{6}{4}$$
$$y = \frac{x}{2} + \frac{3}{2}$$

22. C

The equation is currently in slope y-intercept form. Move all the terms to one side for standard form.

$y = \frac{3}{4}x + \frac{2}{3}$

Multiply each term by 12, the lowest common denominator, to elimate the fractional coefficients.

$12y = 9x + 8$

Subtract $12y$ from both sides of the equation.

$12y - 12y = 9x + 8 - 12y$

$0 = 9x + 8 - 12y$

Rearrange into standard form, $Ax + By + C = 0$.

$9x - 12y + 8 = 0$

23. OR

Isolate y in the given equation.

$x + 3y = 7$

Subtract x from both sides of the equation.

$x - x + 3y = 7 - x$

$3y = -x + 7$

Divide both sides of the equation by 3.

$\frac{3y}{3} = \frac{-x+7}{3}$

$y = -\frac{x}{3} + \frac{7}{3}$

$y = -\frac{1}{3}x + \frac{7}{3}$

24. C

First eliminate alternative D since it does not go through (1, 3).

Rewrite the equation in slope y-intercept form.

$2x + y = 3$

$y = -2x + 3$

The slope of the line $= -2$.

The line you are to find must also have a slope of -2 since it is parallel to the line $2x + y = 3$. Eliminate alternatives A and B with their positive sloping lines.

The graph in alternative C has a line that passes through the points (1, 3) and has a slope of -2.

25. B

Rewrite the equation in slope y-intercept form ($y = mx + b$).

$x - y = 0$

$y = x$

This is direct variation, which means the slope is 1 and the y-intercept is 0. The line passes through the origin.

26. A

In the equation given ($y = 2x - 5$), the y-intercept is -5. Alternatives A and C are the only graphs with this y-intercept.

The rate of change is 2, meaning the line must move in the positive direction. Alternative A has a line in a positive direction.

27. A

The equation of a line in slope y-intercept form is $y = mx + b$, where m is the slope of the line and b is the y-intercept. The given equation of the line is in slope y-intercept form. The line has a slope of 5.

Two parallel lines have the same slope; therefore, the slope of the required line is also 5.

The equation of a line with a slope of 5 and y-intercept of -2 is:

$y = mx + b$

$y = 5x + -2$

$y = 5x - 2$

28. D

The slope of the line $y = \frac{1}{3}x - 6$ is $\frac{1}{3}$. If two lines are perpendicular, then the product of their slopes is -1. The slope of the required line $= -1 \times 3 = -3$.

Find the slope of each alternative.

$x + 3y = 12$

$y = -\frac{1}{3}x + 4$

Slope $= -\frac{1}{3}$

$2x + 5y = 10$

$y = -\frac{2}{5}x + 2$

Slope $= -\frac{2}{5}$

$3x + 6y = 8$

$y = -\frac{1}{2}x + \frac{4}{3}$

Slope $= -\frac{1}{2}$

$6x + 2y = 9$

$y = -3x + \frac{9}{2}$

Slope $= -3$

The line that is perpendicular is $6x + 2y = 9$.

Not for Reproduction

29. A

Substitute the given values into the slope y-intercept form of an equation.

$y = mx + b \rightarrow y = \frac{3}{4}x + \frac{1}{2}$

Eliminate the fractions by multiplying each term by 4. $4y = 3x + 2$

Rewrite in standard form.
$3x - 4y + 2 = 0$

30. OR

The equation of the line passing through points (x_1, y_1) and (x_2, y_2) is found using the following formula:

$\frac{y - y_1}{x - x_1} = \frac{y_2 - y_1}{x_2 - x_1}$

$(x_1, y_1) = (4, 5)$ and $(x_2, y_2) = (3, 2)$

Substitute these values.

$\frac{y - 5}{x - 4} = \frac{2 - 5}{3 - 4}$

Simplify.

$\frac{y - 5}{x - 4} = 3$

Use cross multiplication to eliminate the fractions.
$y - 5 = 3x - 12$

Simplify and write the equation in slope y-intercept form.
$y = 3x - 7$

31. D

The fixed cost of 50 cents for the first day is represented by +50.

The constant rate of change is 25 cents for each additional day, represented by $25n$.

The total cost for the overdue book is represented by the equation $C = 50 + 25n$.

32. B

Slope y-intercept form indicates that the rate of change is the coefficient of x.

The rate of change is calculated with the following formula:

$m = \frac{\Delta y}{\Delta x} = \frac{y_2 - y_1}{x_2 - x_1}$. Take any two points from the graph and substitute them into the equation.

$(x_1, y_1) = (5, 100)$

$(x_2, y_2) = (10, 200)$

$m = \frac{200 - 100}{10 - 5} = \frac{100}{5} = 20$

The correct equation is $I = 20n$.

33. C

The equation of a line in slope y-intercept form is $y = mx + b$, where b represents the y-intercept.

In the equation given, the y-intercept is -25, indicating a debt. Consider each alternative.

Alternative A: While 25 bags of popcorn sell for \$25, they do not cost \$25 to make. The start-up cost is \$25.00. More than 25 bags of popcorn are sold for that cost.

Alternative B: The P-intercept indicates the profit or loss at 0 bags sold, not how many bags sold to break even. The break-even point is (25, 0).

Alternative C: The start-up cost refers to a debt of \$25.00, where no bags have been sold. This value would be $(-25, 0)$, which is the P-intercept.

Alternative D: There is a debt, not a profit, at the start of the fundraiser.

Copyright Protected

34. OR

Points	Sample Answer
4	First find the slope of the relation. Find the coordinates of two points on the graph. $(x_1, y_1) = (0,\ 100)$ $(x_2, y_2) = (3,\ 300)$ $m = \frac{\Delta y}{\Delta x} = \frac{y_2 - y_1}{x_2 - x_1}$ $= \frac{300 - 100}{3 - 0} = \frac{200}{3}$ $= 67$ The y-intercept is 100. The equation of the line in slope y-intercept form $(y = mx + b)$ is $C = 67h + 100$. Slope is the hourly rate that the plumber charges for being at the house. The plumber charges \$67 for each hour worked. The y-intercept $(0,\ 100)$ represents the \$100 that the plumber charges for coming to the house before starting any work.
Application of knowledge and skills involving the meaning of slope and y-intercept in a realistic situation shows a high degree of effectiveness due to: • a thorough understanding of the concepts • an accurate application of the procedures (any minor errors and/or omissions do not detract from the demonstration of a thorough understanding)	
3	The equation is correct, but it is not in slope y-intercept form. The explanations of slope and y-intercept are correct.
Application of knowledge and skills involving the meaning of slope and y-intercept in a realistic situation shows considerable effectiveness due to: • an understanding of most of the concepts • minor errors and/or omissions in the application of the procedures	
2	The equation is correct, but it is not in slope y-intercept form. The explanation of slope or y-intercept is incorrect.
Application of knowledge and skills involving the meaning of slope and y-intercept in a realistic situation shows some effectiveness due to:	

Points	Sample Answer
• minor errors and/or omissions in the application of the procedures • an understanding of most of the concepts	
1	The equation is correct, but it is not in slope y-intercept form. The explanation of slope and y-intercept are incorrect.
Application of knowledge and skills involving the meaning of slope and y-intercept in a realistic situation shows limited effectiveness due to: • a misunderstanding of concepts • an incorrect selection or misuse of procedures	

35. B

The maximum value of N is obtained when the value of p is at its restriction or limit (20).
$N = 15 + 4 \times 20 = 15 + 80 = 95$

The maximum number of people who can watch the race is 95.

36. B

The rate of change (slope) in this situation is −1.4 cm. The original height of the candle (y-intercept) is 21 cm. Substitute these values in the slope y-intercept form of an equation.

$h = -1.4t + 21$, where h is the height of the candle and t is the number of hours burned

To find the maximum burn time, substitute 0 in for the height and solve for t.
$0 = -1.4t + 21$

$0 - 21 = -1.4t + 21 - 21$

$\frac{-21}{-1.4} = \frac{-1.4t}{-1.4}$

$15 = t$

The candle can burn for a maximum of 15 hours.

37. D

The equation of this relation is $D = 30\ 000t$, where D is the distance travelled and t is the time required.

Not for Reproduction

Note that the distance is given in kilometres and the speed is in metres per second.

120 km = 1200 m

Now, substitute the distance into the equation of the line.
1200 = 30 000t

Divide both sides by 300 000 000 to isolate t.
0.04 = t

It will take 0.04 seconds for the signal to travel 12 000 km.

38. D

Use a ruler to extend each line. The solution to a system of equations is the point of intersection. When the lines on the graph are extended, the lines cross at (2, –5).

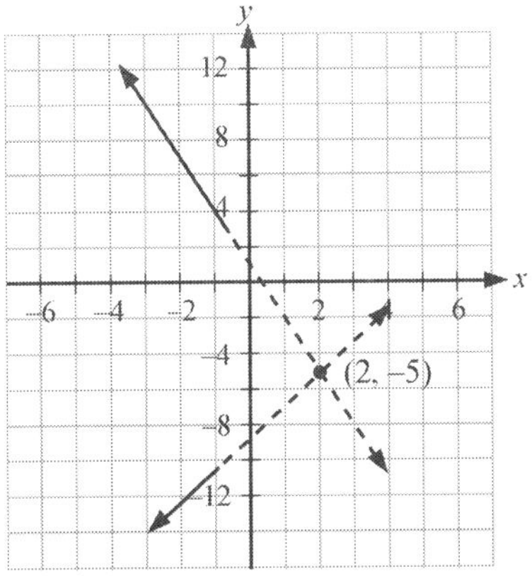

39. D

At x = 10 days, the resorts cost the same amount. This is indicated by the point of intersection. When x > 10 days, Resort I becomes more expensive as the line jumps above the line of Resort II. Thus, at x = 14 days, Resort II is the better value as its line is below the line of Resort I.

40. OR

Bill was given a 5-min head start. This means that the y-intercept would be at (0, 5). This occurs with Line 2. Therefore, Krishna is represented by Line 1. He starts at 0 minutes.

NOTES

Measurement and Geometry

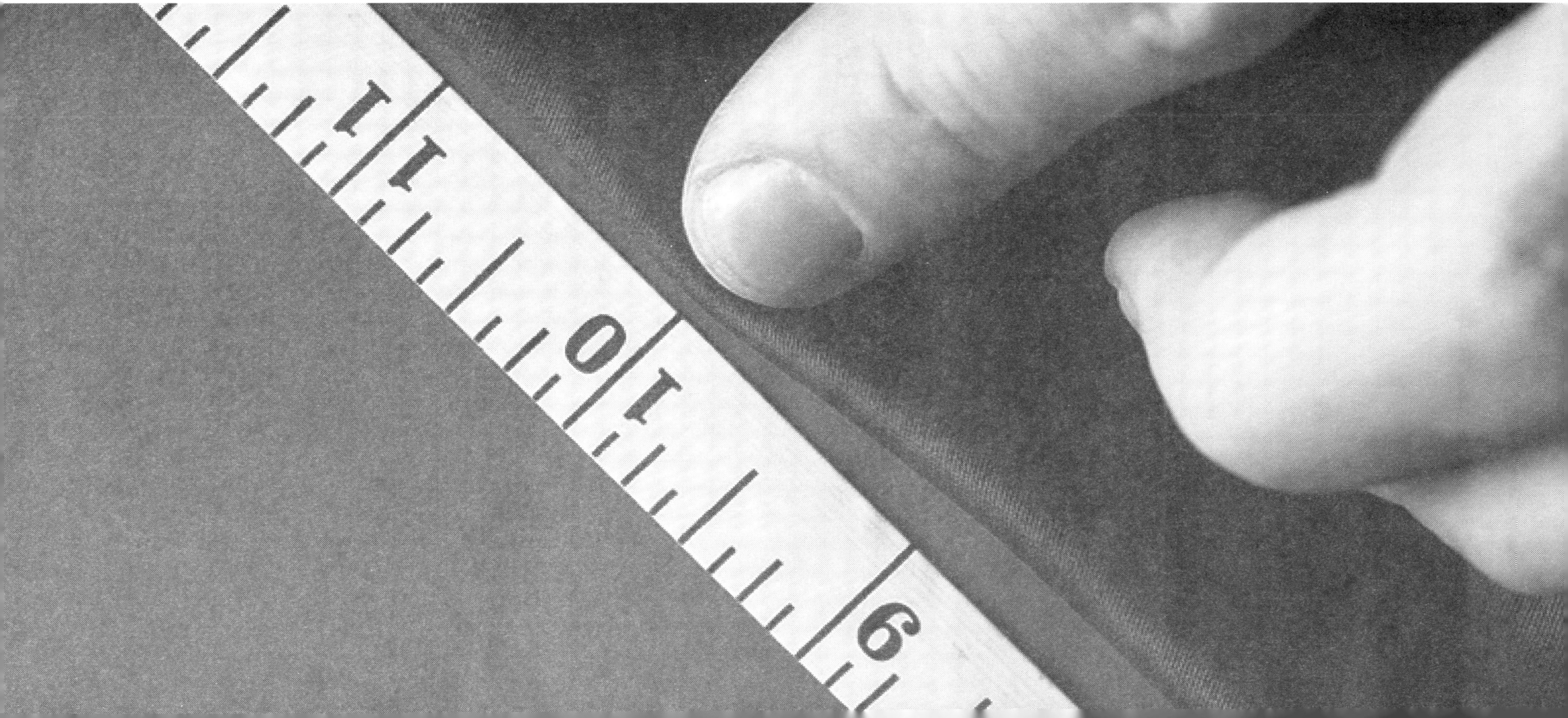

Copyright Protected

MEASUREMENT AND GEOMETRY

Table of Correlations

	Specific Expectation	Practice Questions	Unit Test Questions	Practice Test 1	Practice Test 2
9MGV.01	Investigating the Optimal Values of Measurements				
9MG1.01	*determine the maximum area of a rectangle with a given perimeter by constructing a variety of rectangles, using a variety of tools and by examining various values of the area as the side lengths change and the perimeter remains constant*	1, 2	17, 18	26	
9MG1.02	*determine the minimum perimeter of a rectangle with a given area by constructing a variety of rectangles, using a variety of tools and by examining various values of the side lengths and the perimeter as the area stays constant*	3, 4	19, 20	27	27
9MG1.03	*identify, through investigation with a variety of tools, the effect of varying the dimensions on the surface area [or volume] of square-based prisms and cylinders, given a fixed volume [or surface area]*	5, 6	21, 22		
9MG1.04	*explain the significance of optimal area, surface area, or volume in various applications*	7, 8	23, 24		
9MG1.05	*pose and solve problems involving maximization and minimization of measurements of geometric shapes and figures*	9, 10	25, 26, 27	28, 29	28
9MGV.02	Solving Problems Involving Perimeter, Area, Surface Area, and Volume				
9MG2.01	*relate the geometric representation of the Pythagorean theorem and the algebraic representation* $a^2 + b^2 = c^2$	11, 12	1, 2		
9MG2.02	*solve problems using the Pythagorean theorem, as required in applications*	13, 14, 15	3, 4, 5	12	13
9MG2.03	*solve problems involving the areas and perimeters of composite two-dimensional shapes*	16, 17	6, 7, 8, 9a, 9b	13	14
9MG2.04	*develop, through investigation, the formulas for the volume of a pyramid, a cone, and a sphere*	18, 19	10, 11		
9MG2.05	*determine, through investigation, the relationship for calculating the surface area of a pyramid*	20, 21	12, 13		
9MG2.06	*solve problems involving the surface areas and volumes of prisms, pyramids, cylinders, cones, and spheres, including composite figures*	22, 23	14, 15, 16	14	15, 16
9MGV.03	Investigating and Applying Geometric Relationships				
9MG3.01	*determine, through investigation using a variety of tools and describe the properties and relationships of the interior and exterior angles of triangles, quadrilaterals, and other polygons, and apply the results to problems involving the angles of polygons*	24, 25, 26	28, 29, 30		
9MG3.02	*determine, through investigation using a variety of tools and describe some properties of polygons, and apply the results in problem solving*	27, 28	31, 32, 33, 34		
9MG3.03	*pose questions about geometric relationships, investigate them, and present their findings, using a variety of mathematical forms*	29, 30	35, 36	30	
9MG3.04	*illustrate a statement about a geometric property by demonstrating the statement with multiple examples, or deny the statement on the basis of a counter-example, with or without the use of dynamic geometry software*	31, 32	37, 38		29, 30

Not for Reproduction

9MG1.01 determine the maximum area of a rectangle with a given perimeter by constructing a variety of rectangles, using a variety of tools and by examining various values of the area as the side lengths change and the perimeter remains constant

Determining the Maximum Area of a Rectangle

For a rectangle with width w, and length l, the following formulas can be used to calculate area and perimeter:

$A_{rectangle} = lw$

$P_{rectangle} = 2(l + w)$

Rectangles with equal perimeters can have different areas. For example, a rectangle with a length of 9 cm and a width of 3 cm has a smaller area (27 cm^2) than a rectangle with a length of 6 cm and a width of 6 cm (36 cm^2). They both have a perimeter of 24 cm.

The closer that a rectangle gets to becoming a square, the area of the rectangle increases.

Example

Find the perimeter and area for each of the following rectangles with the given dimensions.

$l = 9$ units, $w = 3$ units

$P_{rectangle} = 2(9 + 3) = 24$ units $A_{rectangle} = 9 \times 3 = 27$ $units^2$

$l = 8$ units, $w = 4$ units

$P_{rectangle} = 2(8 + 4) = 24$ units $A_{rectangle} = 8 \times 4 = 32$ $units^2$

$l = 6$ units, $w = 6$ units

$P_{rectangle} = 2(6 + 6) = 24$ units $A_{rectangle} = 6 \times 6 = 36$ $units^2$

1. The side length of a square is 20 cm. The length and width of a rectangle are 18 cm and 22 cm, respectively. Which of the following statements relating the square and the rectangle is **true**?
   A. The square and the rectangle have equal areas and equal perimeters.
   B. The square and the rectangle have equal areas but different perimeters.
   C. The square and the rectangle have different areas but equal perimeters.
   D. The square and the rectangle have different areas and different perimeters.

2. What is the **maximum** area of a rectangle that can be inscribed in a circle with a radius of 10 cm?
   A. $\sqrt{200}$ cm^2
   B. 100 cm^2
   C. $4\sqrt{200}$ cm^2
   D. 200 cm^2

Copyright Protected

9MG1.02 determine the minimum perimeter of a rectangle with a given area by constructing a variety of rectangles, using a variety of tools and by examining various values of the side lengths and the perimeter as the area stays constant

Determining the Minimum Perimeter of a Rectangle

Rectangles with equal areas can have different perimeters. For example, a rectangle with a length of 12 cm and a width of 3 cm has a larger perimeter (30 cm) than a rectangle with a length of 6 cm and a width of 6 cm(24 cm). They both have an area of 36 cm^2.

The closer that a rectangle gets to becoming a square, the perimeter of the rectangle decreases.

Example

Find the perimeter and area for each of the following rectangles with the given dimensions.

l = 12 units, w = 3 units

$A_{\text{rectangle}} = 12 \times 3 = 36 \text{ units}^2$ $\qquad P_{\text{rectangle}} = 2(12 + 3) = 30 \text{ units}$

l = 9 units, w = 3 units

$A_{\text{rectangle}} = 9 \times 4 = 36 \text{ units}^2$ $\qquad P_{\text{rectangle}} = 2(9 + 4) = 26 \text{ units}$

l = 6 units, w = 6 units

$A_{\text{rectangle}} = 6 \times 6 = 36 \text{ units}^2$ $\qquad P_{\text{rectangle}} = 2(6 + 6) = 24 \text{ units}$

---

3. The area of a rectangle with length l and width w is 120 square units. Which of the following rectangles satisfies the given condition with the **shortest** perimeter?

A. l = 15 units, w = 8 units

B. l = 20 units, w = 6 units

C. l = 10 units, w = 12 units

D. l = 24 units, w = 5 units

4. A rectangular sandbox is fenced in using the existing school's wall as one of its sides. The cost of the material used to construct the fence is \$30 / m. If the area of the sandbox is 200 m^2, then the **minimum** cost of building the fence is

A. \$900 **B.** \$1 200

C. \$3 000 **D.** \$6 000

9MG1.03 identify, through investigation with a variety of tools, the effect of varying the dimensions on the surface area [or volume] of square-based prisms and cylinders, given a fixed volume [or surface area]

Volumes of Rectangular Prisms and Cylinders

Rectangular Prisms

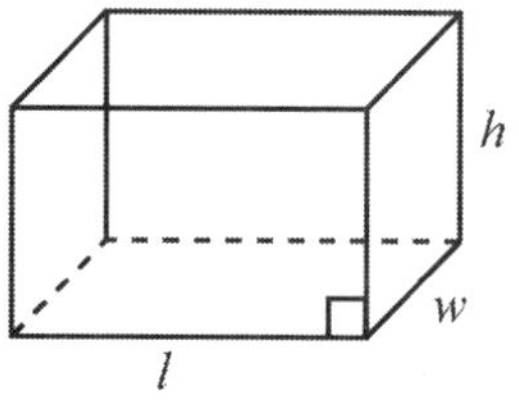

For a rectangular prism with width w, length l, and height h, the following formulas can be used to calculate volume and surface area:

$$V_{\text{rectangular prism}} = (A_{\text{base}})(\text{height}) = lwh$$

$$SA_{\text{rectangular prism}} = 2(wh + lw + lh)$$

Rectangular prisms with equal volumes can have different surface areas. For example, a prism with a length of 8 cm, a width of 4 cm, and a height of 5 cm has the same volume (160 cm^3) as a prism with a length of 10 cm, a width of 2 cm, and a height of 8 cm, but they have two different surface areas.

Minimum surface area for a rectangular prism occurs when the prism is a cube. That is, when all of its side lengths are equal.

Not for Reproduction

Example
Find the surface area and volume for each of the following rectangular prisms with the given dimensions.

$l = 6$ units, $w = 3$ units, $h = 12$ units

$$V_{\text{rectangular prism}} = 6 \times 3 \times 12 = 216 \text{ units}^3$$

$$SA_{\text{rectangular prism}} = 2(3 \times 12 + 6 \times 3 + 6 \times 12) = 252 \text{ units}^2$$

$l = 6$ units, $w = 4$ units, $h = 9$ units

$$V_{\text{rectangular prism}} = 6 \times 4 \times 9 = 216 \text{ units}^3$$

$$SA_{\text{rectangular prism}} = 2(4 \times 9 + 6 \times 4 + 6 \times 9) = 228 \text{ units}^2$$

$l = 6$ units, $w = 6$ units, $h = 6$ units

$$V_{\text{rectangular prism}} = 6 \times 6 \times 6 = 216 \text{ units}^3$$

$$SA_{\text{rectangular prism}} = 2(6 \times 6 + 6 \times 6 + 6 \times 6) = 216 \text{ units}^2$$

As well, rectangular prisms with equal surface areas can have different volumes. Maximum volume for a rectangular prism occurs when the prism is a cube.

Example
Find the surface area and volume for each of the following rectangular prisms with the given dimensions.

$l = 2$ units, $w = 2$ units, $h = 11$ units

$$SA_{\text{rectangular prism}} = 2(2 \times 11 + 2 \times 2 + 2 \times 11) = 96 \text{ units}^2$$

$$V_{\text{rectangular prism}} = 2 \times 2 \times 11 = 44 \text{ units}^3$$

$l = 3$ units, $w = 3$ units, $h = 6.5$ units

$$SA_{\text{rectangular prism}} = 2(3 \times 6.5 + 3 \times 3 + 3 \times 6.5) = 96 \text{ units}^2$$

$$V_{\text{rectangular prism}} = 3 \times 3 \times 6.5 = 58.5 \text{ units}^3$$

$l = 4$ units, $w = 4$units, $h = 4$units

$$SA_{\text{rectangular prism}} = 2(4 \times 4 + 4 \times 4 + 4 \times 4) = 96 \text{ units}^2$$

$$V_{\text{rectangular prism}} = 4 \times 4 \times 4 = 64 \text{ units}^3$$

Cylinders

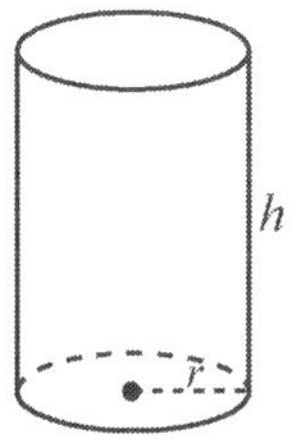

For a cylinder with base radius r and height h, the following formulas can be used to calculate volume and surface area:

$$V_{\text{cylinder}} = (A_{\text{base}})(\text{height}) = (\pi r^2)h$$

$$SA_{\text{cylinder}} = A_{\text{lateral surface}} + A_{\text{bases}} = 2\pi rh + 2\pi r^2$$

Cylinders with equal volumes can have different surface areas. Minimum surface area occurs when the cylinder has a base diameter that is equal to its height.

Example

Find the volume and surface area for each of the following cylinders with the given dimensions.

$d = 3$ units, $h = 13.9$ units

$$V_{\text{cylinder}} = (\pi 1.5^2)13.9$$
$$= 98 \text{ units}^3$$
$$SA_{\text{cylinder}} = 2\pi 1.5 \times 13.9 + 2\pi 1.5^2$$
$$= 145 \text{ units}^2$$

$d = 4$ units, $h = 7.8$ units

$$V_{\text{cylinder}} = (\pi 2^2)7.8$$
$$= 98 \text{ units}^3$$
$$SA_{\text{cylinder}} = 2\pi 2 \times 7.8 + 2\pi 2^2$$
$$= 123 \text{ units}^2$$

$d = 5$ units, $h = 5$ units

$$V_{\text{cylinder}} = (\pi 2.5^2)5$$
$$= 98 \text{ units}^3$$
$$SA_{\text{cylinder}} = 2\pi 2.5 \times 5 + 2\pi 2.5^2$$
$$= 118 \text{ units}^2$$

Cylinders with equal surface areas can have different volumes. Maximum volume occurs when the cylinder has a base diameter that is equal to its height.

Example

Find the volume and surface area for each of the following cylinders with the given dimensions.

$d = 3$ units, $h = 11$ units

$$SA_{\text{cylinder}} = 2\pi 1.5 \times 11 + 2\pi 1.5^2$$
$$= 118 \text{units}^2$$
$$V_{cylinder} = (\pi 1.5^2)11$$
$$= 78 \text{ units}^3$$

$d = 4$ units, $h = 7.35$ units

$$SA_{\text{cylinder}} = 2\pi 2 \times 7.35 + 2\pi 2^2$$
$$= 117 \text{ units}^2$$
$$V_{\text{cylinder}} = (\pi 2^2)7.35$$
$$= 92 \text{ units}^3$$

$d = 5$ units, $h = 5$ units

$$SA_{\text{cylinder}} = 2\pi 2.5 \times 5 + 2\pi 2.5^2$$
$$= 118 \text{ units}^2$$
$$V_{\text{cylinder}} = (\pi 2.5^2)5$$
$$= 98 \text{ units}^3$$

---

5. The manager of a theatre is deciding between two containers to sell peanuts in. One is a rectangular prism with a length of 10 cm, a width of π cm, and a height of 16 cm. The other is a cylinder with a base radius of 4 cm and a height of 10 cm. Both have an open top. Which of the following statements relating the volume and the surface area of the containers is **true**?

A. They have the same surface area and the same volume.

B. They have different surface areas and different volumes.

C. They have equal volumes and the surface area of the prism is greater than the surface area of the cylinder.

D. They have equal volumes and the surface area of the prism is less than the surface area of the cylinder.

Not for Reproduction

6. The volume of a cylinder is 1200π cubic units. The radius is 10 units. If the radius is increased by 40%, the ratio of the new surface area to the original surface area is
   A. 88:52 **B.** 89:53
   C. 90:54 **D.** 91:55

9MG1.04 explain the significance of optimal area, surface area, or volume in various applications

Explaining Optimal Area and Volume

Optimal area and perimeter are important concepts to understand when you come across problems that require the application of area and perimeter formulas to realistic situations.

Example

In what shape would you need to make an enclosed garden to minimize the amount of fencing required while maximizing the amount of area enclosed?

The maximum area and minimum perimeter for a rectangle occurs when the rectangle is a square. Thus, if you were planting an enclosed garden, you would make it in the shape of a square so that you would have the largest garden using the minimum amount of fencing.

Knowing the optimal surface area and volume is helpful when working on a problem involving the cost of packaging.

Example

A company that makes cereal wants to minimize the cost of containers for their product. What shape would the box or cylinder need to be to minimize the packaging while maximizing the volume it will contain?

The maximum volume and minimum surface area for a prism occurs when the prism is a cube. Thus, when creating the packaging, you would make it in the shape of a cube to minimize the required materials and hence, the cost. If the same product were packaged in a cylinder, you would make the diameter of the cylinder the same as the height to minimize the packaging while maximizing the volume.

---

7. If the surface area of a rectangular prism is 294 cm^2, what is the **maximum** possible volume that the prism can have?
   A. 96 cm^3 **B.** 256 cm^3
   C. 294 cm^3 **D.** 343 cm^3

8. What is the change in the lateral surface area of a cone if its radius is halved and its slant height is doubled?
   A. The lateral surface area becomes twice as large.
   B. The lateral surface area becomes 4 times as large.
   C. The lateral surface area becomes 6 times smaller.
   D. There would be no change in the lateral surface area.

9MG1.05 pose and solve problems involving maximization and minimization of measurements of geometric shapes and figures

Solving Problems Involving Maximum and Minimum Perimeter and Area

To solve a problem involving maximization or minimization, apply the principles covered in the previous four lessons regarding maximum and minimum perimeter, area, and volume.

Example

Mr. Johnson purchased 42 m of building material to create the boundary wall for his daughter's rectangular sandbox. He first created an outline of the sandbox on the ground using a 42 m piece of string. What are the dimensions of the sandbox if it is to have a maximum area?

Maximum area occurs when the rectangle is a square.

$$w = l = \frac{P}{4} = \frac{42 \text{ m}}{4} = 10.5 \text{ m}$$

Copyright Protected

9. A circular piece of paper has an area of 154 cm^2. What is the area of the largest square that can be cut out of this circle?

A. 100 cm^2 **B.** 98 cm^2

C. 91 cm^2 **D.** 84 cm^2

10. Bob bought a 1-L bag of candies. Which of the following containers holds all of Bob's candies?

A. Cylinder with a diameter of 14 cm and height of 6 cm

B. Cylinder with a diameter of 14 cm and height of 7 cm

C. Rectangular prism with the dimensions 5 cm by 10 cm by 19 cm

D. Rectangular prism with the dimensions 7 cm by 7 cm by 20 cm

9MG2.01 relate the geometric representation of the Pythagorean theorem and the algebraic representation $a^2 + b^2 = c^2$

Pythagoras' Theorem

Pythagoras' theorem states that in a **right triangle**, the area of the square created by the length of the **hypotenuse** (the longest side of the triangle) is equal to the sum of areas of the squares created by the lengths of the two shorter sides.

$A_{\text{Square 3}} = A_{\text{Square 1}} + A_{\text{Square 2}}$

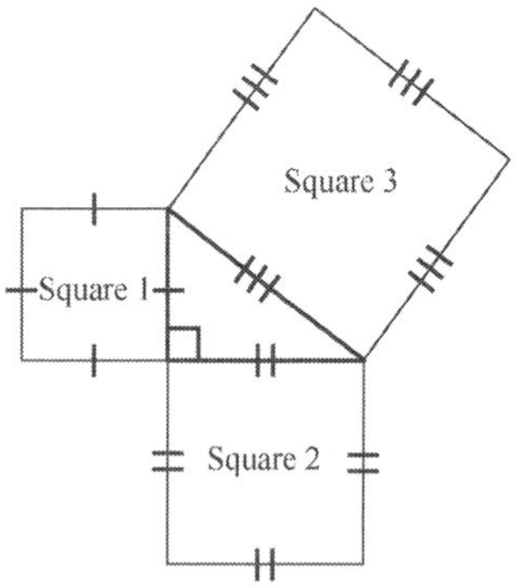

That is, the square of the hypotenuse length (c) equals the sum of the squares of the two shorter side lengths (a and b).

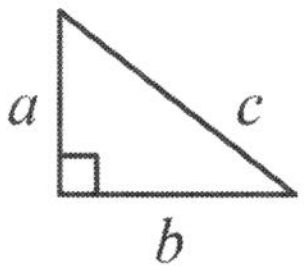

The Pythagorean theorem is written as $c^2 = a^2 + b^2$ or $a^2 + b^2 = c^2$.

Use the following information to answer the next question.

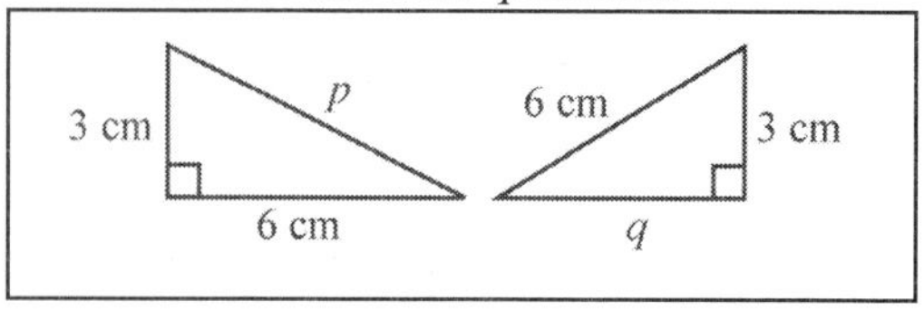

11. What is the value of the expression $p + q$?

A. $\sqrt{3^2 + 6^2} + \sqrt{6^2 + 3^2}$

B. $\sqrt{3^2 + 6^2 + 6^2 + 3^2}$

C. $\sqrt{3^2 + 6^2} + \sqrt{6^2 - 3^2}$

D. $\sqrt{3^2 + 6^2 + 6^2 - 3^2}$

Use the following information to answer the next question.

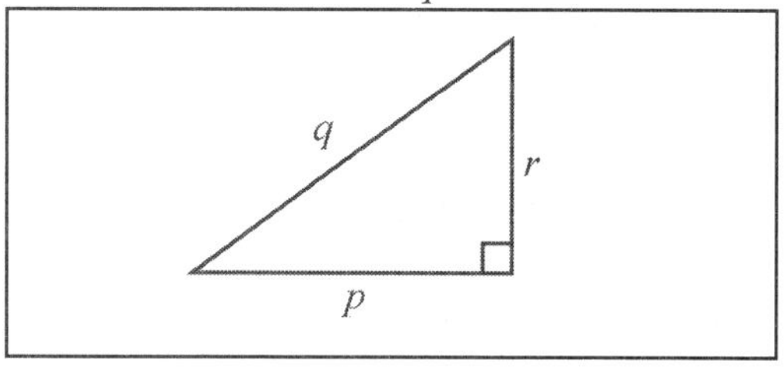

12. The equation that represents the relationship between p, q, and r is

A. $p + r = q$

B. $p + q = r$

C. $p^2 + r^2 = q^2$

D. $p^2 + q^2 = r^2$

9MG2.02 solve problems using the Pythagorean theorem, as required in applications

Solving Problems Using the Pythagorean Theorem

The Pythagorean theorem is used to find the measure of a missing side length when the measures of the other two sides are known. It is only used for right triangles.

In the theorem, $(a^2 + b^2 = c^2)$, c is the hypotenuse. If you are looking for the length of the hypotenuse, you substitute the given values of a and b, then solve for c.

Not for Reproduction

Example
Find the length of c.

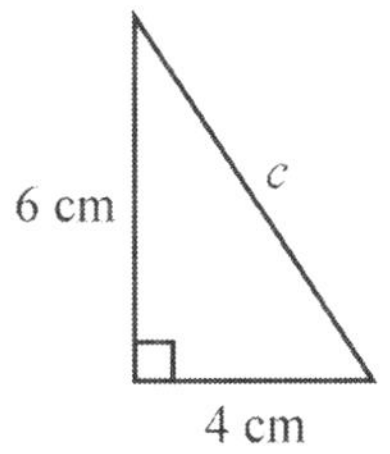

Let $a = 6$ cm and $b = 4$ cm.

$$\begin{aligned} c^2 &= a^2 + b^2 \\ &= 6^2 + 4^2 \\ &= 36 + 16 \\ c^2 &= 52 \\ c &= \sqrt{52} \\ &\approx 7.21 \text{ cm} \end{aligned}$$

If you are looking for one of the shorter sides, the theorem is manipulated to either $c^2 - a^2 = b^2$ or $c^2 - b^2 = a^2$.

Note that the negative square root of 52 is discarded because you cannot have a negative side length.

Example
Find the length of b if $a = 6$ cm and $c = 9$ cm.

$$\begin{aligned} c^2 - a^2 &= b^2 \\ 9^2 - 6^2 &= b^2 \\ 81 - 36 &= b^2 \\ 45 &= b^2 \\ \sqrt{45} &= \sqrt{b^2} \\ 6.71 \text{ cm} &\approx b \end{aligned}$$

Again, the negative square root of 45 is discarded.

---

13. City Q is 100 km due east from city P, and city R is 75 km due north from city P. City S lies on a straight road joining cities Q and R. City S forms the vertex of a right angle between cities P and Q. How far is city S from city P?

A. 30 km **B.** 40 km
C. 50 km **D.** 60 km

14. A ladder is resting against a wall. The bottom of the ladder is 8 m from the wall, and the top of the ladder rests against it at a height of 6 m above the ground. The length of the ladder is

A. 6 m **B.** 8 m
C. 10 m **D.** 12 m

Use the following information to answer the next question.

Mark stands at the top of a cliff. From the edge of the cliff, he can see his base camp in the valley below. Mark calculates that the diagonal distance from the edge of the cliff to his camp is 900 m, and that his position is 61 m above the ground.

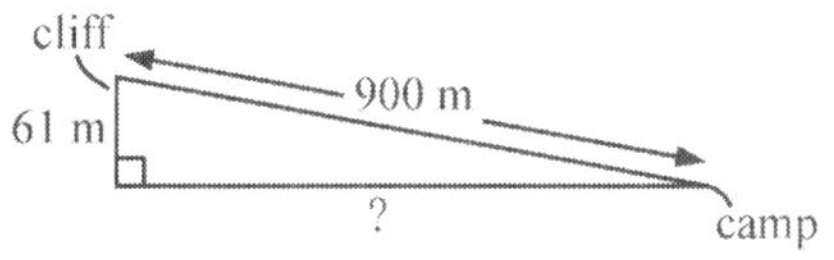

Open Response

15. Mark climbs straight down from the cliff using a rope ladder that forms a right angle with the ground. What is the distance that he must now travel to get to camp?

Show your work.

Copyright Protected

9MG2.03 solve problems involving the areas and perimeters of composite two-dimensional shapes

Solving Problems with Composite Shapes

Composite figures are made up of two or more shapes. Breaking down composite figures into their smaller shapes makes it easier to solve perimeter and area problems. For example, the area of the figure below is solved by finding the areas of the three smaller shapes that compose it: a semicircle, a rectangle, and a right triangle.

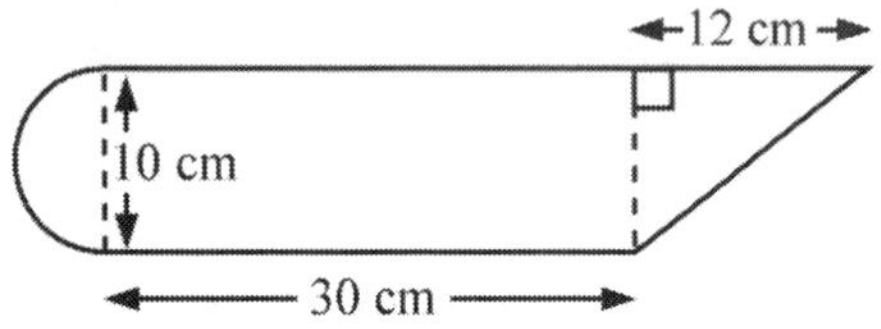

$A_{total} = A_{semicircle} + A_{rectangle} + A_{triangle}$

$= \frac{\pi r^2}{2} + lw + \frac{1}{2}bh$

Calculating the perimeter also involves looking at these three component shapes. To determine the perimeter, first find the length of the unknown side of the right triangle using Pythagoras' theorem.

$P_{total} = C_{semicircle} + 2l_{rectangle}$
$+ \text{side } 1_{triangle} + \text{side } 2_{triangle}$

Use the following information to answer the next question.

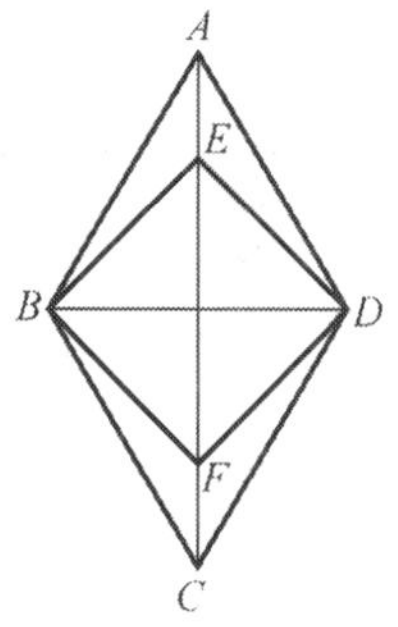

A square flowerbed is constructed inside a rhombus-shaped park. One of the diagonals of the square is the shorter diagonal of the rhombus (*BD*). The portion of the park outside the flowerbed has to be covered with grass. The cost of planting grass is $\$0.20/\text{m}^2$.

16. If the lengths of the park's two diagonals are 30 m and 60 m, then what is the cost of planting grass in the area outside of the flowerbed?

A. \$45 **B.** \$90
C. \$135 **D.** \$180

Use the following information to answer the next question.

Nathan had a piece of wire in the shape of a square with a side length of 5.6 cm. He bent the wire into a circle.

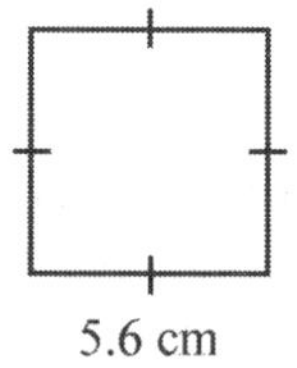

17. If $\pi = 3.14$, what is the area of the circle formed by the wire? Round all intermediate values and final answer to two decimal places.

A. 36.6 cm^2 **B.** 37.6 cm^2
C. 39.9 cm^2 **D.** 40.2 cm^2

Not for Reproduction

9MG2.04 develop, through investigation, the formulas for the volume of a pyramid, a cone, and a sphere

Volumes of 3-D Shapes

Square Pyramid

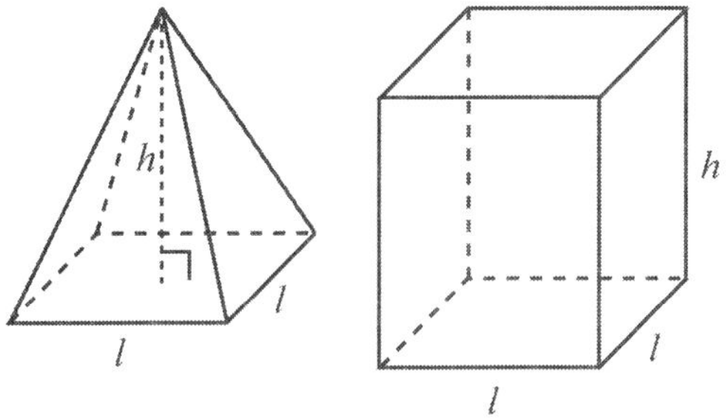

The volume of a square **pyramid** is one-third the volume of a rectangular prism with the same dimensions. The formula for the volume of a square pyramid is the same as that of a rectangular prism with the exception that it is divided by 3.

$$V_{\text{rectangular prism}} = (A_{\text{base}})(\text{height})$$
$$= (l^2)h$$
$$V_{\text{square pyramid}} = \frac{(A_{\text{base}})(\text{height})}{3}$$
$$= \frac{(l^2h)}{3}$$

Cone

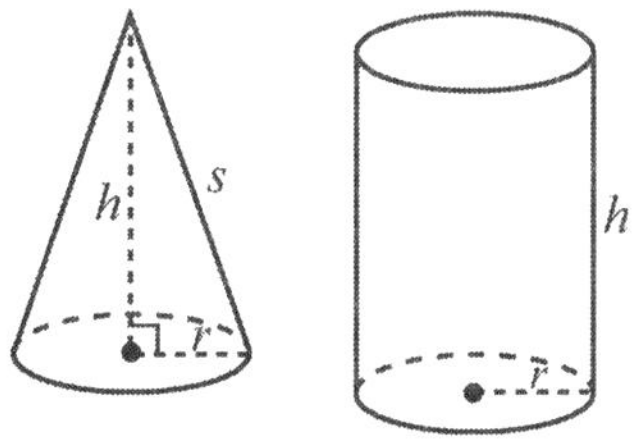

The volume of a **cone** is one-third the volume of a cylinder with the same dimensions. The formula is the same as a cylinder except that it is divided by 3.

$$V_{\text{cylinder}} = (A_{\text{base}})(\text{height})$$
$$= (\pi r^2)h$$
$$V_{\text{cone}} = \frac{(A_{\text{base}})(\text{height})}{3}$$
$$= \frac{(\pi r^2)h}{3}$$

Sphere

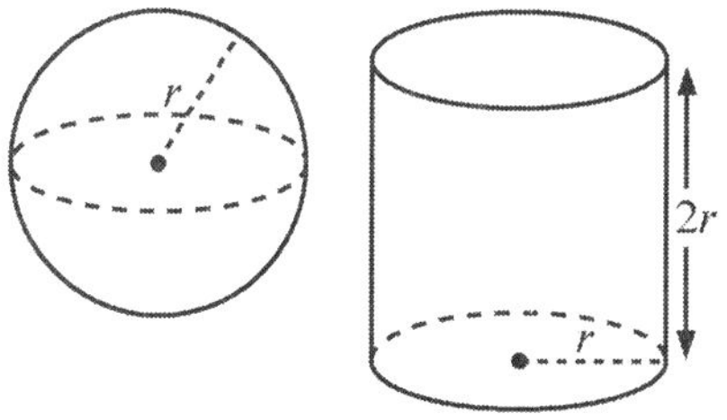

A **sphere**'s volume is two-thirds the volume of a cylinder with the same dimensions. The formula is derived from the formula for the volume of a cylinder:

$$V_{\text{cylinder}} = (A_{\text{base}})(\text{height})$$
$$= (\pi r^2)h$$
$$V_{\text{sphere}} = \frac{2}{3}\left(A_{\text{base}}\right)\left(\text{height}\right)$$
$$V_{\text{sphere}} = \frac{2}{3}\left(\pi r^2\right)\left(2r\right)$$
$$V_{\text{sphere}} = \frac{2 \times 2\pi r^3}{3}$$
$$V_{\text{sphere}} = \frac{4\pi r^3}{3}$$

18. What is the height of a rectangular prism whose base area and volume are equal to those of a square pyramid with a base area of y cm^2 and a height of x cm?

A. $\frac{1}{3}x$ cm **B.** $\frac{1}{3}xy$ cm

C. $3x$ cm **D.** $3xy$ cm

19. The diameters of a cylinder and a cone are both 20 cm. The height of the cone is $\frac{1}{3}$ the height of the cylinder. What is the ratio of the volume of the cylinder to the volume of the cone?

A. 1:1 **B.** 3:1

C. 6:1 **D.** 9:1

9MG2.05 determine, through investigation, the relationship for calculating the surface area of a pyramid

Surface Area of a Pyramid

When a pyramid is opened up and laid flat, its net reveals four **lateral faces**, all of which are triangles, and one **base** of a square or rectangle.

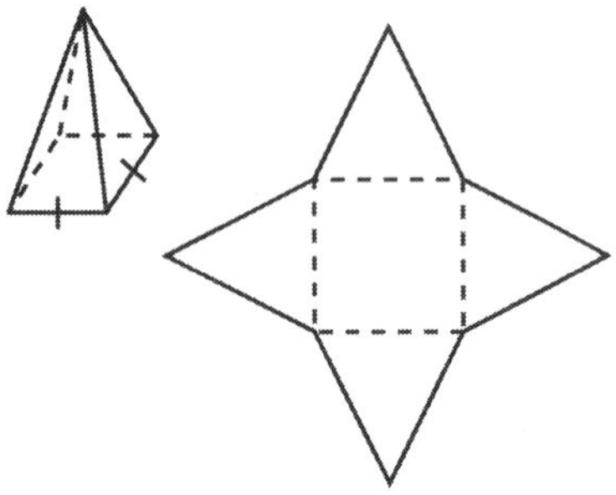

The **slant height** (s) is the height of the pyramid's triangular face.

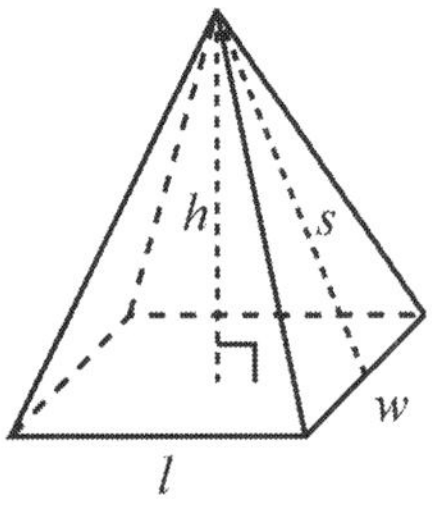

To calculate the surface area of a pyramid, add the areas of the base (lw) and the four lateral faces $\left(\frac{bs}{2}\right)$. Since there are four triangular faces, multiply the area of one triangle by 4. Remember to use s and not h for the height of the face.

$$SA_{\text{pyramid}} = A_{\text{base}} + 4A_{\text{triangle}}$$

$$SA_{\text{pyramid}} = lw + 4\left(\frac{bs}{2}\right)$$

Use the following information to answer the next question.

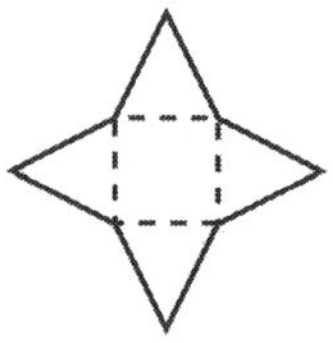

20. Which of the following figures correctly represents the three-dimensional model of the given net?

A. 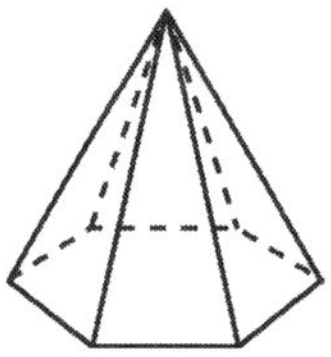

B. 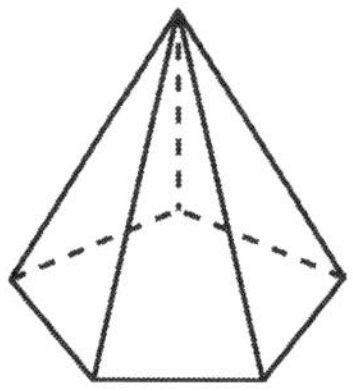

C. 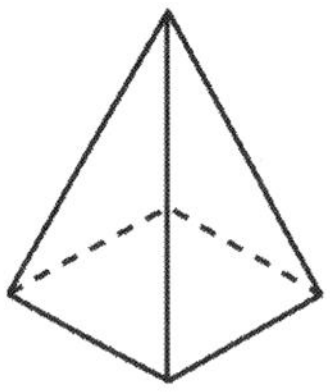

D. 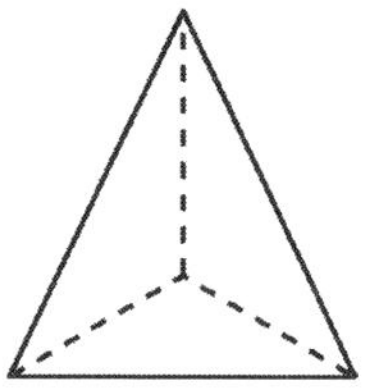

Use the following information to answer the next question.

Ivy creates a triangular pyramid out of this paper net.

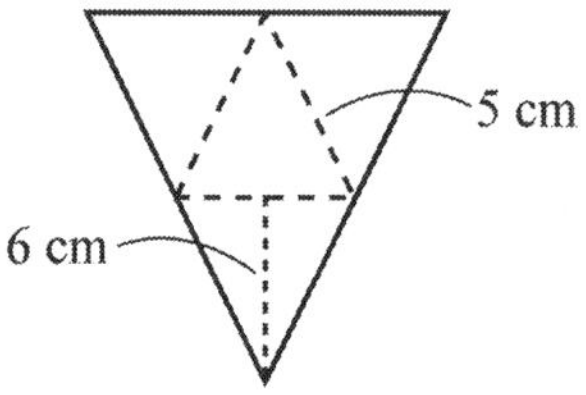

21. What is the lateral surface area of the triangular pyramid?

A. 45 cm^2 **B.** 51 cm^2

C. 52 cm^2 **D.** 104 cm^2

Not for Reproduction

9MG2.06 solve problems involving the surface areas and volumes of prisms, pyramids, cylinders, cones, and spheres, including composite figures

Solving Problems Involving 3-D Composite Shapes

You can solve problems involving the surface area or volume of 3-D composite shapes by breaking down the shapes into smaller, recognizable components. Calculate each of the unknown measurements. Add or subtract the smaller components to determine the required measurement.

Example

A rectangular piece of solid metal has a hole drilled through it in the shape of a cylinder. Calculate the volume of metal remaining.

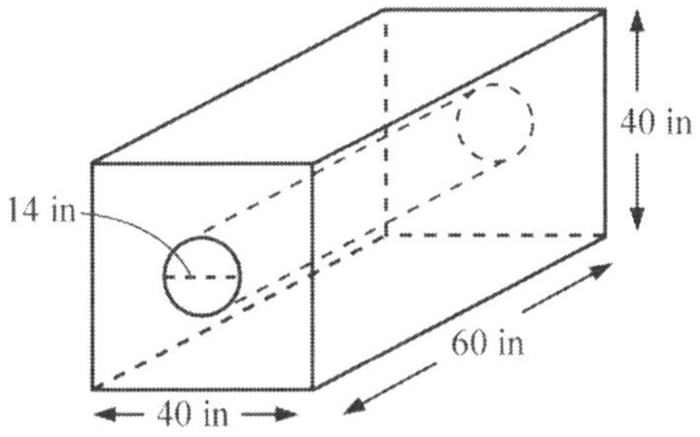

$V_{\text{square prism}} - V_{\text{cylinder}}$

$= s^2h - \pi r^2 h$

$= (40^2 \times 60) - (3.14 \times 7^2 \times 60)$

$= (1600 \times 60) - (3.14 \times 49 \times 60)$

$= 960 - 9231.6$

$= 86\ 768.4\ \text{cm}^3$

Use the following information to answer the next question.

The front cylindrical roller of a road roller has a diameter of 1.75 m and a length of 1.5 m. It has to compact an area of 3 300 m^2.

22. How many complete revolutions must the front roller make to compact the given area?

A. 320 **B.** 329

C. 350 **D.** 401

Use the following information to answer the next question.

This toy has a hemispherical base and a conical top. The perpendicular height of the right cone is 14 cm, and the radius of the hemisphere is 7 cm.

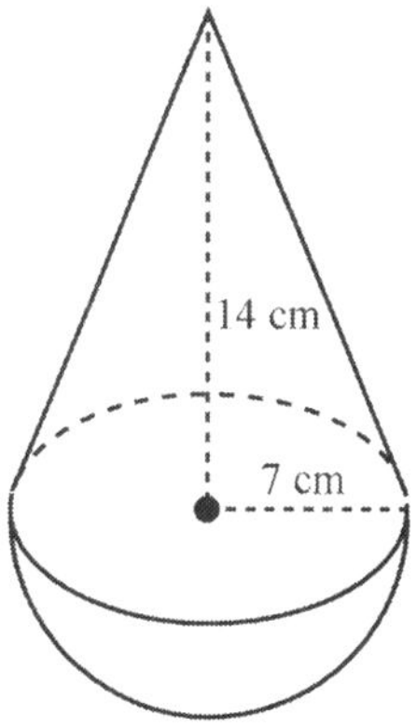

23. What is the approximate volume of the toy, to the nearest whole cubic centimetre?

A. 1 437 cm^3 **B.** 1 337 cm^3

C. 1 117 cm^3 **D.** 1 028 cm^3

9MG3.01 determine, through investigation using a variety of tools and describe the properties and relationships of the interior and exterior angles of triangles, quadrilaterals, and other polygons, and apply the results to problems involving the angles of polygons

Determining the Properties of Interior and Exterior Angles

Triangles

The sum of the measures of all the **interior angles** of any triangle always equals 180°.

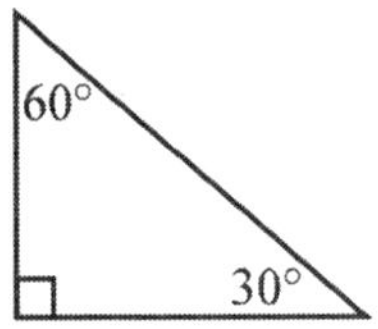

60° + 30° + 90° = 180°

The sum of an interior angle and its **adjacent exterior angle** is always 180°. When two angles make a straight line (180°) they are called **supplementary angles**.

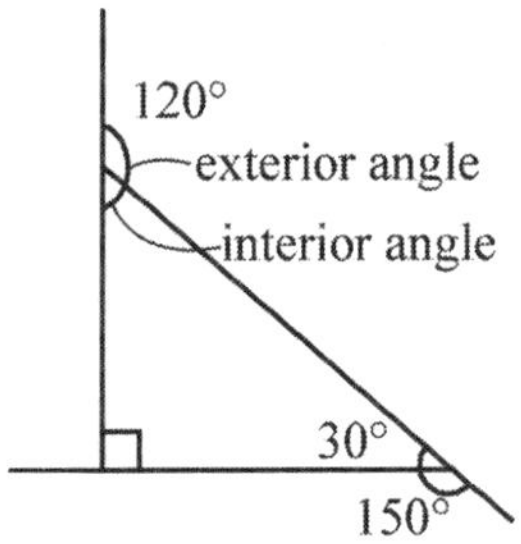

120° + 60° = 180°

30° + 150° = 180°

90° + 90° = 180°

The sum of the measures of all the exterior angles of any triangle always equals 360°.
120° + 150° + 90° = 360°

Quadrilaterals

Divide a **quadrilateral** in half by drawing a line from a corner to its diagonally opposite corner.

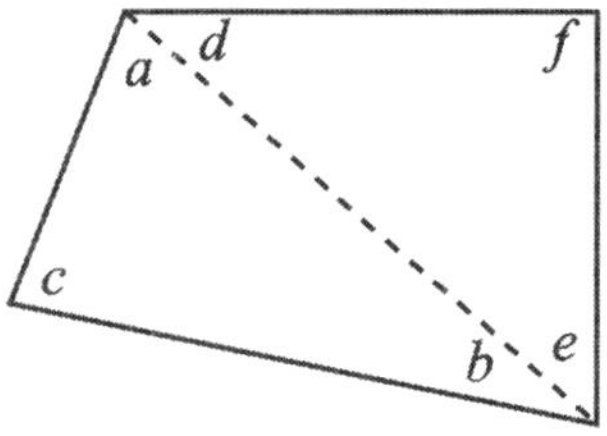

The quadrilateral is now two triangles. The sum of all the angles in a triangle is 180°. It follows that the sum of two triangles together (a quadrilateral) is 360°.

The sum of an interior angle and its adjacent exterior angle equals 180°, and the sum of the exterior angles equals 360°.

Polygons

The sum, S, of the interior angles for a **polygon** with n number of sides can be calculated using the formula $S_{\text{interior angles}} = 180(n - 2)$. The sum of a polygon's exterior angles is 360°.

Example
What is the sum of the angles in this polygon?

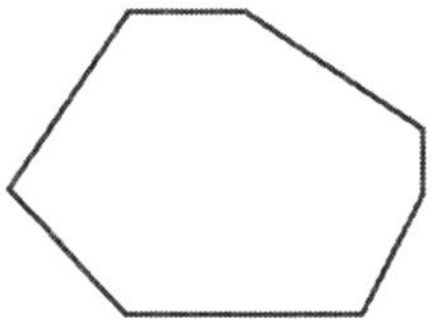

$$
\begin{aligned}
S_{\text{interior angles}} &= 180°(n-2)\\
&= 180°(7-2)\\
&= 180°(5)\\
&= 900°
\end{aligned}
$$

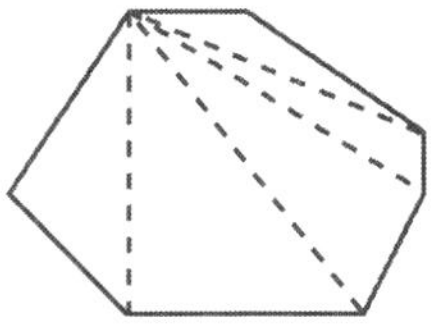

The 5 in the equation represents the 5 triangles within the heptagon.

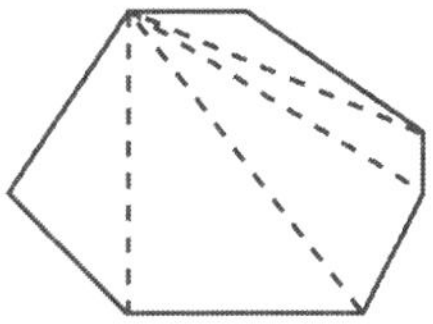

PARALLELOGRAMS

Opposite angles in parallelograms are equal. Adjacent angles within a parallelogram are supplementary.

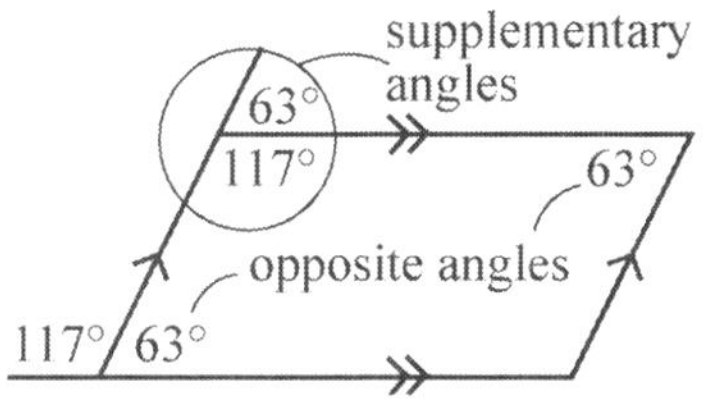

24. If the sum of the internal angles of a polygon is 6 times the sum of its external angles, then how many sides does the polygon have?

A. 8 **B.** 10

C. 12 **D.** 14

Use the following information to answer the next question.

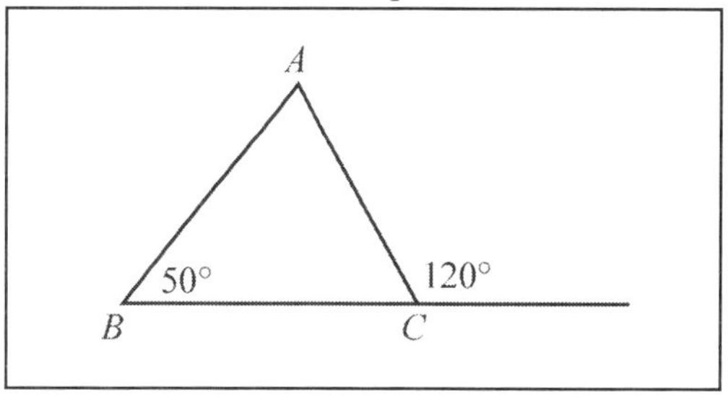

25. What is the measure of $\angle A$?

A. 50° **B.** 70°

C. 90° **D.** 110°

Use the following information to answer the next question.

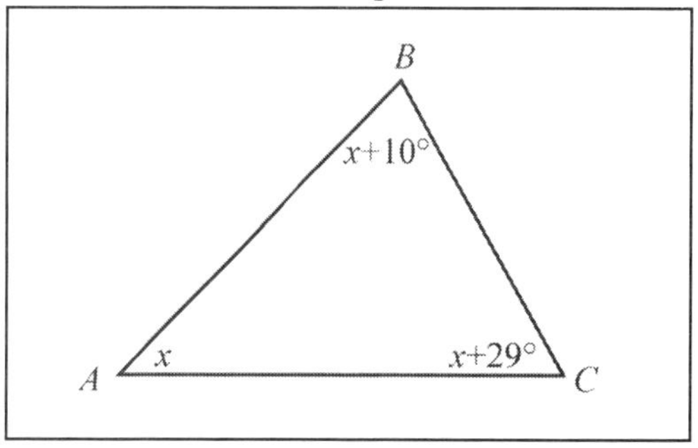

Open Response

26. What is the measure of each of the given angles?

Show your work. Verify that your angles are plausible.

Copyright Protected

9MG3.02 determine, through investigation using a variety of tools and describe some properties of polygons, and apply the results in problem solving

Solving Problems Involving Polygons

When solving problems involving polygons you may be asked to determine an unknown angle. To solve such problems, use the given information and what you know about the properties of and relationships between angles.

Example

A hexagon has two angles that are equal. The sum of these angles is 240°. If the remaining angles are also equal, what is their measure?

Given information: 6-sided figure, sum of two congruent angles is 240°

Known properties of angles:
Use the formula $S = 180°(n - 2)$ to calculate the sum of the interior angle measures.

$S = 180°(6 - 2)$
$= 180°(4)$
$= 720°$

Subtract the known angle measures from this sum to determine the remaining angle measures.
$720° - 240° = 480°$

Divide 480° by 4 to calculate the measure of each remaining angle.
$480° \div 4 = 120°$

Check your work by adding all the angles together to verify they add up to 720°.
$120° + 120° + 120° + 120° + 120° + 120° = 720°$

As all of the angles are equal, this shape is a regular hexagon.

Use the following information to answer the next question.

To solve a problem, John needs to find the sum of the interior angles in the given polygon.

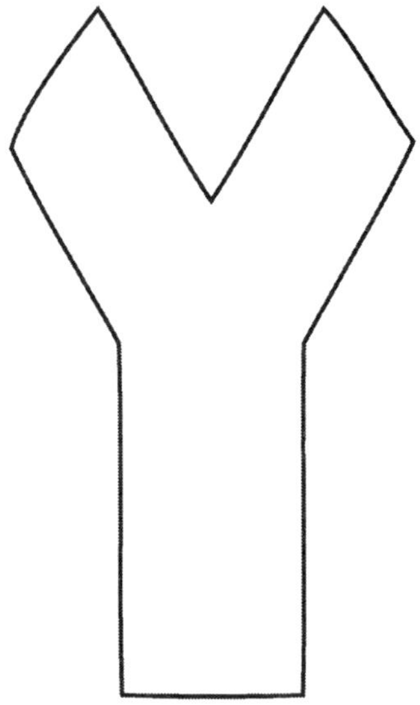

27. The sum of the interior angles in this polygon is

A. 540° **B.** 1 260°

C. 1 440° **D.** 1 620°

28. The ratio of the three interior angles of a triangle is 6:6:8. What is one of the angle measures?

A. 9° **B.** 27°

C. 30° **D.** 54°

Not for Reproduction

9MG3.03 pose questions about geometric relationships, investigate them, and present their findings, using a variety of mathematical forms

Investigating Geometric Relationships

Midpoints and Medians of Triangles

A line segment drawn at the **midpoint** of the two sides of a triangle is half the length and parallel to the base of the triangle.

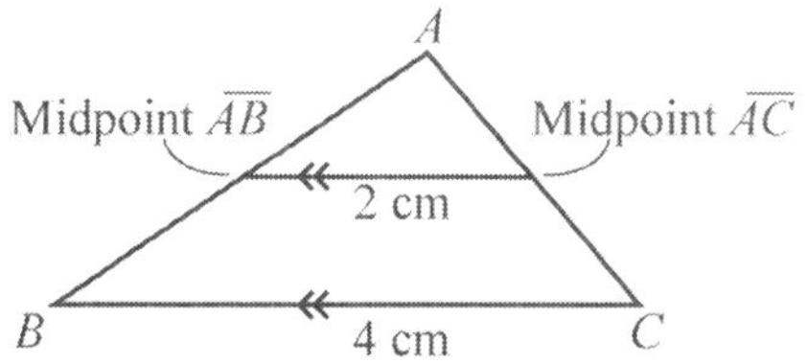

The height of the smaller triangle created on the top is half the height of the original triangle.

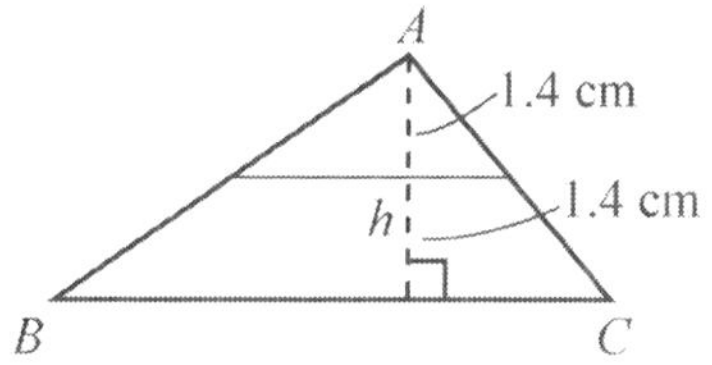

The **median**, a **line segment** joining the **vertex** of a triangle to the midpoint of the opposite side, cuts the area of the triangle in half.

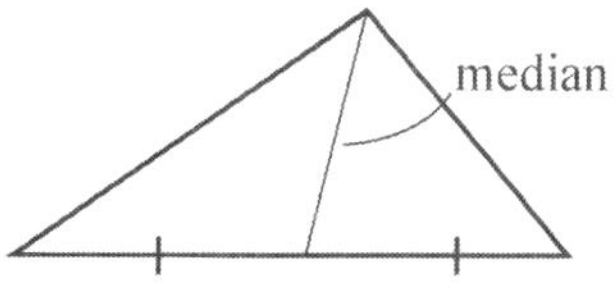

Midpoints and Diagonals of Quadrilaterals

Connecting the midpoints of the adjacent sides of a quadrilateral creates a parallelogram inside the shape.

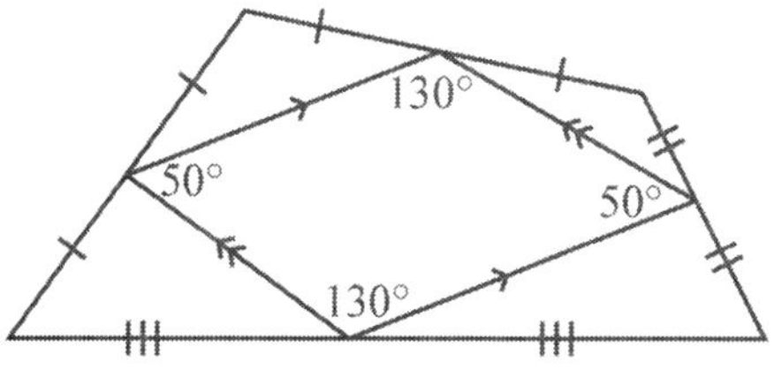

The diagonal lines connecting the two opposite vertices of a parallelogram **bisect** each other.

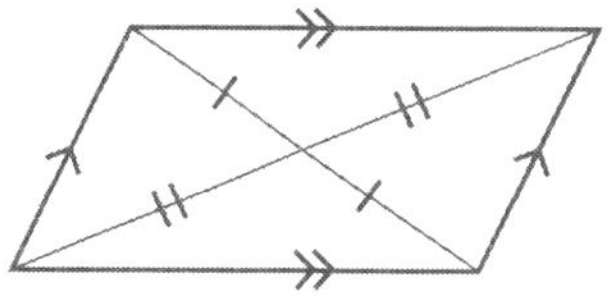

29. A possible length of side AF is

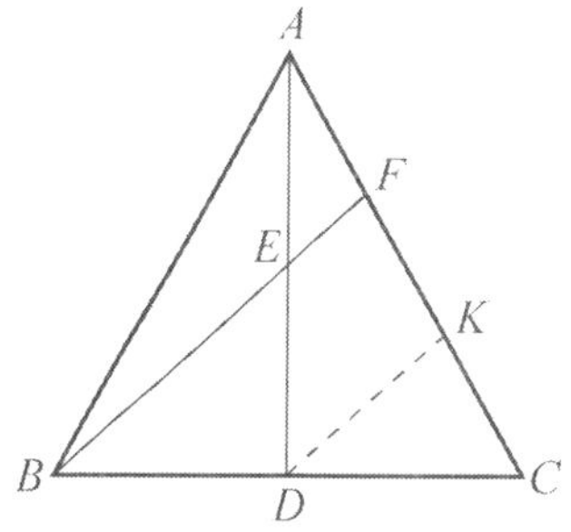

A. 6 units **B.** 8 units
C. 10 units **D.** 11 units

30. Mary has a quadrilateral-shaped garden, all the sides of which are of different lengths. She joined the midpoints of the four sides of the garden and planted bushes in the area enclosed by the lines. The area in which she planted bushes is in the shape of a

A. square **B.** rhombus
C. trapezoid **D.** parallelogram

Copyright Protected

9MG3.04 illustrate a statement about a geometric property by demonstrating the statement with multiple examples, or deny the statement on the basis of a counter-example, with or without the use of dynamic geometry software

ILLUSTRATING GEOMETRIC PROPERTIES

Geometric properties can be proven using counter examples. This means trying to find an example that disproves the property, but in fact demonstrates that the property is true.

Example

Prove that the sum of the measures of all the interior angles of any triangle always equals 180°.

Draw a number of different triangles. Measure the angles. No matter how you draw a triangle, the sum is always 180°.

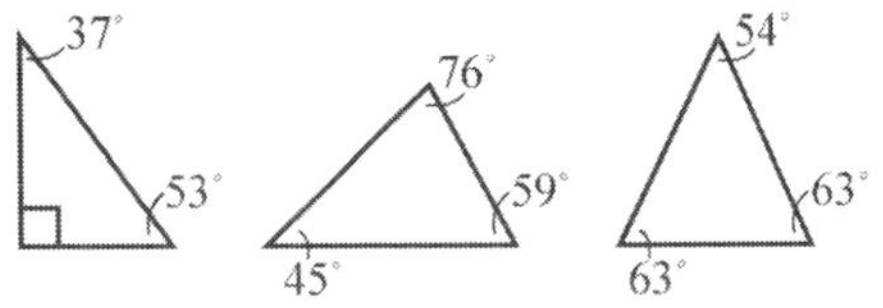

Counter examples can also be used to deny a property. This means finding an example that proves that the property is *not* always true.

Example

Look at the diagram below. Do all medians cut right triangles exactly in half?

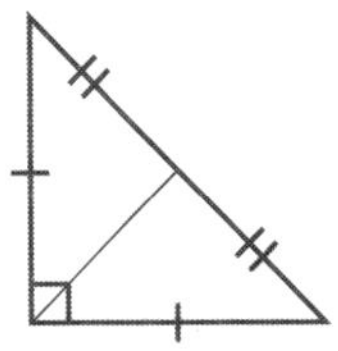

Draw another right triangle with different dimensions to see if this conjecture is true.

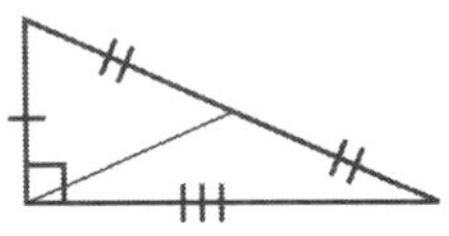

In this triangle, there are three different lengths that prove that medians of right triangles do not always cut a right triangle in half.

Use the following information to answer the next question.

A quadrilateral-shaped field is such that its diagonals are each 10 m long. The diagonals bisect each other at right angles. The quadrilateral is a ___*i*___ and its area is ___*ii*___ m^2.

31. Which of the following rows completes the given statement?

A.

i	*ii*
trapezoid	50

B.

i	*ii*
rectangle	100

C.

i	*ii*
parallelogram	100

D.

i	*ii*
square	50

32. In which of the following types of quadrilaterals do the diagonals **not** bisect each other?

A. Square
B. Rectangle
C. Trapezoid
D. Parallelogram

Not for Reproduction

ANSWERS AND SOLUTIONS
MEASUREMENT AND GEOMETRY

1. C	8. D	15. OR	22. D	29. A
2. D	9. B	16. B	23. A	30. D
3. C	10. B	17. C	24. D	31. D
4. B	11. C	18. A	25. B	32. C
5. D	12. C	19. D	26. OR	
6. D	13. D	20. C	27. B	
7. D	14. C	21. A	28. D	

1. C

$A_{\text{square}} = s^2 = 20^2 = 400\text{ cm}^2$

$A_{\text{rectangle}} = lw = 18 \times 22 = 396\text{ cm}^2$

$P_{\text{square}} = 4s = 4 \times 20 = 80\text{ cm}$

$P_{\text{rectangle}} = 2(l + w) = 2(18 + 22) = 80\text{ cm}$

Thus, the square and the rectangle have different areas but equal perimeters.

2. D

The rectangle assumes its maximum area when it is a square.

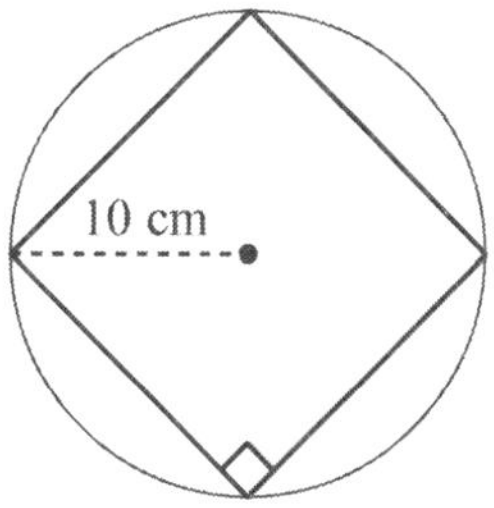

Since the radius of the circle is 10 cm, its diameter is 20 cm, and the diagonal length of the square is 20 cm.

Use the Pythagorean theorem.

$a^2 + b^2 = c^2$

$x^2 + x^2 = 20^2$

$2x^2 = 400$

$x^2 = 200$

$A_{\text{square}} = s^2 = x \times x = x^2$

$x^2 = 200$

The maximum area of the inscribed rectangle is 200 cm^2.

3. C

Alternative A:

Area $= lw$ $= 15 \times 8$ $= 120$ square units

Perimeter $= 2(l+w)$ $= 2(15 + 8)$ $= 2 \times 23$ $= 46$ units

Alternative B:

Area $= lw$ $= 20 \times 6$ $= 120$ square units

Perimeter $= 2(l+w)$ $= 2(20 + 6)$ $= 2 \times 26$ $= 52$ units

Alternative C:

Area $= lw$ $= 10 \times 12$ $= 120$ square units

Perimeter $= 2(l+w)$ $= 2(10 + 12)$ $= 2 \times 22$ $= 44$ units

Alternative D:

Area $= lw$ $= 24 \times 5$ $= 120$ square units

Perimeter $= 2(l+w)$ $= 2(24 + 5)$ $= 2 \times 29$ $= 58$ units

The rectangle with a length of 10 units and a width of 12 units gives the shortest perimeter of 44 units.

4. B

A rectangle created with three lengths of fencing assumes its minimum perimeter when its length is twice its width.

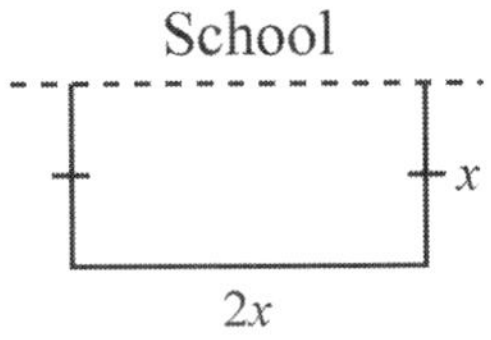

The area is 200 m^2.

$A = lw$

$A = (2x)(x)$

$2x^2 = 200$

$x^2 = 100$

$x = \sqrt{100}$

$x = 10$

Perimeter $= 2w + l$

Perimeter $= (2x + 2x)$

Perimeter $= x + 2x + x = 4x$

When $x = 10$ m:
$P = 4(10)$

$P = 40$ m
Since 40 m is the minimum perimeter of the rectangle and the fencing material costs \$30 / m, the minimum cost of building the fence is (40)(30) = \$1200.

5. D

$V_{prism} = lwh$

$V_{prism} = 10 \times \pi \times 16$

$= 160\pi \text{ cm}^3$

$V_{cylinder} = \pi r^2 h$

$= \pi(4^2) \times 10$

$= 160\pi \text{ cm}^3$

The containers have the same volume. The containers have an open end.

$$\begin{aligned} SA_{prism} &= 2(wh + lw) + wh \\ &= 2(16\pi + 160) + 10\pi \\ &= 32\pi + 320 + 10\pi \\ &= 42\pi + 320 \\ &= 131.95 + 320 \\ &= 451.95cm \end{aligned}$$

$$\begin{aligned} SA_{cylinder} &= \pi r^2 + 2\pi rh \\ &= \pi 4^2 + 2\pi 4 \times 10 \\ &= 16\pi + 80\pi \\ &= 96\pi \\ &= 301.59 \end{aligned}$$

The surface area of the cylinder is greater than the surface area of the prism.

The statement in alternative D is true.

6. D

$V_{cylinder} = 1\ 200\pi \text{ units}^3$
Radius, $r = 10$ units

$\pi r^2 h = 1200\pi$

$10^2 h = 1\ 200$

$h = 1\ 200 \div 100 = 12$ units

$SA_{cylinder} = 2\pi rh + 2\pi r^2 = 2\pi r(h + r)$

$= 2\pi 10(10 + 12)$

$= 20\pi \times 22$

$= 440\pi \text{ units}^2$

New radius $= 10 + \left(\frac{40}{100} \times 10\right) = 10 + 4 = 14$ units

New surface area $= 2\pi r(h + r)$

$= 2\pi(14)(12 + 14)$

$= 28\pi \times 26$

$= 728\pi$

The ratio of the new surface area to the original surface area is:

$\frac{728\pi}{440\pi} = \frac{91}{55}$, or 91:55

7. D

A rectangular prism has a maximum volume when it is a cube. If A is the surface area of one square face of the cube, then $A = \frac{294}{6} = 49\text{ cm}^2$.

If x is th edge length of the cube, then $x = \sqrt{49} = 7$ cm.

The volume, V, of the cube = lwh
$= (x)(x)(x) = x^3 = 7^3 = 343\text{ cm}^3$

8. D

Let the base radius of the cone be r, and let the slant height of the cone be l.
Surface area of the cone $= \pi rl$

After the change, the radius becomes $\frac{r}{2}$ and the slant height becomes $2l$.

New surface area $= \pi \times \frac{r}{2} \times 2l = \pi rl$

Thus, there is no change in the lateral surface area.

9. B

$$A_{\text{circular plate}} = 154\text{ cm}^2$$
$$\pi r^2 = 154$$
$$\frac{\pi r^2}{\pi} = \frac{154}{\pi}$$
$$r^2 = 49$$
$$r = 7\text{ cm}$$

diameter of the circular plate = diagonal of the largest square
14 cm = the diagonal of the square
Let the side of the square be a cm.

$$a^2 + a^2 = 14^2$$
$$2a^2 = 196$$
$$\frac{2a^2}{2} = \frac{196}{2}$$
$$a^2 = 98\text{ cm}$$

$$A_{\text{largest square}} = 98\text{ cm}^2$$

10. B

Calculate the volume for each alternative. The container that holds more than 1 000 cm^3
$= (1\text{ L} = 1\ 0\text{ mL} = 1\ 0\text{ cm}^3)$ will hold all of the candies.

$$V_{\text{cylinder}} = \pi r^2 h$$
$$V_{\text{rectangular prism}} = lwh$$

Alternative A:

$$\begin{aligned} V_{\text{cylinder}} &= \pi 7^2 \times 6 \\ &= \pi 49 \times 6 \\ &= 153.86 \times 6 \\ &= 923.16\text{ cm}^3 \end{aligned}$$

Alternative B:

$$\begin{aligned} V_{\text{cylinder}} &= \pi 7^2 \times 7 \\ &= \pi 49 \times 7 \\ &= 153.86 \times 7 \\ &= 1\ 077.02\text{ cm}^3 \end{aligned}$$

Alternative C:

$$\begin{aligned} V_{\text{rectangular prism}} &= lwh \\ &= 5 \times 10 \times 19 \\ &= 950\text{ cm}^3 \end{aligned}$$

Alternative D:

$$\begin{aligned} V_{\text{rectangular prism}} &= lwh \\ &= 7 \times 7 \times 20 \\ &= 980\text{ cm}^3 \end{aligned}$$

The cylinder with a diameter of 14 cm and a height of 7 cm will hold all of the candies.

11. C

Use Pythagoras' theorem to solve for p.

$$a^2 + b^2 = c^2$$
$$p^2 = 3^2 + 6^2$$
$$p = \sqrt{3^2 + 6^2}$$

Use Pythagoras' theorem to solve for q.

$$a^2 + b^2 = c^2$$
$$q^2 = 6^2 - 3^2$$
$$q = \sqrt{6^2 - 3^2}$$

The value of the expression $p + q$ is equal to $\sqrt{3^2 + 6^2} + \sqrt{6^2 - 3^2}$.

12. C

The Pythagorean theorem states that the square of the hypotenuse length (the longest side of a right triangle) equals the sum of the squares of the two shorter side lengths. In the diagram, q is the hypotenuse. The sum of the squares of p and r are equal to q.

$$p^2 + r^2 = q^2$$

13. D

Sketch the triangles.

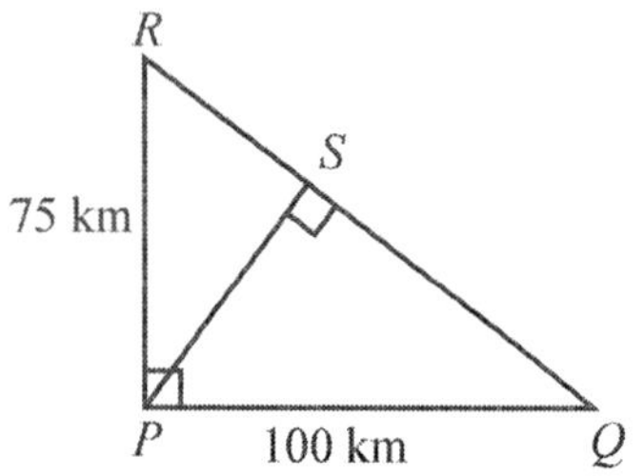

Apply Pythagoras' theorem to the triangle formed with cities R, P, and Q. The line between R and Q is the hypotenuse.

$$c^2 = a^2 + b^2$$

$$\text{RQ}^2 = 75^2 + 100^2$$
$$= 5625 + 100$$
$$= 15\ 625$$
$$\text{RQ} = \sqrt{15\ 625}$$
$$= 125 \text{ km}$$

Calculate the area of this triangle using 75 for the height and 100 as the base.

$$A = \frac{1}{2}bh$$

$$A_{\text{RPQ}} = \frac{1}{2}100 \times 75$$

$$A_{\text{RPQ}} = 3\ \ 750 \text{ km}^2$$

Use $A = 3\ \ 750$ to solve for the distance between cities P and S. The distance between P and S is the height and the distance between cities R and Q (125 km) is the base of the triangle.

$$3750 = \frac{1}{2}\text{PS} \times 125$$

$$2 \times 3\ \ 750 = \text{PS} \times 125$$

$$7\ \ 500 \div 125 = \text{PS}$$

$$\text{PS} = 60$$

Cities P and S are 60 km apart.

14. C

The wall, ground, and ladder form a right triangle with the ladder as the hypotenuse.

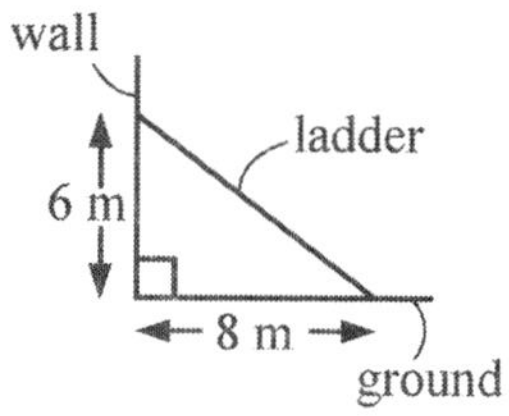

Use Pythagoras' theorem.
$c^2 = a^2 + b^2$

Substitute the wall height for a and the ground distance for b.
$c^2 = 6^2 + 8^2$
$c^2 = 36 + 64$

$c^2 = 100$
Take the square root of both sides to solve for c.
$\sqrt{c^2} = \sqrt{100}$
$c = 10$

The length of the ladder is 10 m.

15. OR

Points	Sample Answer
4	The hypotenuse of the triangle, c, is the 900 m diagonal distance. The height of the triangle, a, is 61 m. Use the Pythagorean theorem to determine the length of the base of the triangle, b. $c^2 = a^2 + b^2$ Algebraically rearrange the equation to have the unknown variable by itself. $b = \sqrt{c^2 - a^2}$ Substitute the known values. $b = \sqrt{900^2 - 61^2}$ $= \sqrt{8100 - 3721}$ $= \sqrt{806279}$ Take the square root. $b = 897.9$ m
Application of knowledge and skills involving the Pythagorean theorem shows a high degree of effectiveness due to: • a thorough understanding of the concepts • an accurate application of the procedures (any minor errors and/or omissions do not detract from the demonstration of a thorough understanding)	

Not for Reproduction

Points	Sample Answer
3	Left the units off the final answer. Miscalculation of the final square root, but most of the procedure is correct.
Application of knowledge and skills involving the Pythagorean theorem shows considerable effectiveness due to • an understanding of most of the concepts • minor errors and/or omissions in the application of the procedures	
2	Subtracted the squares before squaring the numbers. Reversed the a and b values.
Application of knowledge and skills involving the Pythagorean theorem shows some effectiveness due to • a partial understanding of the concepts • minor errors and/or omissions in the application of the procedures	
1	Uses a or b for the hypotenuse value. Equation written correctly, but solution is incomplete.
Application of knowledge and skills involving the Pythagorean theorem shows limited effectiveness due to: • a misunderstanding of concepts • an incorrect selection or misuse of procedures	

16. B

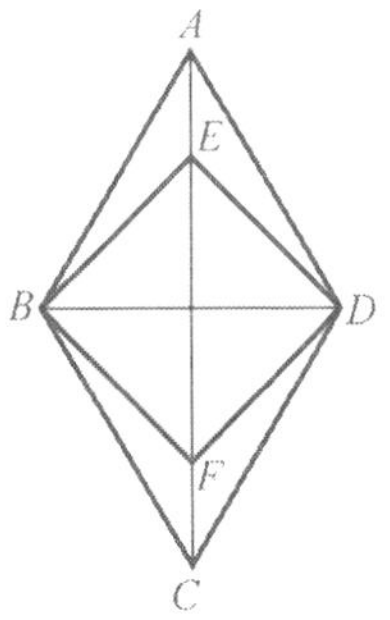

In the given figure, rhombus $ABCD$ represents the park. Square $BFDE$ represents the flowerbed.

Diagonal BD of the square is the short diagonal of the rhombus. The shorter diagonal of the rhombus is given as 30 m, and the longer as 60 m.

$BD = 30$ m

$AC = 60$ m

Find the area of rhombus $ABCD$.

$$A_{\text{rhombus}} = \frac{1}{2}\text{diagonal 1} \times \text{diagonal 2}$$
$$= \frac{1}{2}30 \text{ m} \times 60 \text{ m}$$
$$= \frac{1}{2}\left(1800 \text{ m}^2\right)$$
$$= 900 \text{ m}^2$$

In square $BFDE$, angle BED forms a right angle.

Apply Pythagoras' theorem.

$$a^2 + b^2 = c^2$$
$$BE^2 + ED^2 = BD^2$$

Because the sides of a square are equal, $BE = ED$.

$$2BE^2 = (30 \text{ m})^2$$
$$2BE^2 = 900 \text{ m}^2$$
$$BE^2 = 450 \text{ m}^2$$

$$A_{\text{square}} = s^2$$

$$A_{\text{square } BFED} = BE^2 = 450 \text{ m}^2$$

Area of remaining portion of the park (area for grass)
$= 900 - 450 = 450$ m^2

Cost of planting grass
$=$ area $\times$ cost per area
$= 450 \text{ m}^2 \times \$0.20/\text{m}^2$
$= \$90$

17. C

$$P_{\text{square}} = \text{length of the wire}$$
$$P_{\text{square}} = 4s$$
$$P_{\text{square}} = 4 \times 5.6$$
$$= 22.4 \text{ cm}$$

When the wire is bent into a circle, let its radius be r.

$$C_{\text{circle}} = P_{\text{square}} = 22.4 \text{ cm}$$
$$2\pi r = 22.4$$
$$2(3.14)r = 22.4$$
$$\frac{6.28r}{6.28} = \frac{22.4}{6.28}$$
$$r = 3.5669 \text{ cm}$$

$$A_{\text{circle}} = \pi r^2$$
$$= 3.14(3.5669)^2$$
$$= 3.14 \times 12.7226$$
$$= 39.9489$$
$$= 39.9 \text{ cm}^2$$

Copyright Protected

18. A

Square pyramids are one-third the volume of rectangular prisms with the same dimensions. If the volume of the rectangular pyramid is the same as the prism's, the prism's height must be $\frac{1}{3}$ of the pyramid's height. The height of the pyramid is x cm. The height of the prism is then $\frac{1}{3}x$ cm.

19. D

A cone is one-third the volume of a cylinder with the same dimensions. If the height of the cone is one-third shorter, its volume is going to be yet another one-third smaller. That means the volume of the cylinder will be nine times greater than the volume of the cone.

The correct ratio is 9:1.

This can be proven by substituting 3 cm and 9 cm for the heights of the cone and cylinder, respectively.

$$\begin{aligned} V_{\text{cylinder}} &= A_{\text{base}} \times \text{height} \\ &= \pi r^2 h \\ &= \pi(10 \text{ cm})^2 \times 9 \text{ cm} \\ &= 2826 \text{ cm}^3 \end{aligned}$$

$$\begin{aligned} V_{\text{cone}} &= \frac{A_{\text{base}} \times \text{height}}{3} \\ &= \frac{\pi r^2 h}{3} \\ &= \frac{\pi(10 \text{ cm})^2 \times 3 \text{ cm}}{3} \\ &= 314 \text{ cm}^3 \end{aligned}$$

$2826 \text{ cm}^2 \div 314 \text{ cm}^2 = 9$

The ratio is 9:1.

20. C

The three-dimensional model of the given two-dimensional net should have a square base and four triangular faces. These properties are shown only by the figure drawn in alternative C, which represents a square pyramid.

The other shapes have a hexagon, pentagon, and a triangle as their bases.

21. A

The lateral surface area of the triangular pyramid is equal to the sum of the areas of all its faces. It does not include the area of the figure's base. In the triangular prism, there are three triangular faces.

The area A of a triangle is $\frac{1}{2}bh$, where b is the base length and h is the height of the triangle. Here, $b = 5$ cm and $h = 6$ cm.

$$\begin{aligned} A_{\text{triangle}} &= \frac{bh}{2} \\ &= \frac{5 \times 6}{2} \\ &= \frac{30}{2} \\ &= 15 \text{ cm}^2 \end{aligned}$$

$$\begin{aligned} A_{\text{lateral faces}} &= 3(A_{\text{triangle}}) \\ &= 3(15) \\ &= 45 \text{ cm}^2 \end{aligned}$$

The lateral surface area of the triangular pyramid is 45 cm^2.

22. D

Area covered in one revolution = curved surface area (cylinder with no bases)

$$\text{Number of revolutions} = \frac{\text{total area compacted}}{\text{curved surface area}}$$

$$\text{Number of revolutions} = \frac{\text{total area compacted}}{2\pi rh}$$

Divide the diameter by 2 to calculate radius.
$1.75 \div 2 = 0.875$

Substitute the values into the formula.

$$\begin{aligned} &= \frac{3\ 300}{2 \times \pi \times 0.875 \times 1.5} \\ &= \frac{3300}{8.24} \\ &= 400.49 \end{aligned}$$

The front roller must make 401 complete revolutions to compact all of the given area.

The entire area would not be compacted at only 400 revolutions.

23. A

Determine the volume of the toy.

Using the appropriate volume formulas, add the volume of the right cone to the volume of the hemisphere.

$$V_{\text{toy}} = V_{\text{cone}} + V_{\text{hemisphere}}$$

$$V_{\text{toy}} = \frac{\pi r^2 h}{3} + \frac{2\pi r^3}{3}$$

Notice that in the formula for a hemisphere, $\frac{2}{3}$ is used rather than $\frac{4}{3}$ because you are only calculating half of a sphere.

Substitute the given values into the formulas and solve.

$$\begin{aligned} V_{\text{toy}} &= \frac{\pi \times (7)^2 \times (14)}{3} + \frac{2 \times \pi \times (7)^3}{3} \\ &= \frac{\pi \times 49 \times 14}{3} + \frac{2 \times \pi \times 343}{3} \\ &= 718.38 + 718.38 \\ &\approx 1436.76 \text{ cm}^3 \end{aligned}$$

Therefore, the approximate volume of the toy, to the nearest whole cubic centimetre, is 1 437 cm^3.

24. D

Let the polygon be an n-sided polygon.

$$\begin{aligned} 6 \times 360° &= 2\ 160° \\ 180°(n-2) &= 2\ 160° \\ 180°n - 360° &= 2\ 160° \\ 180°n - 360° + 360° &= 2\ 160° + 360° \\ 180°n &= 1\ 520° \\ \frac{180°n}{180°} &= \frac{1\ 520°}{180°} \\ n &= 14 \end{aligned}$$

25. B

The sum of the interior angles of a triangle is 180°.

The sum of adjacent angles is also 180°.

Calculate $\angle C$ by subtracting the adjacent angle from 180°.
$\angle C = 180° - 120° = 60°$

To solve for the missing angle, subtract $\angle B$ and $\angle C$ from 180°.
$\angle A = 180° - 60° - 50° = 70°$

26. OR

Points	Sample Answer
4	Sum of all angles in a triangle = 180° $x + (x + 10°) + (x + 29°) = 180°$ Group like terms. $3x + 39° = 180°$ $3x + 39° - 39° = 180° - 39°$ $3x = 141°$ Divide both sides of the equation by 3 to solve for x. $\frac{3x}{3} = \frac{141°}{3}$ $x = 47°$ $\angle A = x = 47°$ $\angle B = x + 10° = 57°$ $\angle C = x + 29° = 76°$ To verify these angles, add the three angles together to prove they equal 180°. $47° + 57° + 76° = 180°$
Application of knowledge and problem-solving skills involving angles of polygons shows a high degree of effectiveness due to: • a thorough understanding of the concepts • an accurate application of the procedures (any minor errors and/or omissions do not detract from the demonstration of a thorough understanding)	
3	Wrote the addition statement of all the angles correctly. Calculation errors in solving for the variable lead to errors in calculating the measure for each angle. Procedure correct. Added the measures of the three angles together, but they did not equal 180°.
Application of knowledge and skills problem solving angles of polygons shows considerable effectiveness due to • an understanding of most of the concepts • minor errors and/or omissions in the application of the procedures	
2	Wrote the addition statement of all the angles correctly. Began the process of solving for the variable, but unable to finish it. Because the angle was not determined, there was no verification that the sum of the angles was 180°.

Points	Sample Answer
Application of knowledge and problem-solving skills involving angles of polygons shows some effectiveness due to • a partial understanding of the concepts • minor errors and/or omissions in the application of the procedures	
1	Wrote the addition statement of all the angles, but did not know the next step to solve. Because the angle was not determined, there was no verification that the sum of the angles was 180°.
Application of knowledge and problem-solving skills involving angles of polygons shows limited effectiveness due to: • a misunderstanding of concepts • an incorrect selection or misuse of procedures	

27. B

The shape given is an irregular polygon. Use the formula $S_{\text{interior angles}} = 180°(n - 2)$ to calculate the sum, S, of the interior angles for a polygon with any number of sides, n.

The polygon has 9 sides.

$$\begin{aligned} S_{\text{interior angles}} &= 180°(9 - 2) \\ &= 180°(7) \\ &= 1\ 260° \end{aligned}$$

28. D

The sum of the interior angles of a triangle is 180°. The sum of the ratio is 6 + 6 + 8 = 20. Set up an equivalent proportion to solve for one of the missing angles.

$$\frac{6}{20} = \frac{x}{180°}$$

Cross-multiply to set up an algebraic equation that can be solved.

$$6 \times 180° = 20x$$

$$180° = 20x$$

$$\frac{180°}{20} = \frac{20x}{20}$$

$$x = 54°$$

One of the angles is equal to 54°.

29. A

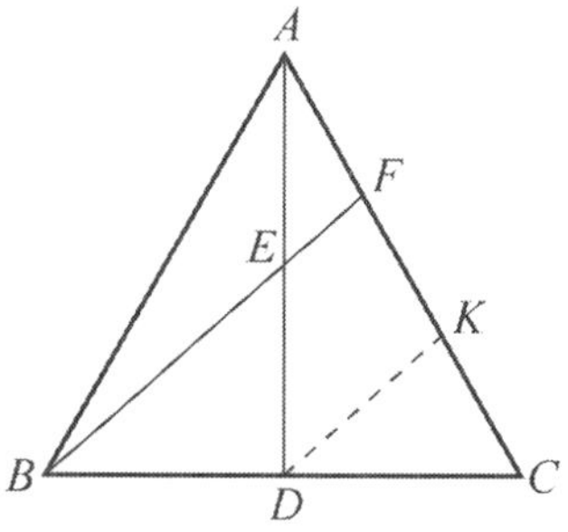

Some properties of this triangle:

- $DK \parallel BF$
- $EF \parallel DK$
- E is the midpoint of AD
- F is the midpoint of AK
- $BD = DC$
- $FK = KC$

$AF = FK = KC$

$\therefore AF = \frac{1}{3}AC$

Because AF is an integer, AC can only take a value that is a multiple of 3.
A possible length of AF is 6 units as that is the only alternative that is a multiple of 3.

30. D

The shape formed as a result of joining the midpoints of a quadrilateral is always a parallelogram.

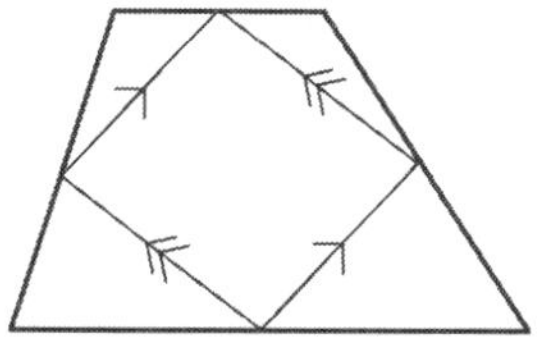

31. D

The diagonals of a square are of equal lengths and bisect each other at right angles. Thus, the field is in the shape of a square.

Not for Reproduction

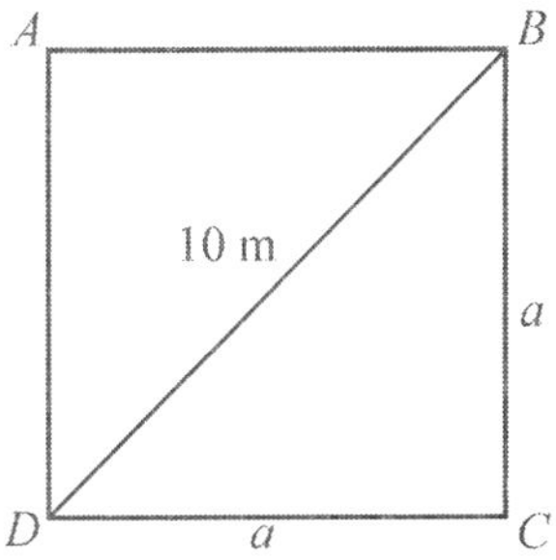

Let the side of the field be a.

In square $ABCD$, $DB^2 = DC^2 + CB^2$.

$(10)^2 = a^2 + a^2$

Hence, $a = \sqrt{50}$ m.

Therefore, the area of the field is $a^2 = 50 \text{ m}^2$.

32. C

The diagonals of parallelograms, rectangles, and squares bisect each other. In a trapezoid, they do not bisect each other.

Copyright Protected

UNIT TEST — MEASUREMENT AND GEOMETRY

Use the following information to answer the next question.

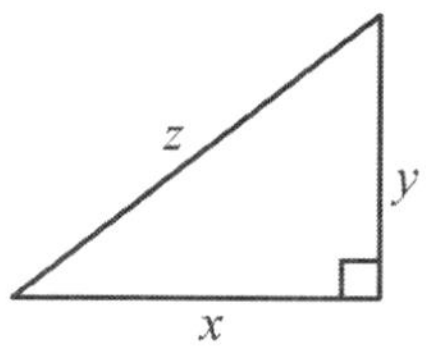

1. Which of the following equations **best** represents this diagram?

A. $x + y = z$

B. $2x + 2y = 2z$

C. $x^2 - y^2 = z^2$

D. $z^2 - y^2 = x^2$

2. Pythagoras' theorem can only be applied to what type of triangle?

A. Obtuse **B.** Acute

C. Isosceles **D.** Right

Use the following information to answer the next question.

Brian leaves his house for school. He first walks 1 km east, then 500 m north, then 200 m east, and finally 100 m south. His house is represented by *H* and his school is *S*.

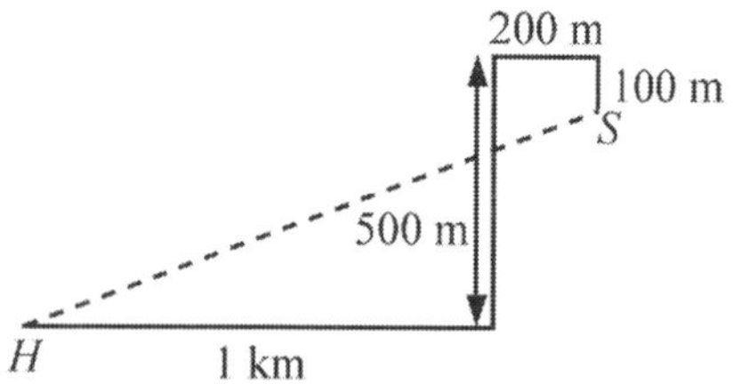

3. If Brian walked the straight diagonal distance from his home to school, how far would he walk?

A. 1 316.25 m **B.** 1 264.91 m

C. 1 225.37 m **D.** 1 200.46 m

Use the following information to answer the next question.

Richard draws a right triangle and then draws squares on each of its sides.

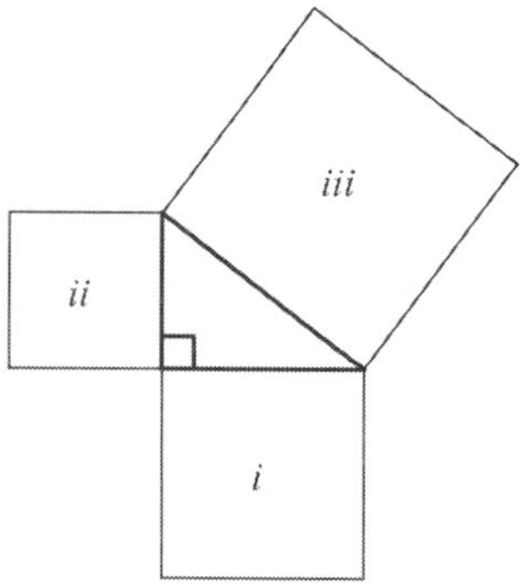

4. If area of square *i* is 9 units^2 and the area of square *ii* is 16 units^2, what is the area of square *iii*?

A. 9 units^2 **B.** 16 units^2

C. 25 units^2 **D.** 32 units^2

Open Response

5. A right triangle has a hypotenuse that is 12 m in length. If the two remaining sides of the right triangle are equal in length, then what is the measure, to the nearest tenth of a metre, of each of these sides?

Show your work.

Not for Reproduction

Use the following information to answer the next question.

The track on which Ben runs each morning has an inner circumference of 374 m and an outer circumference of 440 m.

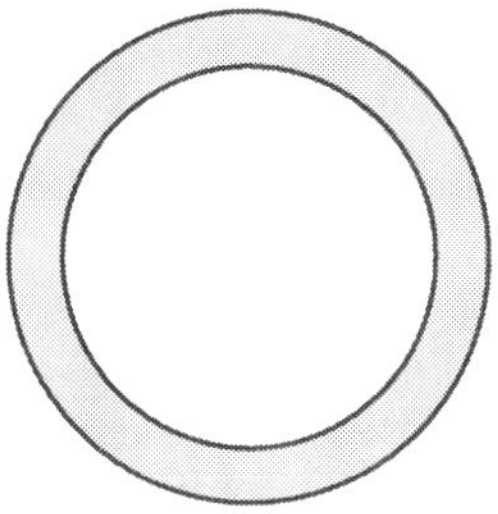

6. How wide, to the nearest tenth of a metre, is the track on which Ben runs?

A. 9.5 m
B. 10.5 m
C. 11.5 m
D. 12.5 m

Use the following information to answer the next question.

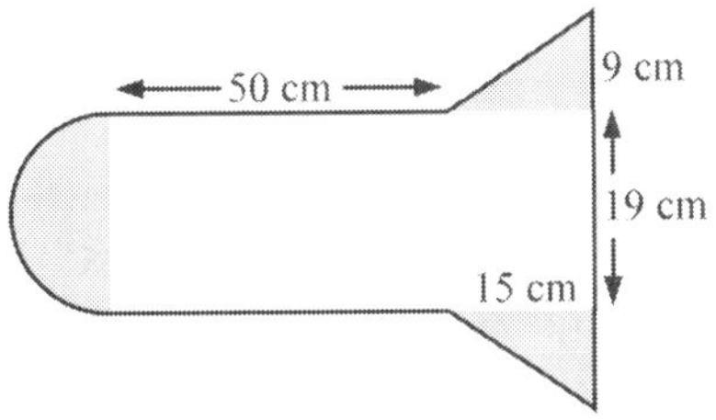

7. What is the total area of the shaded parts of the figure?

A. 176.87 cm^2
B. 276.69 cm^2
C. 512.59 cm^2
D. 987.98 cm^2

Use the following information to answer the next question.

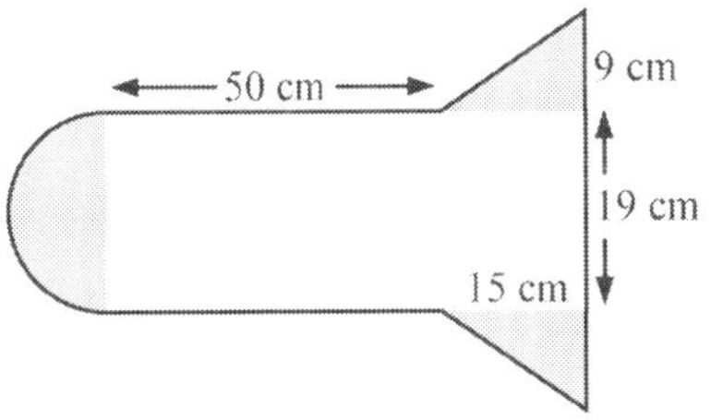

Open Response

8. What is the perimeter of the given figure? Show your work.

Use the following information to answer the next multipart question.

9. The game checkers requires a square board with 64 squares, each having a perimeter of 8 cm. Each player has 12 checkers, which are flat, round disks that fit within the squares. The diameter of each checker is equal to the length of a square on the board.

Open Response

a) What is the perimeter of a checkers board?

b) How much area of the square is exposed when a checker piece rests on a square?

Copyright Protected

Show your work.

Use the following information to answer the next question.

This drawing is of a cylinder circumscribing a sphere.

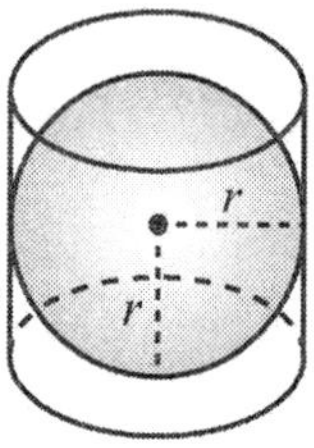

Open Response

10. What is the ratio of the volume of the sphere to the volume of the cylinder?

Show your work.

11. If the volume of a rectangular prism is 300 cm^3, what is the volume of a pyramid with the same base area and height?

A. 100 cm^3 **B.** 150 cm^3

C. 300 cm^3 **D.** 900 cm^3

Use the following information to answer the next question.

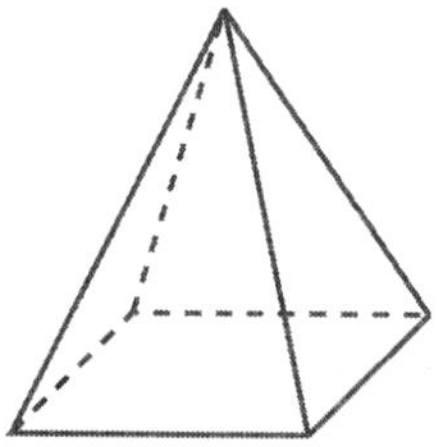

12. Which net can be folded into the given square pyramid?

A. 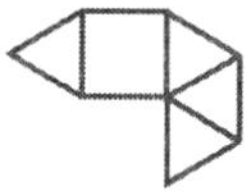 **B.** 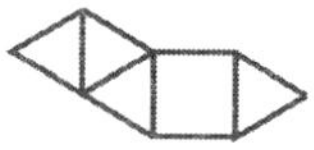

C. 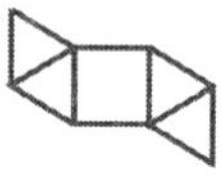 **D.** 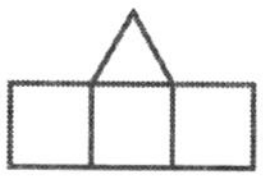

13. The base of a right pyramid is a square. If the length of each side of the base is 25 cm and the slant height of the pyramid is 18 cm, the surface area of the pyramid is

A. 1 536 cm^2 **B.** 1 525 cm^2

C. 1 500 cm^2 **D.** 1 432 cm^2

Use the following information to answer the next question.

The diameter of an iron ball for shot put is 16 cm. The ball is melted, and a solid cone with a height of 10 cm is made from it.

14. What is the diameter of the base of the cylinder?

A. 13.33 cm **B.** 16.67 cm

C. 26.74 cm **D.** 28.62 cm

15. A necklace contains 24 spherical beads of silver, each having a radius of 0.5 cm. The beads are to be coated, and the cost of coating is \$10 per cm^2. What is the approximate total cost, to the nearest dollar, for coating the beads?

A. \$31.00 **B.** \$75.00

C. \$126.00 **D.** \$754.00

Not for Reproduction

Use the following information to answer the next question.

While constructing a bridge, a construction company builds 50 cylindrical pillars. Each concrete pillar is 10 m high and has a radius of 2.5 m.

Open Response

16. If the cost of concrete is $\$1\ 0/\text{m}^3$, what is the total cost of constructing all the pillars?
$\pi = 3.14$
Show your work.

17. What is the **maximum** area of a rectangle that has side lengths that are integers and a perimeter of 36 m?

A. 80 m^2 **B.** 81 m^2
C. 90 m^2 **D.** 91 m^2

Use the following information to answer the next question.

The promoters of a rock concert want to fence off a rectangular area directly in front of the stage for a VIP section. They will use 16 m of fencing. They plan to use the fence for 3 sides of the rectangular area. Part of the stage will be used for the fourth side. The maximum length of the stage that can be used is 12 m.

Open Response

18. What is the **maximum** area that can be fenced off the using the 16 m of fencing? Show your work.

Use the following information to answer the next question.

A rectangle has an area of 196 m^2 and a minimum perimeter.

19. What is the length of the rectangle?

A. 4 m **B.** 7 m
C. 14 m **D.** 28 m

Use the following information to answer the next question.

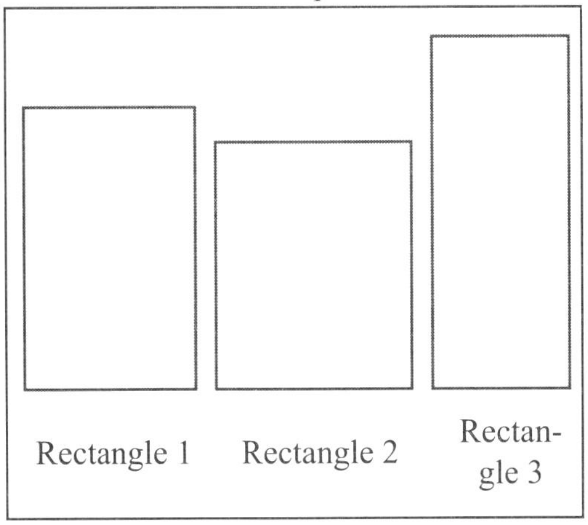

Open Response

20. Each of the given rectangles has the same area. Order the rectangles from the one with the shortest perimeter to the one with the longest perimeter.

Show your work.

Copyright Protected

Use the following information to answer the next question.

A square prism has a width and length of 4 cm and a height of 6 cm.

21. If the length and width are each increased by 1 cm, and the height is decreased by 1 cm, then the new surface area of the prism is

A. 4 cm^2 less than the original surface area

B. equal to the original surface area

C. 22 cm^2 greater than the original surface area

D. 25 cm^2 greater than the original surface area

Use the following information to answer the next question.

Moira constructs a cylinder with a base radius of 6 cm and a height of 8 cm using materials that cost $\$1.20/cm^2$. Gilby constructs a cylinder with a base radius of 5 cm and a height of 9 cm using materials that also cost $\$1.20/cm^2$.

22. Which of the following statements is **true**?

A. Moira and Gilby spend the same amount to construct each of their cylinders.

B. Moira spends approximately $88 more than Gilby to construct her cylinder.

C. Moira spends approximately $106 more than Gilby to construct her cylinder.

D. Moira spends approximately $238 more than Gilby to construct her cylinder.

23. Susan has 150 cm^2 of cardboard to build a box with. Which of the following sets of dimensions will give the box a **maximum** volume?

A. 5 cm by 5 cm by 5 cm

B. 6 cm by 6 cm by 6 cm

C. 2 cm by 2 cm by 17.75 cm

D. 4 cm by 4 cm by 7.38 cm

Open Response

24. A square-based cereal box has a volume of 2 000 cm^3. What dimensions for the box require the **least** amount of packaging?

Show your work.

Open Response

25. A cylinder is built so that it has a maximum volume. The height of the cylinder is 11 cm. What is the radius, to the nearest tenth of a centimetre, of the cylinder's base?

Show your work.

Not for Reproduction

Use the following information to answer the next question.

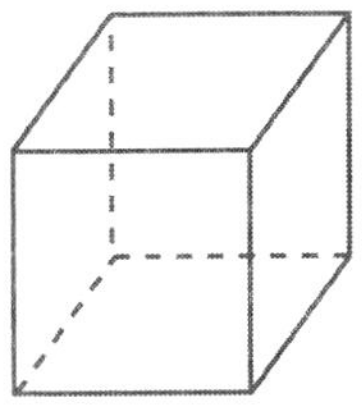

26. The sum of the lengths of all the edges of a rectangular prism is 72 cm. What is the maximum surface area that the prism can have?

A. 96 cm^2 **B.** 216 cm^2

C. 294 cm^2 **D.** 343 cm^2

27. The volume of a cylinder is $250\pi\text{ cm}^3$. What is the **minimum** possible surface area of the cylinder?

A. $100\pi\text{ cm}^2$

B. $125\pi\text{ cm}^2$

C. $150\pi\text{ cm}^2$

D. $200\pi\text{ cm}^2$

Use the following information to answer the next question.

All the interior angles of this hexagon are equal.

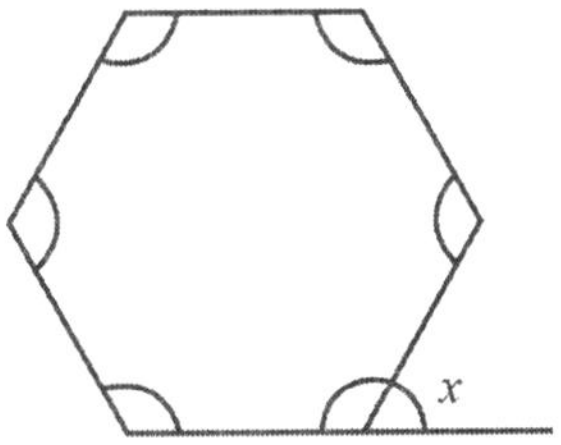

Open Response

28. What is the value of angle x?

Show your work.

29. A park is in the shape of a regular polygon. The measure of each interior angle is double the measure of each exterior angle and all its sides are equal in length. How many sides does the park have?

A. 4 **B.** 6

C. 8 **D.** 9

Use the following information to answer the next question.

All interior angles of this pentagon are equal.

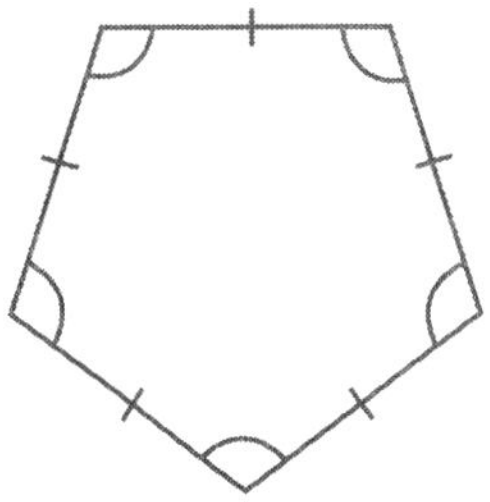

30. What is the sum of any two interior angles of this pentagon?

A. 108° **B.** 180°

C. 216° **D.** 324°

Use the following information to answer the next question.

An artist is cutting pieces for a stained glass window.

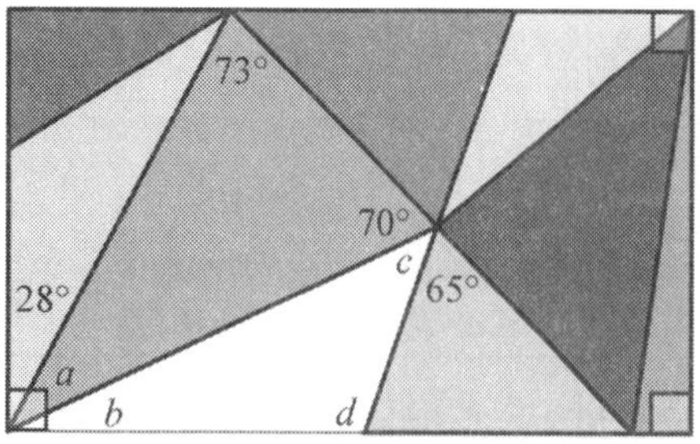

Open Response

31. What are the measures of angles *a*, *b*, *c*, and *d*?

Justify your answer by stating an angle property for each calculation.
Show your work.

32. In triangle *ABC*, if angle *BAC* is decreased by 9° and angle *ABC* is increased by 7°, then angle *ACB*

A. does not change

B. decreases by 5°

C. decreases by 2°

D. increases by 2°

33. In a particular quadrilateral, the opposite angles are equal. If the sum of these two angles is 120°, then the measure of each of the remaining angles is

A. 60° **B.** 90°

C. 120° **D.** 240°

Open Response

34. The ratio of the measure of angle *A* to the measure of angle *B* is 4:5 in a parallelogram. What is the measure of angle *B*?

Show your work.

35. The midpoints of the sides of an equilateral triangle are joined by line segments. These line segments form four triangles within the larger triangle. Each of the triangles formed inside the larger triangle will be

A. a scalene triangle

B. an isosceles triangle

C. similar to the larger triangle

D. congruent to the larger triangle

36. In triangle *PQR*, line *PT* bisects line *QR*, forming a right angle at point *T*. Line segment *PT* is called the perpendicular

A. radius **B.** bisector

C. diagonal **D.** connector

Use the following information to answer the next question.

Martha draws a quadrilateral with the following properties:

- opposite sides are equal
- opposite angles are equal
- diagonals bisect each other at 90°

37. The quadrilateral that Martha draws is a

A. parallelogram **B.** rectangle

C. trapezoid **D.** square

Not for Reproduction

38. Which of the following statements does **not** describe a property of a perpendicular bisector?

A. It divides a line segment into two equal parts.

B. It is perpendicular to the line segment it crosses.

C. It is not located at the midpoint of the line segment.

D. It crosses the line segment at a right angle.

Copyright Protected

ANSWERS AND SOLUTIONS — UNIT TEST

1. D	9. a) OR	16. OR	24. OR	32. D
2. D	b) OR	17. B	25. OR	33. C
3. B	10. OR	18. OR	26. B	34. OR
4. C	11. A	19. C	27. C	35. C
5. OR	12. C	20. OR	28. OR	36. B
6. B	13. B	21. C	29. B	37. D
7. B	14. D	22. C	30. C	38. C
8. OR	15. D	23. A	31. OR	

1. D

The Pythagorean theorem states that the square of the hypotenuse is equal to the sum of the squares of the two shorter sides. The hypotenuse is side *z*. Using the variables indicated, the equation is $z^2 = y^2 + x^2$. This is not one of the alternatives. Manipulate the equation algebraically:

$z^2 - y^2 = y^2 - y^2 + x^2$

$z^2 - y^2 = x^2$

2. D

The Pythagorean theorem applies to right-angled triangles only.

3. B

1 km= 1 000 m

Use Pythagoras' theorem to find the hypotenuse of right triangle *HXS*,

$HX = 1200$ m

$SX = 400$ m

$HS^2 = HX^2 + SX^2$

$= 1200^2 + 400^2$

$= 14\ 400 + 1600$

$\sqrt{HS^2} = \sqrt{14\ 400 + 1600}$

$HS = 1264.91$ m

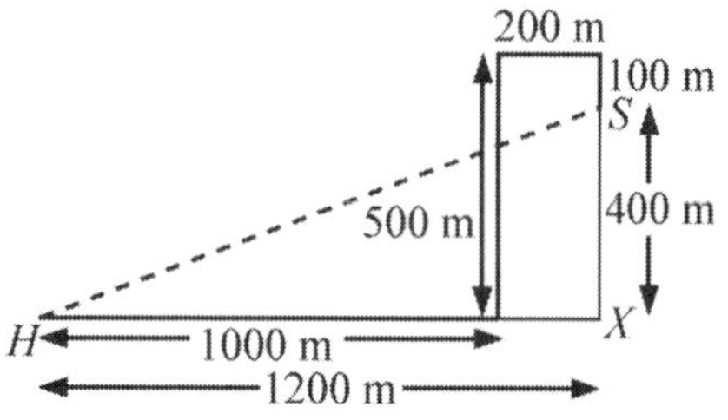

4. C

The areas of two squares on two sides of the right triangle are given. Use the Pythagorean theorem to find the area of the square on the third side.

The theorem is $a^2 + b^2 = c^2$, where a^2 is the area of square *i*, b^2 is the area of square *ii*, and c^2 is the area of square *iii*.

In this case, $16 + 9 = c^2$.

$25 = c^2$

The area of the square *iii* is 25 units².

5. OR

According to the Pythagorean theorem, $a^2 + b^2 = c^2$, where *c* is the hypotenuse of a right triangle and *a* and *b* are the legs of the triangle. Because the two remaining legs are equal, let *a* and *b* each be represented as *x*.

Apply the Pythagorean theorem.

$x^2 + x^2 = 12^2$

Combine like terms.

$2x^2 = 144$

Divide both sides by 2 to isolate the variable.

$\frac{2x^2}{2} = \frac{144}{2}$

$x^2 = 72$

Take the square root of both sides to solve for *x*.

$\sqrt{x^2} = \sqrt{72}$

$x = 8.485\ 281\ 374$ m

Each side is 8.5 m in length.

6. B

Let the outer radius be *R* and the inner radius be*r*.

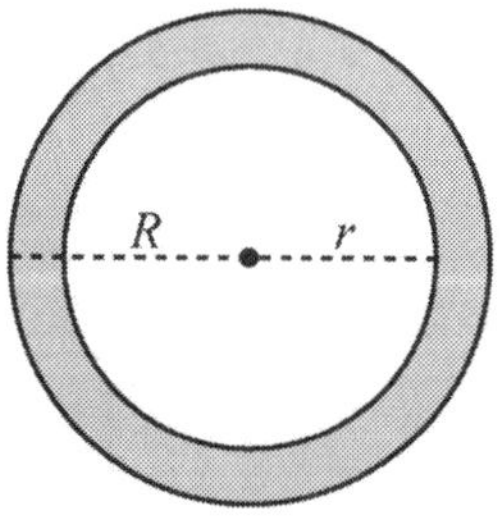

Not for Reproduction

Use the formula for circumference to find the radius of the outer circle.

$$C = 2\pi r$$
$$2\pi R = 440 \text{ m}$$
$$2(3.14)R = 440 \text{ m}$$
$$6.28R = 440 \text{ m}$$
$$R = 70.0637 \text{ m}$$

Now, find the radius of the inner circle.

$$C = 2\pi r$$
$$2\pi r = 374 \text{ m}$$
$$2(3.14)r = 374 \text{ m}$$
$$6.28r = 374 \text{ m}$$
$$r = 59.5541 \text{ m}$$

The difference of the two radii is the width of the track.

$$\begin{aligned}\text{Width} &= R - r\\ &= 70.0637 - 59.5541\\ &= 10.5096\\ &= 10.5 \text{ m}\end{aligned}$$

7. B

The shaded parts include a semicircle and two triangles of the same dimensions.

Find the area of one shaded triangle.

$$A_{\text{triangle}} = \frac{1}{2}bh$$

$$A_{\text{triangle}} = 0.5 \times 15 \times 9$$
$$= 67.5 \text{ cm}^2$$

Find the area of the semicircle.

$$\text{radius} = \frac{\text{diameter}}{2} = \frac{19}{2} = 9.5 \text{ cm}$$

$$\begin{aligned}A_{\text{semicircle}} &= \frac{1}{2}\pi r^2\\ &= \frac{1}{2}\pi(9.5 \text{ cm})^2\\ &= \frac{3.14 \times 90.25}{2}\\ &= 141.69 \text{ cm}^2\end{aligned}$$

Add the two areas together.

$$\begin{aligned}A_{\text{total}} &= A_{\text{semicircle}} + 2A_{\text{triangle}}\\ &= 141.69 + 2(67.5)\\ &= 276.69 \text{ cm}^2\end{aligned}$$

8. OR

Calculate the perimeter of the various parts of the composite shape.

$$P_{\text{total}} = C_{\text{semicircle}} + 2l_{\text{rectangle}} + 2(\text{hypotenuse}_{\text{triangle}}) + \text{long end}$$

First, find the circumference of the semicircle.

$$\begin{aligned}C_{\text{semicircle}} &= \pi\frac{d}{2}\\ &= \pi\frac{19}{2}\\ &= 29.83 \text{ cm}\end{aligned}$$

The length of each side of the unshaded rectangle is 50 cm.

Find the length of the hypotenuse using Pythagoras' theorem.

$$c^2 = a^2 + b^2$$
$$c^2 = 9^2 + 15^2$$
$$= 81 + 225$$
$$\sqrt{c^2} = \sqrt{306}$$
$$c = 17.49 \text{ cm}$$

Length of the long end on the right side of the figure $= 9 + 19 + 9 = 37$ cm

$$\begin{aligned}P_{\text{total}} &= C_{\text{semicircle}} + 2l_{\text{rectangle}} + 2(\text{hypotenuse}_{\text{triangle}}) + \text{long end}\\ &= 29.83 + 2(50) + 2(17.49) + 37\\ &= 201.81 \text{ cm}\end{aligned}$$

9. a) OR

Each square on the board has a perimeter of 8 cm. A square has four equal sides. Divide the perimeter by 4 to determine the length of one side.

$8 \div 4 = 2$

Therefore, each square has a length of 2 cm.

The board has 64 squares and is in the shape of a square. The square root will give the number of squares along each side of the board.

$\sqrt{64} = 8$

There are 8 squares on each side.

Length of the board = square length × number of squares

$= 2 \times 8 = 16$ cm

$$\begin{aligned}P_{\text{square}} &= 4s\\ &= 4 \times 16\\ &= 64 \text{ cm}\end{aligned}$$

b) OR

Points	Sample Answer
4	First, find the area of a checker piece. $\text{diameter}_{\text{circle}} = l_{\text{square}}$ $d = 2$ cm $r = d \div 2 = 2 \div 2 = 1$ cm 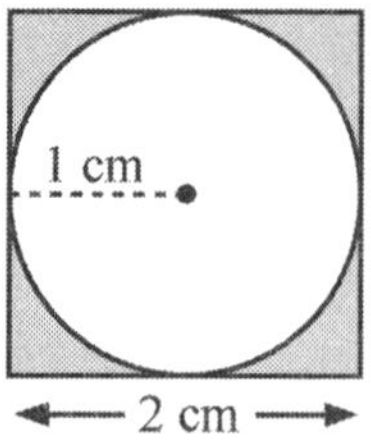 $A_{\text{circle}} = \pi r^2$ $A_{\text{circle}} = \pi 1^2$ $= \pi 1$ $= 3.14 \text{ cm}^2$ Find the area of a square. $A_{\text{square}} = lw$ $A_{\text{square}} = 2 \times 2$ $= 4 \text{ cm}^2$ Subtract the area of the circle from the area of the square to determine how much of the square is exposed. $A_{\text{exposed}} = A_{\text{square}} - A_{\text{circle}}$ $= 4 - 3.14$ $= 0.86 \text{ cm}^2$
	Application of knowledge and skills involving area and perimeter of composite figures shows a high degree of effectiveness due to • a thorough understanding of the concepts • an accurate application of the procedures (any minor errors and/or omissions do not detract from the demonstration of a thorough under-standing)
3	Calculates the perimeter using 8 cm as the measurement rather than 16 cm. Calculates the two areas, but does not subtract them to determine the exposed area.
	Application of knowledge and skills involving area and perimeter of composite figures shows consid-erable effectiveness due to • an understanding of most of the concepts • minor errors and/or omissions in the application of the procedures
2	Calculates the perimeter using a diagram rather than algebraically. Calculates one area correctly and the second area with errors.
	Application of knowledge and skills involving area and perimeter of composite figures shows some effectiveness due to • a partial understanding of the concepts • minor errors and/or omissions in the application of the procedures
1	Unable to correctly calculate perimeter with a diagram or algebraically. Begins calculations of areas but unable to complete them.
	Application of knowledge and skills involving area and perimeter of composite figures shows limited effectiveness due to: • a misunderstanding of the concepts • an incorrect selection or misuse of procedures

10. OR

The radius of the sphere is r.
The radius of the cylinder is also r, and its height is $2r$.

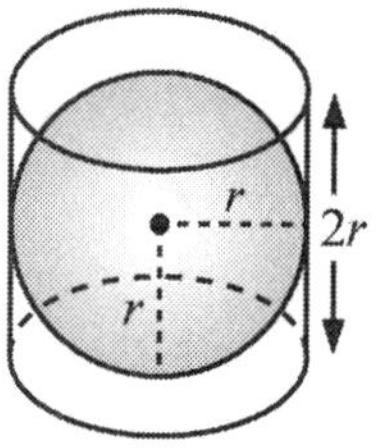

Not for Reproduction

$V_{sphere} = \frac{4}{3}\pi r^3$

$V_{cylinder} = \text{(base area)(height)}$

$V_{cylinder} = (\pi r^2)\text{(height)}$

Substitute the values in for r and h.

$V_{cylinder} = (\pi r^2)(2r)$

Set up the ratio and solve.

$$\frac{V_{sphere}}{V_{cylinder}} = \frac{\frac{4}{3}\pi r^3}{\pi r^2 \times 2r} = \frac{\frac{4}{3}\pi r^3}{2\pi r^3}$$

$$= \frac{4}{3} \div \frac{2}{1} = \frac{4}{3} \times \frac{1}{2}$$

$$= \frac{2}{3}$$

Therefore, the ratio of the volume of the sphere to the circumscribing cylinder is 2:3.

11. A

A pyramid is one-third the volume of a rectangular prism with the same dimensions.

$V_{rectangular\ prism} = A_{base} \times \text{height}$

$$V_{pyramid} = \frac{A_{base} \times \text{height}}{3}$$

If the volume of the prism is 300 cm^3, divide it by 3 to calculate the volume of the pyramid.

$300 \div 3 = 100 \text{ cm}^3$

12. C

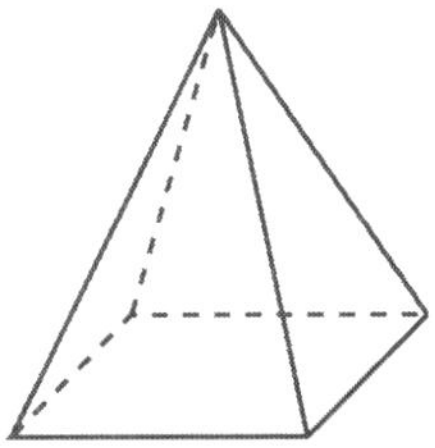

The square pyramid shown has one square base and four lateral triangular faces. Alternative D does not satisfy these requirements.

In order to fold the pieces into the pyramid, each triangular piece must be able to touch a separate edge of the square base. In alternative A three lateral faces are attached, but the middle face has no edge that will touch the base. In alternative B, the leftmost lateral face will not touch the base.

13. B

$SA_{pyramid} = A_{base} + 4A_{triangle}$

$SA_{pyramid} = lw + 4\left(\frac{1}{2}bs\right)$

$= (25 \times 25) + 4\left(\frac{1}{2} \times 25 \times 18\right)$

$= 625 + 4(225)$

$= 625 + 900$

$= 1525 \text{ cm}^2$

14. D

Let the radius of the cylinder be R cm.

The two volumes are equal to each other.

$V_{cone} = V_{sphere}$

$$\frac{\pi r^2 h}{3} = \frac{4\pi r^3}{3}$$

Substitute in the known values.

$$\frac{\pi R^2 10}{3} = \frac{4\pi 8^3}{3}$$

Solve for R.

$10.47R^2 = 2\ 143.57$

$R^2 = 204.73$

$\sqrt{R^2} = \sqrt{204.73}$

$R = 14.31 \text{ cm}$

The diameter is twice the length of the radius.

$14.31 \times 2 = 28.62 \text{ cm}$

15. D

Calculate the surface area of one bead.

$SA_{sphere} = 4\pi r^2$

$= 4\pi 0.5^2$

$= 4\pi 0.25$

$= 3.14 \text{ cm}^2$

There are 24 beads, so multiply the area by 24.

$3.14 \times 24 = 75.4 \text{ cm}^2$

The cost of coating is \$10 per cm^2 so multiply the total area by \$10 for the total cost.

$75.4 \times 10 = \$754.00$

Copyright Protected

16. OR

Calculate the volume of each cylinder.

$V_{cylinder}$$V$ cylinder $= (A_{base}$$A$base)(height)

$V_{cylinder}$$V$ cylinder $= \pi r^2 h$

$= \pi \times 2.5^2 \times 10$

$= \pi \times 6.25 \times 10$

$= 196.25 \text{ m}^3$

Calculate the cost of constructing each pillar by multiplying the volume by $1 000.
196.25 × 1 0 = $196 250

There are 50 pillars. Multiply the cost of one pillar by 50 to get the total cost.
$196 250 × 50 = $9 812 500

17. B

$P_{rectangle} = 2(l + w)$

$36 \text{ cm} = 2(l + w)$

$\frac{36}{2} = \frac{2(l + w)}{2}$

$18 \text{ cm} = l + w$

$A_{rectangle} = lw$

Use guess and check with a chart to determine the different combinations possible.

The maximum area occurs when the rectangle is a square (four equal sides). The dimensions of the square are 9 m × 9 m.

Therefore, the maximum area is 81 m^2.

18. OR

To determine the maximum area, let l equal the length of the fenced area and w the width.

The perimeter is equal to three sides only.

$P_{fenced\ area} = 2l + w$

$A_{rectangle} = lw$

Width (m)	Length (m)	Perimeter (m)	Area (m^2)
1	14	16	14
2	12	16	24
3	10	16	30
4	8	16	32
5	6	16	30
6	4	16	24

The maximum area is 32 m^2.

19. C

The minimum perimeter is obtained when the rectangle is a square (four equal sides).

$A_{square} = s^2$

$A_{square} = 196$

$s^2 = 196$

$\sqrt{s^2} = \sqrt{196}$

$s = 14$

The length of the rectangle is 14 m.

20. OR

A rectangle with a given area has a minimum perimeter when it is a square. Rectangle 2 is most like a square and most likely has the smallest perimeter.

Rectangle 1 is more like a square than Rectangle 3. The perimeter of Rectangle 3 is most likely longer than Rectangle 1.

The rectangles in correct order are Rectangle 2, Rectangle 1, Rectangle 3.

21. C

Calculate the surface area of the original prism, where $l = 4$, $w = 4$, and $h = 6$.

$SA = 2(wh + lw + lh)$

$= 2(4 \times 6 + 4 \times 4 + 4 \times 6)$

$= 2(24 + 16 + 24)$

$= 2 \times 64$

$= 128 \text{ cm}^2$

Calculate the surface area of the new prism where l, w, and $h = 5$.

$SA = 2(wh + lw + lh)$

$= 2(5 \times 5 + 5 \times 5 + 5 \times 5)$

$= 2(25 + 25 + 25)$

$= 2 \times 75$

$= 150 \text{ cm}^2$

Subtract the surface area of the two prisms.

$150 - 128 = 22 \text{ cm}^2$

The new surface area is 22 cm^2 greater than the original surface area.

Not for Reproduction

22. C

First find the area of Moira's cylinder.

$$SA_{\text{cylinder}} = 2\pi r(h + r)$$
$$= 2\pi(6)(8 + 6)$$
$$= 12\pi \times 14$$
$$= 168\pi \text{ cm}^2$$

Find the cost of constructing Moira's cylinder.

Cost = area × price

$168\pi \times 1.20 = \$633.35$

Find the area of Gilby's cylinder.

$$SA_{\text{cylinder}} = 2\pi r(h + r)$$
$$= 2\pi(5)(9 + 5)$$
$$= 10\pi \times 14$$
$$= 140\pi \text{ cm}^2$$

Find the cost of constructing Gilby's cylinder.

Cost = area × price

$140\pi \times 1.20 = \$527.79$

The approximate difference in the cost of the two cylinders is 633.35 – 527.79 = \$105.56.

Moira's cylinder costs approximately \$106 more than Gilby's to construct.

23. A

The maximum volume is achieved when the rectangular prism is a cube. Only alternatives A and B give the dimensions of a cube (all sides are equal).

Find the surface area for each of these two sets. The maximum amount of cardboard possible to use is given.

$$A_{\text{face1}} = 5 \times 5 = 25 \text{ cm}^2$$
$$SA_{\text{cube}} = A_{\text{face}} \times 6$$
$$= 25 \times 6$$
$$= 150 \text{ cm}^2$$

$$A_{\text{face2}} = 6 \times 6 = 36 \text{ cm}^2$$
$$SA_{\text{cube}} = A_{\text{face}} \times 6$$
$$= 36 \times 6$$
$$= 216 \text{ cm}^2$$

The required dimensions are 5 cm by 5 cm by 5 cm.

24. OR

Calculate the side length of the cube.

$$V_{\text{cube}} = l^3$$
$$2\ 000 = l^3$$
$$\sqrt[3]{2\ 000} = \sqrt[3]{l^3}$$
$$12.6 \text{ cm} = l$$

The dimensions of a cube are all the same. Therefore, the volume dimensions (length, width, and height) are 12.6 cm by 12.6 cm by 12.6 cm.

25. OR

A cylinder has a maximum volume when its base diameter equals its height. If r is the base radius and h is the height, then the base diameter is $2r$ and the height is $2r$. Since $h = 2r$ and $h = 11$ cm, $r = \frac{11}{2} = 5.5$ cm.

26. B

A rectangular prism will have a maximum surface area when it is a cube.

A rectangular prism has 12 edges. The 6 faces of the cube are squares. The edge length is equal to $\frac{72}{12} = 6$ cm.

$$A_{\text{face}} = lw$$
$$= 6 \times 6$$
$$= 36 \text{ cm}^2$$

$$SA_{\text{cube}} = A_{\text{face}} \times 6$$
$$= 36 \times 6$$
$$= 216 \text{ cm}^2$$

27. C

A cylinder has a minimum surface area when its height and diameter are equal. If the radius of the base of the cylinder is r, then the diameter d and the height h are each equal to $2r$.

$V_{\text{cylinder}} = \pi r^2 h$

$250\pi = \pi r^2 2r$

$250\pi = 2\pi r^3$

Divide both sides by 2π.

$\frac{250\pi}{2\pi} = \frac{2\pi r^3}{2\pi}$

$125 = r^3$

$\sqrt[3]{125} = \sqrt[3]{r^3}$

$r = 5$ cm

Using the formula for the surface area of a cylinder:

$SA_{\text{cylinder}} = 2\pi r(h + r)$

$= 2\pi 5(10 + 5)$

$= 10\pi \times 15$

$= 150\pi \text{ cm}^2$

28. OR

Use the formula $S = 180°(n - 2)$ to determine the sum of the angles.

$S = 180°(6 - 2)$

$= 180°(4)$

$= 720°$

Divide the sum of the angles by 6 to determine the measure of one angle.

$\frac{720°}{6} = 120°$

Adjacent angles equal 180°. Subtract the interior angle from this measure to determine the exterior angle.

$180° - 120° = 60°$

29. B

The sum of an interior angle and its adjacent exterior angle is 180°.

If x is the measure of the exterior angle, then $2x$ is the measure of the interior angle since it is twice the measure. Write an algebraic equation to solve for the value of x.

$180° = x + 2x$

$180° = x + 2x$

$180° = 3x$

Divide both sides by 3 to isolate the variable and solve for x.

$\frac{180°}{3} = \frac{3x}{3}$

$60° = x$

The sum of the exterior angles of a polygon is 360°. Divide this sum by 60° to determine the number of sides.

$360° \div 60° = 6$ sides

30. C

Sum of interior angles of a polygon having n sides:

$S_{\text{interior angles}} = 180°(n - 2)$

A pentagon has 5 sides.

$S_{\text{interior angles}} = 180°(5 - 2)$

$= 180°(3)$

$= 540°$

All interior angles are equal. Divide the total measure of the angles by the number of sides.

$\frac{540°}{5} = 108°$

Sum of any two interior angles:

$108° + 108° = 216°$

31. OR

Points	Sample Answer
4	$\angle a$ $180° - 73° - 70° = 37°$ Angle property: 180° is the sum of all interior angles of a triangle $\angle b$ $90° - 28° - 37° = 25°$ Angle property: 90° is the measure of a right angle $\angle c$ $180° - 70° - 65° = 45°$ Angle property: 180° is the sum of supplementary angles $\angle d$ $180° - 25° - 45° = 110°$ Angle property: 180° is the sum of all interior angles of a triangle
Application of knowledge and skills involving properties of polygons shows a high degree of effectiveness due to:	

Not for Reproduction

Points	Sample Answer
	• a thorough understanding of the concepts • an accurate application of the procedures (any minor errors and/or omissions do not detract from the demonstration of a thorough understanding)
3	Angle measures are calculated correctly. Justification of one of the calculations using the properties is omitted.
	Application of knowledge and skills involving properties of polygons shows considerable effectiveness due to: • an understanding of most of the concepts • minor errors and/or omissions in the application of the procedures
2	Calculation of one angle is incorrect but the procedure followed is correct. The remaining calculations are correct based on the mistake of the first calculation. Justification of two of the calculations using the properties is omitted.
	Application of knowledge and skills involving properties of polygons shows some effectiveness due to: • a partial understanding of the concepts • minor errors and/or omissions in the application of the procedures
1	Application of knowledge and skills involving properties of polygons shows limited effectiveness due to:
	Only one angle is correctly calculated. No justifications are given. • a misunderstanding of concepts • an incorrect selection or misuse of procedures

32. D

The sum of the interior angles of a triangle is 180°. If angle BAC is decreased by 9° and angle ABC is increased by 7°, there are 2° missing from the 180° sum of the angle measures.

$180° - 9° + 7° = 178°$

Angle ACB must be increased by 2° to keep the sum of 180°.

$180° - 9° + 7° + 2° = 180°$

33. C

Sum of all four angles of a quadrilateral $= 360°$
Sum of its two equal and opposite angles $= 120°$

Sum of the remaining two angles $= 360° - 120° = 240°$

In a quadrilateral, if two opposite angles are equal, the remaining angles will also be equal.

$$\text{Each remaining angle} = \frac{240°}{2} = 120°$$

34. OR

Set up the ratio.

$$\frac{A}{B} = \frac{4}{5}$$

The sum of the interior angles in a parallelogram is 360°. The sum of the ratio of the angles is $4 + 5 + 4 + 5 = 18$.

Set up the proportion, solving for B.

$$\frac{5}{18} = \frac{x}{360°}$$

Multiply across to create an algebraic equation that can be solved.

$$5 \times 360° = 18x$$
$$1\ 800° = 18x$$
$$\frac{1\ 800°}{18} = \frac{18x}{18}$$
$$100° = x$$

35. C

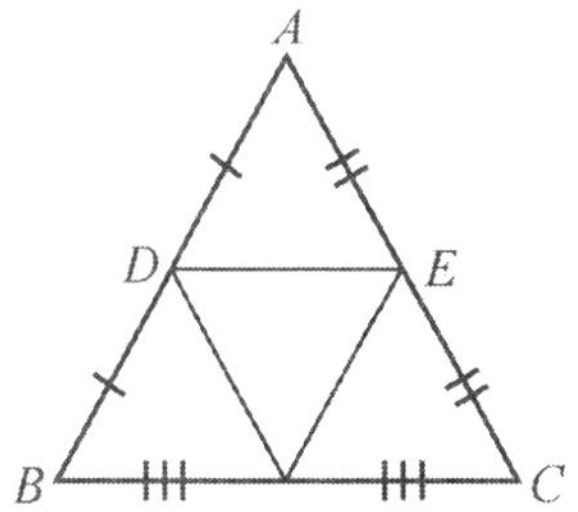

The four triangles formed are ΔADE, ΔDBF, ΔDEF and ΔEFC. The four triangles are similar to the larger triangle, ΔABC.

36. B

A line that bisects any side of a triangle and makes a right angle at the midpoint is known as the perpendicular bisector. Thus, PT is the perpendicular bisector of side QR.

Copyright Protected

37. D

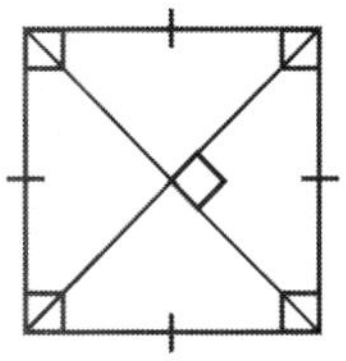

The given properties describe a square.

38. C

A perpendicular bisector divides a line segment into two equal parts at its midpoint (alternative A) and extends from the line segment at 90 degrees (alternatives B and D).

Alternative C does not describe a property of a perpendicular bisector because the bisector is located at the midpoint.

Key Strategies for Success on Tests

Copyright Protected

KEY STRATEGIES FOR SUCCESS ON TESTS

THINGS TO CONSIDER WHEN TAKING A TEST

It is normal to feel anxious before you write a test. You can manage this anxiety by using the following strategies:

- Think positive thoughts. Imagine yourself doing well on the test.
- Make a conscious effort to relax by taking several slow, deep, controlled breaths. Concentrate on the air going in and out of your body.
- Before you begin the test, ask questions if you are unsure of anything.
- Jot down key words or phrases from any instructions your teacher gives you.
- Look over the entire test to find out the number and kinds of questions on the test.
- Read each question closely, and reread if necessary.
- Pay close attention to key vocabulary words. Sometimes, these words are **bolded** or *italicized*, and they are usually important words in the question.
- If you are putting your answers on an answer sheet, mark your answers carefully. Always print clearly. If you wish to change an answer, erase the mark completely, and ensure that your final answer is darker than the one you have erased.
- Use highlighting to note directions, key words, and vocabulary that you find confusing or that are important to answering the question.
- Double-check to make sure you have answered everything before handing in your test.
- When taking tests, students often overlook the easy words. Failure to pay close attention to these words can result in an incorrect answer. One way to avoid this is to be aware of these words and to underline, circle, or highlight them while you are taking the test.
- Even though some words are easy to understand, they can change the meaning of the entire question, so it is important that you pay attention to them. Here are some examples.

all	always	most likely	probably	best	not
difference	usually	except	most	unlikely	likely

Example

1. Which of the following expressions is **incorrect**?

A. $3 + 2 \geq 5$

B. $4 - 3 < 2$

C. $5 \times 4 < 15$

D. $6 \times 3 \geq 18$

Not for Reproduction

Test Preparation and Test-Taking Skills

Helpful Strategies for Answering Multiple-Choice Questions

A multiple-choice question gives you some information and then asks you to select an answer from four choices. Each question has one correct answer. The other choices are distractors, which are incorrect.

The following strategies can help you when answering multiple-choice questions:

- Quickly skim through the entire test. Find out how many questions there are, and plan your time accordingly.
- Read and reread questions carefully. Underline key words, and try to think of an answer before looking at the choices.
- If there is a graphic, look at the graphic, read the question, and go back to the graphic. Then, you may want to underline the important information from the question.
- Carefully read the choices. Read the question first and then each choice that goes with it.
- When choosing an answer, try to eliminate those choices that are clearly wrong or do not make sense.
- Some questions may ask you to select the best answer. These questions will always include words like *best*, *most appropriate*, or *most likely*. All of the choices will be correct to some degree, but one of the choices will be better than the others in some way. Carefully read all four choices before choosing the answer you think is the best.
- If you do not know the answer, or if the question does not make sense to you, it is better to guess than to leave it blank.
- Do not spend too much time on any one question. Make a mark (*) beside a difficult question, and come back to it later. If you are leaving a question to come back to later, make sure you also leave the space on the answer sheet, if you are using one.

- Remember to go back to the difficult questions at the end of the test; sometimes, clues are given throughout the test that will provide you with answers.
- Note any negative words like *no* or *not*, and be sure your answer fits the question.
- Before changing an answer, be sure you have a very good reason to do so.
- Do not look for patterns on your answer sheet, if you are using one.

Copyright Protected

HELPFUL STRATEGIES FOR ANSWERING WRITTEN-RESPONSE QUESTIONS

A written response requires you to respond to a question or directive indicated by words such as explain, predict, list, describe, show your work, solve, or calculate. The following strategies can help you when answering written-response questions:

- Read and reread the question carefully.
- Recognize and pay close attention to directing words such as *explain*, *show your work*, and *describe*.
- Underline key words and phrases that indicate what is required in your answer, such as *explain*, *estimate*, *answer*, *calculate*, or *show your work*.
- Write down rough, point-form notes regarding the information you want to include in your answer.
- Think about what you want to say, and organize information and ideas in a coherent and concise manner within the time limit you have for the question.
- Be sure to answer every part of the question that is asked.
- Include as much information as you can when you are asked to explain your thinking.
- Include a picture or diagram if it will help to explain your thinking.
- Try to put your final answer to a problem in a complete sentence to be sure it is reasonable.
- Reread your response to ensure you have answered the question.
- Ask yourself if your answer makes sense.
- Ask yourself if your answer sounds right.
- Use appropriate subject vocabulary and terms in your response.

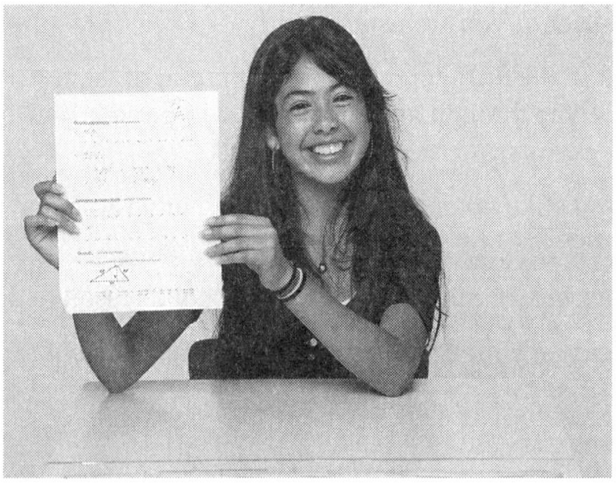

Not for Reproduction

About Mathematics Tests

What You Need to Know about Mathematics Tests

To do well on a mathematics test, you need to understand and apply your knowledge of mathematical concepts. Reading skills can also make a difference in how well you perform. Reading skills can help you follow instructions and find key words, as well as read graphs, diagrams, and tables. They can also help you solve mathematics problems.

Mathematics tests usually have two types of questions: questions that ask for understanding of mathematics ideas and questions that test how well you can solve mathematics problems.

How You Can Prepare for Mathematics Tests

The following strategies are particular to preparing for and writing mathematics tests:

- Know how to use your calculator, and, if it is allowed, use your own for the test.
- Note taking is a good way to review and study important information from your class notes and textbook.
- Sketch a picture of the problem, procedure, or term. Drawing is helpful for learning and remembering concepts.
- Check your answer to practice questions by working backward to the beginning. You can find the beginning by going step by step in reverse order.
- Use the following steps when answering questions with graphics (pictures, diagrams, tables, or graphs):
  1. Read the title of the graphic and any key words.
  2. Read the test question carefully to figure out what information you need to find in the graphic.
  3. Go back to the graphic to find the information you need.
  4. Decide which operation is needed.
- Always pay close attention when pressing the keys on your calculator. Repeat the procedure a second time to be sure you pressed the correct keys.

Copyright Protected

TEST PREPARATION COUNTDOWN

If you develop a plan for studying and test preparation, you will perform well on tests.

Here is a general plan to follow seven days before you write a test.

COUNTDOWN: 7 DAYS BEFORE THE TEST

1. Use "Finding Out about the Test" to help you make your own personal test preparation plan.
2. Review the following information:
   - Areas to be included on the test
   - Types of test items
   - General and specific test tips
3. Start preparing for the test at least seven days before the test. Develop your test preparation plan, and set time aside to prepare and study.

COUNTDOWN: 6, 5, 4, 3, 2 DAYS BEFORE THE TEST

1. Review old homework assignments, quizzes, and tests.
2. Rework problems on quizzes and tests to make sure you still know how to solve them.
3. Correct any errors made on quizzes and tests.
4. Review key concepts, processes, formulas, and vocabulary.
5. Create practice test questions for yourself, and answer them. Work out many sample problems.

COUNTDOWN: THE NIGHT BEFORE THE TEST

1. Use the night before the test for final preparation, which includes reviewing and gathering materials needed for the test before going to bed.
2. Most importantly, get a good night's rest, and know you have done everything possible to do well on the test.

TEST DAY

1. Eat a healthy and nutritious breakfast.
2. Ensure you have all the necessary materials.
3. Think positive thoughts, such as "I can do this," "I am ready," and "I know I can do well."
4. Arrive at your school early, so you are not rushing, which can cause you anxiety and stress.

Not for Reproduction

Summary of How to Be Successful during a Test

You may find some of the following strategies useful for writing a test:

- Take two or three deep breaths to help you relax.
- Read the directions carefully, and underline, circle, or highlight any important words.
- Look over the entire test to understand what you will need to do.
- Budget your time.
- Begin with an easy question or a question you know you can answer correctly rather than follow the numerical question order of the test.
- If you cannot remember how to answer a question, try repeating the deep breathing and physical relaxation activities. Then, move on to visualization and positive self-talk to get yourself going.
- When answering questions with graphics (pictures, diagrams, tables, or graphs), look at the question carefully, and use the following steps:
    1. Read the title of the graphic and any key words.
    2. Read the test question carefully to figure out what information you need to find in the graphic.
    3. Go back to the graphic to find the information you need.
- Write down anything you remember about the subject on the reverse side of your test paper. This activity sometimes helps to remind you that you do know something and are capable of writing the test.
- Look over your test when you have finished, and double-check your answers to be sure you did not forget anything.

NOTES

Practice Tests

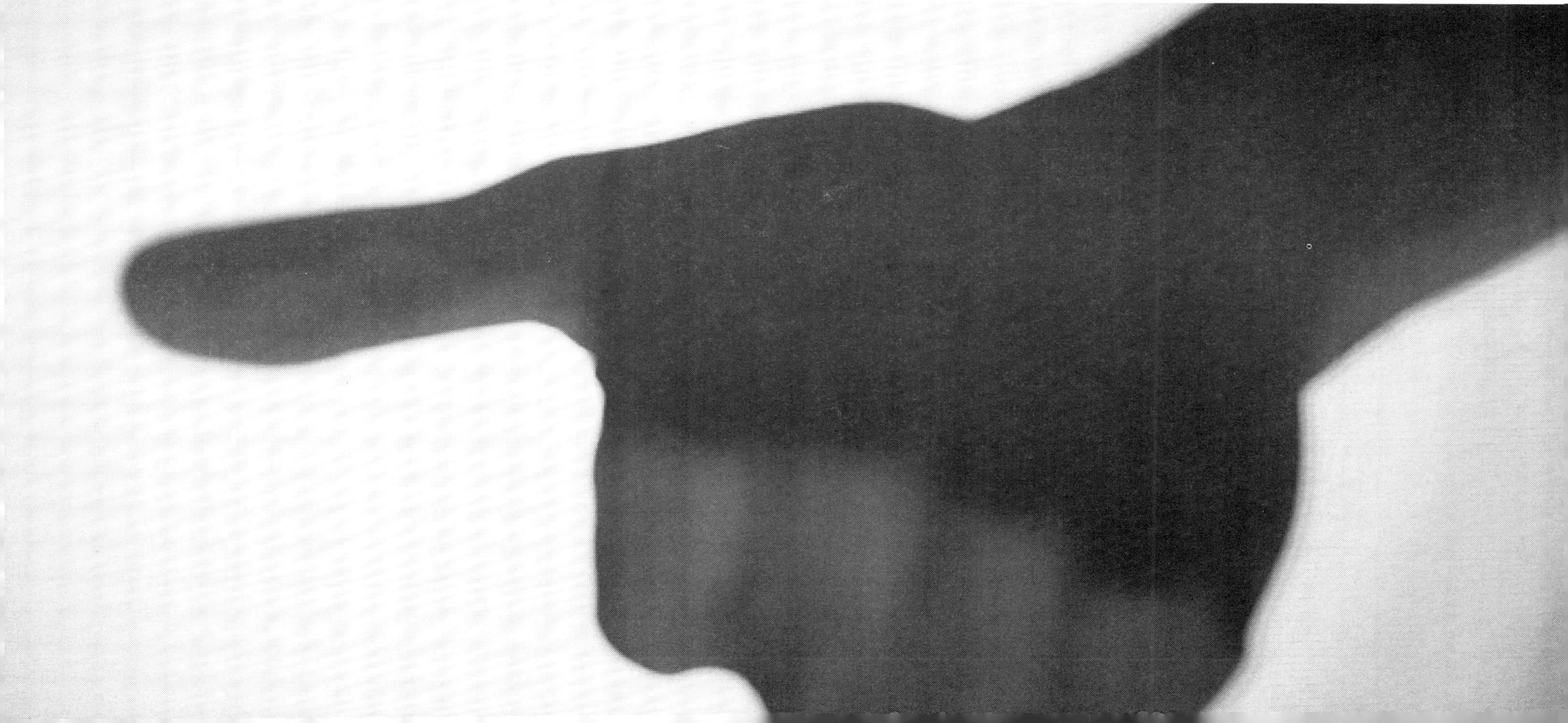

PRACTICE TEST 1

1. Which of the following graphs represents a linear relation?

A.

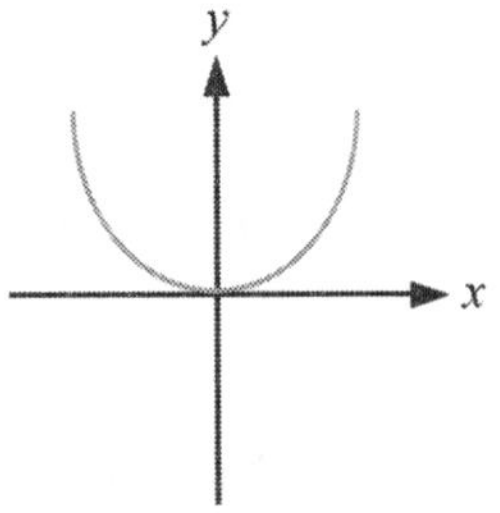

B.

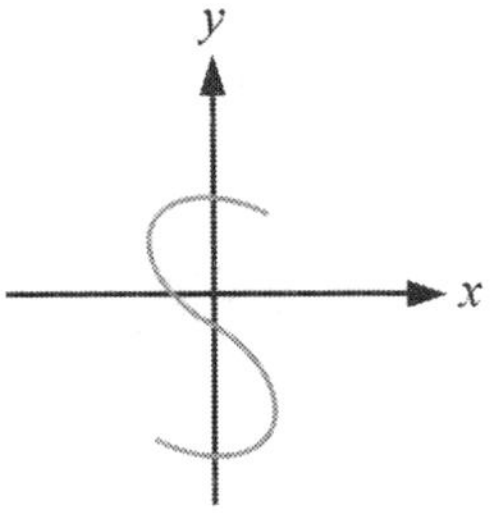

C.

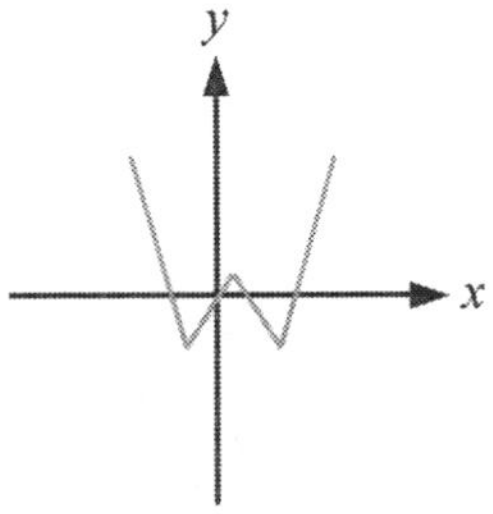

D.

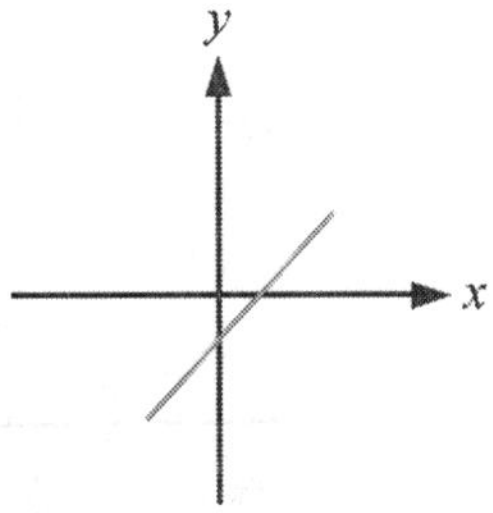

2. Which of the following equations represents a non-linear relation?

   A. $(n - 1)(n + 1) = 3$

   B. $x + y + z = 3$

   C. $n + m = 3$

   D. $x = 2y$

Use the following information to answer the next question.

Consider the two graphs below.

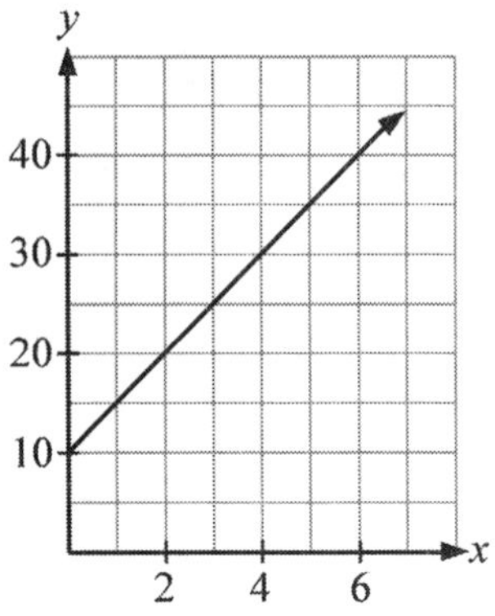

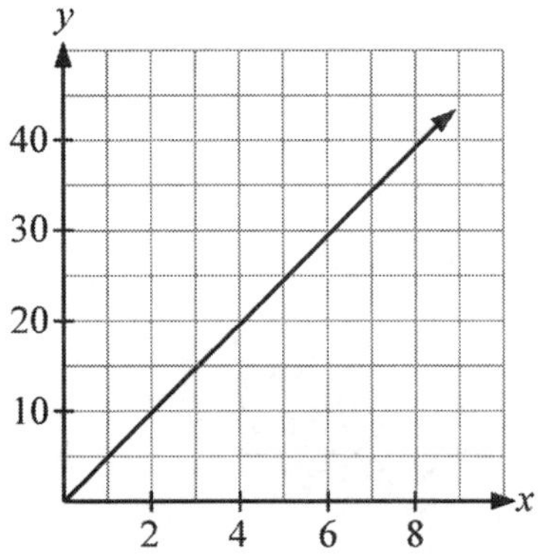

Open Response

3. Identify what type of variation is shown in each graph.

   Justify your answer.

Not for Reproduction

Use the following information to answer the next question.

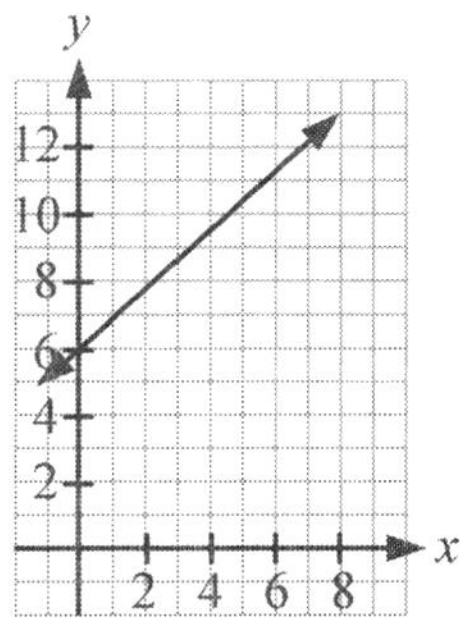

4. What is the equation of the given line?

A. $y = x + 3$

B. $y = x - 3$

C. $y = x + 6$

D. $y = x - 6$

Use the following information to answer the next question.

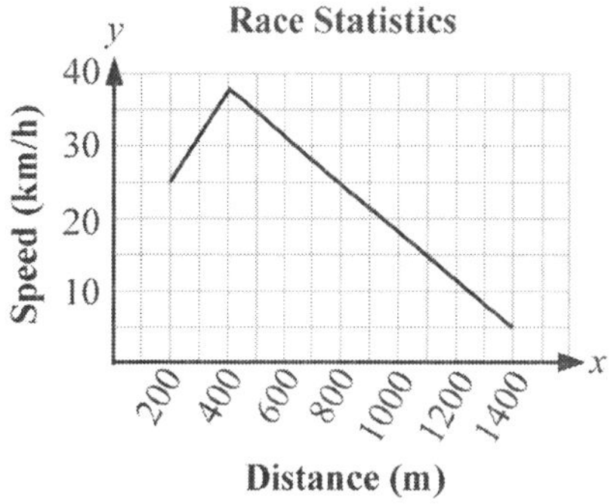

5. Which of the following statements about the graph is **not** true?

A. Interpolation would involve analyzing races that were between 200 m and 1 400 m.

B. Extrapolation would involve analyzing races that were between 200 m and 1 400 m.

C. The negative rate of change between 400 m and 1 400 m indicates a constant decrease in speed as the length of the race increases.

D. The positive rate of change between 200 m and 400 m indicates a constant increase in speed as the length of the race increases.

6. Which of the following tables gives correct x- and y-values for the expression $y = \frac{2x}{3}$?

A.

x	0	3	6	9
y	0	2	4	6

B.

x	2	4	6	8
y	3	6	9	12

C.

x	3	6	8	21
y	2	4	12	14

D.

x	0	3	4	14
y	0	2	6	21

Copyright Protected

Use the following information to answer the next question.

The owners of a new racquetball club are trying to decide on what the monthly fees for the club should be.
Plan I – \$20 per month plus \$3 per court rental
Plan II – \$15 per month plus \$4 per court rental

Open Response

7. Describe the difference in the graphs of plans I and II.

Which is the better plan to begin with for someone who wants to join the club? At what point does the other plan become the better deal?

Use a table of values to justify your answer.

8. The height to which a ball rebounds varies directly with the height from which it was dropped. A ball dropped from a height of 35 cm rebounds to a height of 21 cm. If the ball is dropped from a height of 100 cm, then what is the rebound height?

A. 166 cm

B. 75 cm

C. 60 cm

D. 47 cm

Use the following information to answer the next question.

Line	Slope
I	3
II	-1
III	-3
IV	$-\frac{1}{3}$

9. Which two of the given lines are perpendicular?

A. I and II

B. I and IV

C. II and III

D. II and IV

10. Which of the following equations represents a straight line on a graph?

A. $y^4 = 4x^2$

B. $x + 4 = y$

C. $x^3 + y^2 = 3$

D. $4xy + 5 = 0$

11. What is the equation $3x + 2y + 6 = 0$ expressed in slope y-intercept form?

A. $y = -\frac{3}{2}x - 3$

B. $y = -\frac{3}{2}x + 3$

C. $y = \frac{3}{2}x - 3$

D. $y = \frac{3}{2}x + 3$

12. The hypotenuse of a right triangle is 17 cm and the difference between the other two sides is 7 cm. What are the lengths of the two unknown sides?

A. 5 cm and 12 cm

B. 6 cm and 13 cm

C. 7 cm and 14 cm

D. 8 cm and 15 cm

Not for Reproduction

Use the following information to answer the next question.

This diagram represents a rectangular envelope.

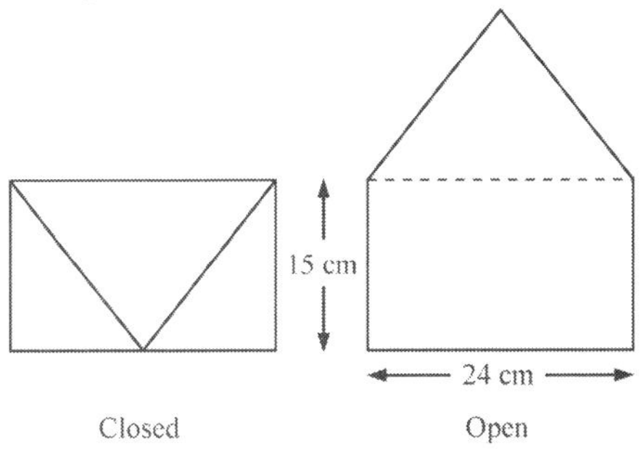

13. What is the total area of one side of the opened envelope?

A. 720 cm^2

B. 540 cm^2

C. 360 cm^2

D. 180 cm^2

14. If a lead cylinder is 24 cm high and has a base radius of 6.0 cm, how many spheres that are 1.2 cm in diameter can be made from it when it is melted down? Use $\pi = 3.14$.

A. 2 534

B. 2 853

C. 3 000

D. 3 200

15. What is the volume of a cube, to the nearest hundredth, with an edge length of 9.8 mm?

A. 29.40 mm^3

B. 94.12 mm^3

C. 96.04 mm^3

D. 941.19 mm^3

16. The expression $(-a^2)^{-3}$ is simplified to

A. a^{-6}

B. $-3a^2$

C. $-a^{-6}$

D. $-a^{-1}$

17. At a garden centre, two 1-L buckets are each being filled by a different tap. The first tap flows at a rate of 100 mL / min and the second tap flows at a rate of 200 mL / min. What is the ratio of the tap flows?

A. 1:1

B. 1:2

C. 1:3

D. 1:4

18. Expanding the expression $(x-3)(x^2+2x-4)$ results in which of the following polynomials?

A. $x^3+x^2-10x+7$

B. $x^3-x^2-10x+12$

C. $x^3+5x^2+10x-7$

D. $x^3-5x^2+10x-12$

Use the following information to answer the next multipart question.

19. $2x+3$ is multiplied by $3x+4$.

Open Response

a) What is the product of $2x+3$ and $3x+4$?

Show your work.

b) Justify your answer using algebra tiles, FOIL strategy, or vertical multiplication.

Copyright Protected

Show your work.

Use the following information to answer the next question.

On a cool spring day, the wind is blowing at 30 km/h. A small aircraft can fly 600 km with this wind in the same time that it takes to fly 500 km against this wind.

20. Which of the following rational equations determines the speed of the aircraft in still air?

A. $600x + 30 = 500x - 30$

B. $600(x + 30) = 500(x - 30)$

C. $\dfrac{600}{x+30} = \dfrac{500}{x-30}$

D. $\dfrac{600}{x+30} = \dfrac{500}{x-30} + x$

Open Response

21. Use the x- and y-intercept method to graph the equation $3x - 6y - 12 = 0$.

Show your work.

22. Which equation represents the line that has an x-intercept of 4 and a y-intercept of 12?

A. $y = -3x + 12$

B. $y = -12x - 3$

C. $y = 3x + 12$

D. $y = -12x + 3$

Not for Reproduction

Open Response

23. Determine the equation of the given line in slope y-intercept form and standard form.

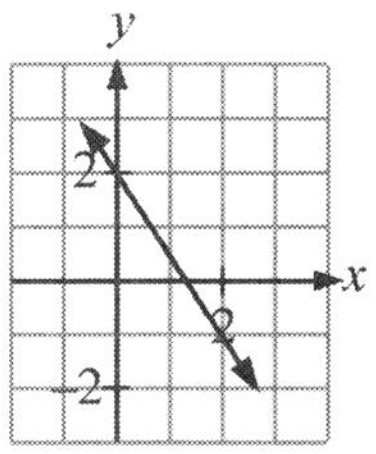

Show your work.

Use the following information to answer the next question.

> Lenny and Julie have a car-washing business. If P represents the profit, in dollars, from the car wash and n represents the number of cars washed, the equation that represents their situation is $P = 5n - 50$.

24. Which of the following statements about this relation is **false**?

A. The rate of change is 50.

B. The slope of the relation is 5.

C. Washing 10 cars will allow Lenny and Julie to break even.

D. The P-intercept corresponds to a business start-up cost of $50.

Use the following information to answer the next question.

> The total cost of transporting a group of students on a field trip from Hamilton to Niagra Falls is made up of a fixed initial cost for the bus plus a cost per student.
> Line I represents the total cost of the field trip last year.
> Line II represents the total cost of the field trip this year.

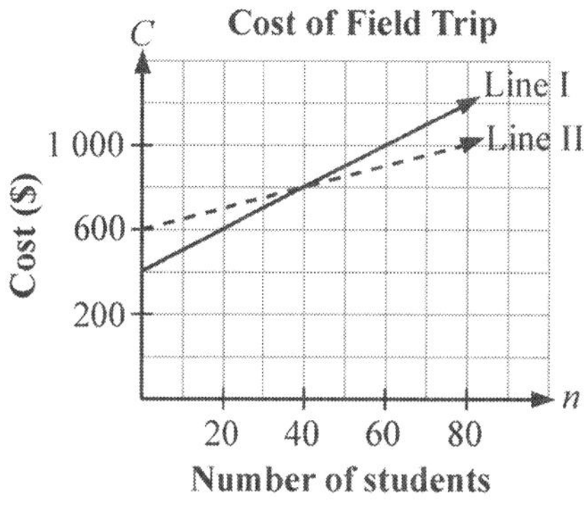

25. Which statement is **true**?

A. The fixed cost for the bus last year is the same as the fixed cost for the bus this year.

B. The point of intersection determines the number of students for which the total cost of the field trip in each year is the same.

C. If 40 students go on the field trip each year, the total cost was more last year than it is this year.

D. If more than 50 students go on the field trip each year, then the cost per student last year was less than the cost per student this year.

Copyright Protected

Use the following information to answer the next question.

A rectangle has a perimeter of 32 cm and side lengths that are integers.

26. What is the measure of one of the sides of the rectangle that is required in order to obtain the **maximum** area?

A. 6 cm

B. 7 cm

C. 8 cm

D. 9 cm

Open Response

27. A rectangle has a width of 7 cm and a length of 10 cm. If the rectangle is reconfigured such that it has a maximum area and minimum perimeter, what will the length of each side of the rectangle be?

Show your work.

Use the following information to answer the next question.

Some students want to wrap the four sides of this box.

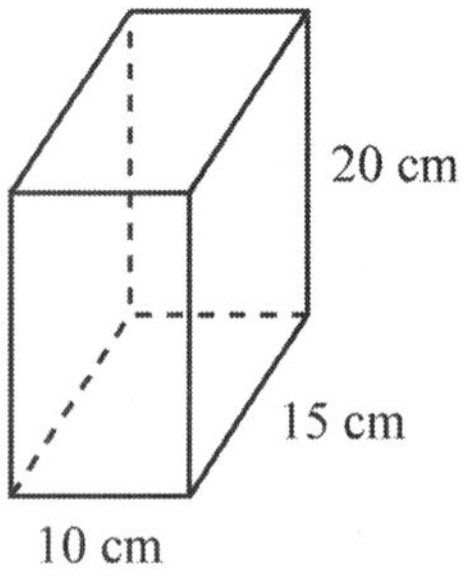

28. Which expression can be used to calculate the total amount of paper needed?

A. $2(10 \times 20) + 4(15 \times 20)$

B. $2(10 \times 20) + 2(15 \times 20)$

C. $4(10 \times 20)$

D. $4(15 \times 20)$

Use the following information to answer the next question.

A company packages blank CDs that are 2 mm thick and 12 cm in diameter.
The company determines that the most cost effective packaging is a cylinder with a height of 12.2 cm.

Open Response

29. What is the surface area of a cylindrical package with a **maximum** volume?
How many CDs would fit into it?

Show your work.

Use the following information to answer the next question.

In the given figure, line *DE* is parallel to *BC*, and *D* and *E* are the midpoints of sides *AB* and *AC*, respectively.

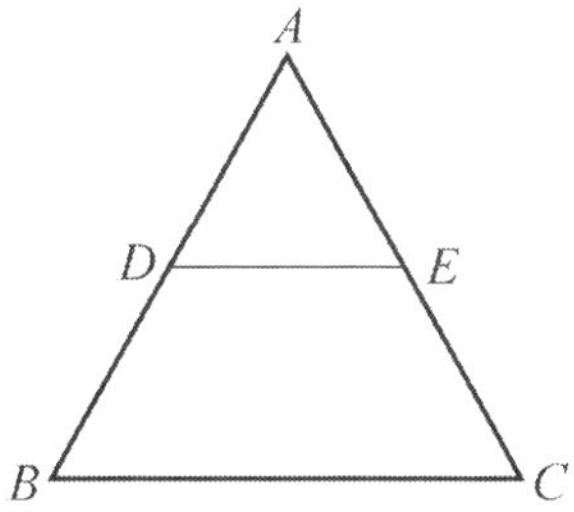

30. What is ratio of the length of *DE* to that of *BC*?

A. 1:1

B. 1:2

C. 2:2

D. 3:2

Use the following information to answer the next question.

The given scatter plot shows the approximate amount of snowfall received each day over a period of seven days at one location.

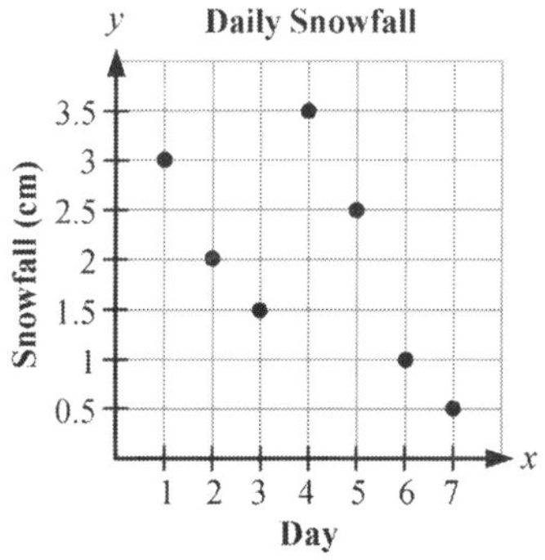

31. On which day was the snowfall 1 cm?

A. Day 3

B. Day 4

C. Day 5

D. Day 6

Copyright Protected

PRACTICE TEST 2

Use the following information to answer the next question.

The following scatter plot shows the profits for a computer software company over five years.

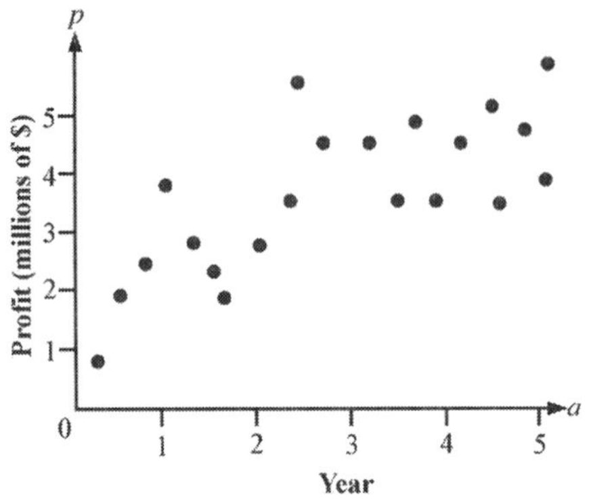

1. Which of the following statements regarding the line of best fit for the scatter plot shown is **true**?
   A. The line of best fit steadily falls from left to right.
   B. The line of best fit steadily rises from left to right.
   C. The line of best fit fluctuates.
   D. There is no line of best fit.

Open Response

2. Complete the table below and show your work. Then, identify the type of relation present and justify your answer based on the properties that are evident.

x	$y = 3x + 1$	**First Differences**
0		
1		
2		
3		

Use the following information to answer the next question.

Memory on a computer is measured in kilobytes (KB), megabytes (MB), or gigabytes (GB). A memory device has a capacity of 2 048 KB, which is equivalent to 2 MB. When there are 4 096 KB on the device, the equivalent memory is 4 MB.

3. How can the relationship between kilobytes (KB) and megabytes (MB) be described?
   A. A direct variation with a positive correlation
   B. A direct variation with a negative correlation
   C. A partial variation with a positive correlation
   D. A partial variation with a negative correlation

Not for Reproduction

4. Which of the following graphs represents a line with a rate of change of $\frac{3}{2}$ and that passes through the point $(-3, -1)$?

A.
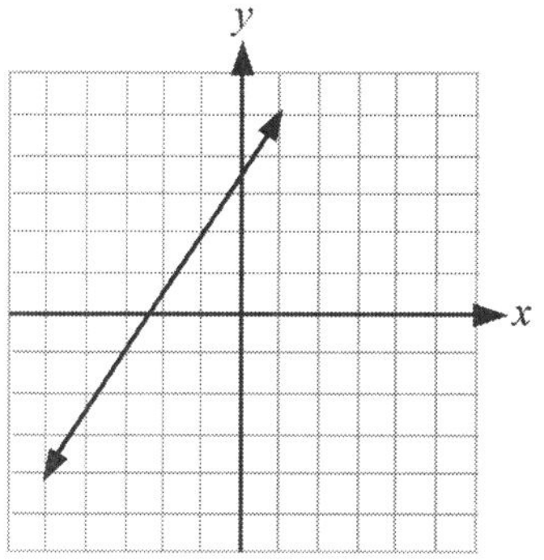

B.
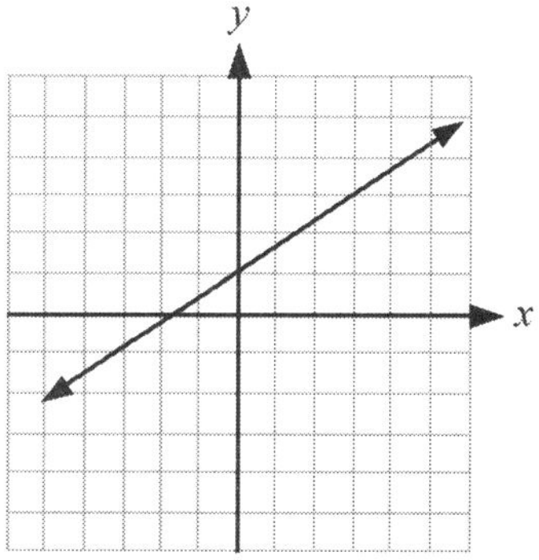

C.
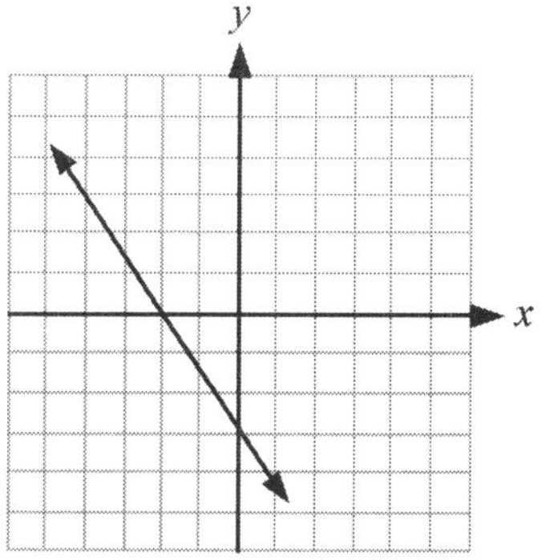

D.
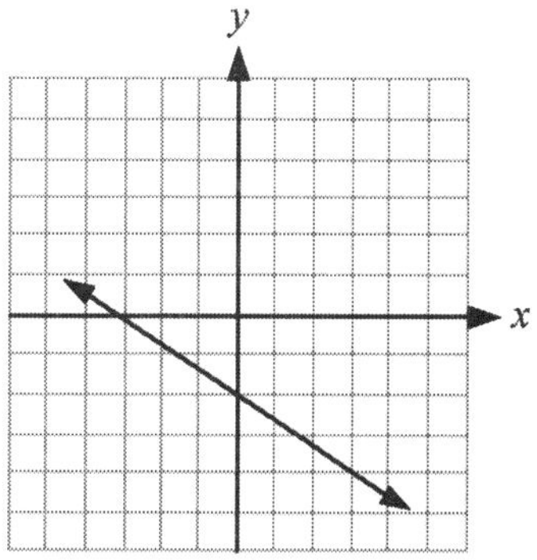

Use the following information to answer the next question.

A tour boat will leave its port and make a total of three stops. Two stops allow the passengers to go snorkeling and one stop is at an island village for lunch. The boat will then return to port.

5. Which of the following graphs **best** represents the distance that the tour boat is from port versus the time of day?

A.
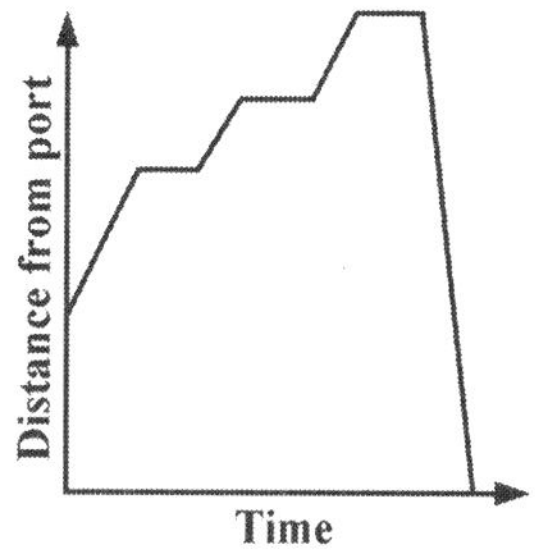

B.
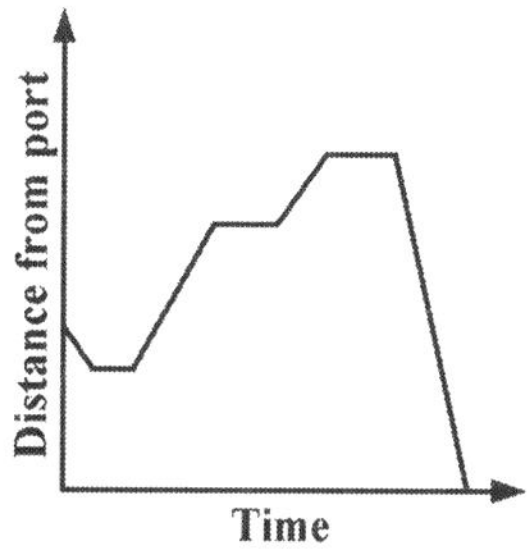

C.
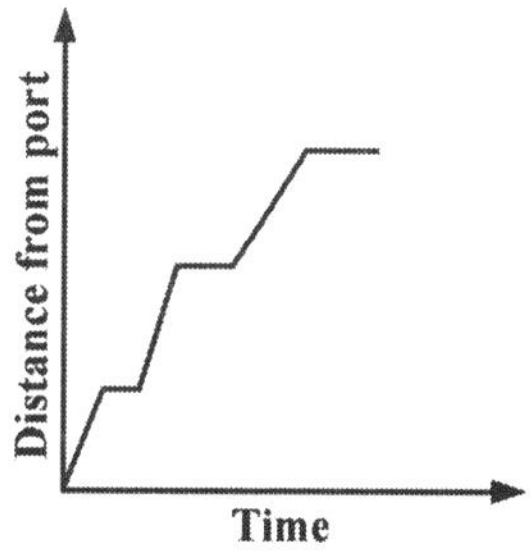

D.
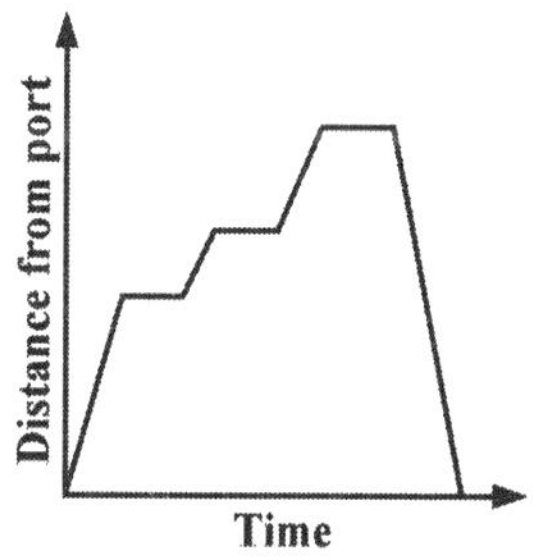

Copyright Protected

Use the following information to answer the next question.

Jet Ski Rentals
The data shows the cost of renting a Jet Ski at a local lake.

Time (h)	1	2	3	4	5	6	7
Cost ($)	28	36	44	52	60	68	76

Open Response

6. Graph the relation and determine the equation of the line.

Show your work.

Use the following information to answer the next question.

Two mechanics advertise the following labour costs for car repairs.
Company I: Service charge of $40 plus $25 per hour
Company II: Service charge of $80 plus $20 per hour

7. How would the graph representing the repair costs of company II be different than the graph of company I?

A. The y-intercept would be lower and the graph would have a steeper line from left to right.

B. The y-intercept would be higher and the graph would have a steeper line from left to right.

C. The y-intercept would be lower and the graph would have a less steep line from left to right.

D. The y-intercept would be higher and the graph would have a less steep line from left to right.

Use the following information to answer the next question.

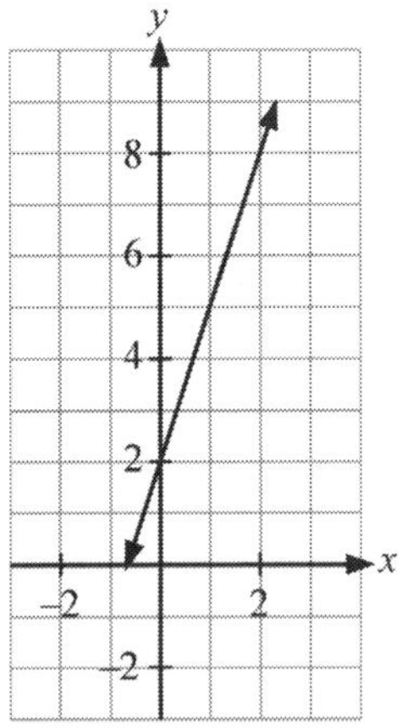

8. What is the **most likely** equation of this line?

A. $y = 3x + 1$

B. $y = 3x + 2$

C. $y + 3 - 1 = 0$

D. $y + 3x - 2 = 0$

Not for Reproduction

Use the following information to answer the next question.

x	y
1	–3.5
2	–4
3	–4.5
4	–5

9. Which graph correctly shows the rate of change for the given data?

A. 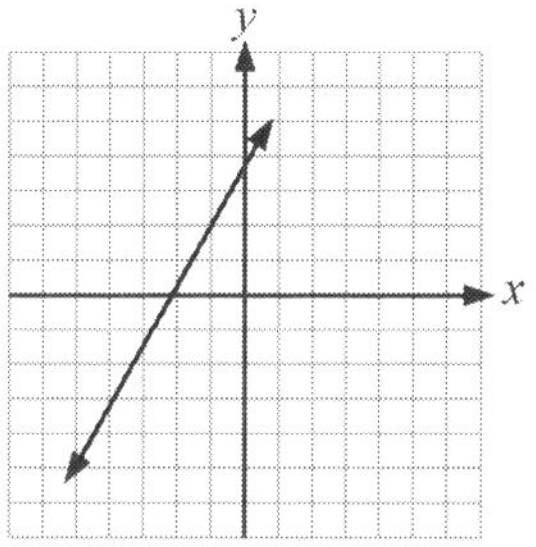

B. 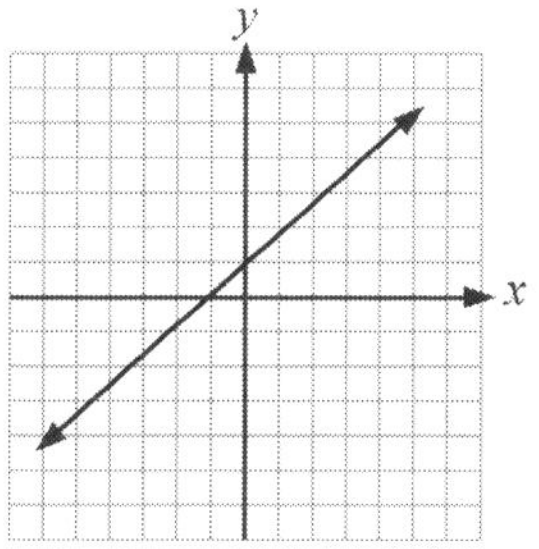

C. 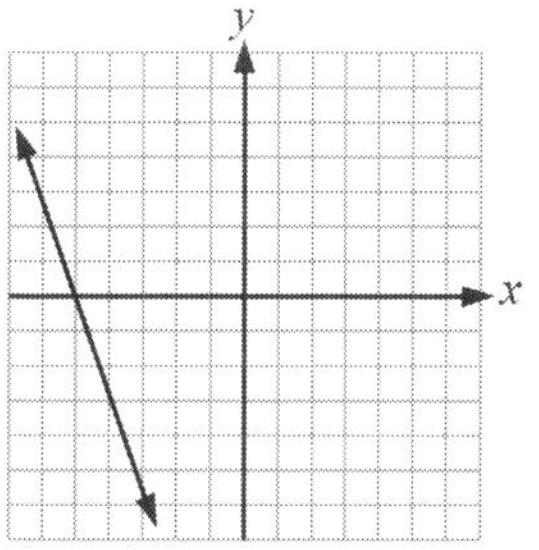

D. 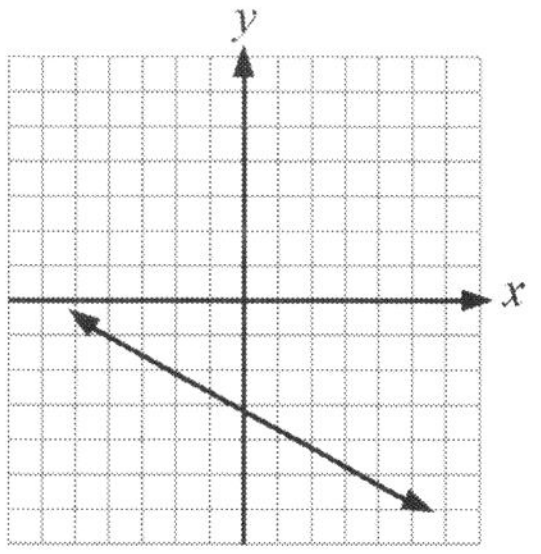

10. Which of the following statements describes the line defined by the equation $y = -2x + 5$?

A. The line rises toward the right and intersects the x-axis at +5.

B. The line falls toward the right and intersects the y-axis at –5.

C. The line falls toward the right and intersects the y-axis at +5.

D. The line rises toward the right and intersects the y-axis at –5.

11. Which of the following equations describes a vertical line?

A. $y = 4$

B. $x = 4$

C. $y = 2x$

D. $x = -5y$

Copyright Protected

Use the following information to answer the next question.

Graphing Equations
The slope of a line is 2, and the y-intercept is 3.

Open Response

12. Write the equation of this line in slope y-intercept form and standard form. Graph the relation. Then, compare the characteristics of this graph with the graph of $y = 3$.

Show your work.

13. The length of the hypotenuse of a right triangle is 30.5 cm and the length of one of the other sides is 5.5 cm. What is the length of the third side?

A. 25 cm

B. 30 cm

C. 31 cm

D. 36 cm

14. Four semicircles are attached on the four sides of a rectangle such that their diameters are equal to the sides of the rectangles. The side lengths of the rectangle are 30 m and 50 m. What is the perimeter of this composite figure?

A. 30π m

B. 60π m

C. 80π m

D. 90π m

Use the following information to answer the next question.

A circus tent is cylindrical up to a height of 3.5 m and conical above it.
The diameter of the base is 102 m, and the slant height of the conical part is 55 m.

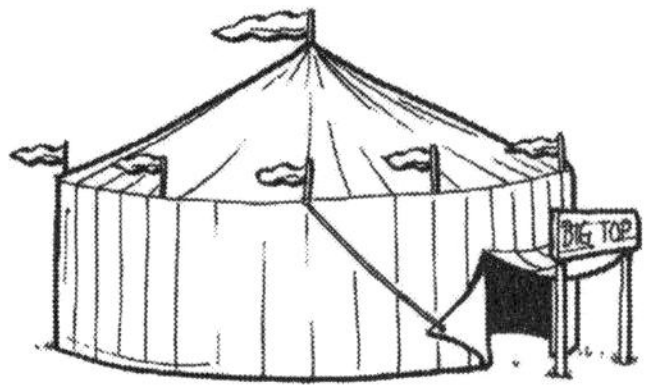

15. What is the total canvas used in making the tent?

$\pi = 3.14$

A. 9 052.23 m^2

B. 9 372.15 m^2

C. 9 928.68 m^2

D. 9 948.25 m^2

Not for Reproduction

Use the following information to answer the next question.

John is considering purchasing juice in one of these containers. They both cost \$1.50 and are completely filled with juice.

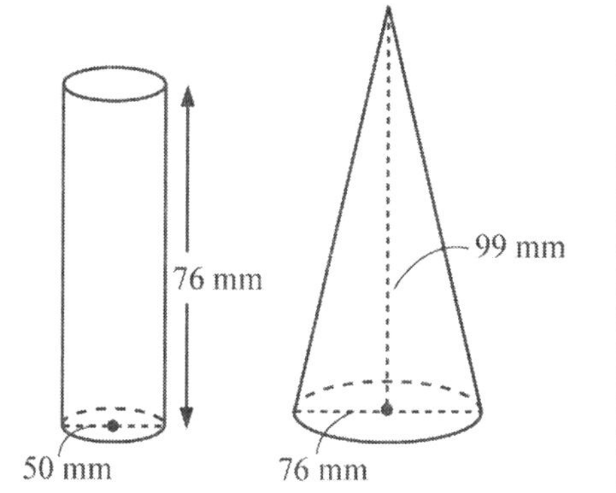

Open Response

16. Which juice container is the better deal?

Show your work and justify your answer.

17. The side length of the given cube is $3x^3y^4$. What is the simplified expression for the volume of this cube?

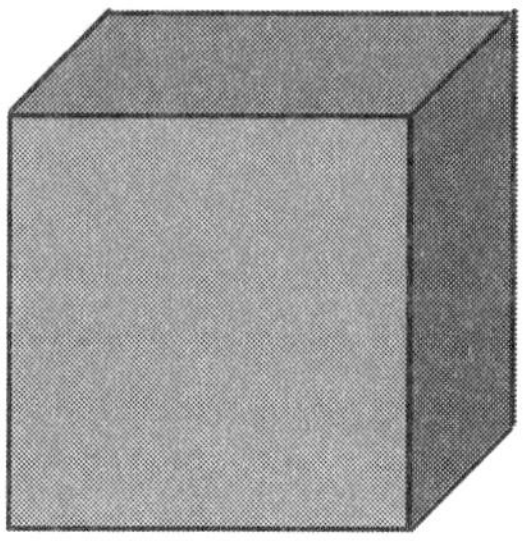

A. $9x^9y^{12}$

B. $9x^6y^{12}$

C. $27x^{27}y^{64}$

D. $27x^9y^{12}$

18. What is the product of x^{17} and x^{25}?

A. x^{425}

B. x^{42}

C. x^{32}

D. x^{52}

19. While travelling in northern Ontario, John asked a gas attendant to give him \$10.00 worth of gas. If the attendant put 6.25 L of gas in John's car, what was the price of gas per litre?

A. \$0.63 / L

B. \$1.60 / L

C. \$3.75 / L

D. \$62.50 / L

Use the following information to answer the next question.

A copy of a newspaper purchased from a newspaper box costs \$0.50 Monday through Saturday, and \$1.00 on Sunday. Subscribing to the newspaper for daily delivery costs \$3.65 per week.

Open Response

20. For one full week of newspapers, what is the amount as a percentage that a newspaper subscriber saves compared with a person who buys the newspaper each day from a newspaper box?

Show your work.

Use the following information to answer the next question.

The pyramids of Egypt are ancient tombs built by pharaohs 4 000 years ago. Pharaohs built these tombs to protect their bodies as they prepared for the afterlife. The pyramids were built with amazing precision. Their bases are perfect squares, and the limestone blocks fit so well together that in many places you cannot slide a piece of paper between them.

21. If the base of a pyramid covers an area of 100 m^2, what is the length of one side of the base?

A. 500 m

B. 400 m

C. 250 m

D. 100 m

22. Ms. Carlson put $3.75 into a parking meter. She used twice as many nickels as quarters, and 3 fewer dimes than quarters. How many nickels did she use?

A. 3

B. 6

C. 9

D. 18

23. Which of the following equations represents the line that passes through point $(-2, -6)$ and has slope of -1?

A. $y + x = 6$

B. $y + x = 8$

C. $y + x = -6$

D. $y + x = -8$

Use the following information to answer the next question.

The publisher of a high school yearbook charges $24 per yearbook plus a layout fee of $475.

24. The yearbook committee has decided that the publisher will receive no more than $6100. What is the **maximum** number of yearbooks that can be sold?

A. 234

B. 235

C. 273

D. 274

Use the following information to answer the next question.

Car Rental Plans

Walter is researching the cost of renting a car for one week for when he has to get his car repainted. Company I charges $75 per week plus $0.20 for each kilometre driven. Company II charges $100 per week plus $0.10 for each kilometre driven.

Open Response

25. Write the equation of the line for both relations and solve graphically. Explain the conditions under which each plan is better.

Show your work and justify your answer.

Not for Reproduction

Use the following information to answer the next question.

A company wants to rent a hall for a holiday party.

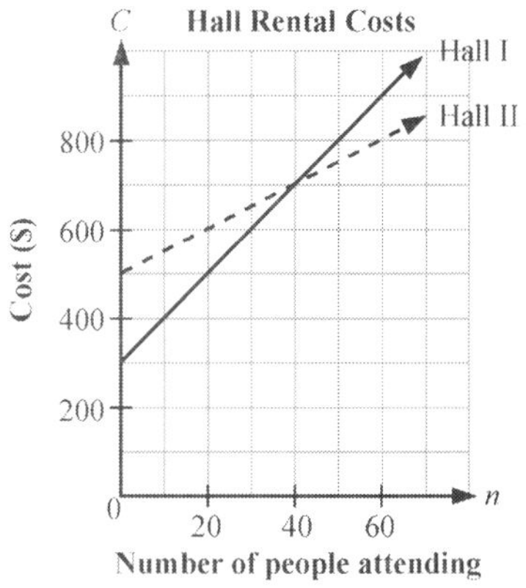

26. Which of the following statements is **true**?

A. The equation for Hall I is $C = 500 + 5n$, and it is the better value if 40 or less people attend.

B. The equation for Hall II is $C = 500 - 5n$, and it is the better value if 40 or less people attend.

C. The equation for Hall I is $C = 300 + 10n$, and it is the better value if 40 or less people attend.

D. The equation for Hall II is $C = 300 - 10n$, and it is the better value if 40 or less people attend.

27. The area of a rectangle with length l and width w is 90 square units. Which of the following sets of dimensions has a **minimum** perimeter and the given area?

A. $l = 10$ units
$w = 9$ units

B. $l = 15$ units
$w = 6$ units

C. $l = 18$ units
$w = 5$ units

D. $l = 30$ units
$w = 3$ units

Use the following information to answer the next question.

Cylinder 1 and Cylinder 2 have approximately the same volume. Susan needs to figure out which cylinder has the least amount of surface area to paint.

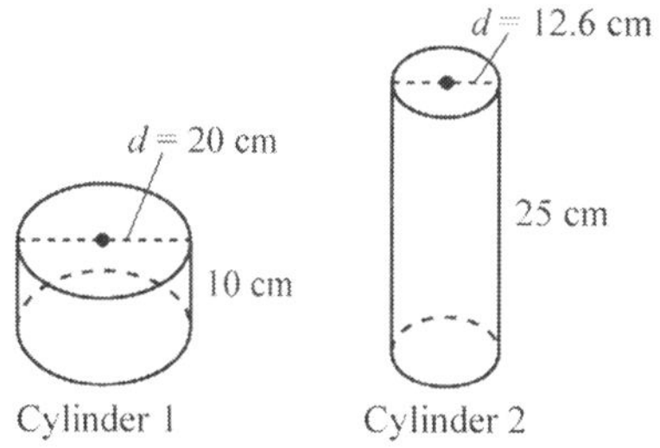

28. Which of the following statements is **true**?

A. Cylinder 1 has 18 cm^2 more surface area to paint.

B. Cylinder 2 has 18 cm^2 more surface area to paint.

C. Cylinder 1 has 25 cm^2 more surface area to paint.

D. Cylinder 2 has 25 cm^2 more surface area to paint.

Open Response

29. Prove the median of the triangle bisects the total area of the triangle.

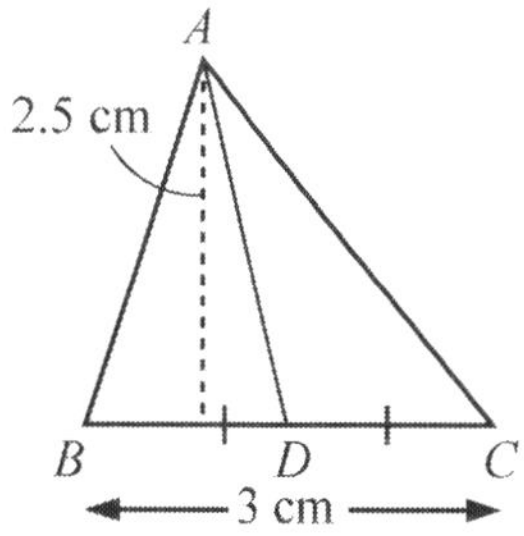

Show your work.

Copyright Protected

30. In which of the following shapes are the diagonals perpendicular to each other?

A. Rhombus

B. Rectangle

C. Trapezoid

D. Parallelogram

31. Two variables are related to each other in such a way that an increase in one results in an increase of the other. Which of the following scatter plots represents the two variables?

A.

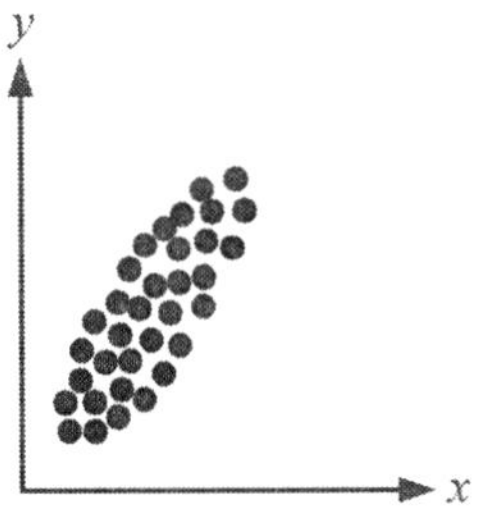

B.

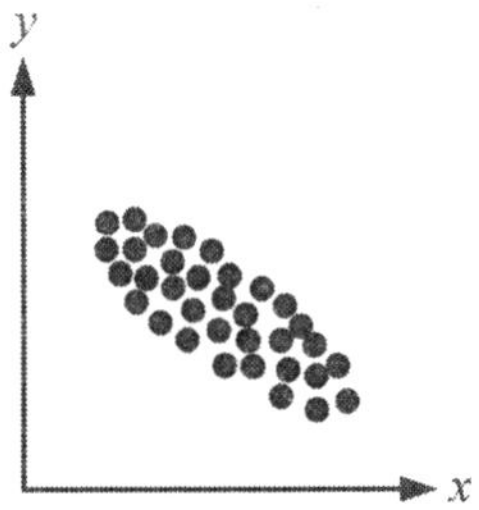

C.

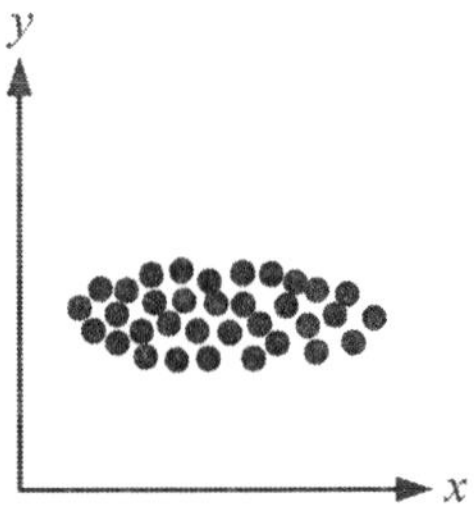

D.

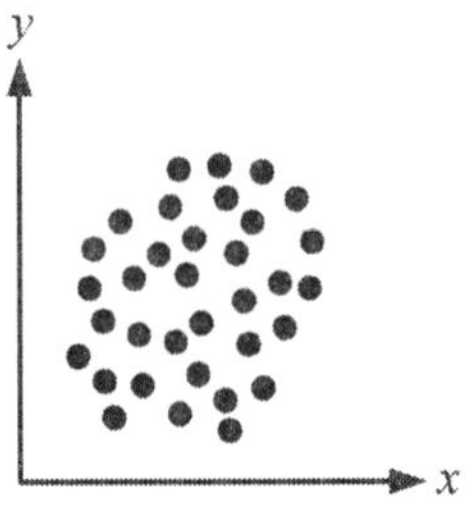

Not for Reproduction

ANSWERS AND SOLUTIONS — PRACTICE TEST 1

1. D	8. C	15. D	21. OR	28. B
2. A	9. B	16. C	22. A	29. OR
3. OR	10. B	17. B	23. OR	30. B
4. C	11. A	18. B	24. A	31. D
5. B	12. D	19. a) OR	25. B	
6. A	13. B	b) OR	26. C	
7. OR	14. C	20. C	27. OR	

1. D

The graph of a linear relation is always in the shape of a straight line. Only the graph in alternative D displays this type of relation.

2. A

A non-linear relation is represented by an equation with a degree greater than one. When the two binomials in alternative A are factored, the expression will have a degree of 2 ($n^2 - 1 = 3$), indicating that it is non-linear. The remaining alternatives are all of the first degree, which means they represent linear relations.

3. OR

Points	Sample Answer
4	Graph *A* shows partial variation because it has a constant rate of change (1) and an initial value of 10, which means that the line does not pass through the origin. Graph *B* shows direct variation because it has a constant rate of change (1) and the line does pass through the origin (0, 0).
	Application of knowledge and skills involving properties of variations shows a high degree of effectiveness due to: • a thorough understanding of the concepts • an accurate application of the procedures (any minor errors and/or omissions do not detract from the demonstration of a thorough understanding)
3	Identifies graphs correctly. Justifies answers correctly but does not use numbers from the graph for support.
	Application of knowledge and skills involving properties of variations shows considerable effectiveness due to: • an understanding of most of the concepts • minor errors and/or omissions in the application of the procedures
2	Identifies graphs correctly. Identifies and justifies one graph correctly. The second graph does not have a justification.
	Application of knowledge and skills involving properties of variations shows some effectiveness due to: • a partial understanding of the concepts • minor errors and/or omissions in the application of the procedures
1	Identifies graphs correctly but cannot support the answer with a justification.
	Application of knowledge and skills involving properties of variations shows limited effectiveness due to: • a misunderstanding of concepts • an incorrect selection or misuse of procedures

4. C

Write the equation of the line in the form $y = mx + b$.

The initial value is +6.

To calculate the rate of change, use the points (0, 6) and (2, 8).

$$\text{rate of change} = \frac{y_2 - y_1}{x_2 - x_1} = \frac{8-6}{2-0} = \frac{2}{2} = 1$$

The equation of the line is $y = x + 6$.

5. B

Interpolation involves looking at data on the line. Extrapolation involves looking at data when the line is extended. Therefore, alternative B is the false statement because race lengths of 200 m and 1 400 m are on the line, which is interpolation.

Copyright Protected

6. A

To determine which table corresponds to the equation $y = \frac{2x}{3}$, substitute some of the given x-values and solve for y. If the resulting y-values are the same as shown in one of the tables, then that table is the correct answer.

Solve for y for the x-values of 0, 2, 3, 6, and 8 as they are representative of the four tables.

- If $x = 0$, then $y = \frac{2x}{3} = \frac{2(0)}{3} = \frac{0}{3} = 0$.
- If $x = 2$, then $y = \frac{2x}{3} = \frac{2(2)}{3} = \frac{4}{3}$.
- If $x = 3$, then $y = \frac{2x}{3} = \frac{2(3)}{3} = 2$.
- If $x = 6$, then $y = \frac{2x}{3} = \frac{2(6)}{3} = \frac{12}{3} = 4$.
- If $x = 8$, then $y = \frac{2x}{3} = \frac{2(8)}{3} = \frac{16}{3}$.

Ordered pairs of this expression are $(0, 0)$, $\left(2, \frac{4}{3}\right)$, $(3, 2)$, $(6, 4)$, and $\left(8, \frac{16}{3}\right)$.

Only the values of the table in alternative A correspond to the given expression.

7. OR

<table>
<tr><th>Points</th><th>Sample Answer</th></tr>
<tr><td>4</td><td>Plan I: The initial value is $20 and the rate of change is $3. The equation of the line is $C = 3n + 20$.
Plan II: The initial value is $15 and the rate of change is $4. The equation of the line is $C = 4n + 15$.

The y-intercept would start lower on the graph of plan II, at $15. This line would slightly steeper since the rate of change is greater.

To determine the better plan, create a table of values.
<table>
<tr><th>Number of Court Rentals (x)</th><th>Monthly Fee Plan I
$C = 3n + 20$</th><th>Monthly Fee Plan II
$C = 4n + 15$</th></tr>
<tr><td>1</td><td>23</td><td>19</td></tr>
<tr><td>2</td><td>26</td><td>23</td></tr>
<tr><td>3</td><td>29</td><td>27</td></tr>
<tr><td>4</td><td>32</td><td>31</td></tr>
<tr><td>5</td><td>35</td><td>35</td></tr>
<tr><td>6</td><td>38</td><td>39</td></tr>
</table>
Plan II is the better deal if renting a court less than 5 times per month. Plan I is better if renting more than 5 times. If renting exactly 5 times per month, the plans cost the same.</td></tr>
<tr><td colspan="2">Application of knowledge and skills involving changes to a linear equation and graph when the conditions they represent are varied shows a high degree of effectiveness due to:
• a thorough understanding of the concepts
• an accurate application of the procedures (any minor errors and/or omissions do not detract from the demonstration of a thorough understanding)</td></tr>
<tr><td>3</td><td>Equations of the lines are correct.
Description of how the graph would change is correct.
Table is constructed correctly with some mathematical errors. Conclusions based on the table are correct using the miscalculated values.</td></tr>
<tr><td colspan="2">Application of knowledge and skills involving changes to a linear equation and graph when the conditions they represent are varied shows considerable effectiveness due to:
• an understanding of most of the concepts
• minor errors and/or omissions in the application of the procedures</td></tr>
<tr><td>2</td><td>Equations of the line are correct.
Descriptions of how the graph would change are incorrect.
Table is constructed correctly. Conclusions based on the table are incorrect.</td></tr>
<tr><td colspan="2">Application of knowledge and skills involving changes to a linear equation and graph when the conditions they represent are varied shows some effectiveness due to:
• a partial understanding of the concepts
• minor errors and/or omissions in the application of the procedures</td></tr>
<tr><td>1</td><td>Equations of the line are correct.
Descriptions of how the graph would change are incorrect.
Table is not completed correctly. Conclusions of the better plan are incorrect.</td></tr>
<tr><td colspan="2">Application of knowledge and skills involving changes to a linear equation and graph when the conditions they represent are varied shows limited effectiveness due to:
• a misunderstanding of concepts
• an incorrect selection or misuse of procedures</td></tr>
</table>

8. C

To solve the problem, find the rate of change and apply it to the equation of the line.

This is direct variation, meaning the line passes through (0, 0). Another known point is (35, 21). Calculate the rate of change.

$$\text{Rate of change} = \frac{\Delta y}{\Delta x}$$

$$\text{Rate of change} = \frac{21 - 0}{35 - 0} = \frac{21}{35} = \frac{21 \div 7}{35 \div 7} = \frac{3}{5}$$

Not for Reproduction

The equation of the line is $y = \frac{3}{5}x$.

Since the ball is dropped from 100 cm, substitute 100 into the equation and solve for y.

$y = \frac{3}{5}(100)$

$y = \frac{3 \times 100}{5} = \frac{300}{5} = 60$

The rebound height is 60 cm.

9. B

Recall that two lines are perpendicular if their slopes are negative reciprocals; that is, the product of their slopes is -1.
When the slopes of equations I and IV are multiplied, they have a product of -1.

$3 \times -\frac{1}{3} = -1$

10. B

A straight line is always represented by a linear equation, which is always an equation of the first degree. Only the equation given in alternative B represents a straight line.

Alternative A: y^4 makes the equation a degree of 4.

Alternative B: $x + 4 = y$ is a degree of 1 and therefore linear.

Alternative C: x^3 makes the equation a degree of 3.

Alternative D: the exponents xy added together make the equation a degree of 2.

11. A

Isolate y in the given equation.

$3x + 2y + 6 = 0$
Subtract $3x$ and 6 from both sides of the equation (inverse operation).
$3x - 3x + 2y + 6 - 6 = 0 - 3x - 6$

$2y = -3x - 6$

Divide both sides of the equation by 2 to isolate y.

$y = -\frac{3x}{2} - 3$

12. D

Use Pythagoras' theorem to check which alternative satisfies the condition that the hypotenuse is 17 cm.
$a^2 + b^2 = c^2$

$a^2 + b^2 = 17^2 = 289$

Substitute the values in each alternative for a and b.

Alternative A
$5^2 + 12^2 = 169$

Alternative B
$6^2 + 13^2 = 205$

Alternative C
$7^2 + 14^2 = 245$

Alternative D
$8^2 + 15^2 = 289$

The unknown sides are 8 cm and 15 cm.

13. B

$A_{\text{total}} = A_{\text{rectangle}} + A_{\text{triangle}}$

$A_{\text{rectangle}} = lw$

$A_{\text{rectangle}} = 24 \times 15$

$= 360 \text{ cm}^2$

$A_{\text{triangle}} = \frac{bh}{2}$

$A_{\text{triangle}} = \frac{24 \times 15}{2}$

$= 180 \text{ cm}^2$

$A_{\text{total}} = A_{\text{rectangle}} + A_{\text{triangle}}$

$A_{\text{total}} = 360 + 180$

$= 540 \text{ cm}^2$

Therefore, the total area of one side of the opened envelope is 540 cm^2.

14. C

$V_{\text{cylinder}} = \pi r^2 h$

$= \pi 6^2 \times 24$

$= 2712.96 \text{ cm}^2$

$V_{\text{sphere}} = \frac{4}{3}\pi r^3$

$= \frac{4}{3}\pi(0.6 \text{ cm})^3$

$= 0.904\ 32 \text{ cm}^2$

Number of spheres $= \frac{V_{\text{cylinder}}}{V_{\text{sphere}}}$

$= \frac{2712.96}{0.904\ 32}$

$= 3\ 0$

15. D

$V = l \times w \times h$

The object is a cube, so all three measurements are the same. Substitute the values into the formula.
$V = 9.8 \times 9.8 \times 9.8$
$V = 941.192 \text{ mm}^3$

Now, round to the nearest hundredth. There is a 9 in the hundredths place. As the 2 following the 9 is less than 5, you do not round up.

$V = 941.19 \text{ mm}^3$

16. C

According to the exponent laws, you must raise both the coefficient and the variable to the exponent outside the brackets. There are two methods that can be used to derive the answer.

Method 1

$$\left(-a^2\right)^{-3} = \left(-1a^2\right)^{-3} = (-1)^{-3} \times \left(a^2\right)^{-3}$$
$$= -1 \times a^{-6} = -a^{-6}$$

Method 2

Since there is a negative exponent, $\left(-a^2\right)^{-3}$ can be rewritten as $\dfrac{1}{\left(-a^2\right)^3} = \dfrac{1}{-a^6} = -a^{-6}$.

17. B

Ratios are a comparison of two quantities with the same unit. In this question, rates in mL / min are being compared.

Set up the ratio keeping the order of the buckets consistent. The alternatives are given in ratio form, so it is a good idea to set up the solution in the same form.
100:200

Ratios are always reduced to lowest terms. Both numbers are multiples of 100; therefore, divide both sides by 100 to get the ratio in lowest terms.
$\dfrac{100}{100} : \dfrac{200}{100} = 1:2$

18. B

Use the distributive property to distribute the x and -3 through the second set of brackets.
Then, collect like terms and simplify.

$$(x-3)\left(x^2+2x-4\right)$$
$$= \left(\begin{array}{l} x(x^2) + x(2x) + x(-4) + (-3)(x^2) \\ +(-3)(2x) + (-3)(-4) \end{array}\right)$$
$$= x^3 + 2x^2 - 4x - 3x^2 - 6x + 12$$
$$= x^3 - x^2 - 10x + 12$$

19. a) OR

$$(2x+3)(3x+4)$$
$$= 6x^2 + 8x + 9x + 12$$
$$= 6x^2 + 17x + 12$$

b) OR

There are three strategies that can be used to justify the answer.

Algebra tiles strategy:

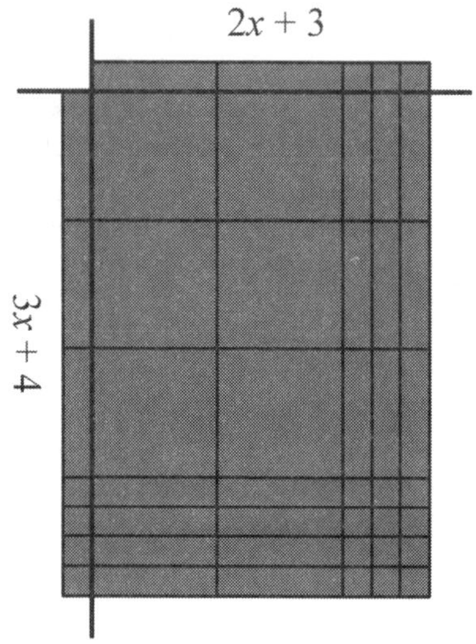

FOIL strategy:

First	$2x \times 3x = 6x^2$
Outside	$2x \times 4 = 8x$
Inside	$3 \times 3x = 9x$
Last	$3 \times 4 = 12$

Collect like terms.

$$= 6x^2 + 17x + 12$$

Vertical multiplication strategy:

$$\begin{array}{l} 2x + 3 \\ \underline{3x + 4} \\ 6x^2 + 9x \\ \underline{\qquad 8x + 12} \\ 6x^2 + 17x + 12 \end{array}$$

Not for Reproduction

20. C

Let x be the speed of the aircraft in still air.

Speed of the airplane against the wind = $x - 30$ (aircraft is travelling slower)

distance = rate × time

$\dfrac{\text{distance}}{\text{rate}} = \text{time}$

The time taken by the aircraft to travel 600 km downwind is $\dfrac{600}{x+30}$.

The time taken by the aircraft to travel 500 km against the wind is $\dfrac{500}{x-30}$.

Since the time taken by the airplane to travel 600 km downwind is the same as the time it takes to travel 500 km against the wind, a rational equation that can be solved to determine the speed of the aircraft in still air is $\dfrac{600}{x+30} = \dfrac{500}{x-30}$.

21. OR

Points	Sample Answer
4	Find the value of y when $x = 0$. $3x - 6y - 12 = 0$ $3(0) - 6y - 12 = 0$ $-6y = 12$ $\dfrac{-6y}{-6} = \dfrac{12}{-6}$ $y = -2$ (0, −2) Find the value of x when $y = 0$. $3x - 6y - 12 = 0$ $3x - 6(0) - 12 = 0$ $3x = 12$ $\dfrac{3x}{3} = \dfrac{12}{3}$ $x = 4$ (4, 0) Plot these two points on the grid. Connect the points with a straight edge, extend the line, and put arrowheads on each end of the line. 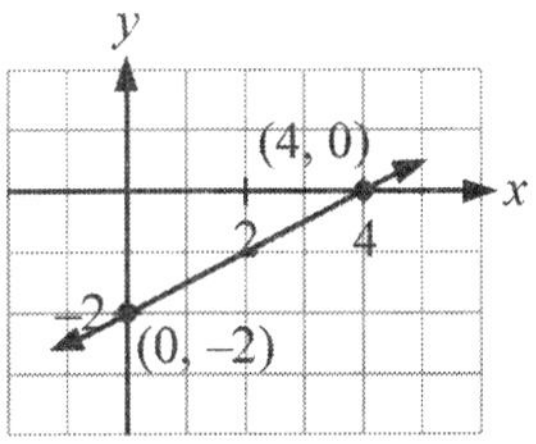

Points	Sample Answer
	Application of knowledge and skills involving graphing shows a high degree of effectiveness due to: • a thorough understanding of the concepts • an accurate application of the procedures (any minor errors and/or omissions do not detract from the demonstration of a thorough understanding)
3	Small errors in the graph, such as missing arrowheads on the line or axes. Correct method is used, but only the points are plotted, not the graph. Calculation error in finding the x- or y-intercept, but they are graphed correctly based on the numbers calculated.
	Application of knowledge and skills involving graphing shows considerable effectiveness due to: • an understanding of most of the concepts • minor errors and/or omissions in the application of the procedures
2	Slope and y-intercept method used, but the line is not graphed correctly. Only one of the intercepts is calculated.
	Application of knowledge and skills involving graphing shows some effectiveness due to: • minor errors and/or omissions in the application of the procedures • an understanding of most of the concepts
1	No calculations for the x- and y-intercept are shown. One of the points is graphed correctly, but no line is present on the graph.
	Application of knowledge and skills involving graphing shows limited effectiveness due to: • a misunderstanding of concepts • an incorrect selection or misuse of procedures

22. A

Two points are given: the x-intercept (4, 0) and the y-intercept (0, 12).
In the equation $y = mx + b$, b is the y-intercept and m is the slope of the line. Since the y-intercept is equal to 12, then $b = 12$. Alternative B and D can be eliminated.

Copyright Protected

The slope of the equation can be found if two points on the line are given. Use (0, 12) as (x_1, y_1) and (4, 0) as (x_2, y_2) in the following slope equation.

$$\begin{aligned} m &= \frac{y_2 - y_1}{x_2 - x_1} \\ &= \frac{0 - 12}{4 - 0} \\ &= \frac{-12}{4} \\ &= -3 \end{aligned}$$

Substituting m and b into the slope y-intercept form gives the equation $y = -3x + 12$.

23. OR

Points	Sample Answer
4	Slope y-intercept form: $y = mx + b$ Notice the y-intercept: $b = 2$ Note that the slope is negative. By counting units from the y-intercept, the slope can be determined as follows. $m = \frac{\text{rise}}{\text{run}} = \frac{3 \text{ units down}}{2 \text{ units right}} = \frac{-3}{2}$ 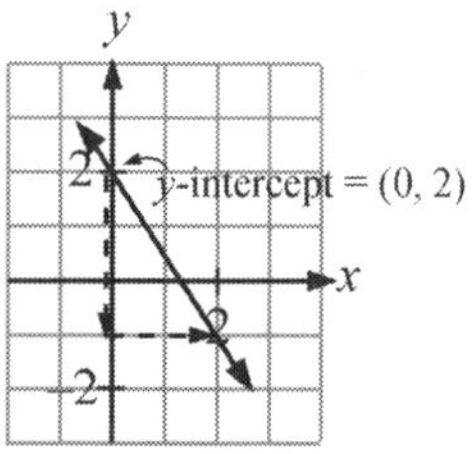 Substitute the values into the slope y-intercept form of the equation: $y = -\frac{3}{2}x + 2$ Standard form: $Ax + By + C = 0$ Multiply all the terms by 2 to eliminate the fractional coefficients. $2(y) = 2\left(\frac{-3}{2}x\right) + 2(2)$ $2y = -3x + 4$ Equate one side to 0, making sure the variables are in the correct order. $2y = -3x + 4$ $2y + 3x - 4 = -3x + 3x + 4 - 4$ $3x + 2y - 4 = 0$
Application of knowledge and skills in determining the equation of a line shows a high degree of effectiveness due to • a thorough understanding of the concepts • an accurate application of the procedures (any minor errors and/or omissions do not detract from the demonstration of a thorough understanding)	
3	Small calculation error, but all the procedures are done correctly and the equations are correct based on the calculation done.
Application of knowledge and skills in determining the equation of a line shows considerable effectiveness due to • an understanding of most of the concepts • minor errors and/or omissions in the application of the procedures	
2	Only one of the two forms of equations are completed correctly. The second form is partially started and the work shown is correct.
Application of knowledge and skills in determining the equation of a line shows some effectiveness due to: • minor errors and/or omissions in the application of the procedures • an understanding of most of the concepts	
1	Only one of the two forms of the equation is completed correctly.
Application of knowledge and skills in determining the equation of a line shows limited effectiveness due to: • a misunderstanding of concepts • an incorrect selection or misuse of procedures	

24. A

The equation $P = 5n - 50$ is in slope y-intercept form ($y = mx + b$).

The slope is represented by m and the y-intercept is b.

$m =$ slope = rate of change = 5

Profit = 0 = break-even point
$0 = 5n - 50$
$5n = 50$
$n = 10$ washes

The P-intercept at -50 indicates a loss or start-up cost of $50.

The statement in alternative A is false.

Not for Reproduction

25. B

The fixed cost was \$400 last year and \$600 this year, as indicated by the two different y-intercepts.
The total cost was the same for both years when 40 students go on the field trip.
When looking at $x = 50$ for both lines, Line I is higher, indicating that the charge per student was higher last year.

When the lines intersect at (40, 800), the values for both lines are the same.

26. C

$$P_{\text{rectangle}} = 2(l + w)$$
$$\frac{32}{2} = \frac{2(l+w)}{2}$$
$$16 \text{ cm} = l + w$$

The maximum area is obtained when the rectangle has 4 equal sides: a square. The dimensions of the square are 8 cm × 8 cm.

Therefore, the maximum area is 64 m^2.

27. OR

Points	Sample Answer
4	A rectangle has a maximum area and a minimum perimeter when it is a square. $P_{\text{rectangle}} = 2(l + w)$ $= 2(10 + 7)$ $= 34$ cm A square has equal sides. Take the total perimeter and divide it by 4 to get the length. $34 \div 4 = 8.5$ cm $A_{\text{square}} = lw$ $= 8.5 \times 8.5$ $= 72.25 \text{ cm}^2$
Application of knowledge and skills involving minimum perimeter shows a high degree of effectiveness due to: • a thorough understanding of the concepts • an accurate application of the procedures (any minor errors and/or omissions do not detract from the demonstration of a thorough understanding)	
3	Units are omitted in the calculations or incorrect.
Application of knowledge and skills involving minimum perimeter shows considerable effectiveness due to: • an understanding of most of the concepts • minor errors and/or omissions in the application of the procedures	
2	Calculates the perimeter correctly, but does not show the area increasing.
Application of knowledge and skills involving minimum perimeter shows some effectiveness due to: • a partial understanding of the concepts • minor errors and/or omissions in the application of the procedures	
1	Calculates a new perimeter that is a little smaller and with greater area, but not that of a square.
Application of knowledge and skills involving minimum perimeter shows limited effectiveness due to: • a misunderstanding of concepts • an incorrect selection or misuse of procedures	

28. B

You need to find the surface area of the four sides.

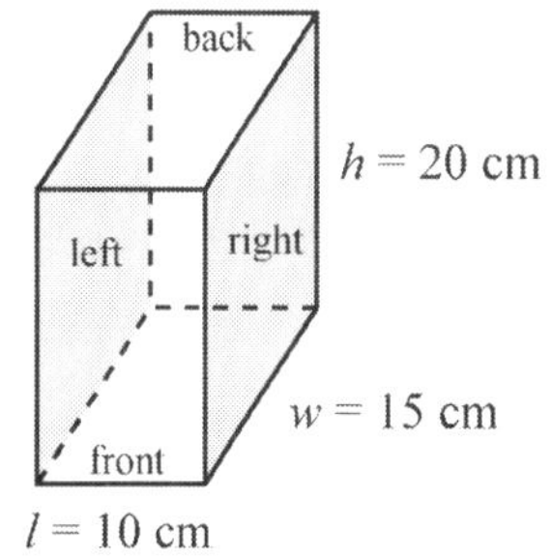

Multiply length l and height h for the front and back sides of the box. Then, multiply the width w and height h for the left and right sides of the box.

$$SA_{\text{rectangular prism}} = 2(l \times h) + 2(w \times h)$$
$$= 2(10 \times 20) + 2(15 \times 20)$$

Copyright Protected

29. OR

<table>
<tr><th>Points</th><th>Sample Answer</th></tr>
<tr><td>4</td><td>A cylinder with a maximum volume has the same height as its diameter. Use these measurements to calculate the surface area of the container.
$SA = 2\pi r^2 + 2\pi rh$
$= 2(3.14)(6.1)^2 + 2(3.14)(6.1)(12.2)$
$= 233.68 + 4\ 667.36$
$= 701.04\ \text{cm}^2$
If the height of the cylinder is 12.2 cm, divide that by the thickness to determine the number of CDs that will fit into the cylinder.
$12.2 \div 0.2 = 61$
A total of 61 CDs will fit into the cylinder with a height of 12.2 cm.</td></tr>
<tr><td colspan="2">Application of knowledge and skills involving maximization and minimization of measurements of geometric shapes and figures shows a high degree of effectiveness due to:
• a thorough understanding of the concepts
• an accurate application of the procedures (any minor errors and/or omissions do not detract from the demonstration of a thorough understanding)</td></tr>
<tr><td>3</td><td>Calculated the surface area correctly, but the units are left off or the incorrect units are used.
Divided the thickness of CDs correctly using mm instead of cm to get an answer of 6 CDs.</td></tr>
<tr><td colspan="2">Application of knowledge and skills involving maximization and minimization of measurements of geometric shapes and figures shows considerable effectiveness due to:
• an understanding of most of the concepts
• minor errors and/or omissions in the application of the procedures</td></tr>
<tr><td>2</td><td>Incorrectly substituted diameter into the values for radius for the surface area formula but calculated the answer correctly with the values.
Divided the thickness of CDs correctly using mm instead of cm to get an answer of 6 CDs.</td></tr>
<tr><td colspan="2">Application of knowledge and skills involving maximization and minimization of measurements of geometric shapes and figures shows some effectiveness due to:
• a partial understanding of the concepts
• minor errors and/or omissions in the application of the procedures</td></tr>
<tr><td>1</td><td>Substituted diameter into the values for radius for the surface area formula. Did not complete calculations correctly.
Used volume formula rather than surface area formula.
Unable to calculate the number of CDs in the cylinder.</td></tr>
<tr><td colspan="2">Application of knowledge and skills involving maximization and minimization of measurements of geometric shapes and figures shows limited effectiveness due to:
• a misunderstanding of concepts
• an incorrect selection or misuse of procedures</td></tr>
</table>

30. B

The length of the line joining the midpoints of two sides of a triangle is half of the length of the third side.

$$DE = \frac{1}{2}BC$$

The ratio of the length of DE to that of BC is 1:2.

31. D

Move up the y-axis to 1 cm. Then move right until you reach the corresponding point. Move down to the x-axis to determine the day, which is day 6.

Not for Reproduction

ANSWERS AND SOLUTIONS — PRACTICE TEST 2

1. B	8. B	15. C	22. D	29. OR
2. OR	9. D	16. OR	23. D	30. A
3. A	10. C	17. D	24. A	31. A
4. A	11. B	18. B	25. OR	
5. D	12. OR	19. B	26. C	
6. OR	13. B	20. OR	27. A	
7. D	14. C	21. D	28. A	

1. B

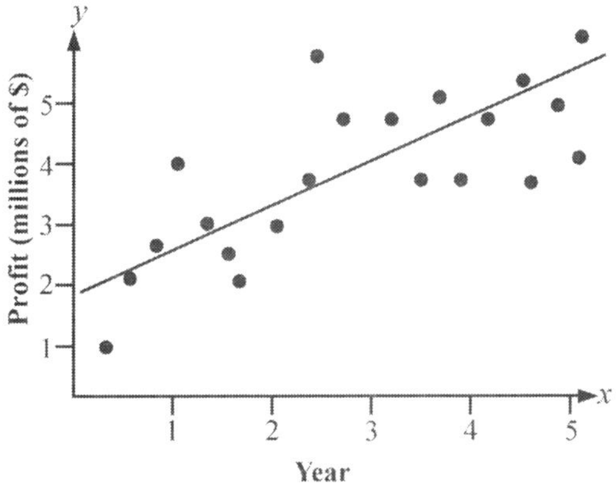

The data points show a general positive correlation: as the time increases, the profits also generally increase. The line of best fit is a trend line and would rise from left to right.

2. OR

<table>
<tr><th>Points</th><th>Sample Answer</th></tr>
<tr><td>4</td><td>
<table>
<tr><th>x</th><th>y = 3x + 1</th><th>First Differences</th></tr>
<tr><td>0</td><td>y = 3(0) + 1 = 1</td><td></td></tr>
<tr><td>1</td><td>y = 3(1) + 1 = 4</td><td>4 – 1 = 3</td></tr>
<tr><td>2</td><td>y = 3(2) + 1 = 7</td><td>7 – 4 = 3</td></tr>
<tr><td>3</td><td>y = 3(3) + 1 = 10</td><td>10 – 7 = 3</td></tr>
</table>
The relation is linear because the first differences are all the same and the equation is of the first degree.</td></tr>
<tr><td colspan="2">Application of knowledge and skills involving properties of relations shows a high degree of effectiveness due to:
• a thorough understanding of the concepts
• an accurate application of the procedures (any minor errors and/or omissions do not detract from the demonstration of a thorough understanding)</td></tr>
<tr><td>3</td><td>Table completed with some small errors.
Justification of relation is correct with respect to the answers in the table.</td></tr>
<tr><td colspan="2">Application of knowledge and skills involving properties of relations shows considerable effectiveness due to:
• an understanding of most of the concepts
• minor errors and/or omissions in the application of the procedures</td></tr>
<tr><td>2</td><td>Table completed with some small errors.
Justification is partly correct or complete with respect to the table.</td></tr>
<tr><td colspan="2">Application of knowledge and skills involving properties of relations shows some effectiveness due to:
• a partial understanding of the concepts
• minor errors and/or omissions in the application of the procedures</td></tr>
<tr><td>1</td><td>Table incomplete or incorrect.
Justification is incomplete or incorrect.</td></tr>
<tr><td colspan="2">Application of knowledge and skills involving properties of relations shows limited effectiveness due to:
• a misunderstanding of concepts
• an incorrect selection or misuse of procedures</td></tr>
</table>

3. A

When there is no memory on the device, the initial value is 0. Therefore, this situation represents direct variation.

As the kilobytes increase, the megabytes also increase, so the correlation is positive.

4. A

The rate of change is given as $\frac{3}{2}$, which is a positive value. The graph of the line must rise toward the right. Only the graphs in alternatives A and B fulfill this requirement. Now, determine which of these two graphs passes through the point (–3, –1).

Only the graph in alternative A passes through this point with the given rate of change.

5. D

The trip starts at port, so the graph must start at (0, 0). Alternatives A and B are eliminated.

There are three stops, so there must be three plateaus where the distance does not increase. Alternatives C and D indicate this. Finally, the boat must return to port where the distance will once again have a *y*-value of zero. Alternative C is eliminated as it does not show the boat returning to port.

Copyright Protected

6. OR

Points	Sample Answer
4	Application of knowledge and skills involving various representations of a linear relation shows a high degree of effectiveness due to: • a thorough understanding of the concepts • an accurate application of the procedures (any minor errors and/or omissions do not detract from the demonstration of a thorough understanding) Possible Solution The independent variable is the time, so it must go on the x-axis; cost must go on the y-axis. **Cost of Renting a Jet Ski** 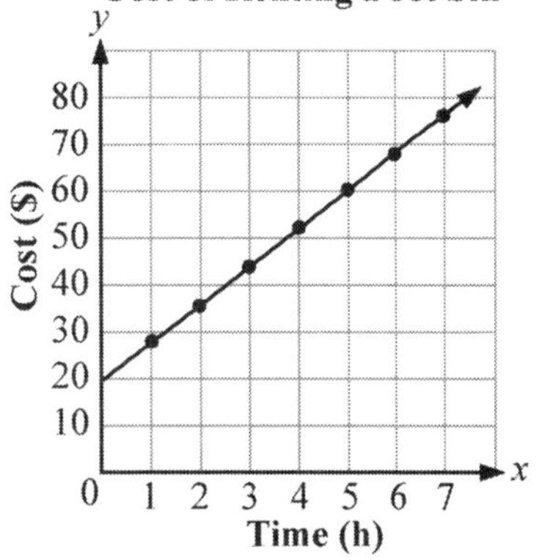 First differences: $36-28=8$ $44-36=8$ $52-44=8$ $60-52=8$ $68-60=8$ $76-68=8$ The values increase by \$8 each hour. The rate of change is 8. When the Jet Ski is rented for the first hour, the \$8 rate applies, but the initial value also applies. Subtracting 8 from 28 gives the initial value of \$20. The equation of the line is $y=8x+20$.
3	Application of knowledge and skills involving various representations of a linear relation shows considerable effectiveness due to: • an understanding of most of the concepts • minor errors and/or omissions in the application of the procedures Example Plots the graph correctly. Some of the labels are missing on the graph. Equation of the line is correct.
2	Application of knowledge and skills involving various representations of a linear relation shows some effectiveness due to: • a partial understanding of the concepts • minor errors and/or omissions in the application of the procedures Example Plots the graph correctly with axes reversed (cost on x-axis and time on y-axis). Equation of the line does not include the initial value.
1	Application of knowledge and skills involving various representations of a linear relation shows limited effectiveness due to: • a misunderstanding of concepts • an incorrect selection or misuse of procedures Example Plots the graph correctly, but with no labels. No equation of the line.

7. D

Company II has a greater initial value of \$80. This would cause the y-intercept to shift up. Company II has a lower rate of change (\$20 per hour) than company I (\$25 per hour). This would be shown on the graph as a less steep line from left to right.

Not for Reproduction

8. B

Pick two distinguishable points on the graph, such as (0, 2) and (2, 8).

Let (x_1, y_1) be (0, 2).

Let (x_2, y_2) be (2, 8).

Substitute the values into the slope formula.

$$m = \frac{\text{rise}}{\text{run}} = \frac{y_2 - y_1}{x_2 - x_1}$$

$$\frac{8-2}{2-0} = \frac{6}{2} = 3$$

The y-intercept (b) is 2.

Substitute the slope and y-intercept into the slope y-intercept form of the equation of a line.
$y = 3x + 2$

9. D

Use first differences to calculate the rate of change.

x	y	First differences
1	−3.5	(−4)−(−3.5) = (−0.5)
2	−4	
3	−4.5	(−4.5) − (−4) = (−0.5)
4	−5	(−5)−(−4.5) = (−0.5)

The rate of change is −0.5 or $-\frac{1}{2}$. The line descends 1 unit on the y-axis and runs across 2 units on the x-axis.

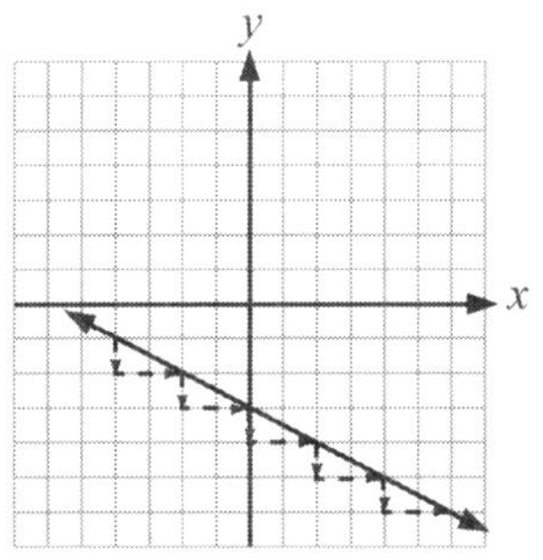

10. C

The coefficient of x is the slope of the line when the equation is in the form $y = mx + b$. Negative slopes fall toward the right, and the slope is −2. The constant (+5) is the y-intercept.

Therefore, the line falls toward the right and intersects the y-axis at 5.

11. B

A vertical line is parallel to the y-axis and intersects the x-axis. The basic form of a vertical equation is $x = a$. Only the equation $x = 4$ satisfies these requirements.

Alternative A is a horizontal line, and alternatives C and D are lines that intersect both axes.

12. OR

<table>
<tr><th>Points</th><th>Sample Answer</th></tr>
<tr><td>4</td><td>
Application of knowledge and skills involving the equation of a line shows a high degree of effectiveness due to

- a thorough understanding of the concepts
- an accurate application of the procedures (any minor errors and/or omissions do not detract from the demonstration of a thorough understanding)

Solution
Slope y-intercept form is $y = mx + b$.

Slope $= m = 2$
y-intercept $= b = 3$

Substitute these values into the equation of the line in slope y-intercept form:
$y = 2x + 3$.
To change the equation in standard form, move y to the other side of the equation and make it equal to 0.

Standard form is $Ax + By + C = 0$.

$$y = 2x + 3$$
$$y - y = 2x - y + 3$$
$$0 = 2x - y + 3$$

Create a table of values and then plot the points.

x	$y = 2x + 3$
−3	−3
−2	−1
−1	1
0	3
1	5
2	7
3	9
</td></tr>
</table>

Copyright Protected

Points	Sample Answer
	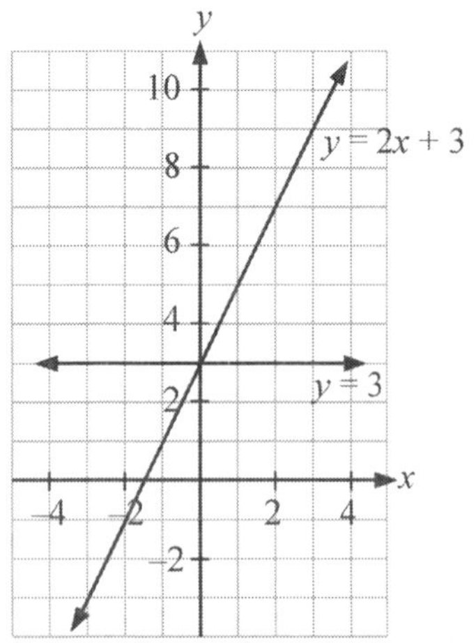 The graph of $y = 2x + 3$ is a line with a positive slope of 2. It intersects the y-axis at 3. The line $y = 3$ also intersects the y-axis at the same point, but it is a horizontal line.
3	Application of knowledge and skills involving the equation of a line shows considerable effectiveness due to • an understanding of most of the concepts • minor errors and/or omissions in the application of the procedures Example Writes the equation of the line correctly in y-intercept form. In standard form, the A value is negative rather than positive. Creates a correct table of values. Graphs the line correctly but leaves off the arrows on either end. Does not compare the characteristics of the two lines.
2	Application of knowledge and skills involving the equation of a line shows some effectiveness due to: • minor errors and/or omissions in the application of the procedures • an understanding of most of the concepts Example Writes the equation of the line correctly in one form. Creates a correct table of values. Graphs the line correctly but leaves off the arrows on either end. Does not compare the characteristics of the two lines.
1	Application of knowledge and skills involving the equation of a line shows limited effectiveness due to: • a misunderstanding of concepts • an incorrect selection or misuse of procedures Example Writes the equation of the line correctly in one form. Creates an incorrect table of values. Graphs the line incorrectly or does not graph the line at all. Does not compare the characteristics of the two lines.

13. B

Use Pythagoras' theorum to calculate the measure of the third side of the right triangle.

$a^2 + b^2 = c^2$

$5.5^2 + b^2 = 30.5^2$

$30.25 + b^2 = 930.25$

$30.25 - 30.25 + b^2 = 930.25 - 30.25$

$b^2 = 900$

$b = \sqrt{900}$

$b = 30$ cm

Not for Reproduction

14. C

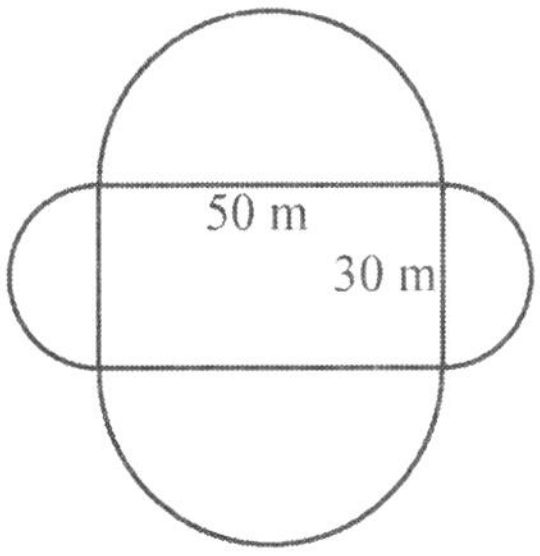

The perimeter of the figure is the sum of the circumferences of the four semicircles.

$$C_{\text{semicircle}} = \pi r = \pi \frac{d}{2}$$

$$P_{\text{shape}} = \frac{30\pi}{2} + \frac{50\pi}{2} + \frac{30\pi}{2} + \frac{50\pi}{2}$$
$$= 15\pi + 25\pi + 15\pi + 25\pi$$
$$= 80\pi \text{ m}$$

15. C

total canvas used= curved surface area of cylinder + curved surface area of cone

$$SA_{\text{total}} = A_{\text{cylinder's lateral face}} + A_{\text{cone's lateral face}}$$
$$SA_{\text{total}} = 2\pi rh + \pi rs$$

The diameter is 102 m. Therefore, the radius is 51 m.

Substitute the values into the formulas. Be careful to assign the correct height for each of the shapes.

$$SA_{\text{total}} = (2\pi 51 \times 3.5) + (\pi 51 \times 55)$$
$$= 1120.98 + 8807.7$$
$$= 9928.68 \text{ m}^2$$

16. OR

<table>
<tr><th>Points</th><th>Sample Answer</th></tr>
<tr><td>4</td><td>Calculate the radius of both shapes.
$r_{\text{cylinder}} = 50 \div 2 = 25$ mm
$r_{\text{cone}} = 76 \div 2 = 38$ mm
Calculate the volume of each container.
$V_{\text{cylinder}} = (A_{\text{base}})(\text{height})$
$V_{\text{cylinder}} = \pi r^2 h$
$= \pi \times 25^2 \times 76$
$= \pi \times 625 \times 76$
$= 149\ 150 \text{ mm}^3$
$V_{\text{cone}} = \frac{(A_{\text{base}})(\text{height})}{3}$
$V_{\text{cone}} = \frac{\pi r^2 h}{3}$
$= \frac{\pi \times 38^2 \times 99}{3}$
$= \frac{\pi \times 1444 \times 99}{3}$
$= \frac{448\ 881.84}{3}$
$= 149\ 627.28 \text{ mm}^3$
Find the difference between the two volumes.
$149\ 627.28 - 149\ 150 = 477.28 \text{ mm}^3$
The cone's volume is larger by 477.28 mm^3. John will get more juice for $1.50 if he purchases the cone-shaped container. It is the better deal.</td></tr>
<tr><td colspan="2">Application of knowledge and problem-solving skills involving volumes of 3-D shapes shows a high degree of effectiveness due to:
• a thorough understanding of the concepts
• an accurate application of the procedures (any minor errors and/or omissions do not detract from the demonstration of a thorough understanding)</td></tr>
<tr><td>3</td><td>Calculates the two volumes using diameter rather than radius, but completes the calculations correctly with those measurements.
Leaves units off the final calculations.
Justifies the answer thoroughly showing the difference between the two volumes.</td></tr>
</table>

Points	Sample Answer
Application of knowledge and problem-solving skills involving volumes of 3-D shapes shows considerable effectiveness due to: • an understanding of most of the concepts • minor errors and/or omissions in the application of the procedures	
2	Calculates the volume of one shape correctly; the second shape incorrectly. Based on the calculations, chooses the correct shape as the larger volume. Does not justify through subtraction that it is the larger volume.
Application of knowledge and problem-solving skills involving volumes of 3-D shapes shows some effectiveness due to: • a partial understanding of the concepts • minor errors and/or omissions in the application of the procedures	
1	Calculations for the two shapes are not shown. Justification for the purchase is based on the idea that a cone has a smaller volume than a cylinder. The student forgets that the principle only applies when the measurements of the two shapes are the same.
Application of knowledge and problem-solving skills involving volumes of 3-D shapes shows limited effectiveness due to: • a misunderstanding of concepts • an incorrect selection or misuse of procedures	

17. D

All the sides of a cube are equal.
Volume = length × width × height

$= (3x^3y^4)(3x^3y^4)(3x^3y^4)$

$= (3 \times 3 \times 3)(x^3 \times x^3 \times x^3)(y^4 \times y^4 \times y^4)$

$= 27x^9y^{12}$

18. B

One of the exponent law states that when multiplying two powers with the same base, the exponents are added together.
$x^{17} \times x^{25} = x^{17+25} = x^{42}$

19. B

A rate is a comparison of two quantities with different units. In this question, money and litres are being compared. $\frac{\$10.00}{6.25\text{ L}}$

A unit rate is a rate where the second term is 1. To calculate the unit rate (price per litre), divide the first term by the second term.
$\$10.00 \div 6.25\text{ L} = \$1.60/\text{L}$

20. OR

Points	Sample Answer
4	The cost of a subscription to the newspaper is \$3.65 per week. The cost of buying the newspaper each day from a newspaper box is \$0.50 per day for 6 days (Monday to Saturday) plus \$1.00 for the Sunday edition. Therefore, $(\$0.50 \times 6) + \$1.00 = \$4.00$. It costs \$4.00 per week to buy the newspaper from a newspaper box. Subscription savings $= \$4.00 - \$3.65 = \$0.35$ per week To find the amount saved as a percentage, divide the amount saved (\$0.35) by the cost of buying the newspaper from a newspaper box (\$4.00). $\frac{0.35}{4.00} = 0.0875$ To convert the decimal to a percentage multiply by 100 %. $0.0875 \times 100\% = 8.75\%$ Therefore, a person who subscribes to the newspaper saves 8.75% compared with a person who buys the newspaper every day from a newspaper box.
Application of knowledge and skills involving solving problems requiring the manipulation of expressions arising from applications of percent shows a high degree of effectiveness due to: • a thorough understanding of the concepts • an accurate application of the procedures (any minor errors and/or omissions do not detract from the demonstration of a thorough understanding)	

Not for Reproduction

Points	Sample Answer
3	Does not include the \$1.00 for the Sunday edition, but completes the rest of the procedures correctly. (\$0.50 × 7) = \$3.50 \$4.00 – \$3.50 = \$0.50 $\frac{0.50}{4.00} = 0.13$ 0.13 × 100% = 13%
Application of knowledge and skills involving solving problems requiring the manipulation of expressions arising from applications of percent shows considerable effectiveness due to: • minor errors and/or omissions in the application of the procedures • an understanding of most of the concepts	
2	Does not include \$1.00 for the Sunday edition, but completes the rest of the procedures correctly. (\$0.50 × 7) = \$3.50 \$4.00 – \$3.50 = \$0.50 $\frac{0.50}{4.00} = 0.13$ 0.13 × 100 = 13% Multiplies 0.0875 × 100 = 0.875% and then round the answer to 1%.
Application of knowledge and skills involving solving problems requiring the manipulation of expressions arising from applications of percent shows some effectiveness due to: • minor errors and/or omissions in the application of the procedures • an understand of most of the concepts	
1	(\$0.50 × 6) + \$1.00 ÷ 100 = 0.04 0.04 × 100 = 4%
An application of knowledge and skills involving solving problems requiring the manipulation of expressions arising from applications of percent shows limited effectiveness due to: • a misunderstanding of concepts • an incorrect selection or misuse of procedures	

21. D

Area for the bottom of a pyramid, $A = 100 \text{ m}^2$

Formula for the area of a square, $A = s^2$, where s is the length of one of the sides.

$s^2 = 100 \text{ m}^2$

To find the number that multiplied by itself equals 10 000, take the square root of both sides.

$\sqrt{s^2} = \sqrt{100} \text{ m}^2$

$s = 100$ m

Therefore, the length of one side of the base of the pyramid is 100 m.

22. D

Define the variable.
Let x be the number of quarters.
Twice as many nickels $= 2x$
3 less dimes $= x - 3$

Write the equation.
$(0.25x) + (0.05 \times 2x) + 0.1(x - 3) = 3.75$

Solve for x.
$0.25x + 0.1x + 0.1x - 0.3 = 3.75$
Combine like terms.
$0.45x - 0.3 = 3.75$
Use the inverse to remove the constant.
$0.45x = 4.05$
Divide both sides by 0.45 to determine the value of x.
$x = 9$

Ms. Carlson used 9 quarters. The question asks for how many nickels she used in the parking meter.

Number of nickels $= 2x$

$2 \times 9 = 18$

Therefore, Ms. Carlson used 18 nickels.

23. D

The equation of a line can be found with the formula $(y - y_1) = m(x - x_1)$.
In this case, $m = -1$, $x_1 = -2$, and $y_1 = -6$.

Substitute these values.
$y-(-6)=-1(x-(-2))$

Rewrite the subtraction to addition.
$y+6=-1(x+2)$

Distribute the -1 through the brackets and then simplify.

$$y+6=-x-2$$
$$y+6-6=-x-2-6$$
$$y=-x-8$$
$$y+x=-x+x-8$$
$$y+x=-8$$

24. A

Rate of change = slope = $m = 24$
Layout fee = y-intercept = $b = 475$
Write an equation of this realistic situation in slope y-intercept form.

$C = 24n + 475$, where C is the total ($), and n is the number of yearbooks sold.

Substitute the maximum total cost into the equation.
$6\ 100 = 24n + 475$

Solve for n.
$6100 - 475 = 24\text{ n} + 475 - 475$

$5625 \div 24 = 24n \div 24$
$234.38 = n$
A partial yearbook cannot be sold so 234 yearbooks is the maximum.

25. OR

Points	Sample Answer
4	Application of knowledge and skills for solving a linear system shows a high degree of effectiveness due to: • a thorough understanding of the concepts • an accurate application of the procedures (any minor errors and/or omissions do not detract from the demonstration of a thorough understanding) Solution The equation for each company can be written in slope y-intercept form ($y = mx + b$) as the y-intercept is the weekly charge and the slope is the rate per kilometre.

Points	Sample Answer
	Company I: y-intercept $= 75$; $m = 0.20$ The equation of the line is $y = 0.2x + 75$. Company II: y-intercept $= 100$; $m = 0.10$ The equation of the line is $y = 0.1x + 100$. Graph each relation by first plotting the y-intercept. Use the slope or substitute values into the equation to determine other points on the line. 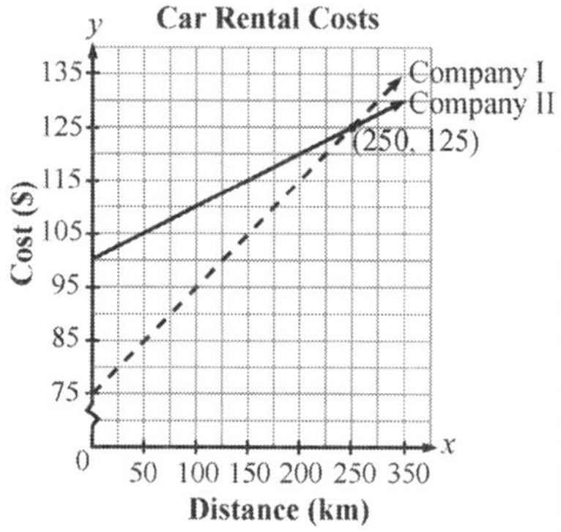 Company I is the better value if Walter travels less than 250 km. Company II is the better value if Walter travels more than 250 km.
3	Application of knowledge and skills for solving a linear system shows considerable effectiveness due to: • an understanding of most of the concepts • minor errors and/or omissions in the application of the procedures The equations of both relations are written correctly and graphed correctly. A label may be missing from one of the axes. Only one plan is discussed in the interpretation of the relation.
2	Application of knowledge and skills for solving a linear system shows some effectiveness due to: • minor errors and/or omissions in the application of the procedures • an understanding of most of the concepts

Not for Reproduction

Points	Sample Answer
	The equation of one relation is written correctly. Both relations are graphed correctly according to the equations written. Labels are missing on the axes. Only one plan is discussed in the interpretation of the relation. The interpretation is correct given the equations used.
1	Application of knowledge and skills for solving a linear system shows limited effectiveness due to: • a misunderstanding of concepts • an incorrect selection or misuse of procedures The equation of one relation is written correctly. Both relations are graphed incorrectly according to the equations written. Labels are missing on the axes. The interpretation of the best plan is reversed.

26. C

The line for Hall I has a y-intercept of 300 and the slope is $\frac{100}{10} = 10$. The equation of the line is $C = 300 + 10\text{ n}$.

Looking at the line for Hall II, the y-intercept is 500 and the slope is $\frac{100}{20} = 5$. The equation of the line is $C = 500 + 5\text{ n}$.

When $n < 40$, the line for Hall II is lower, so it is the better deal.

27. A

Alternative A:

Perimeter $= 2(10 + 9) = 2 \times 19 = 38$ units
Area $= 10 \times 9 = 90$ units^2

Alternative B:

Perimeter $= 2(15 + 6) = 2 \times 21 = 42$ units
Area $= 15 \times 6 = 90$ units^2

Alternative C:

Perimeter $= 2(18 + 5) = 2 \times 23 = 46$ units
Area $= 18 \times 5 = 90$ units^2

Alternative D:

Perimeter $= 2(30 + 3) = 2 \times 33 = 66$ units
Area $= 30 \times 3 = 90$ units^2

The required dimensions are 10 units and 9 units.

28. A

Calculate the surface area of each cylinder.

$$SA_{\text{Cylinder 1}} = 2\pi r(h + r)$$
$$= 2\pi(10)(10 + 10)$$
$$= 1256\text{ cm}^2$$

$$SA_{\text{Cylinder 2}} = 2\pi r(h + r)$$
$$= 2\pi(6.3)(25 + 6.3)$$
$$= 1238.4\text{ cm}^2$$

Subtract the smaller surface area (Cylinder 2) from the larger surface area (Cylinder 1).

$1256 - 1238.4 = 17.6\text{ cm}^2$

Cylinder 1 has approximately 18 cm^2 more surface area to paint.

29. OR

Points	Sample Answer
4	Calculate the area of triangle ABC and the area of triangle ABD to prove that the smaller triangle is half of the area of the larger one. $A_{\triangle ABC} = \frac{bh}{2}$ $= \frac{3 \times 2.5}{2}$ $= \frac{7.5}{2}$ $= 3.75\text{ cm}^2$ $A_{\triangle ABD} = \frac{bh}{2}$ $= \frac{1.5 \times 2.5}{2}$ $= \frac{3.75}{2}$ $= 1.875\text{ cm}^2$ Note that the base is bisected by the median. To calculate half of the area of triangle ABC, divide the area by 2. $3.75 \div 2 = 1.875\text{ cm}^2$ Half of the area of triangle ABC divided by 2 is equal to the area of triangle ABD, proving that the median of a triangle bisects the area of a triangle.
	Application of knowledge and skills illustrating a geometric property shows a high degree of effectiveness due to:

Copyright Protected

Points	Sample Answer
• a thorough understanding of the concepts • an accurate application of the procedures (any minor errors and/or omissions do not detract from the demonstration of a thorough understanding)	
3	Calculates the two areas correctly but does not explain how the two areas prove the median bisects the area of a triangle. No units on the final answer.
Application of knowledge and skills illustrating a geometric property shows considerable effectiveness due to: • an understanding of most of the concepts • minor errors and/or omissions in the application of the procedures	
2	Calculates the area of triangle *ABC* but does not bisect the base for area *ABD*. Calculations are correct based on the incorrect base unit used. Does not explain how the two areas prove the median bisects the area of a triangle.
Application of knowledge and skills illustrating a geometric property shows some effectiveness due to: • a partial understanding of the concepts • minor errors and/or omissions in the application of the procedures	
1	Makes a statement about the area of the large triangle being double that of the smaller triangle, but does not show any work to verify the statement.
Application of knowledge and skills illustrating a geometric property shows limited effectiveness due to: • a misunderstanding of concepts • an incorrect selection or misuse of procedures	

30. A

Perpendicular diagonals means the angle of the crossing lines is 90°. Only the diagonals of a rhombus bisect each other at right angles.

Rhombus

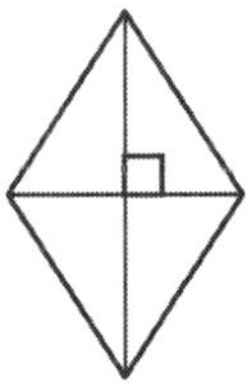

Rectangle

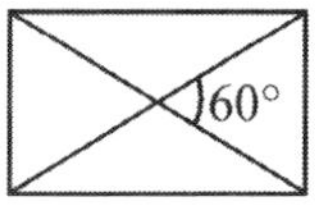

Trapezoid

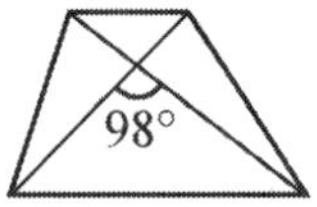

Parallelogram

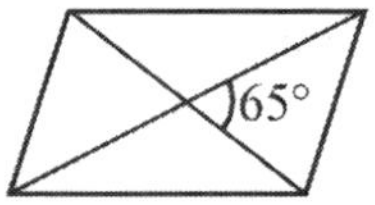

31. A

For every increase in x, there must be an increase in y. Alternative A follows this pattern.

Appendices

Copyright Protected

Formula Sheet

2-D Shape	Perimeter	Area
Rectangle 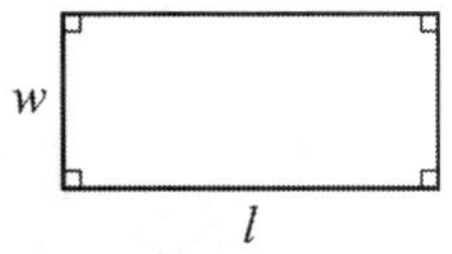	$P_{\text{rectangle}} = 2(l + w)$	$A_{\text{rectangle}} = lw$
Parallelogram 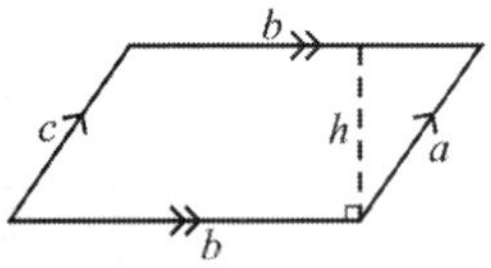	$P_{\text{parallelogram}} = 2(b + a)$	$A_{\text{parallelogram}} = bh$
Triangle 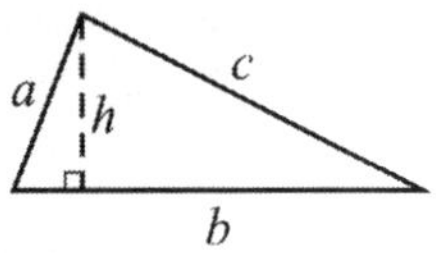	$P_{\text{triangle}} = a + b + c$	$A_{\text{triangle}} = \frac{bh}{2}$
Trapezoid 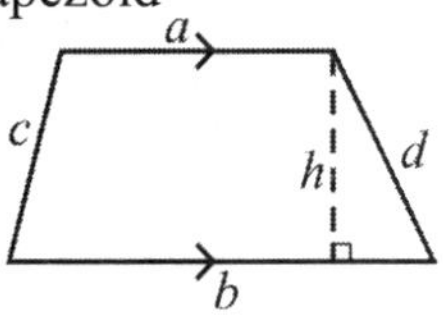	$P_{\text{trapezoid}} = a + b + c + d$	$A_{\text{trapezoid}} = \frac{(a + b)h}{2}$
Circle 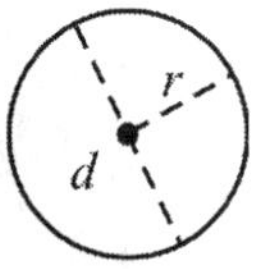	$C_{\text{circle}} = 2\pi r$ $C_{\text{circle}} = \pi d$	$A_{\text{circle}} = \pi r^2$

Not for Reproduction

Formula Sheet

3-D Shape	Surface Area	Volume
Rectangular Prism 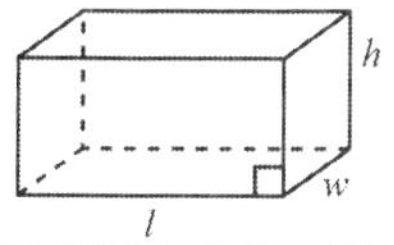	$SA_{\text{rectangular prism}} = 2(wh + lw + lh)$	$V_{\text{rectangular prism}} = (A_{\text{base}})(\text{height})$ $= lwh$
Triangular Prism 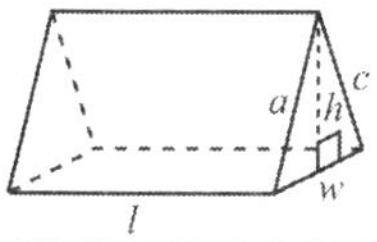	$SA_{\text{triangular prism}} = A_{\text{rectangles}} + A_{2\text{ bases}}$ $= al + cl + wl + wh$	$V_{\text{triangular prism}} = (A_{\text{base}})(\text{height})$ $= \dfrac{lwh}{2}$
Square Pyramid 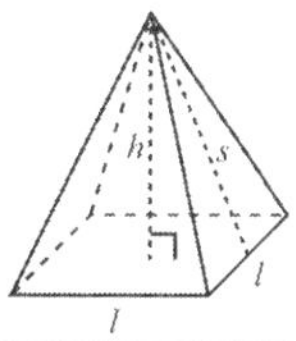	$SA_{\text{square pyramid}} = A_{4\text{ lateral surfaces}} + A_{\text{base}}$ $= 2ls + l^2$	$V_{\text{pyramid}} = \dfrac{(A_{\text{base}})(\text{height})}{3}$ $= \dfrac{l^2h}{3}$
Cylinder 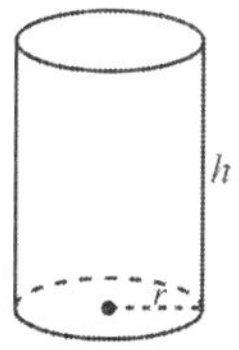	$SA_{\text{cylinder}} = A_{\text{lateral surface}} + A_{2\text{ bases}}$ $= 2\pi rh + 2\pi r^2$ $= 2\pi r(h + r)$	$V_{\text{cylinder}} = (A_{\text{base}})(\text{height})$ $= \pi r^2 h$
Cone 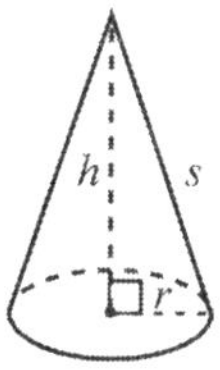	$SA_{\text{cone}} = A_{\text{lateral surface}} + A_{\text{base}}$ $= \pi rs + \pi r^2$	$V_{\text{cone}} = \dfrac{(A_{\text{base}})(\text{height})}{3}$ $= \dfrac{\pi r^2 h}{3}$
Sphere 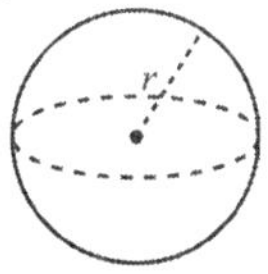	$SA_{\text{sphere}} = 4\pi r^2$	$V_{\text{sphere}} = \dfrac{2}{3}(A_{\text{base}})(\text{height})$ $= \dfrac{4\pi r^3}{3}$

Every effort has been made to provide proper acknowledgement of the original source and to comply with copyright law. However, some attempts to establish original copyright ownership may have been unsuccessful. If copyright ownership can be identified, please notify Castle Rock Research Corp so that appropriate corrective action can be taken.

Some images in this document are from www.clipart.com, © 2013 Clipart.com, a division of Getty Images.